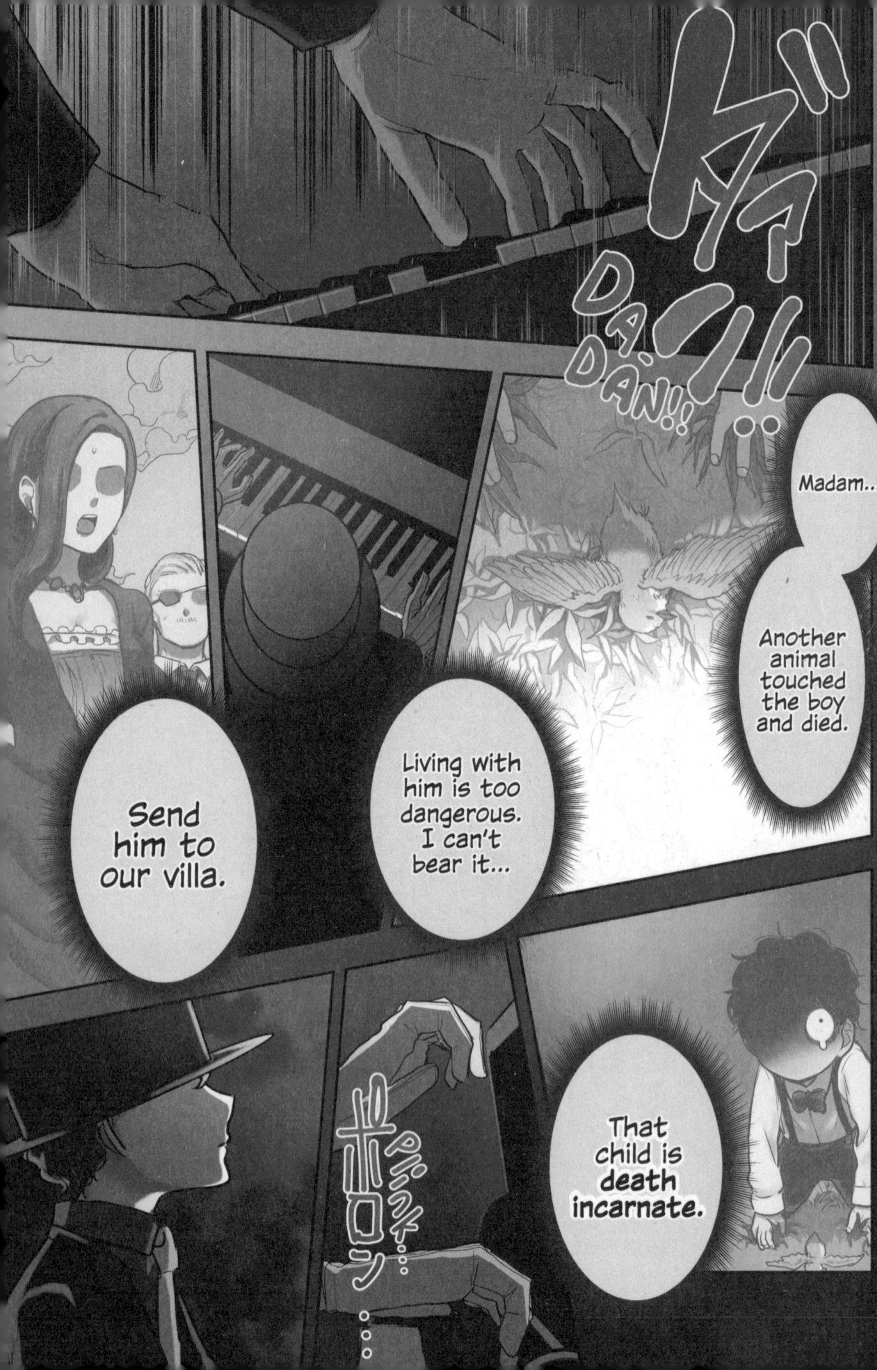
ドダァン!!
DA-DAN!!
Madam...
Another animal touched the boy and died.
Living with him is too dangerous. I can't bear it...
Send him to our villa.
That child is death incarnate.
ポロン…
Plink...

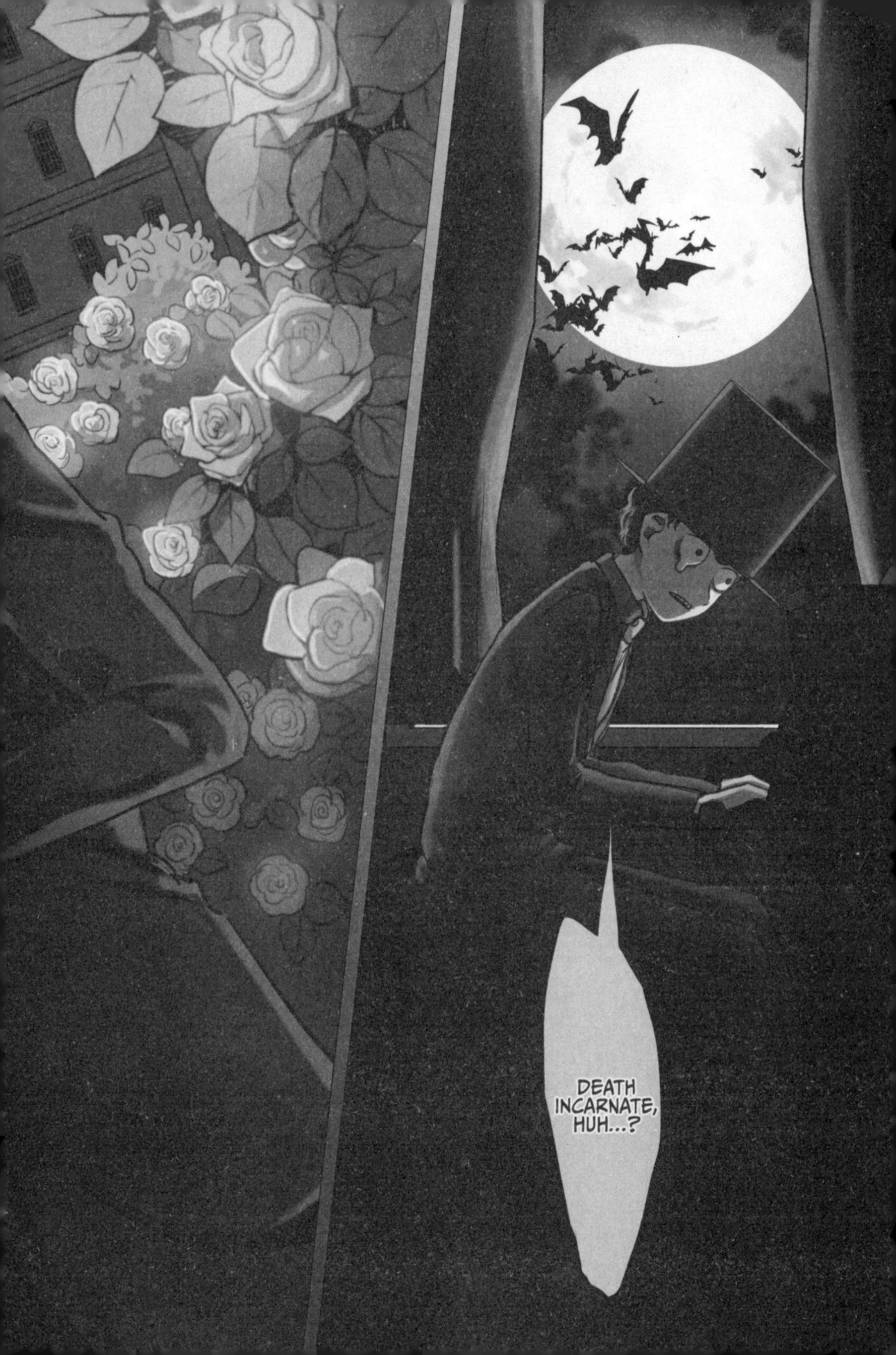
DEATH INCARNATE, HUH...?

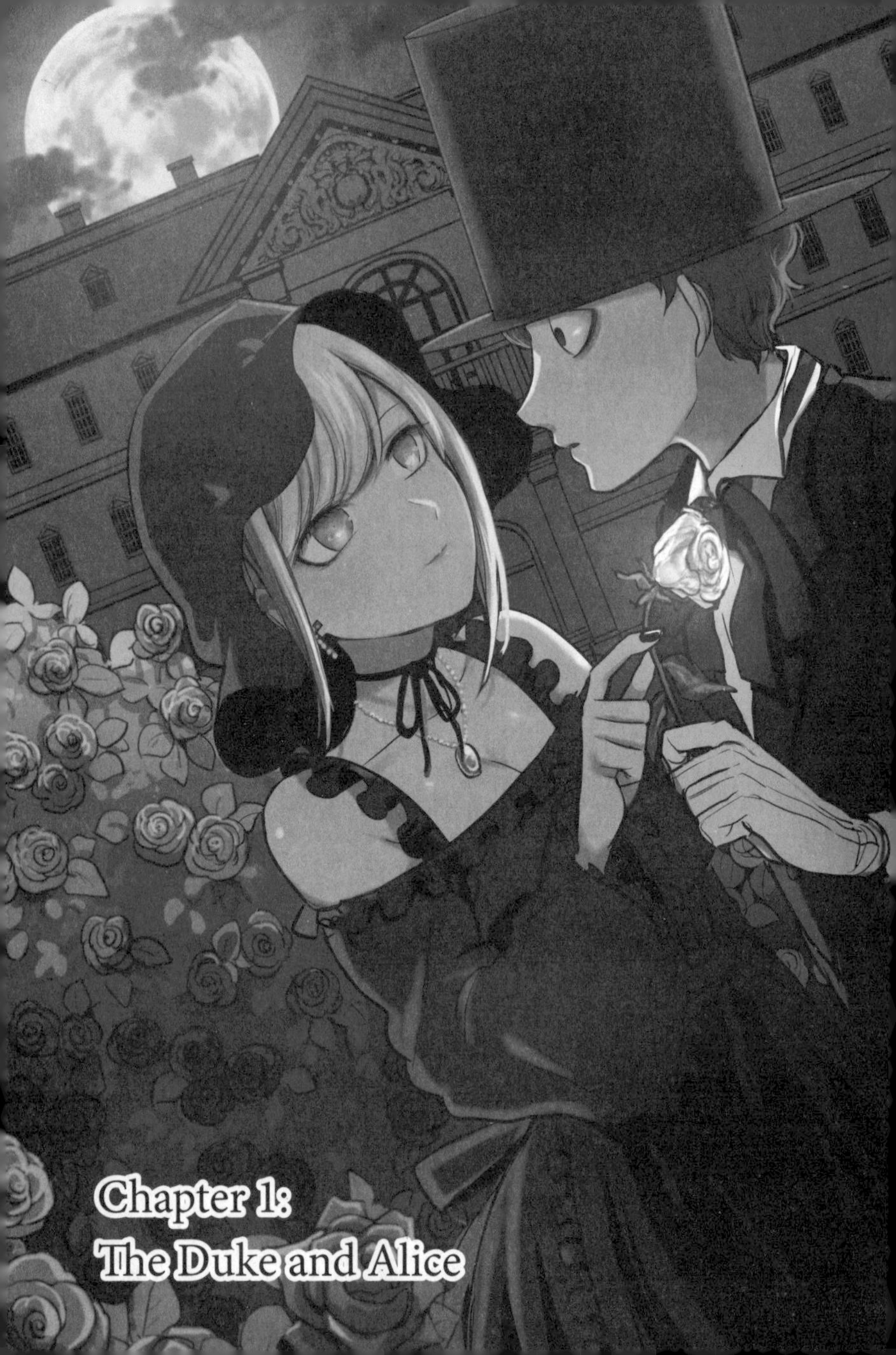
Chapter 1:
The Duke and Alice

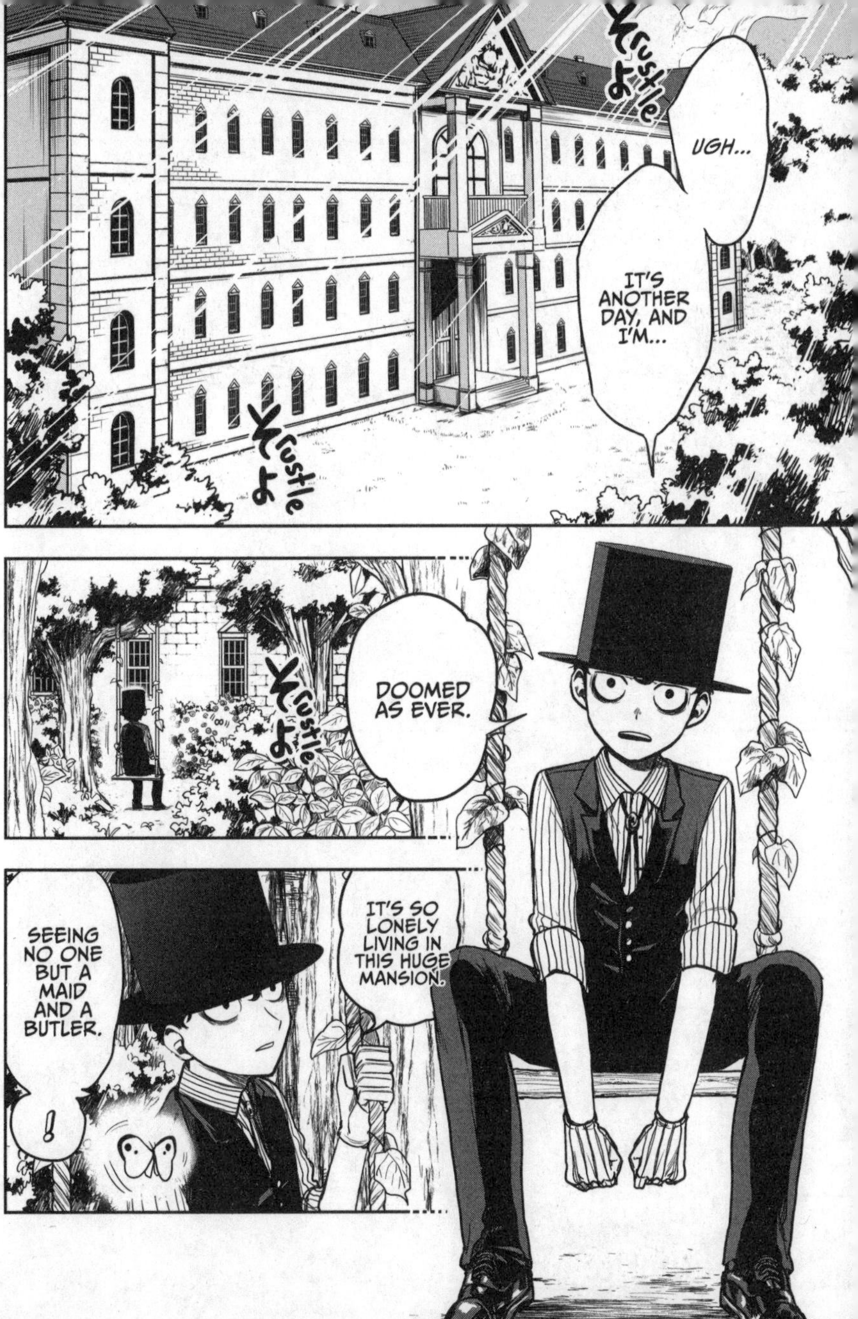

そよ rustle
UGH...
IT'S ANOTHER DAY, AND I'M...
そよ rustle
DOOMED AS EVER.
そよ rustle
IT'S SO LONELY LIVING IN THIS HUGE MANSION.
SEEING NO ONE BUT A MAID AND A BUTLER.
!

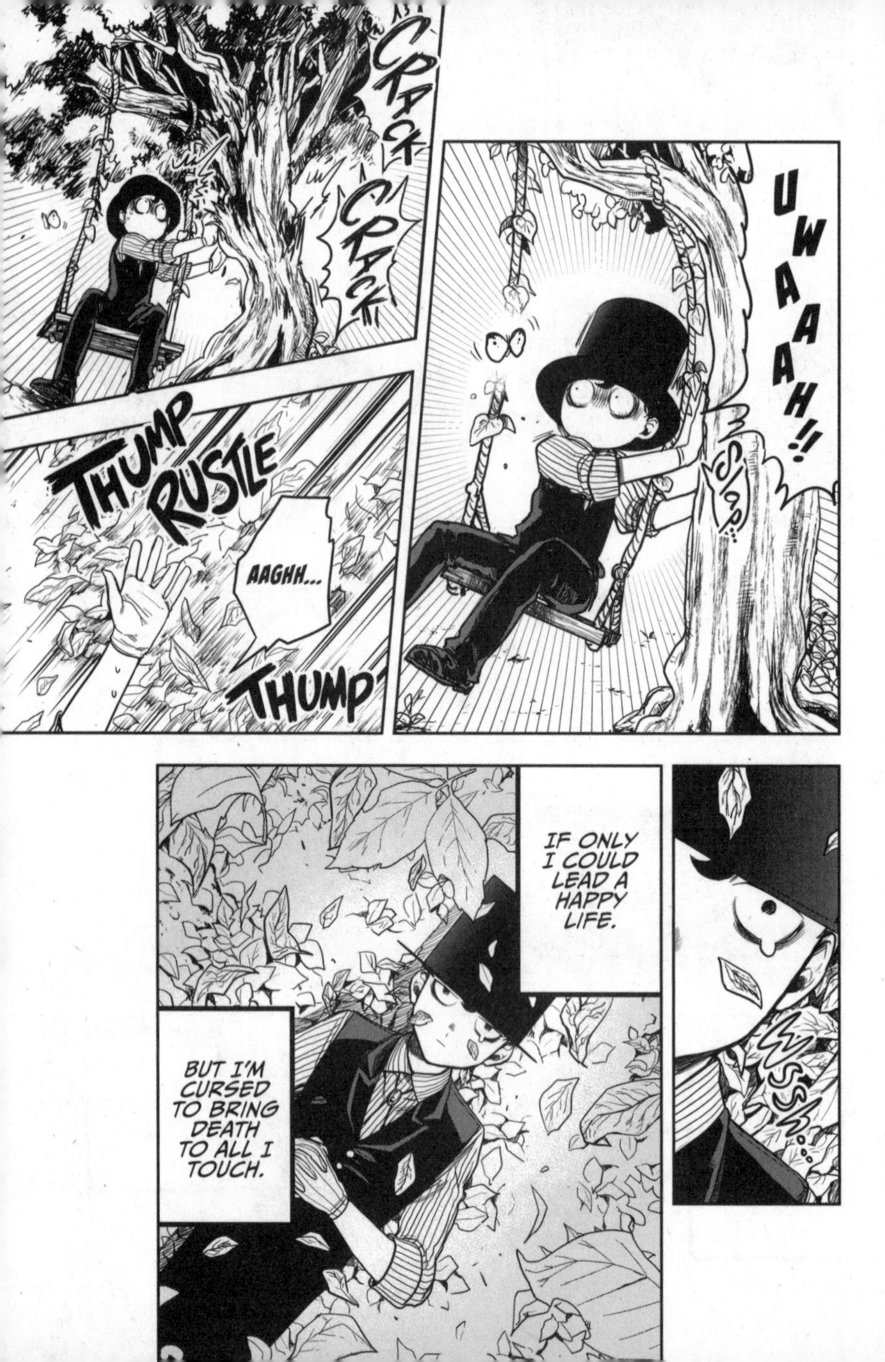
UWAAAH!!
Slap...
CRACK
CRACK
THUMP
RUSTLE
AAGHH...
THUMP
WSSSH...
IF ONLY I COULD LEAD A HAPPY LIFE.
BUT I'M CURSED TO BRING DEATH TO ALL I TOUCH.

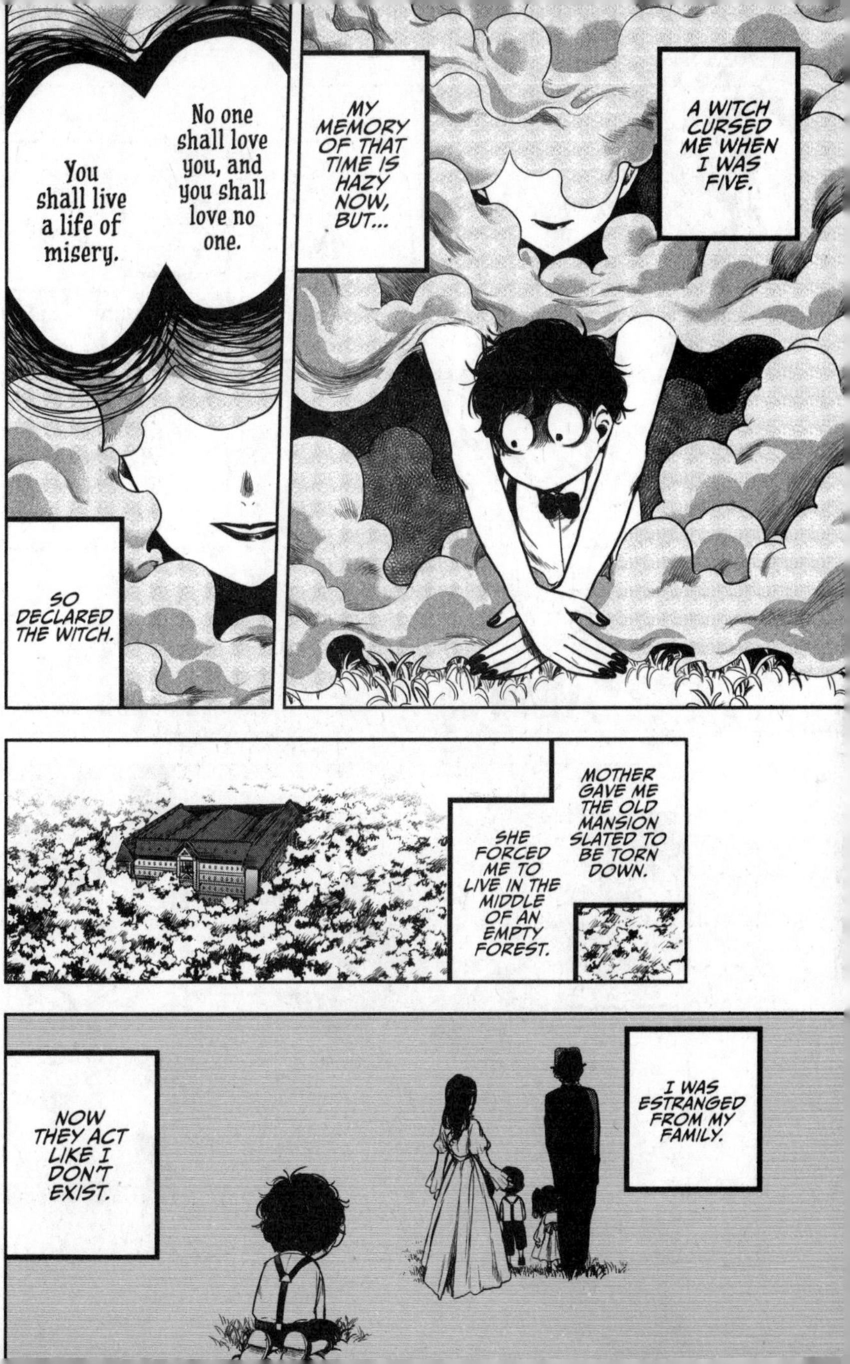
A WITCH CURSED ME WHEN I WAS FIVE.
MY MEMORY OF THAT TIME IS HAZY NOW, BUT...
No one shall love you, and you shall love no one.
You shall live a life of misery.
SO DECLARED THE WITCH.
MOTHER GAVE ME THE OLD MANSION SLATED TO BE TORN DOWN.
SHE FORCED ME TO LIVE IN THE MIDDLE OF AN EMPTY FOREST.
I WAS ESTRANGED FROM MY FAMILY.
NOW THEY ACT LIKE I DON'T EXIST.

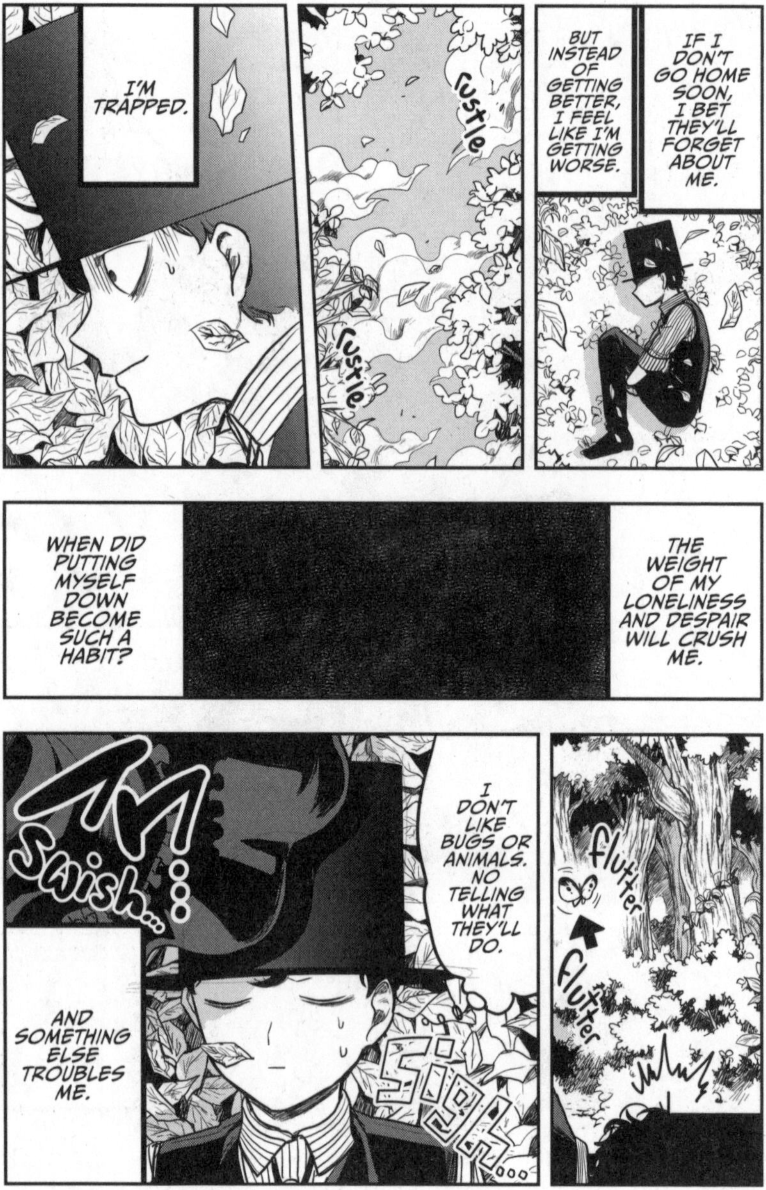
IF I DON'T GO HOME SOON, I BET THEY'LL FORGET ABOUT ME.
BUT INSTEAD OF GETTING BETTER, I FEEL LIKE I'M GETTING WORSE.
rustle
rustle
I'M TRAPPED.
THE WEIGHT OF MY LONELINESS AND DESPAIR WILL CRUSH ME.
WHEN DID PUTTING MYSELF DOWN BECOME SUCH A HABIT?
flutter
flutter
I DON'T LIKE BUGS OR ANIMALS. NO TELLING WHAT THEY'LL DO.
SWISH...
SIGH...
AND SOMETHING ELSE TROUBLES ME.

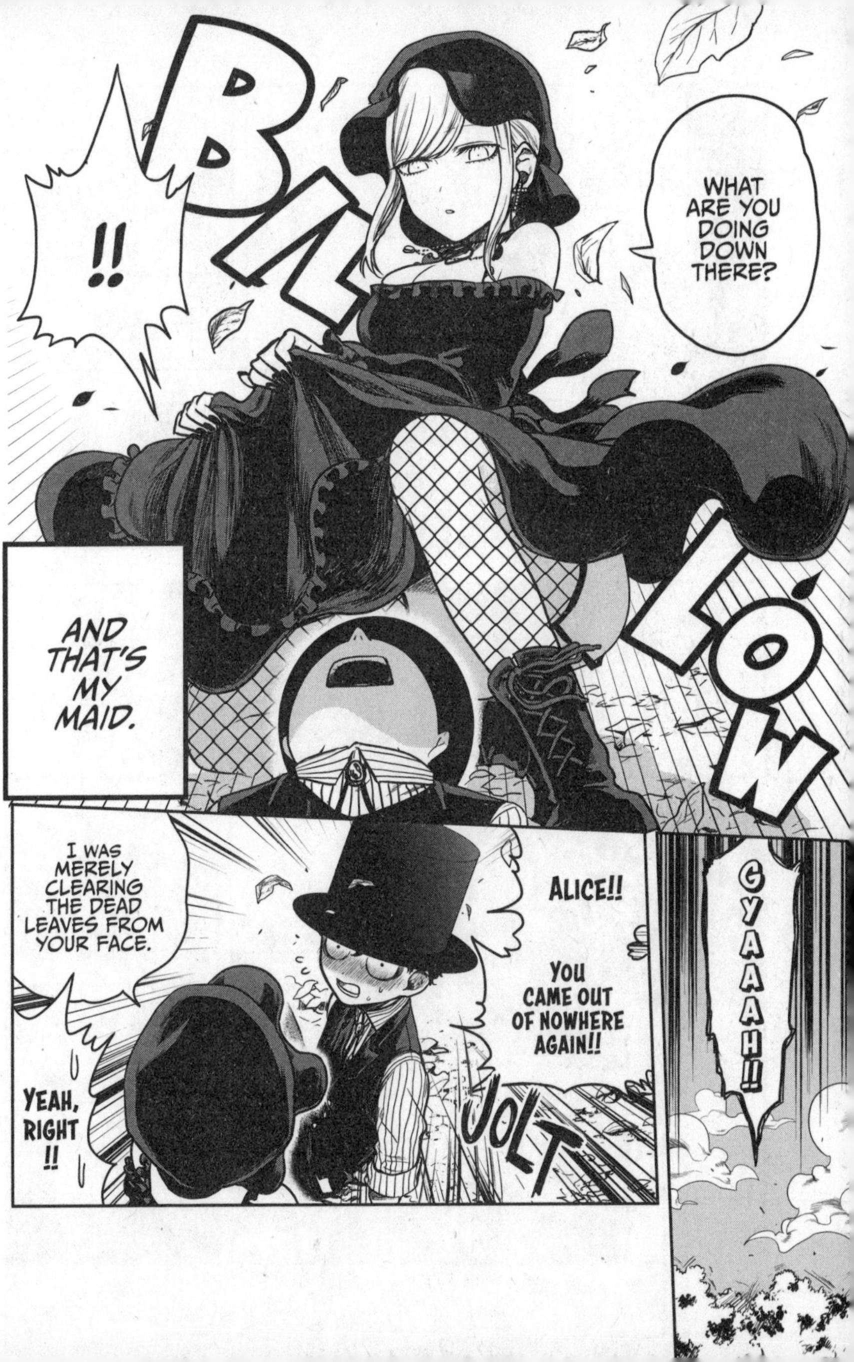
WHAT ARE YOU DOING DOWN THERE?
BL
LOW
!!
AND THAT'S MY MAID.
GYAAAAH!!
ALICE!!
YOU CAME OUT OF NOWHERE AGAIN!!
JOLT
I WAS MERELY CLEARING THE DEAD LEAVES FROM YOUR FACE.
YEAH, RIGHT!!

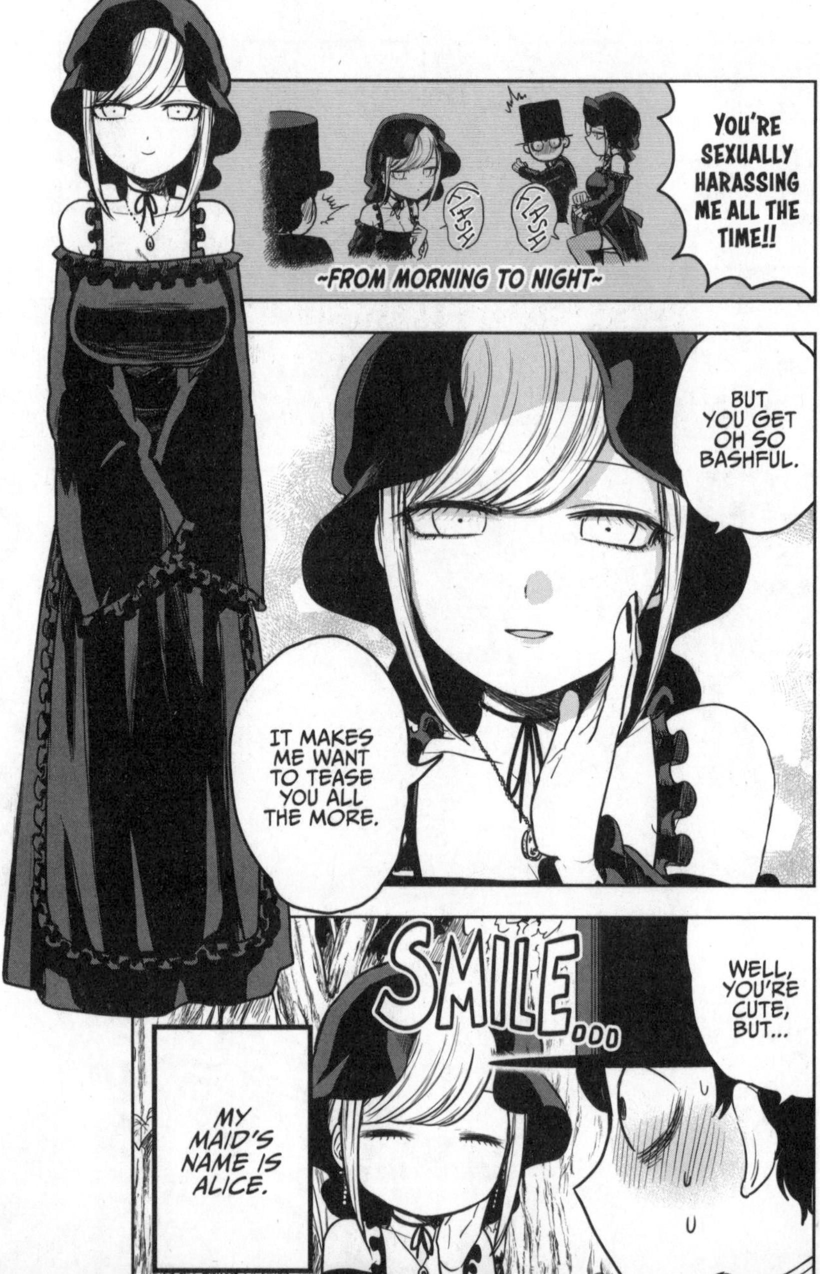

YOU'RE SEXUALLY HARASSING ME ALL THE TIME!!
FLASH
FLASH
~FROM MORNING TO NIGHT~
BUT YOU GET OH SO BASHFUL.
IT MAKES ME WANT TO TEASE YOU ALL THE MORE.
WELL, YOU'RE CUTE, BUT...
SMILE...
MY MAID'S NAME IS ALICE.

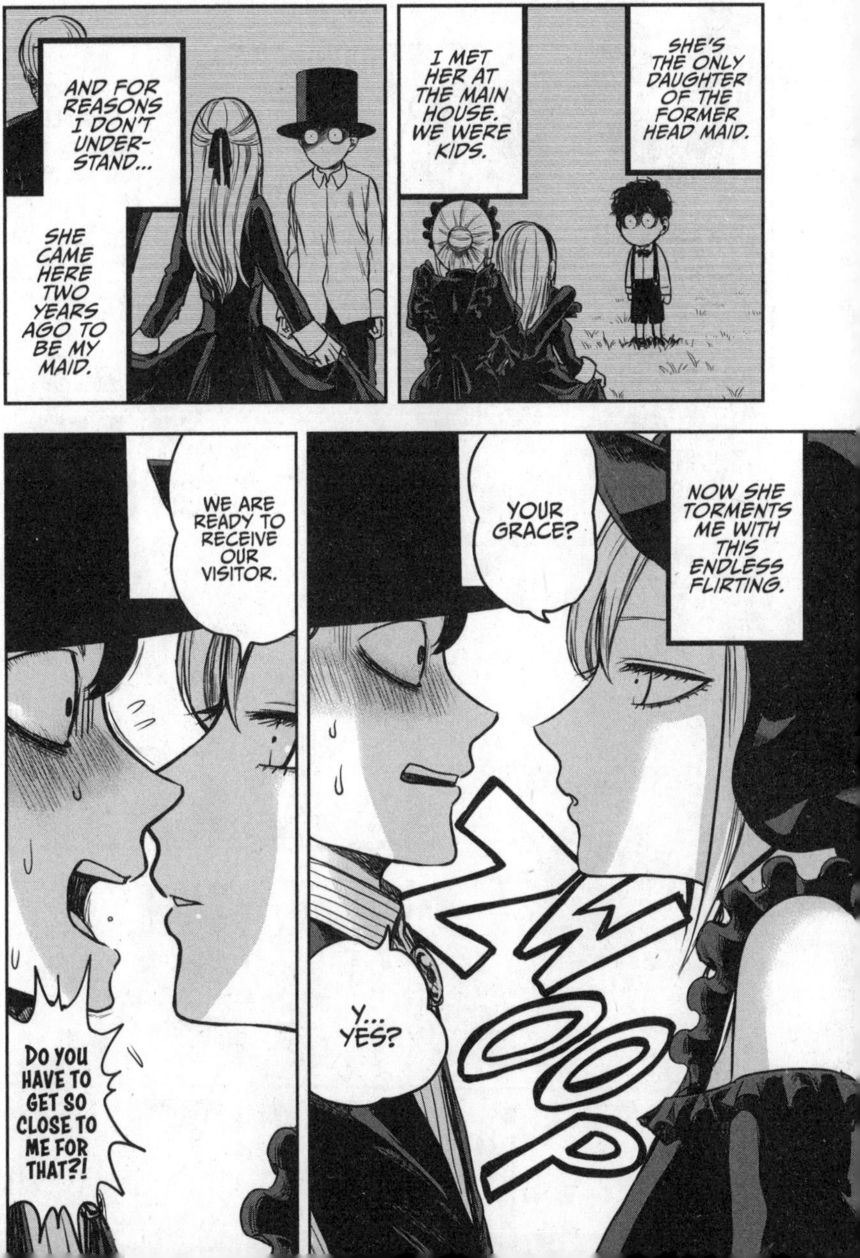
SHE'S THE ONLY DAUGHTER OF THE FORMER HEAD MAID.
I MET HER AT THE MAIN HOUSE. WE WERE KIDS.
AND FOR REASONS I DON'T UNDER-STAND...
SHE CAME HERE TWO YEARS AGO TO BE MY MAID.
NOW SHE TORMENTS ME WITH THIS ENDLESS FLIRTING.
YOUR GRACE?
SWOOP
Y... YES?
WE ARE READY TO RECEIVE OUR VISITOR.
DO YOU HAVE TO GET SO CLOSE TO ME FOR THAT?!

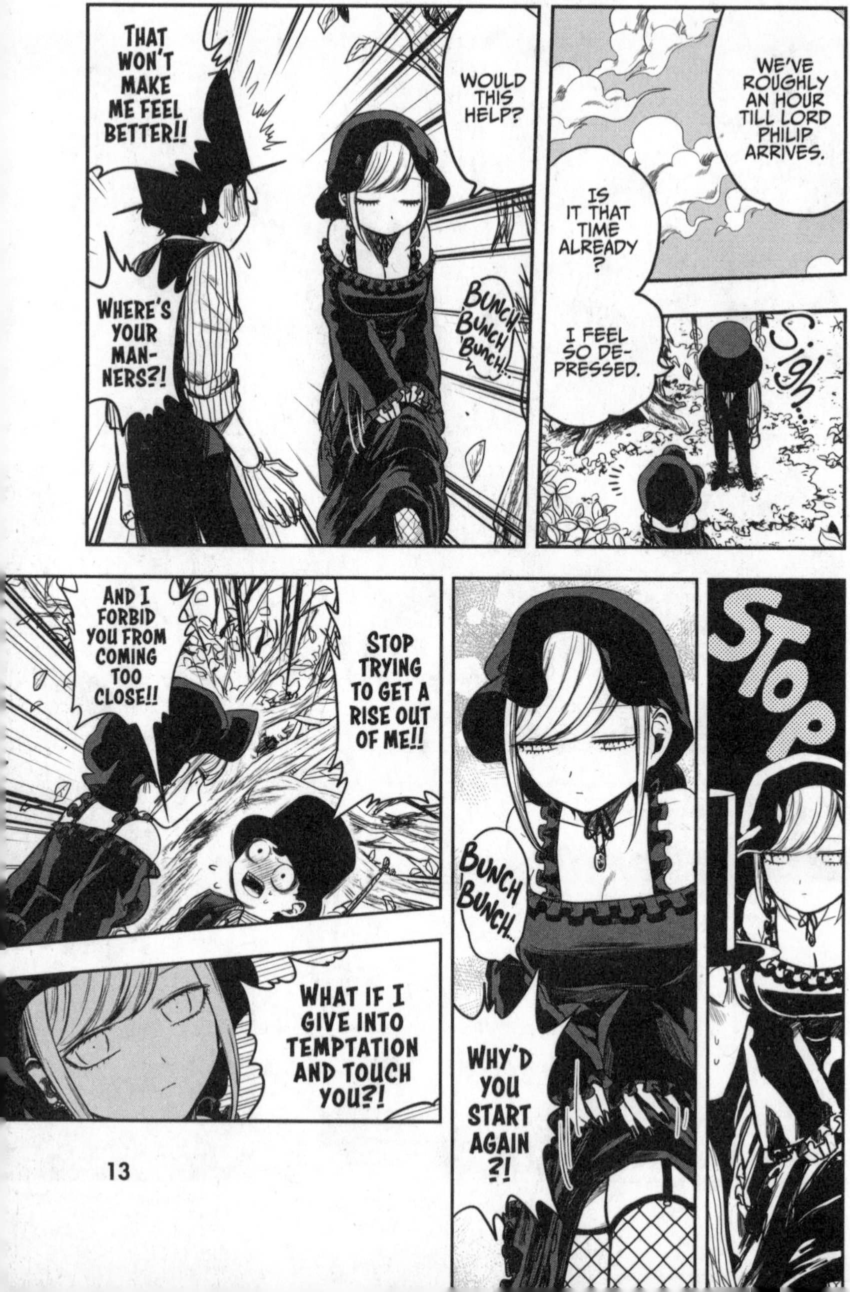

WE'VE ROUGHLY AN HOUR TILL LORD PHILIP ARRIVES.
IS IT THAT TIME ALREADY?
I FEEL SO DE-PRESSED.
Sigh...
WOULD THIS HELP?
THAT WON'T MAKE ME FEEL BETTER!!
BUNCH BUNCH BUNCH...
WHERE'S YOUR MAN-NERS?!
STOP
BUNCH BUNCH...
WHY'D YOU START AGAIN?!
STOP TRYING TO GET A RISE OUT OF ME!!
AND I FORBID YOU FROM COMING TOO CLOSE!!
WHAT IF I GIVE INTO TEMPTATION AND TOUCH YOU?!

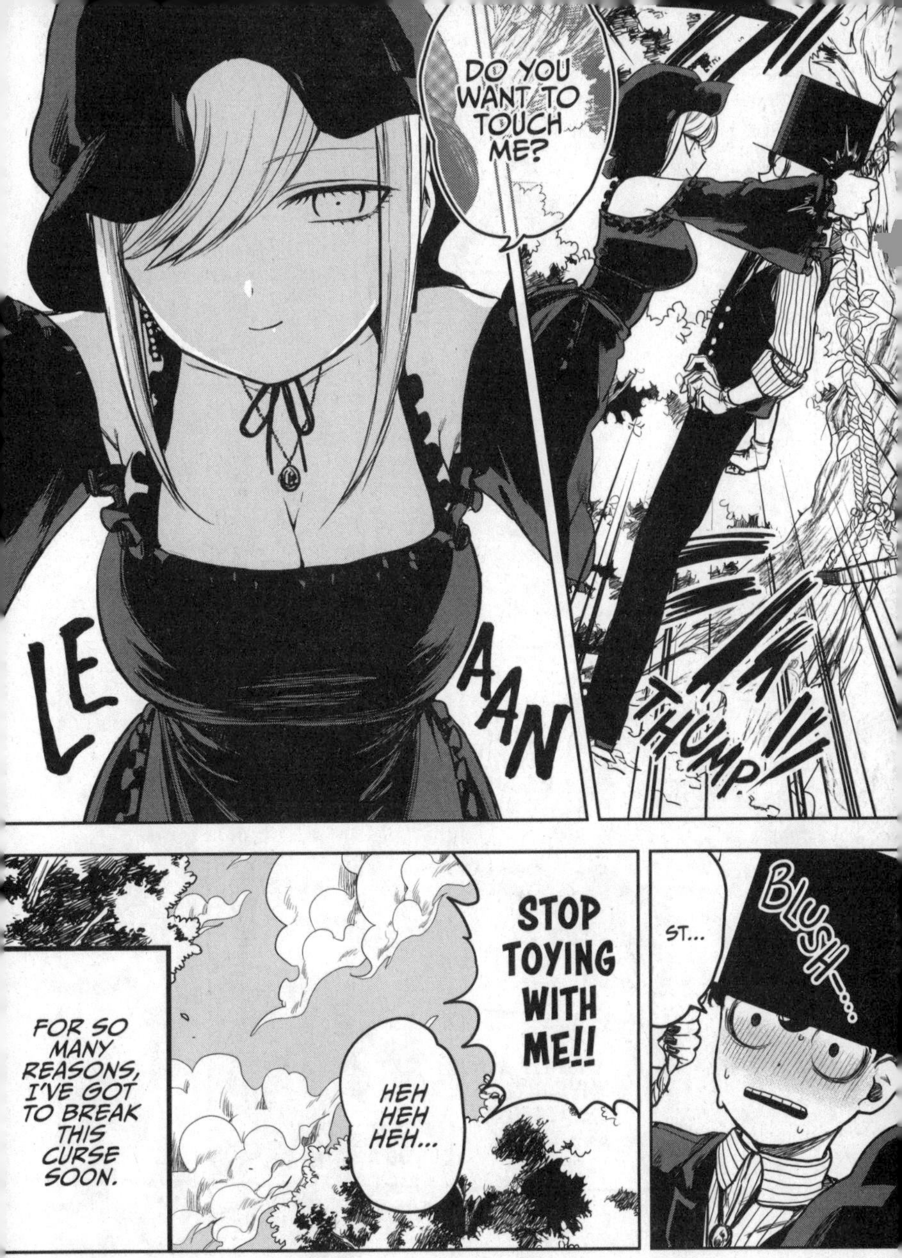
THUMP!
DO YOU WANT TO TOUCH ME?
LE
AAN
BLUSH...
ST...
STOP TOYING WITH ME!!
HEH HEH HEH...
FOR SO MANY REASONS, I'VE GOT TO BREAK THIS CURSE SOON.

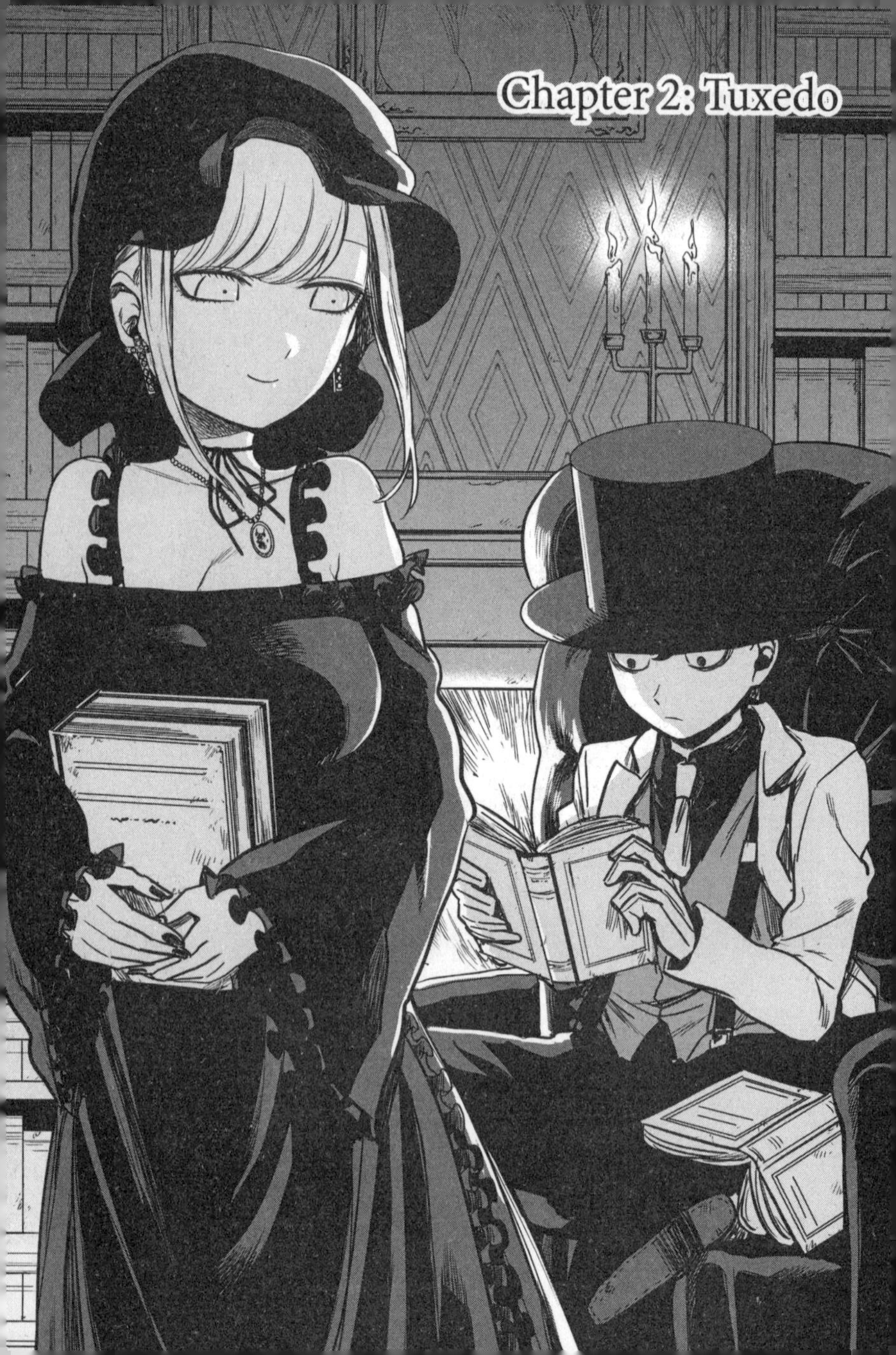
Chapter 2: Tuxedo

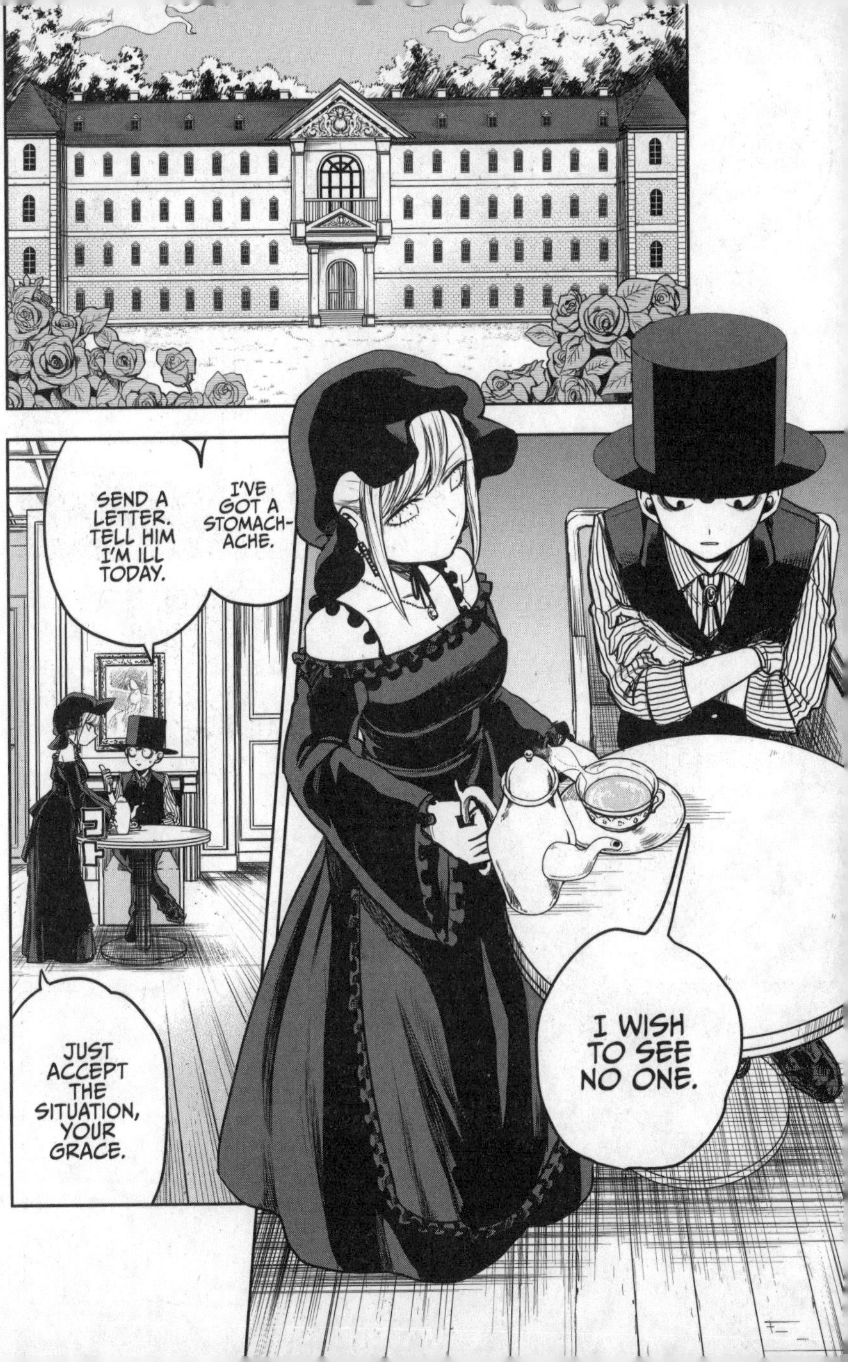
I'VE GOT A STOMACH-ACHE.
SEND A LETTER. TELL HIM I'M ILL TODAY.
I WISH TO SEE NO ONE.
JUST ACCEPT THE SITUATION, YOUR GRACE.

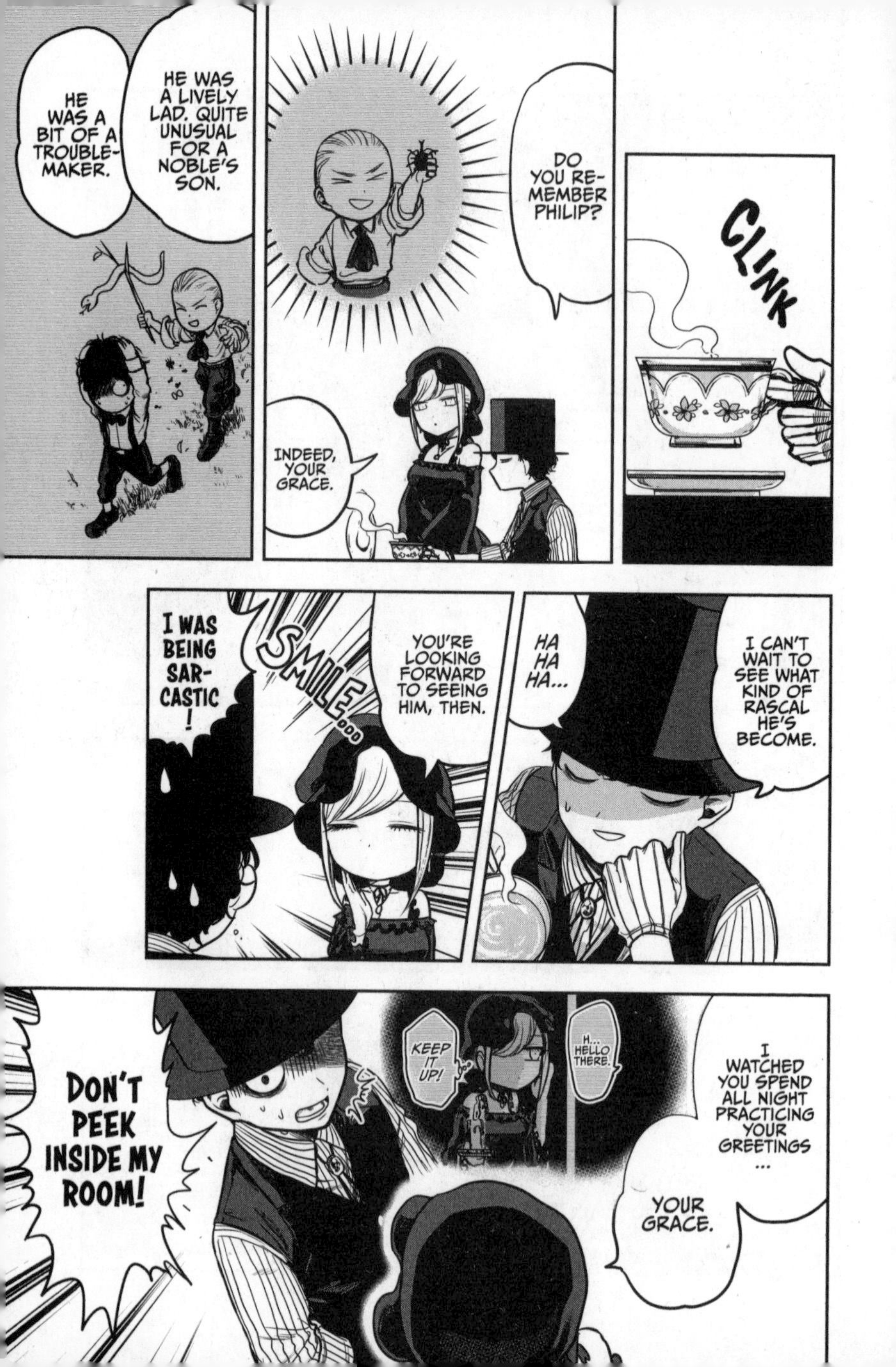
CLINK
DO YOU RE-MEMBER PHILIP?
INDEED, YOUR GRACE.
HE WAS A LIVELY LAD. QUITE UNUSUAL FOR A NOBLE'S SON.
HE WAS A BIT OF A TROUBLE-MAKER.
I CAN'T WAIT TO SEE WHAT KIND OF RASCAL HE'S BECOME.
HA HA HA...
YOU'RE LOOKING FORWARD TO SEEING HIM, THEN.
SMILE...
I WAS BEING SAR-CASTIC!
I WATCHED YOU SPEND ALL NIGHT PRACTICING YOUR GREETINGS...
YOUR GRACE.
H... HELLO THERE.
KEEP IT UP!
DON'T PEEK INSIDE MY ROOM!

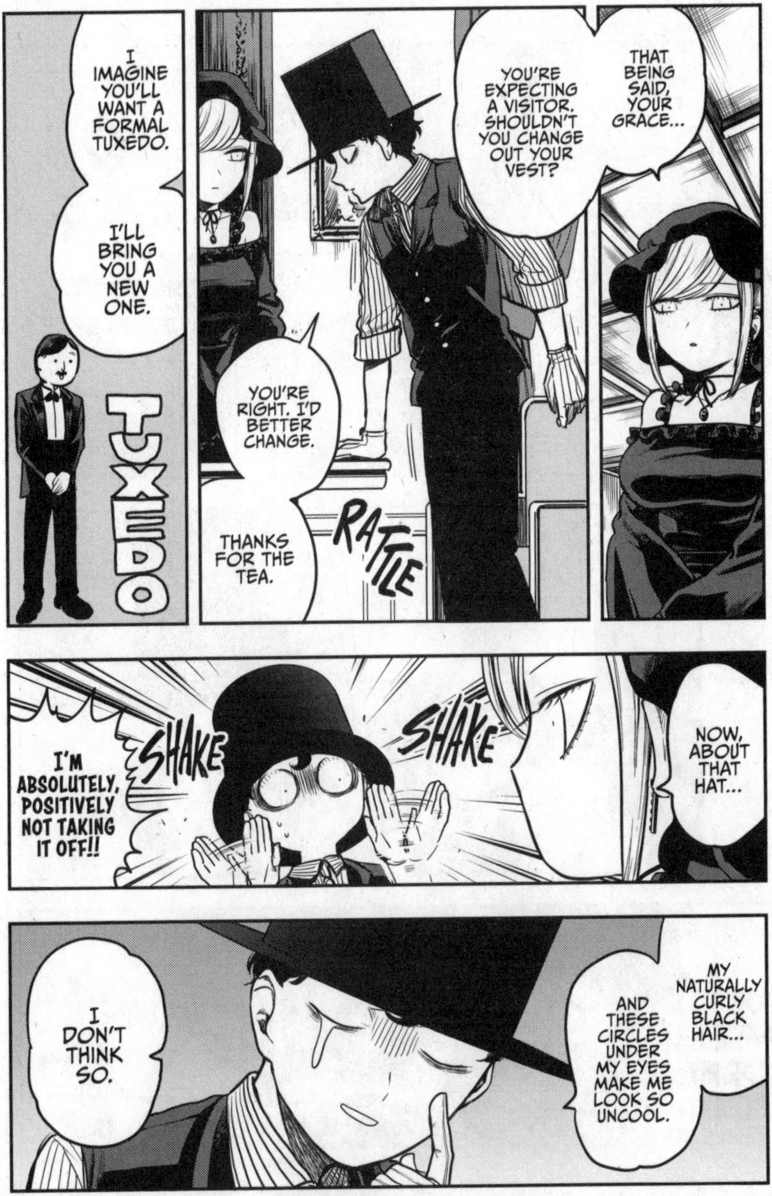
THAT BEING SAID, YOUR GRACE...
YOU'RE EXPECTING A VISITOR. SHOULDN'T YOU CHANGE OUT YOUR VEST?
YOU'RE RIGHT. I'D BETTER CHANGE.
THANKS FOR THE TEA.
RATTLE
I IMAGINE YOU'LL WANT A FORMAL TUXEDO.
I'LL BRING YOU A NEW ONE.
TUXEDO
NOW, ABOUT THAT HAT...
SHAKE
SHAKE
I'M ABSOLUTELY, POSITIVELY NOT TAKING IT OFF!!
MY NATURALLY CURLY BLACK HAIR...
AND THESE CIRCLES UNDER MY EYES MAKE ME LOOK SO UNCOOL.
I DON'T THINK SO.

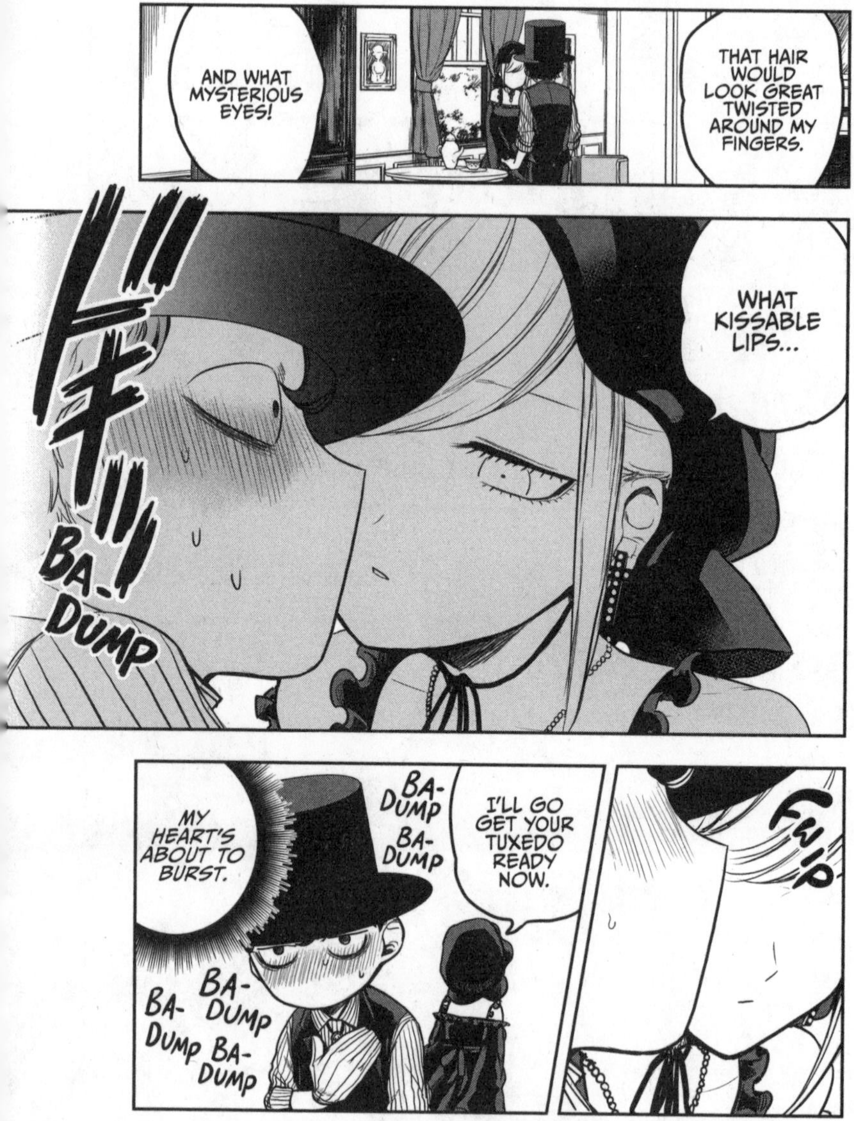
THAT HAIR WOULD LOOK GREAT TWISTED AROUND MY FINGERS.
AND WHAT MYSTERIOUS EYES!
WHAT KISSABLE LIPS...
BA-DUMP
FWIP
I'LL GO GET YOUR TUXEDO READY NOW.
BA-DUMP BA-DUMP
MY HEART'S ABOUT TO BURST.
BA-DUMP BA-DUMP BA-DUMP

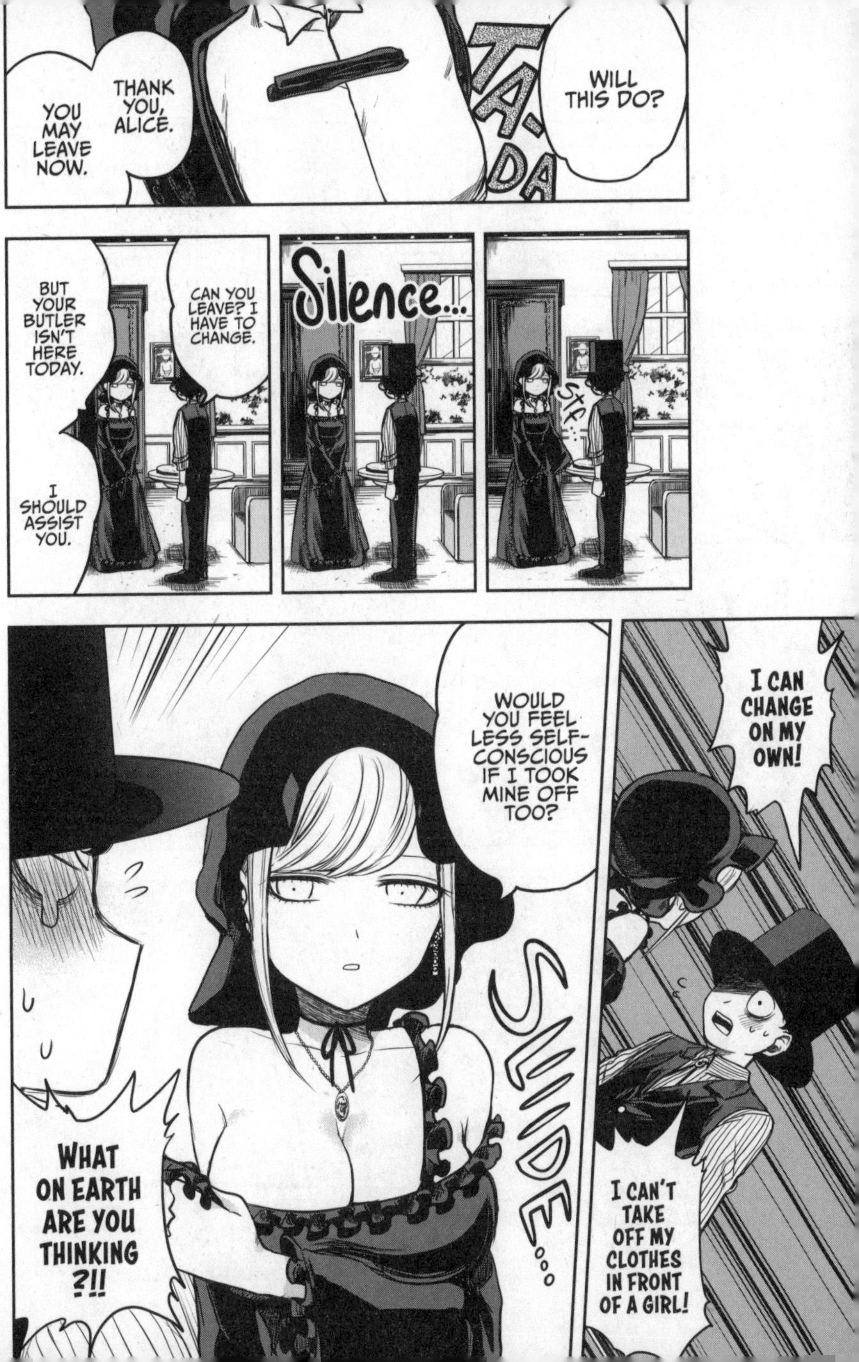
WILL THIS DO?
TA-DA
THANK YOU, ALICE.
YOU MAY LEAVE NOW.
Stf...
Silence...
CAN YOU LEAVE? I HAVE TO CHANGE.
BUT YOUR BUTLER ISN'T HERE TODAY.
I SHOULD ASSIST YOU.
I CAN CHANGE ON MY OWN!
I CAN'T TAKE OFF MY CLOTHES IN FRONT OF A GIRL!
WOULD YOU FEEL LESS SELF-CONSCIOUS IF I TOOK MINE OFF TOO?
SLIIDE...
WHAT ON EARTH ARE YOU THINKING?!!

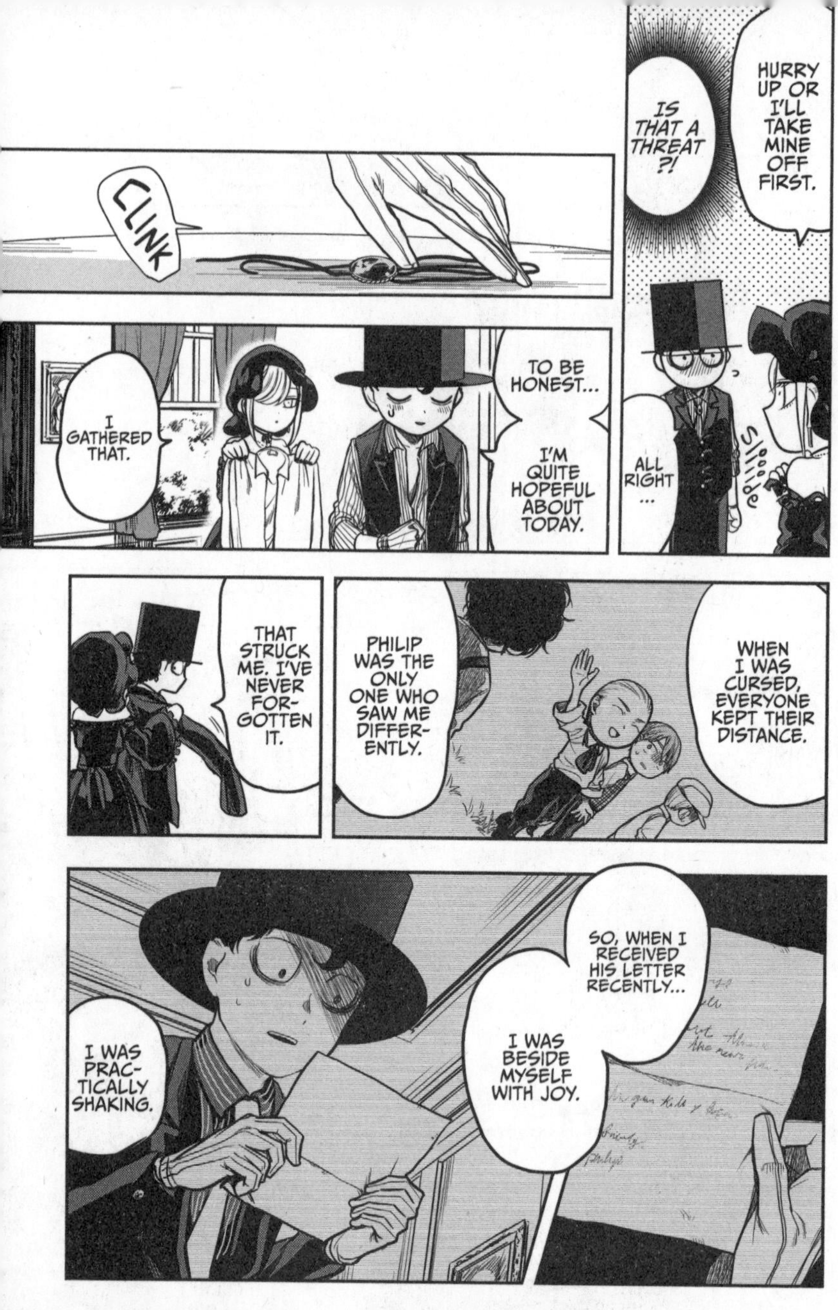
HURRY UP OR I'LL TAKE MINE OFF FIRST.
IS THAT A THREAT?!
ALL RIGHT...
Sliiide
CLINK
TO BE HONEST...
I'M QUITE HOPEFUL ABOUT TODAY.
I GATHERED THAT.
WHEN I WAS CURSED, EVERYONE KEPT THEIR DISTANCE.
PHILIP WAS THE ONLY ONE WHO SAW ME DIFFER-ENTLY.
THAT STRUCK ME. I'VE NEVER FOR-GOTTEN IT.
SO, WHEN I RECEIVED HIS LETTER RECENTLY...
I WAS BESIDE MYSELF WITH JOY.
I WAS PRAC-TICALLY SHAKING.

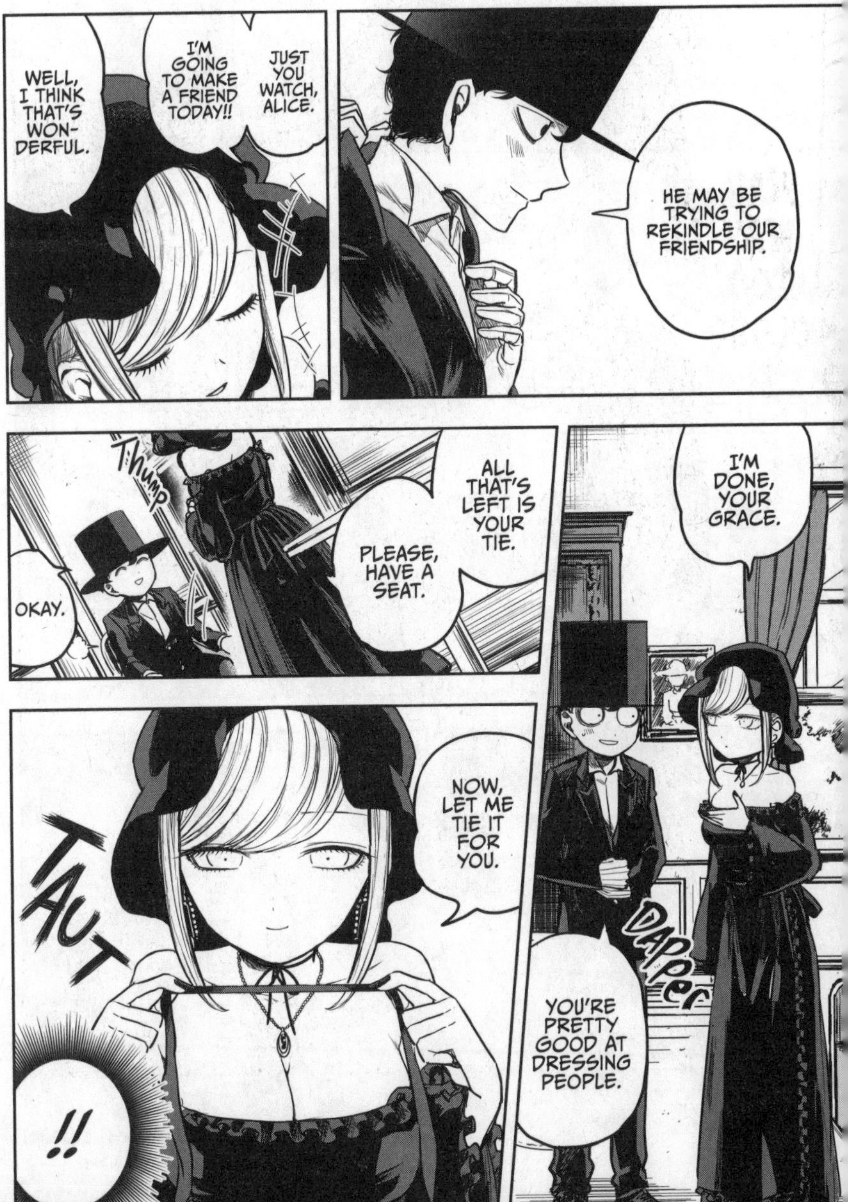
HE MAY BE TRYING TO REKINDLE OUR FRIENDSHIP.
JUST YOU WATCH, ALICE.
I'M GOING TO MAKE A FRIEND TODAY!!
WELL, I THINK THAT'S WON-DERFUL.
I'M DONE, YOUR GRACE.
DAPPER
YOU'RE PRETTY GOOD AT DRESSING PEOPLE.
ALL THAT'S LEFT IS YOUR TIE.
PLEASE, HAVE A SEAT.
Thump
OKAY.
NOW, LET ME TIE IT FOR YOU.
TAUT
!!

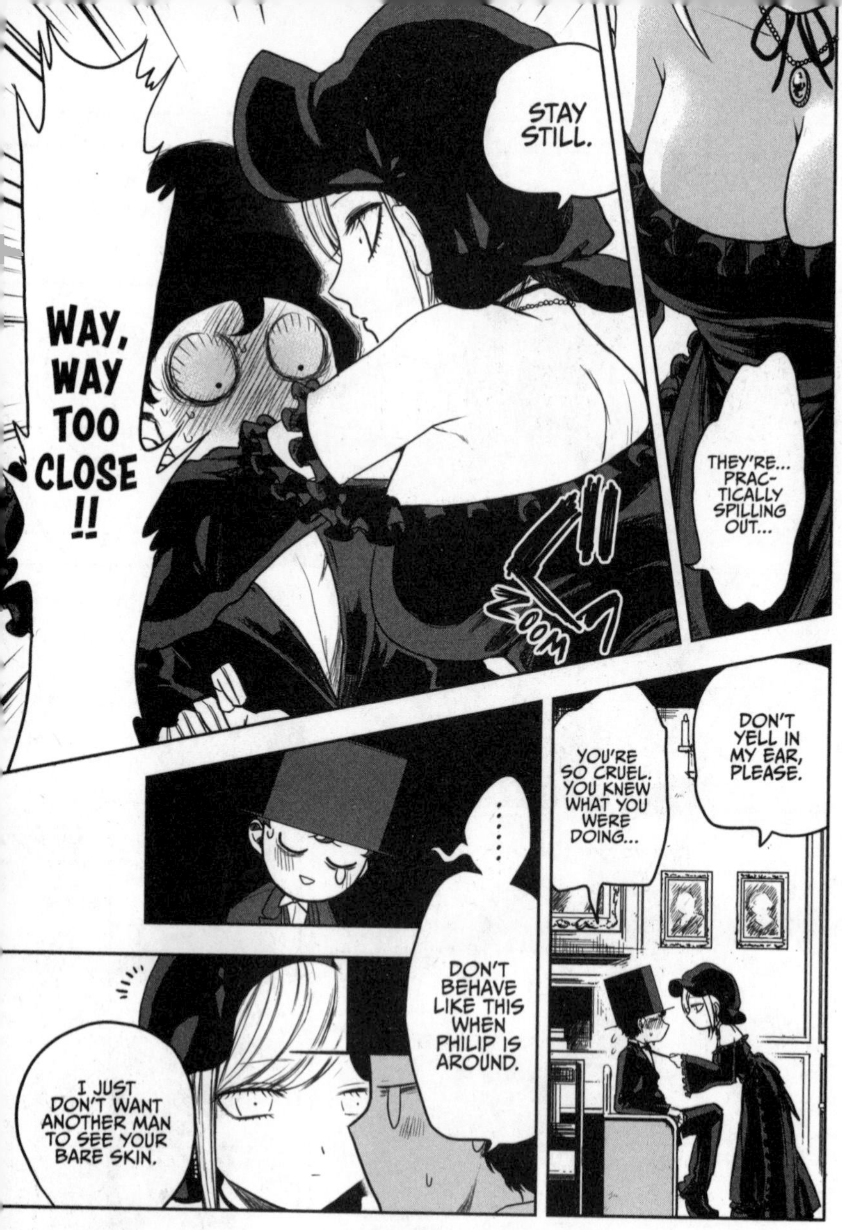
THEY'RE... PRAC-TICALLY SPILLING OUT...
STAY STILL.
WAY, WAY TOO CLOSE!!
ZOOM
DON'T YELL IN MY EAR, PLEASE.
YOU'RE SO CRUEL. YOU KNEW WHAT YOU WERE DOING...
......
DON'T BEHAVE LIKE THIS WHEN PHILIP IS AROUND.
I JUST DON'T WANT ANOTHER MAN TO SEE YOUR BARE SKIN.

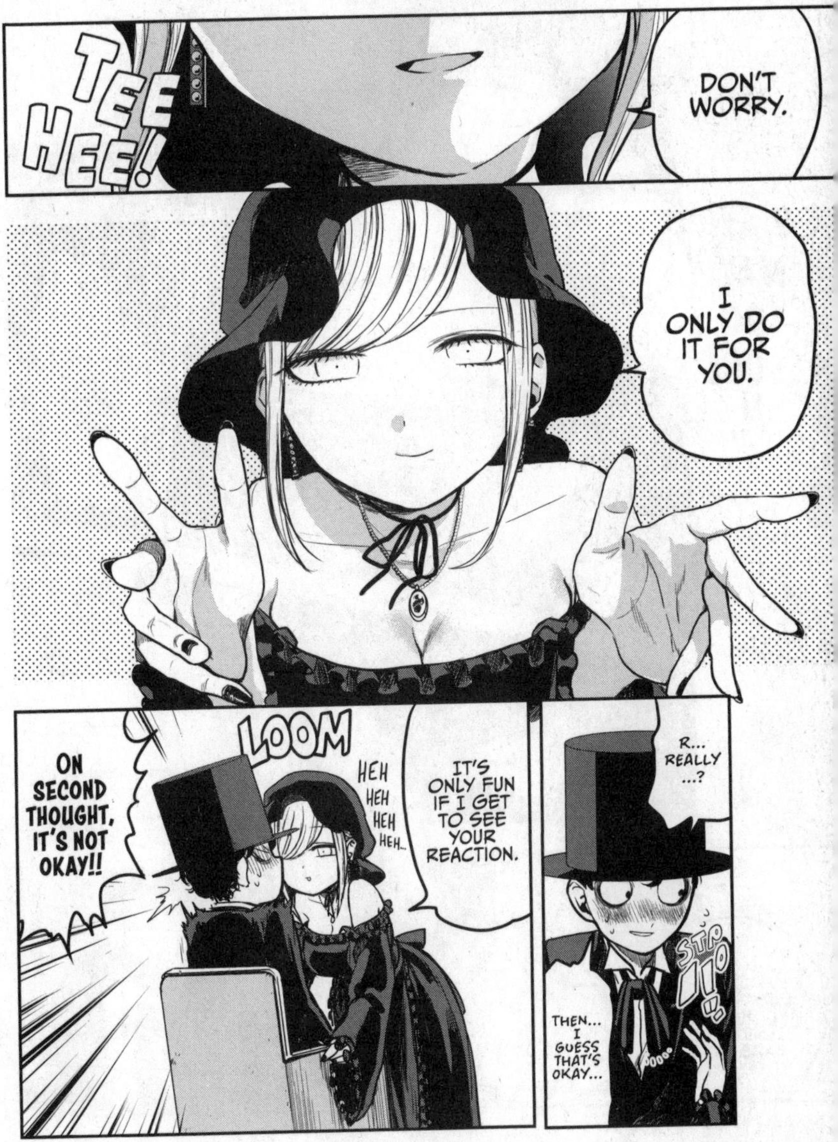
DON'T WORRY.
TEE HEE!
I ONLY DO IT FOR YOU.
R... REALLY ...?
THEN... I GUESS THAT'S OKAY...
IT'S ONLY FUN IF I GET TO SEE YOUR REACTION.
HEH HEH HEH HEH...
LOOM
ON SECOND THOUGHT, IT'S NOT OKAY!!

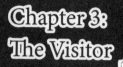

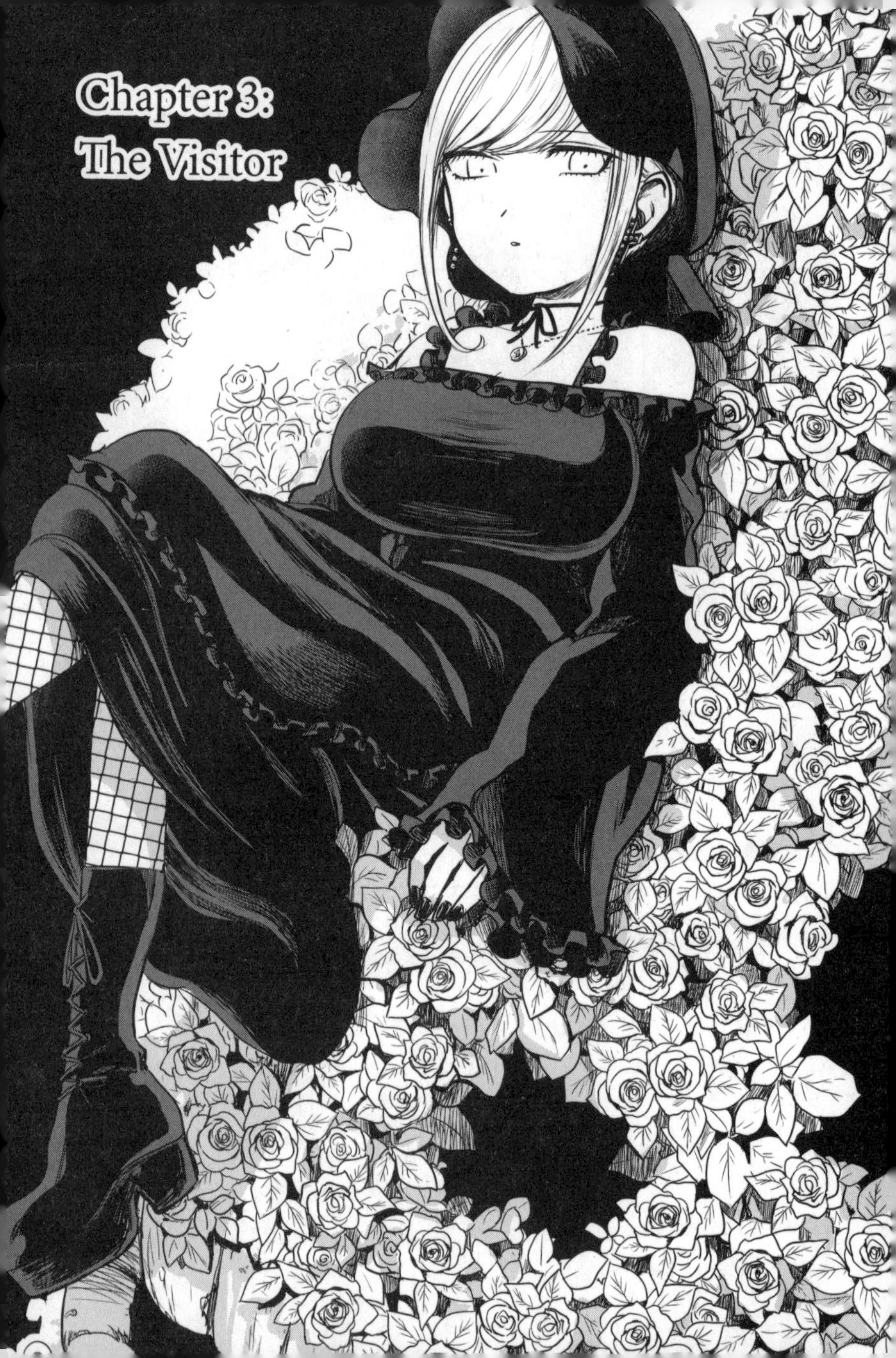

Chapter 3:
The Visitor

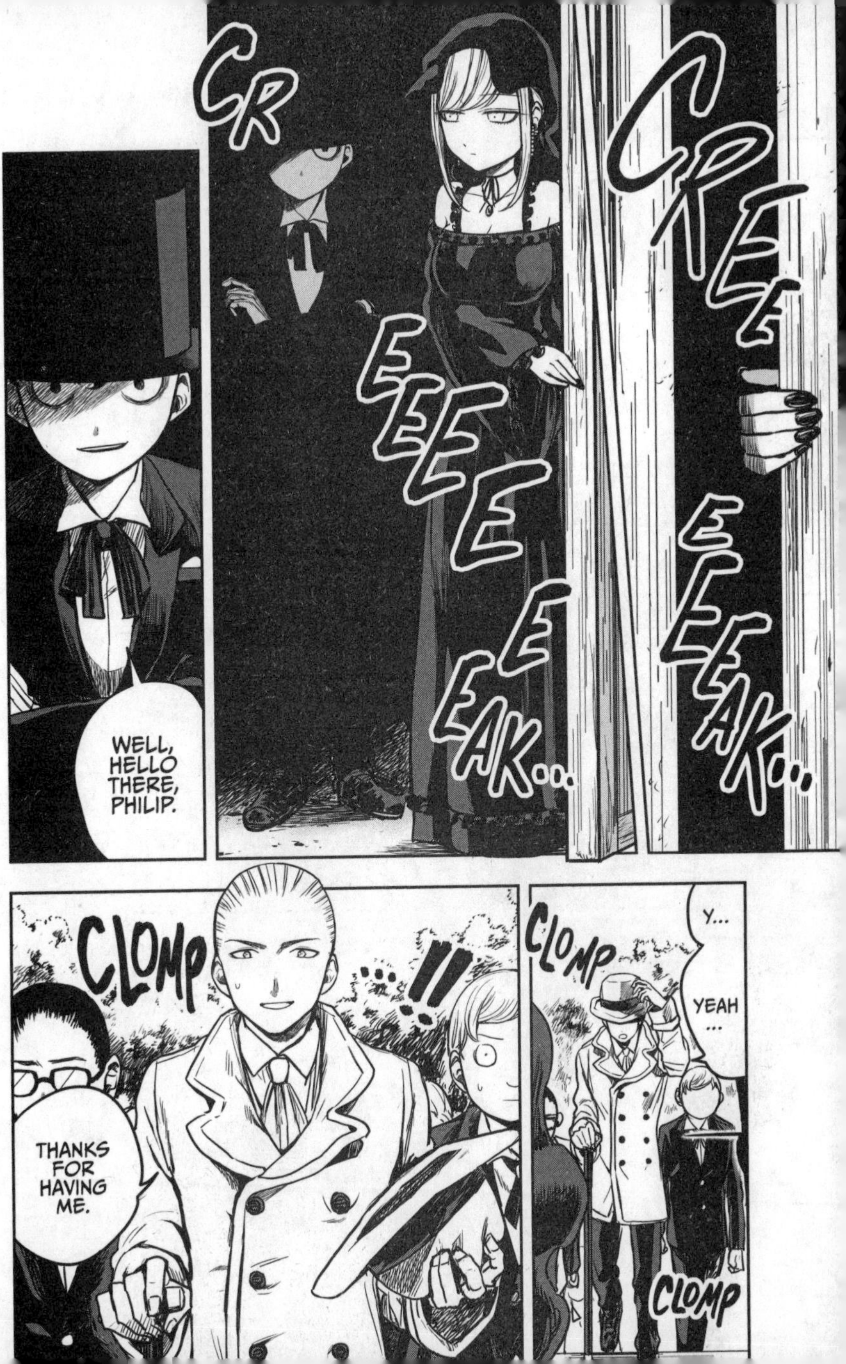
CREE
EEEEAK...
CR
EEEEEEAK...
WELL, HELLO THERE, PHILIP.
Y...
YEAH...
CLOMP
CLOMP
CLOMP
...!!
THANKS FOR HAVING ME.

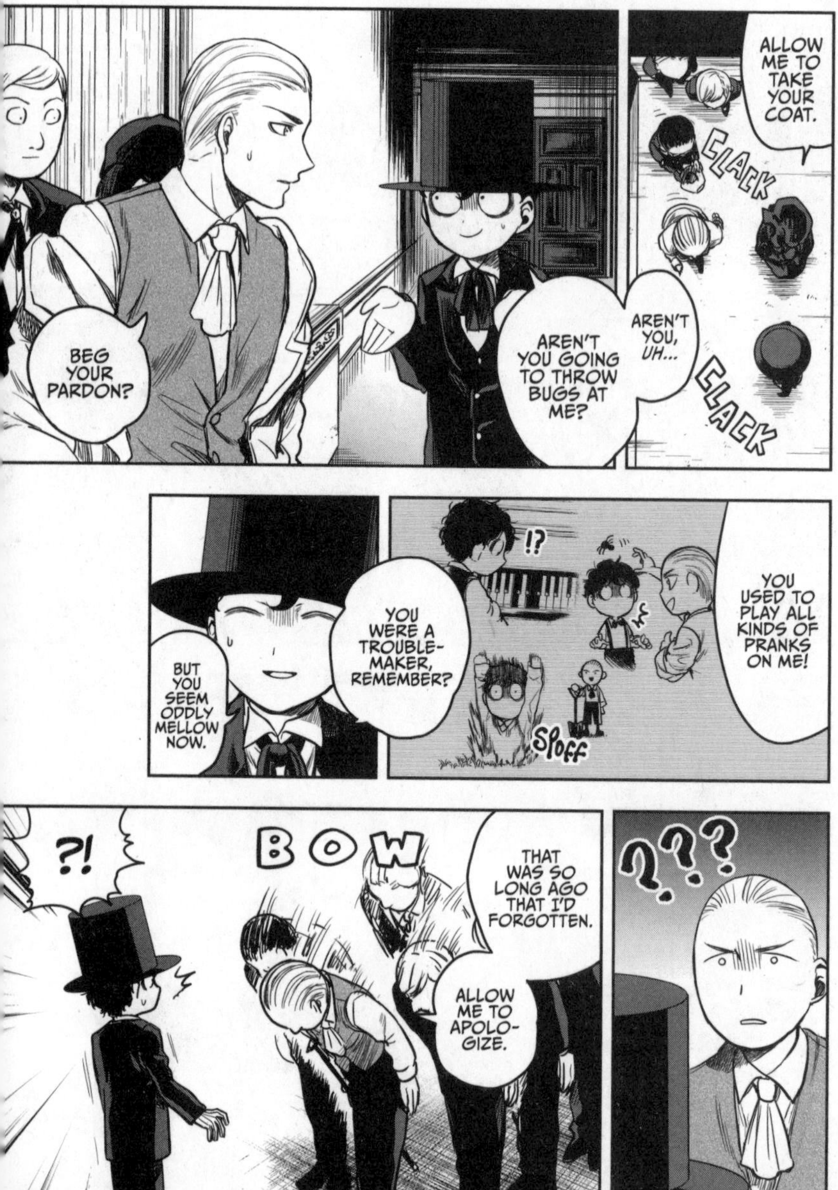
ALLOW ME TO TAKE YOUR COAT.
CLACK
CLACK
AREN'T YOU, UH...
AREN'T YOU GOING TO THROW BUGS AT ME?
BEG YOUR PARDON?
YOU USED TO PLAY ALL KINDS OF PRANKS ON ME!
!?
SPOFF
YOU WERE A TROUBLE-MAKER, REMEMBER?
BUT YOU SEEM ODDLY MELLOW NOW.
???
THAT WAS SO LONG AGO THAT I'D FORGOTTEN.
ALLOW ME TO APOLOGIZE.
BOW
?!

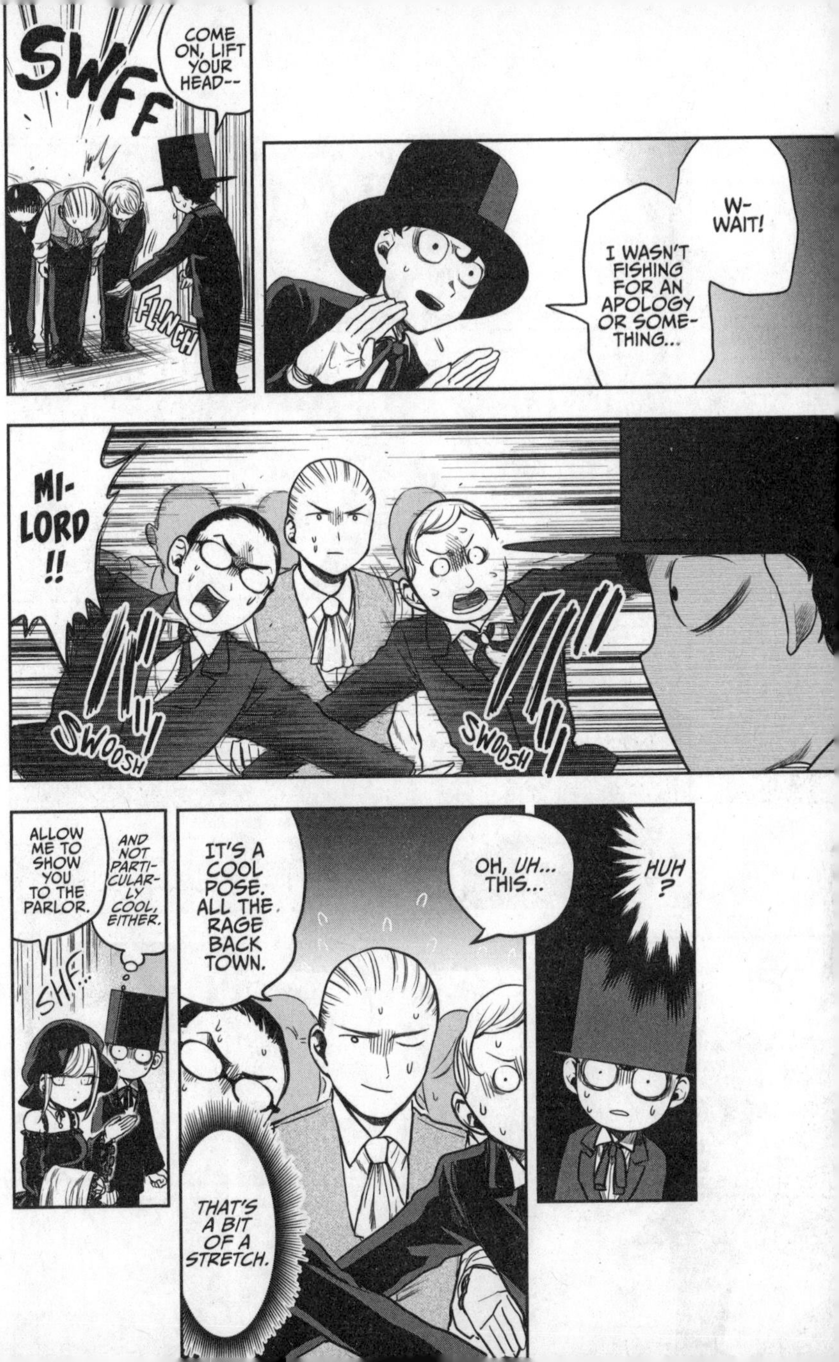
W-WAIT!
I WASN'T FISHING FOR AN APOLOGY OR SOMETHING...
COME ON, LIFT YOUR HEAD--
SWFF
FLINCH
MI-LORD!!
SWOOSH
SWOOSH
HUH?
OH, UH... THIS...
IT'S A COOL POSE. ALL THE RAGE BACK TOWN.
THAT'S A BIT OF A STRETCH.
AND NOT PARTICULARLY COOL, EITHER.
ALLOW ME TO SHOW YOU TO THE PARLOR.
SHF...

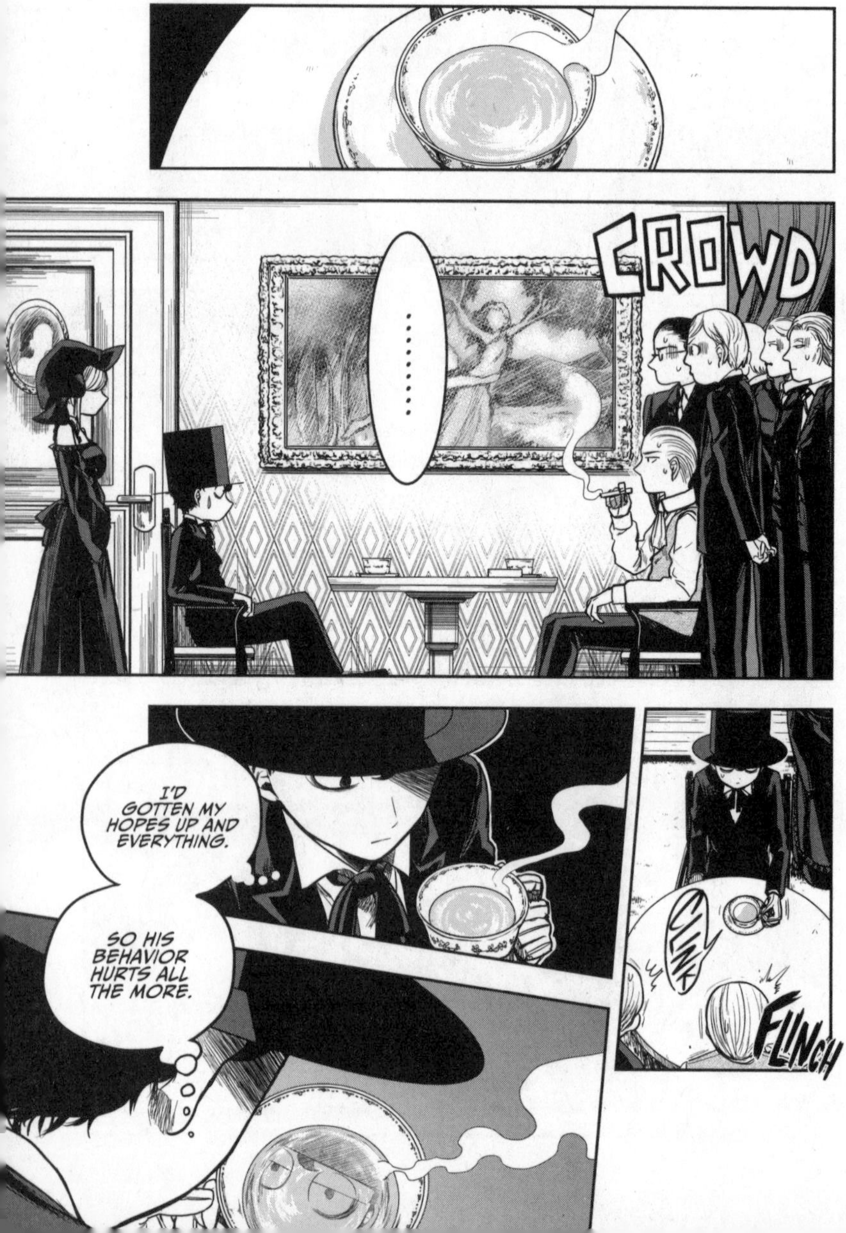
CROWD
......
CLINK
FLINCH
I'D GOTTEN MY HOPES UP AND EVERYTHING.
SO HIS BEHAVIOR HURTS ALL THE MORE.

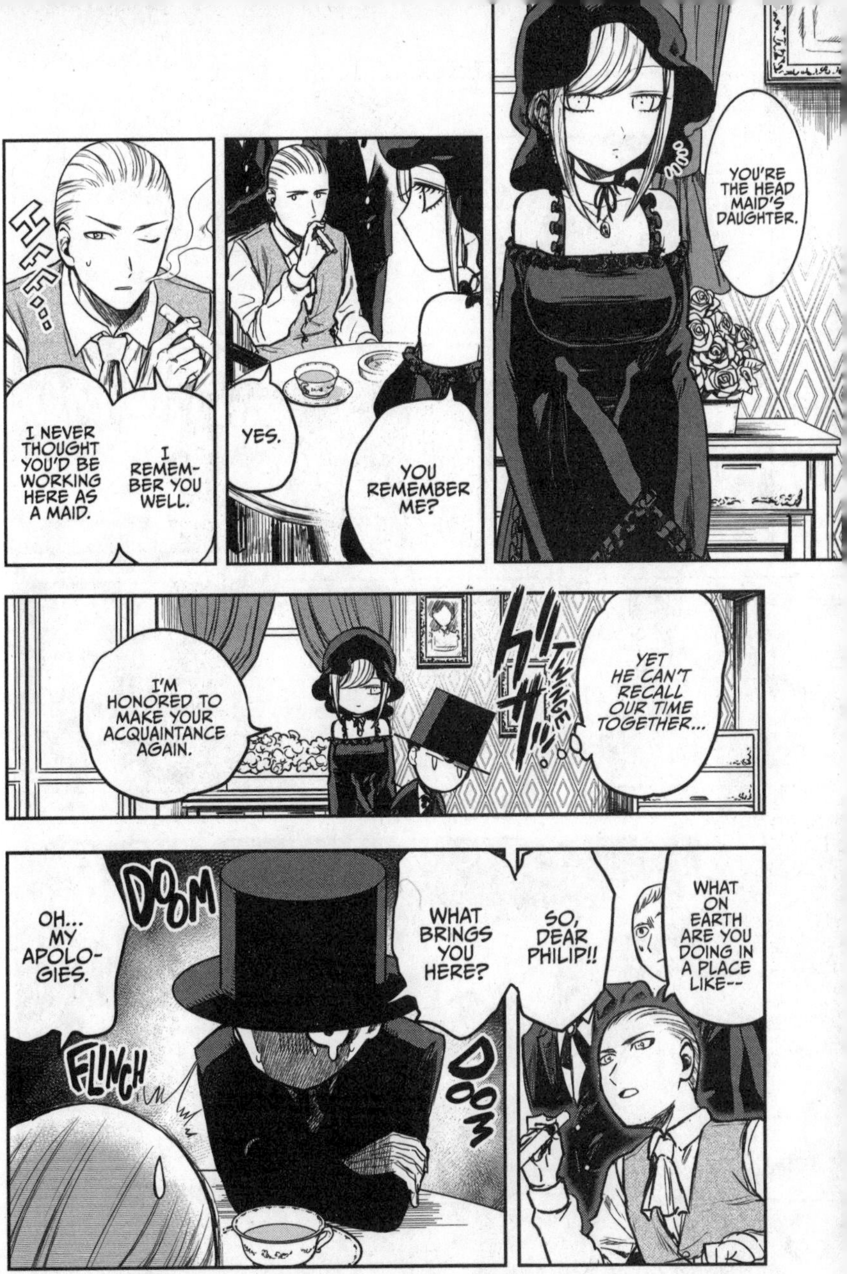
YOU'RE THE HEAD MAID'S DAUGHTER.
YOU REMEMBER ME?
YES.
I REMEMBER YOU WELL.
I NEVER THOUGHT YOU'D BE WORKING HERE AS A MAID.
YET HE CAN'T RECALL OUR TIME TOGETHER...
TWINGE
I'M HONORED TO MAKE YOUR ACQUAINTANCE AGAIN.
WHAT ON EARTH ARE YOU DOING IN A PLACE LIKE--
SO, DEAR PHILIP!!
WHAT BRINGS YOU HERE?
DOOM
DOOM
OH... MY APOLOGIES.
FLINCH

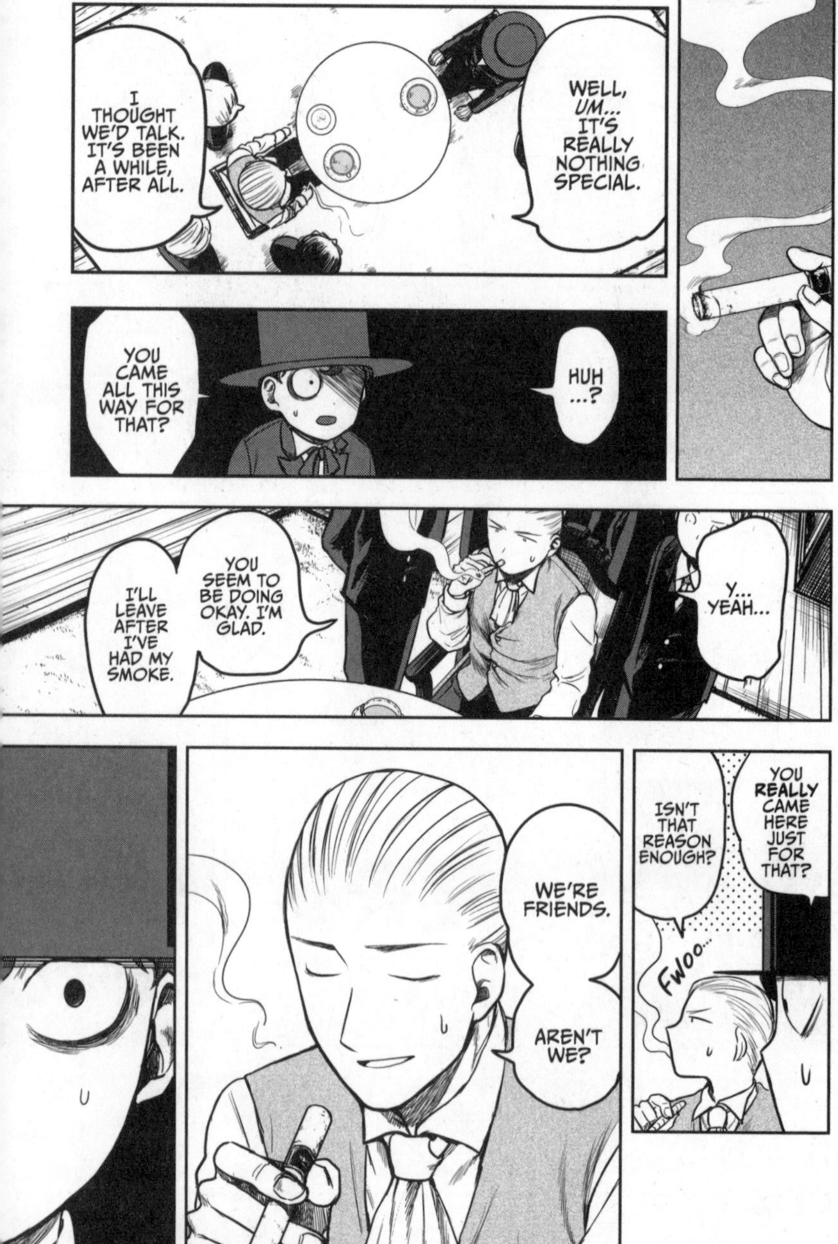
WELL, UM... IT'S REALLY NOTHING SPECIAL.
I THOUGHT WE'D TALK. IT'S BEEN A WHILE, AFTER ALL.
HUH ...?
YOU CAME ALL THIS WAY FOR THAT?
Y... YEAH...
YOU SEEM TO BE DOING OKAY. I'M GLAD.
I'LL LEAVE AFTER I'VE HAD MY SMOKE.
YOU **REALLY** CAME HERE JUST FOR THAT?
ISN'T THAT REASON ENOUGH?
FWOO...
WE'RE FRIENDS.
AREN'T WE?

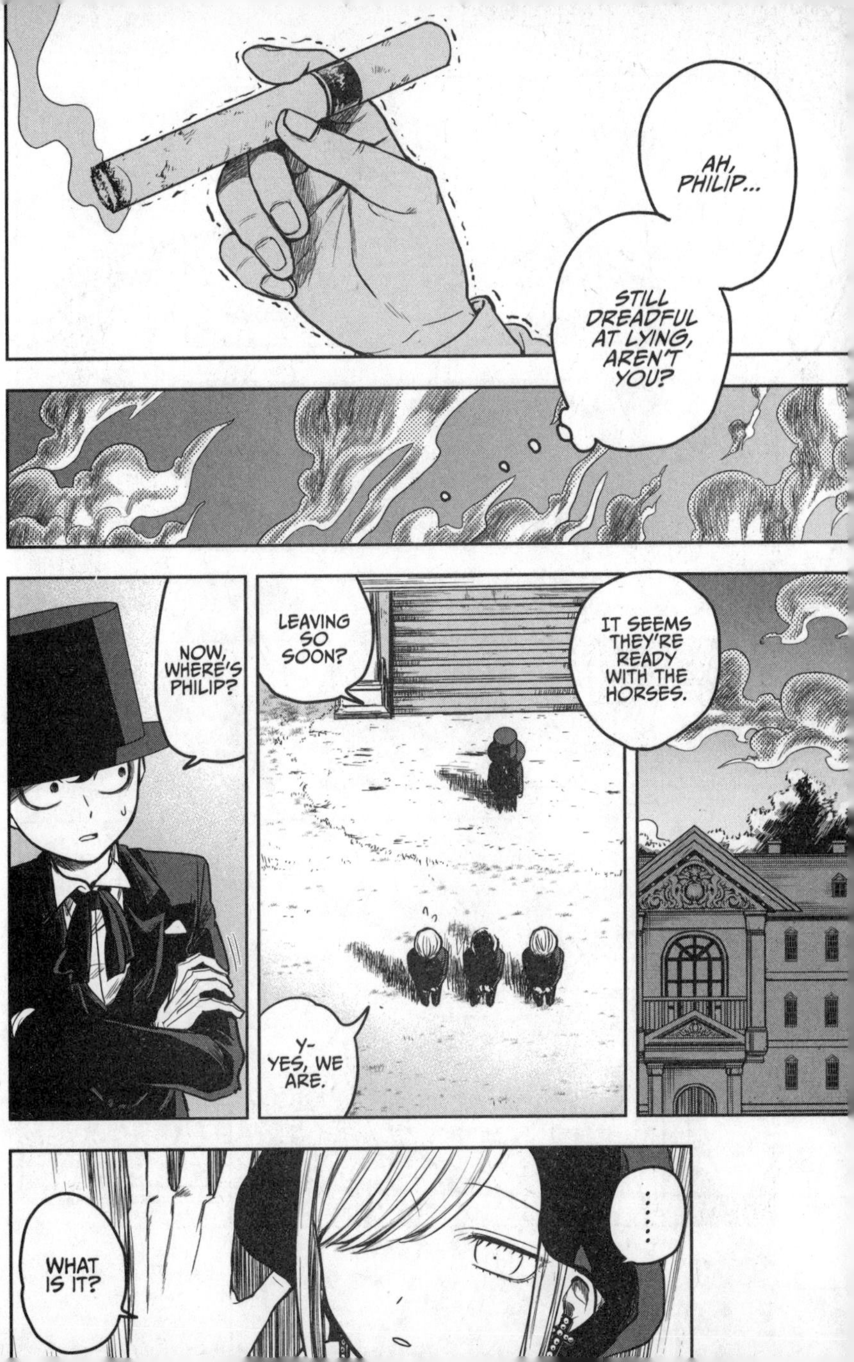
AH, PHILIP...
STILL DREADFUL AT LYING, AREN'T YOU?
IT SEEMS THEY'RE READY WITH THE HORSES.
LEAVING SO SOON?
Y- YES, WE ARE.
NOW, WHERE'S PHILIP?
......
WHAT IS IT?

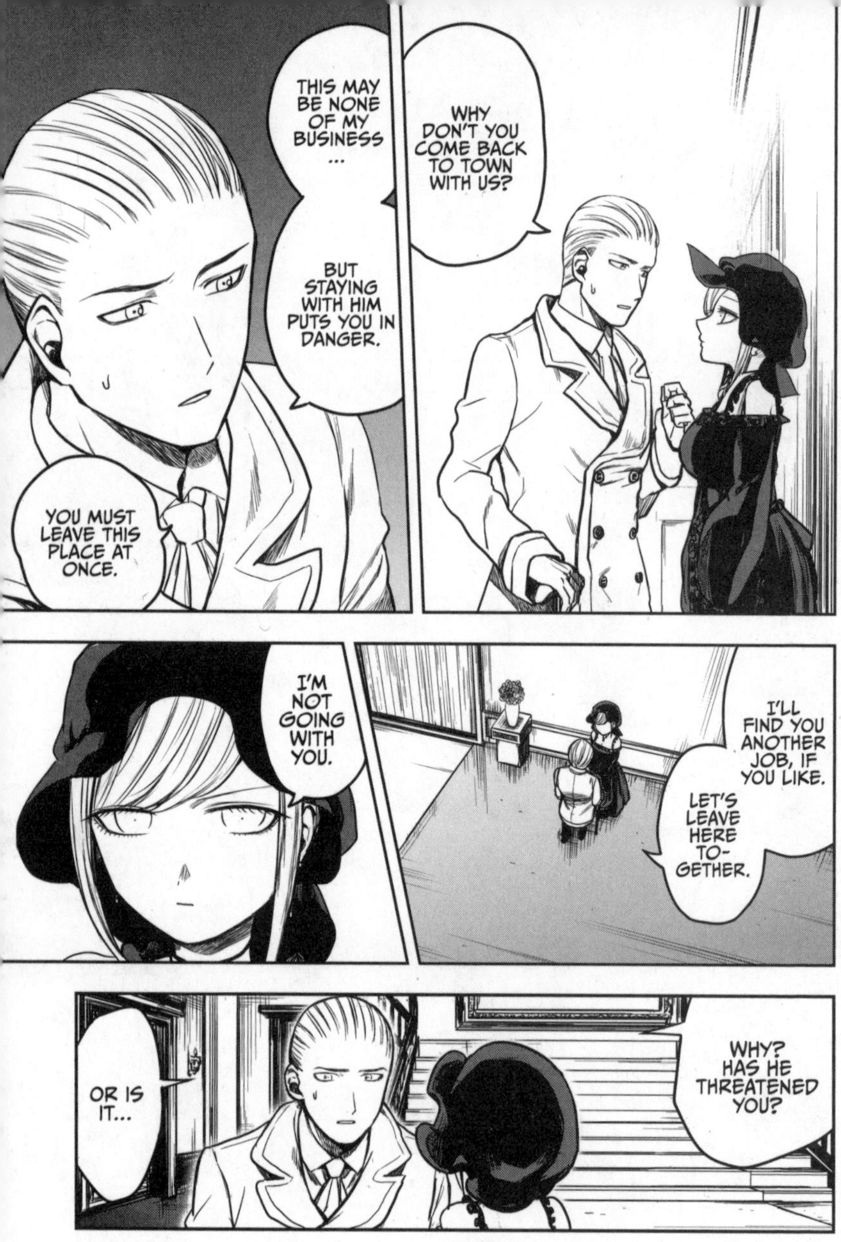
WHY DON'T YOU COME BACK TO TOWN WITH US?
THIS MAY BE NONE OF MY BUSINESS...
BUT STAYING WITH HIM PUTS YOU IN DANGER.
YOU MUST LEAVE THIS PLACE AT ONCE.
I'LL FIND YOU ANOTHER JOB, IF YOU LIKE.
LET'S LEAVE HERE TO-GETHER.
I'M NOT GOING WITH YOU.
WHY? HAS HE THREATENED YOU?
OR IS IT...

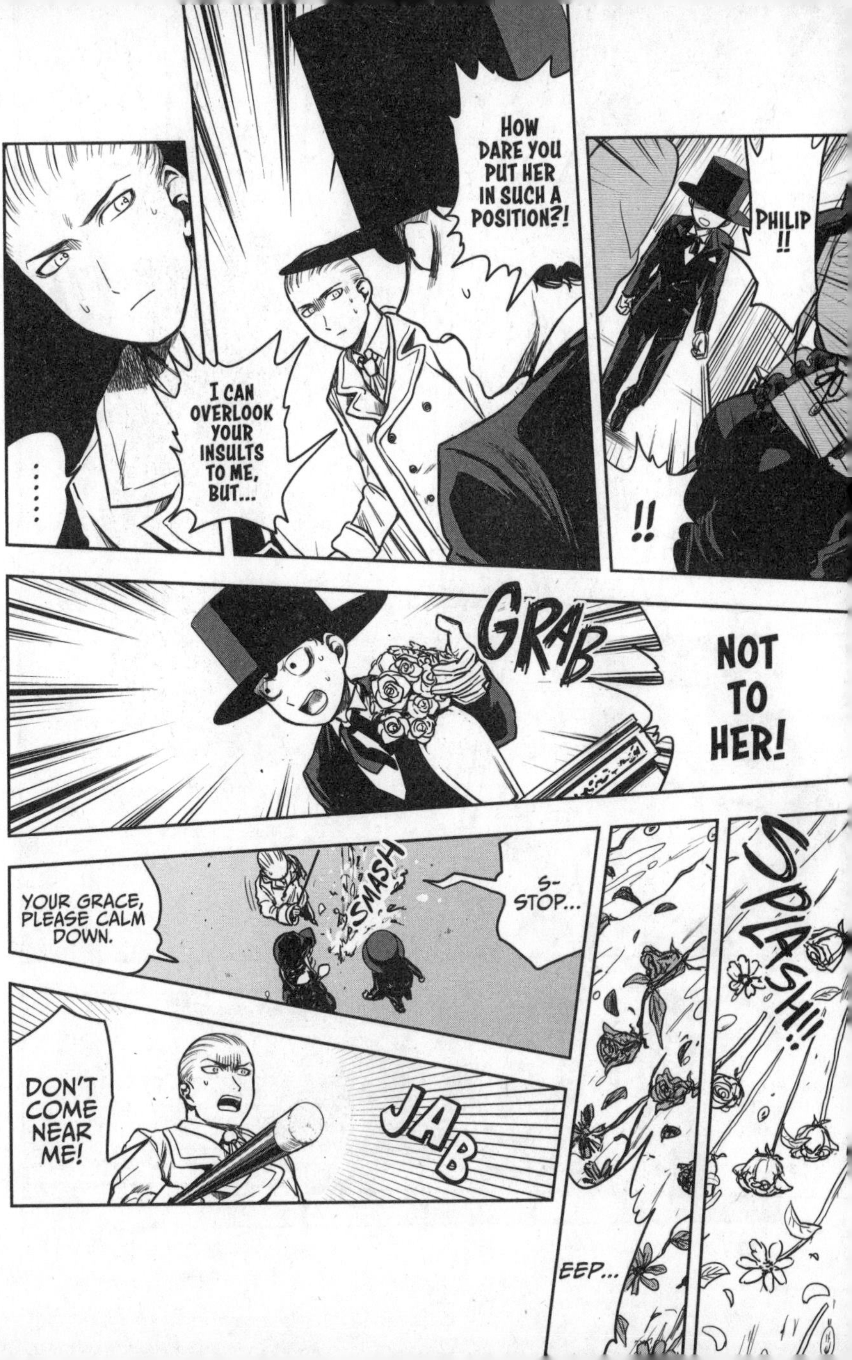
PHILIP !!
!!
HOW DARE YOU PUT HER IN SUCH A POSITION?!
I CAN OVERLOOK YOUR INSULTS TO ME, BUT...
......
GRAB
NOT TO HER!
SPLASH!!!
EEP...
S-STOP...
SMASH
YOUR GRACE, PLEASE CALM DOWN.
JAB
DON'T COME NEAR ME!

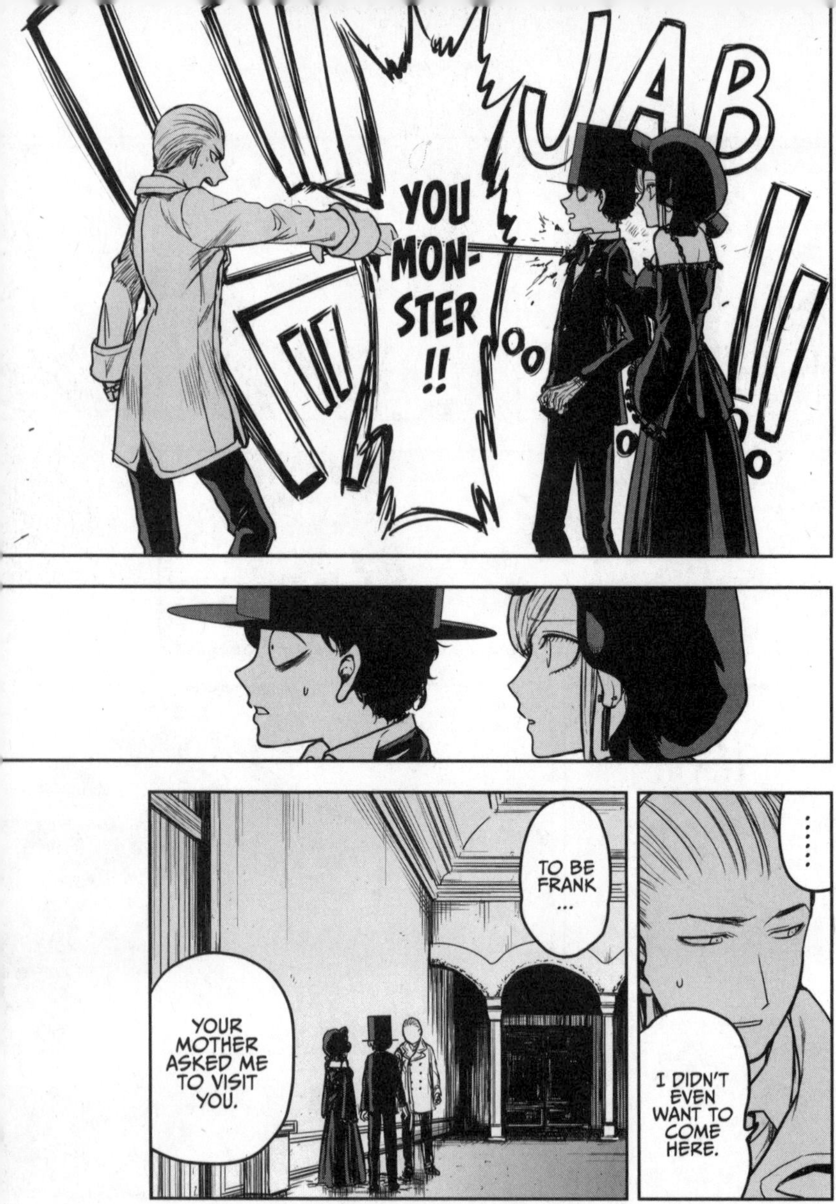
JAB
YOU MON-STER!!
......
I DIDN'T EVEN WANT TO COME HERE.
TO BE FRANK ...
YOUR MOTHER ASKED ME TO VISIT YOU.

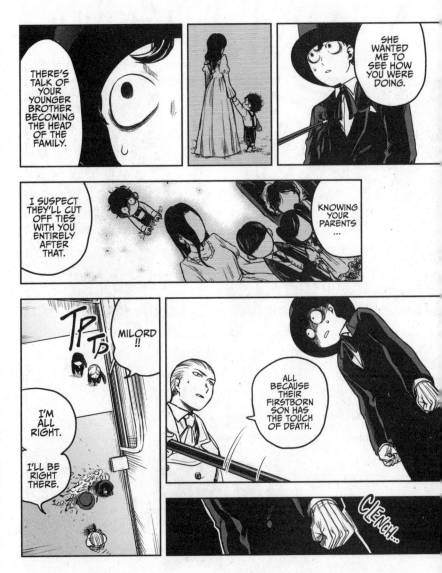

SHE WANTED ME TO SEE HOW YOU WERE DOING.
THERE'S TALK OF YOUR YOUNGER BROTHER BECOMING THE HEAD OF THE FAMILY.
KNOWING YOUR PARENTS...
I SUSPECT THEY'LL CUT OFF TIES WITH YOU ENTIRELY AFTER THAT.
ALL BECAUSE THEIR FIRSTBORN SON HAS THE TOUCH OF DEATH.
CLENCH...
TP TP
MILORD!!
I'M ALL RIGHT.
I'LL BE RIGHT THERE.

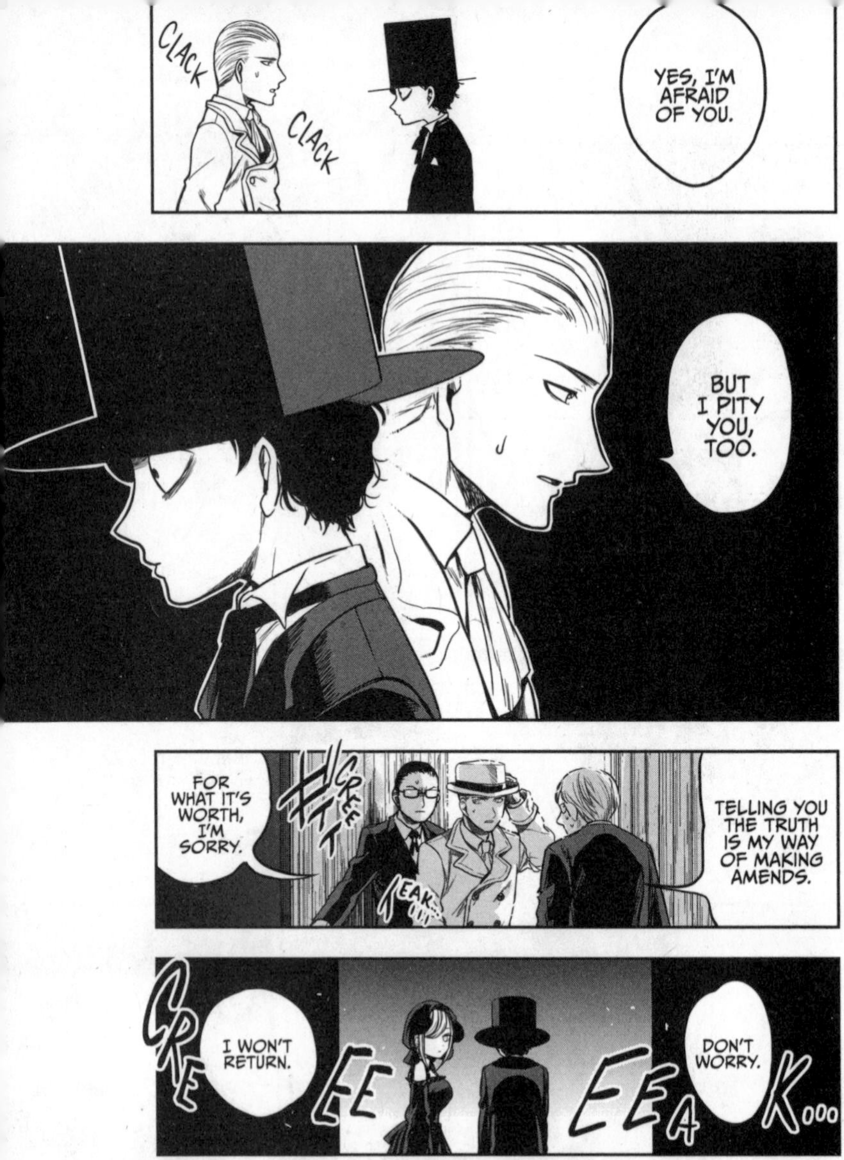
YES, I'M AFRAID OF YOU.
CLACK
CLACK
BUT I PITY YOU, TOO.
TELLING YOU THE TRUTH IS MY WAY OF MAKING AMENDS.
FOR WHAT IT'S WORTH, I'M SORRY.
DON'T WORRY.
I WON'T RETURN.
CREEEEEAK...

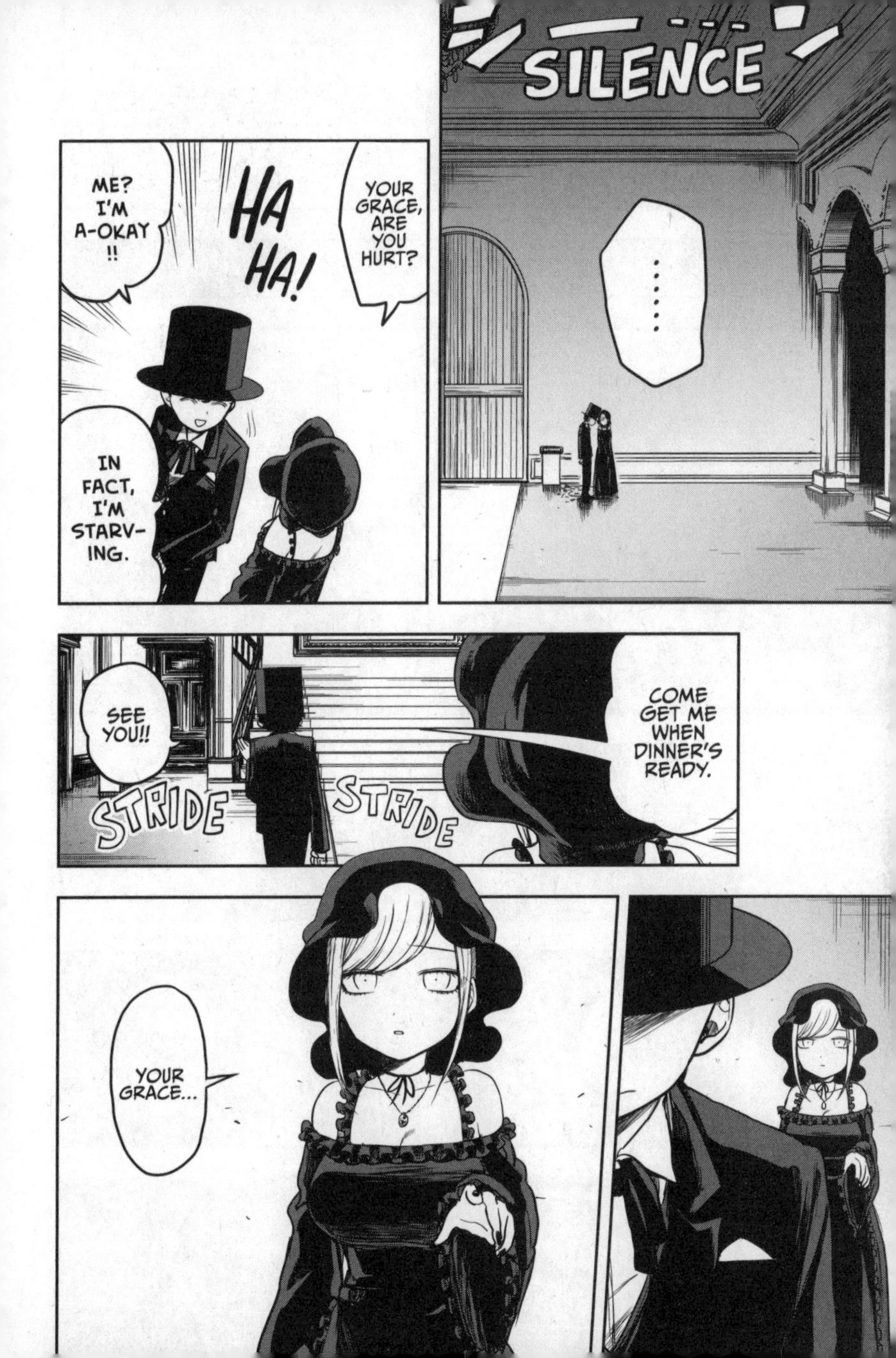
SILENCE
......
YOUR GRACE, ARE YOU HURT?
HA HA!
ME? I'M A-OKAY !!
IN FACT, I'M STARVING.
COME GET ME WHEN DINNER'S READY.
STRIDE
STRIDE
SEE YOU!!
YOUR GRACE...

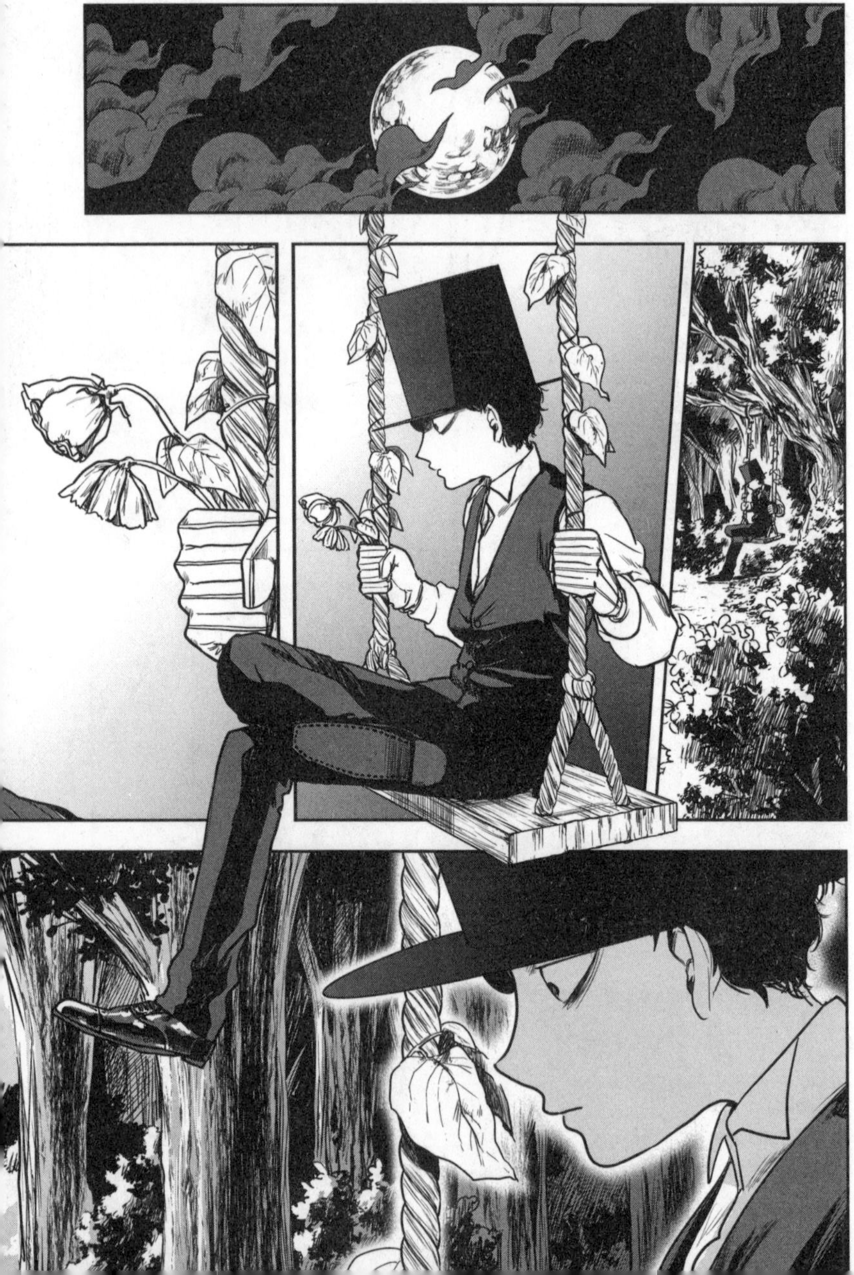

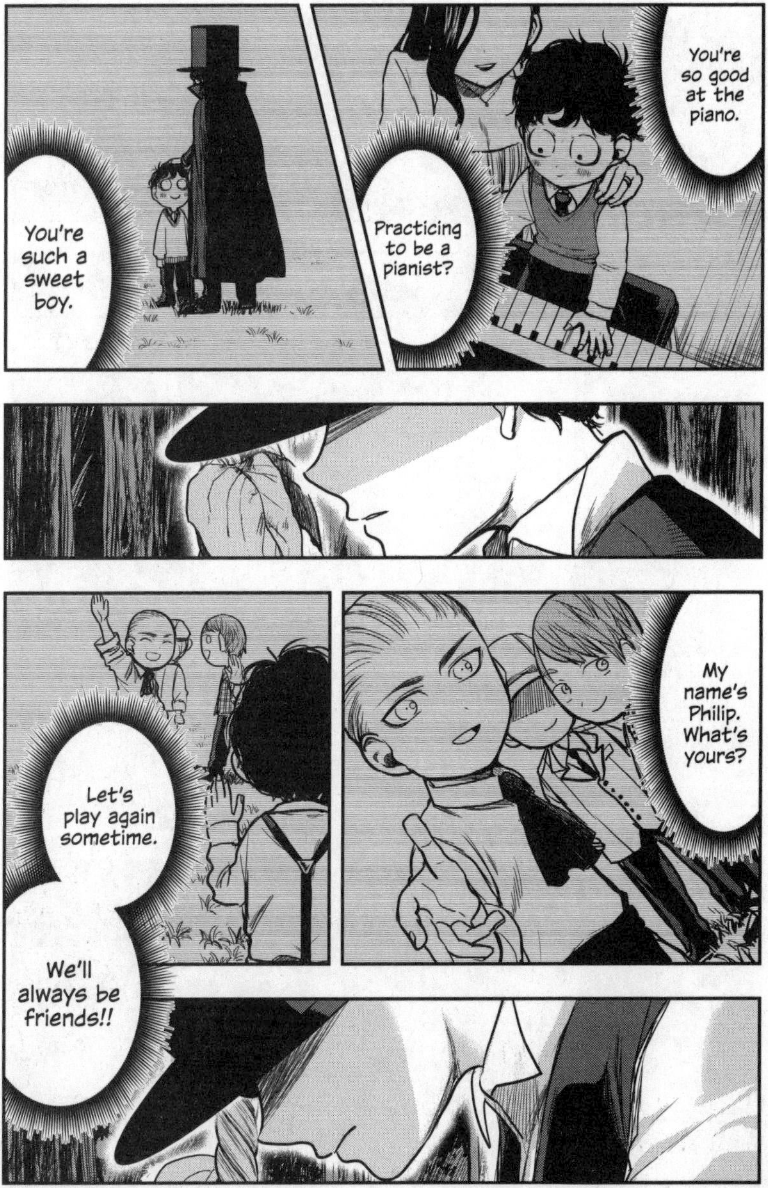
You're so good at the piano.
Practicing to be a pianist?
You're such a sweet boy.
My name's Philip. What's yours?
Let's play again sometime.
We'll always be friends!!

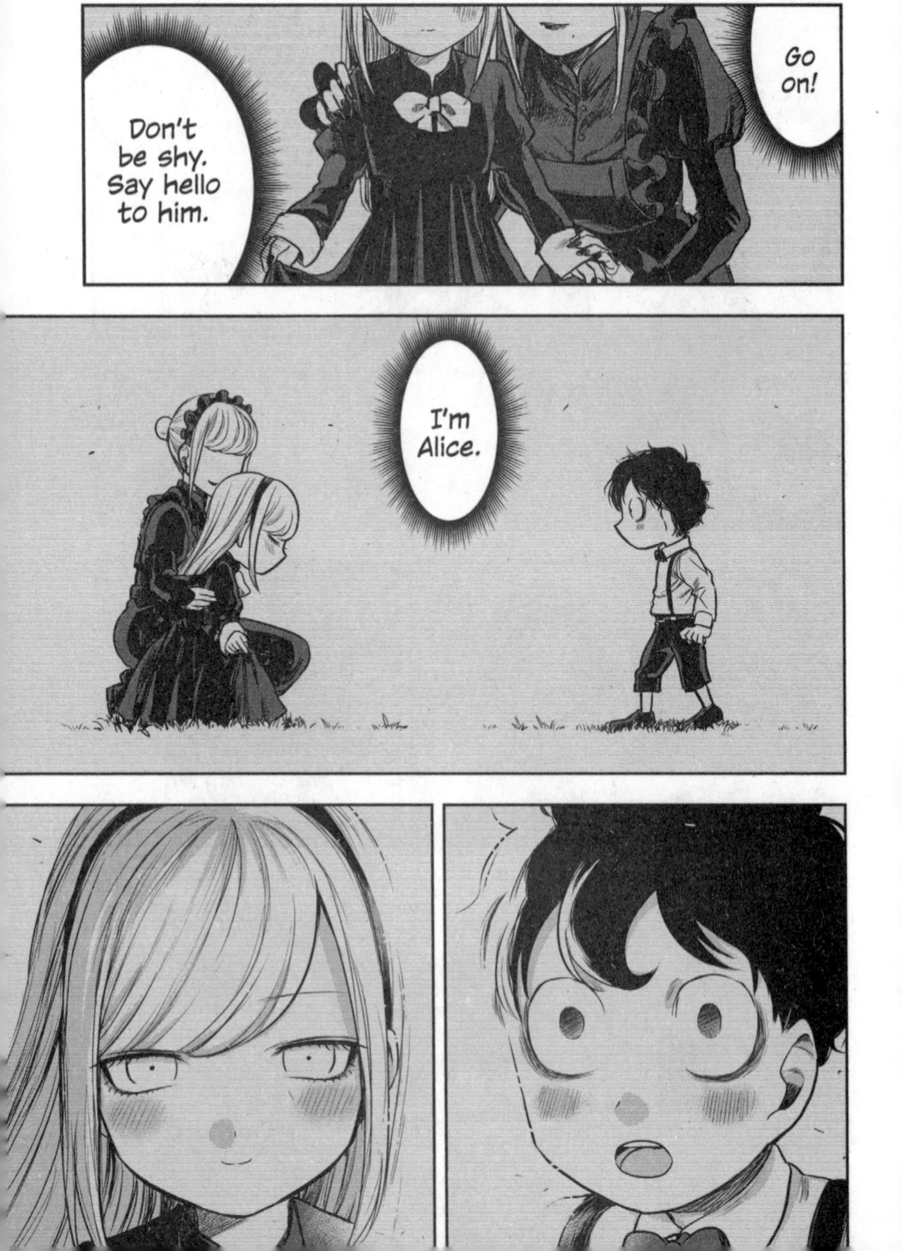
Go on!
Don't be shy. Say hello to him.
I'm Alice.

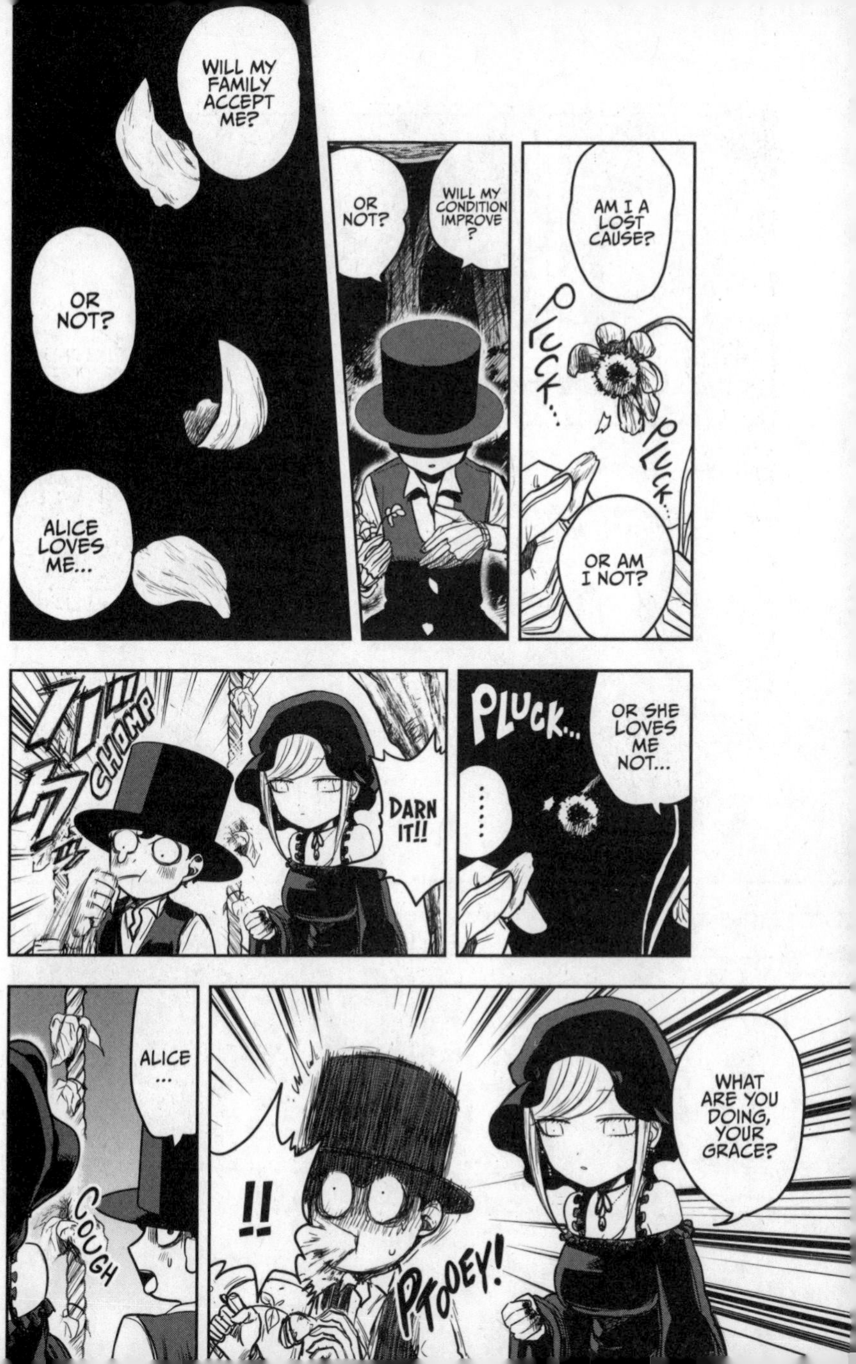
AM I A LOST CAUSE?
PLUCK...
PLUCK...
OR AM I NOT?
WILL MY CONDITION IMPROVE?
OR NOT?
WILL MY FAMILY ACCEPT ME?
OR NOT?
ALICE LOVES ME...
PLUCK...
OR SHE LOVES ME NOT...
......
CHOMP
DARN IT!!
WHAT ARE YOU DOING, YOUR GRACE?
!!
PTOOEY!
ALICE...
COUGH

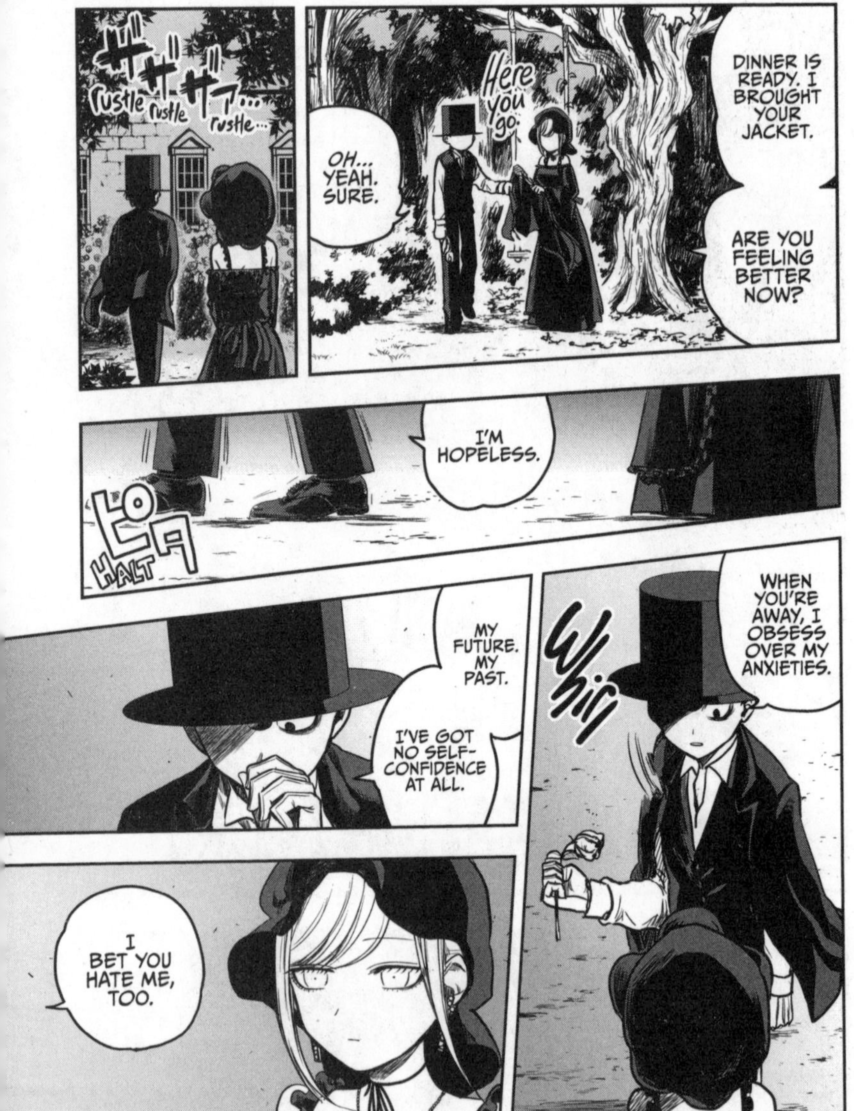
DINNER IS READY. I BROUGHT YOUR JACKET.
ARE YOU FEELING BETTER NOW?
Here you go.
OH... YEAH. SURE.
rustle rustle rustle...
I'M HOPELESS.
HALT
WHEN YOU'RE AWAY, I OBSESS OVER MY ANXIETIES.
Whirl
MY FUTURE. MY PAST.
I'VE GOT NO SELF-CONFIDENCE AT ALL.
I BET YOU HATE ME, TOO.

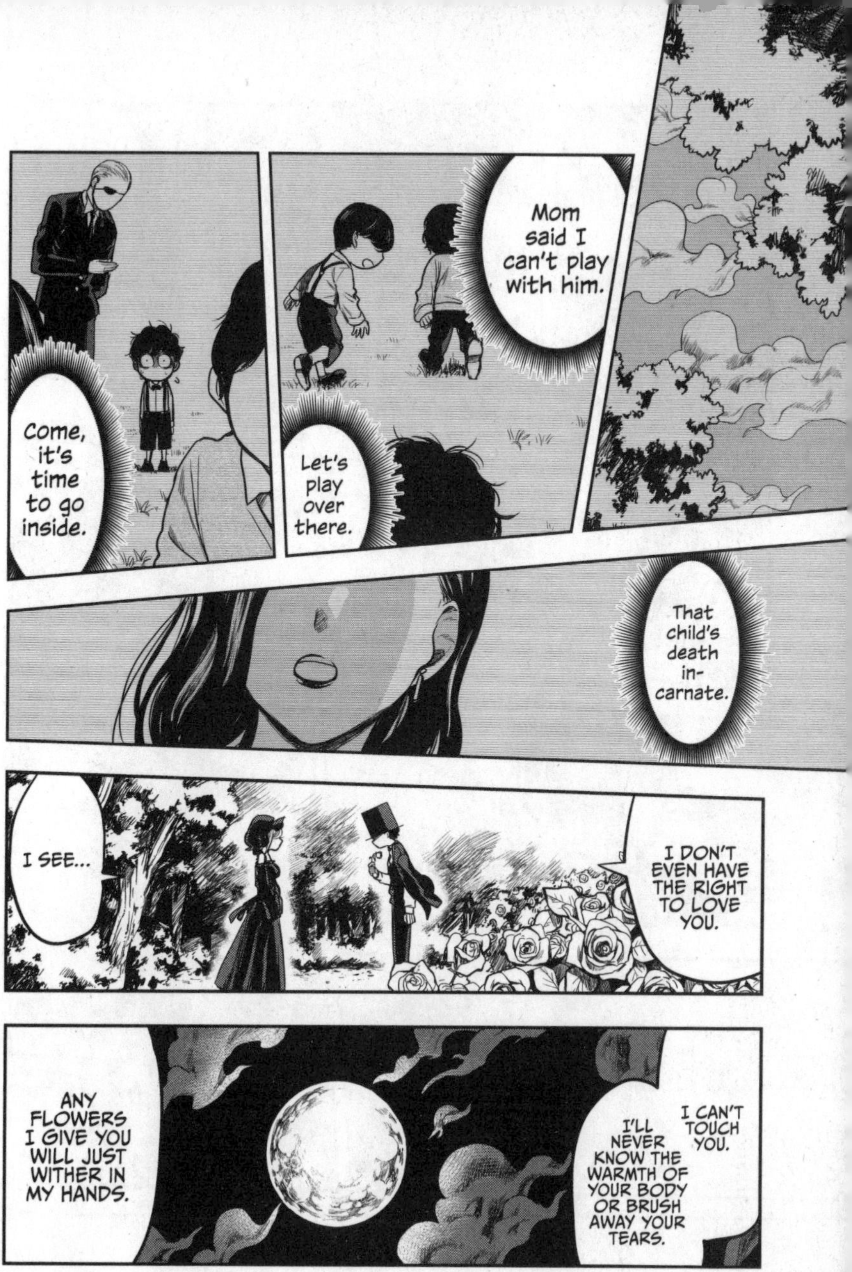
Mom said I can't play with him.
Let's play over there.
Come, it's time to go inside.
That child's death in-carnate.
I DON'T EVEN HAVE THE RIGHT TO LOVE YOU.
I SEE...
I CAN'T TOUCH YOU.
I'LL NEVER KNOW THE WARMTH OF YOUR BODY OR BRUSH AWAY YOUR TEARS.
ANY FLOWERS I GIVE YOU WILL JUST WITHER IN MY HANDS.

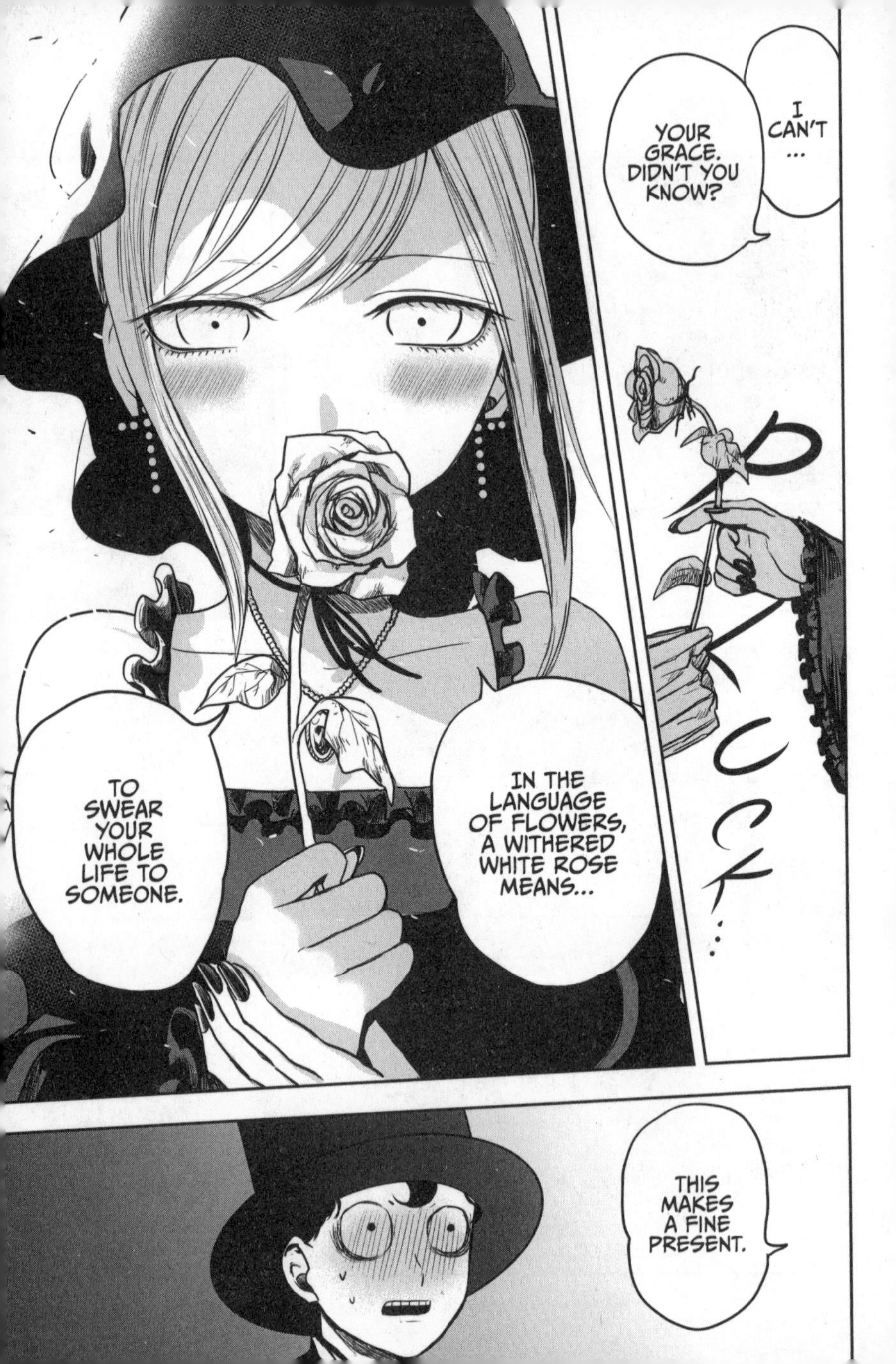
I CAN'T ...
YOUR GRACE. DIDN'T YOU KNOW?
IN THE LANGUAGE OF FLOWERS, A WITHERED WHITE ROSE MEANS...
TO SWEAR YOUR WHOLE LIFE TO SOMEONE.
THIS MAKES A FINE PRESENT.

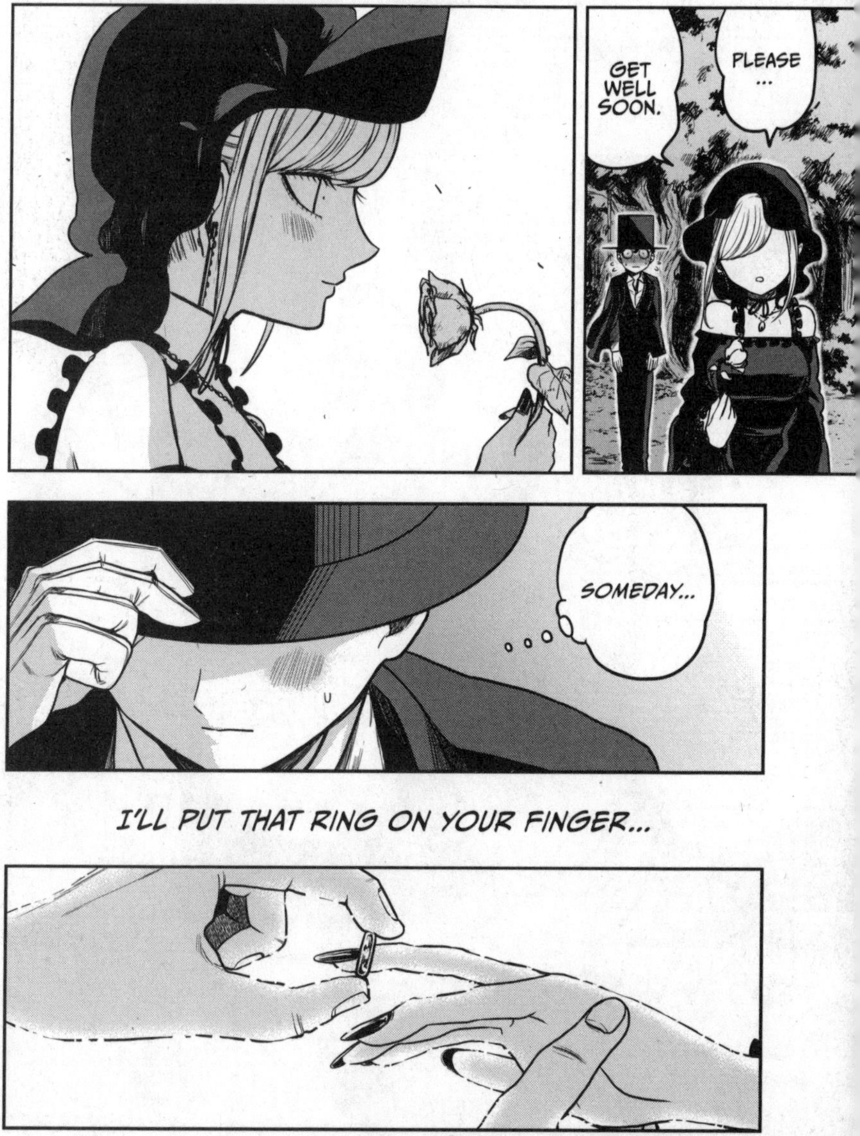
PLEASE ...
GET WELL SOON.
SOMEDAY...
I'LL PUT THAT RING ON YOUR FINGER...
WITH MY OWN HANDS.

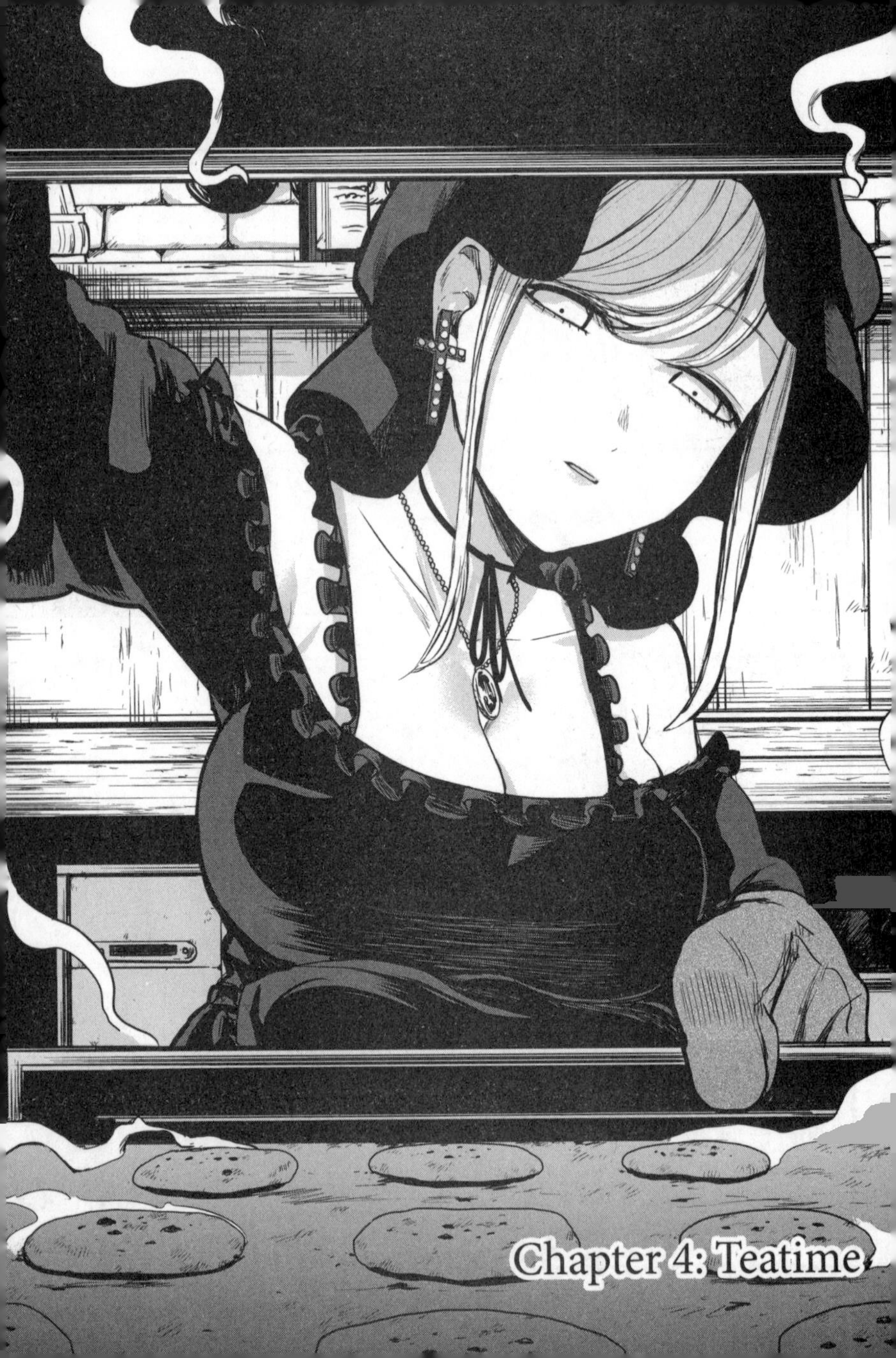
Chapter 4: Teatime

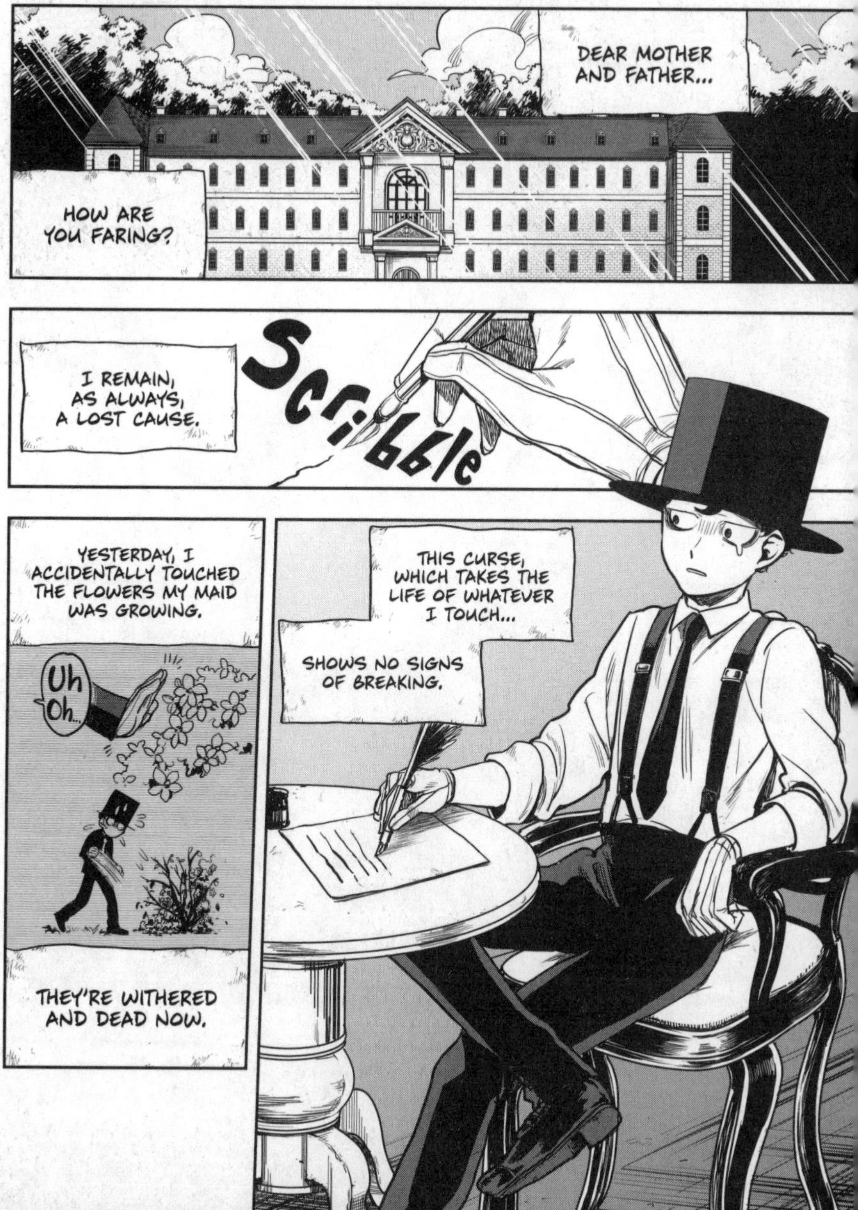
DEAR MOTHER AND FATHER...
HOW ARE YOU FARING?
Scribble
I REMAIN, AS ALWAYS, A LOST CAUSE.
THIS CURSE, WHICH TAKES THE LIFE OF WHATEVER I TOUCH...
SHOWS NO SIGNS OF BREAKING.
YESTERDAY, I ACCIDENTALLY TOUCHED THE FLOWERS MY MAID WAS GROWING.
Uh Oh...
THEY'RE WITHERED AND DEAD NOW.

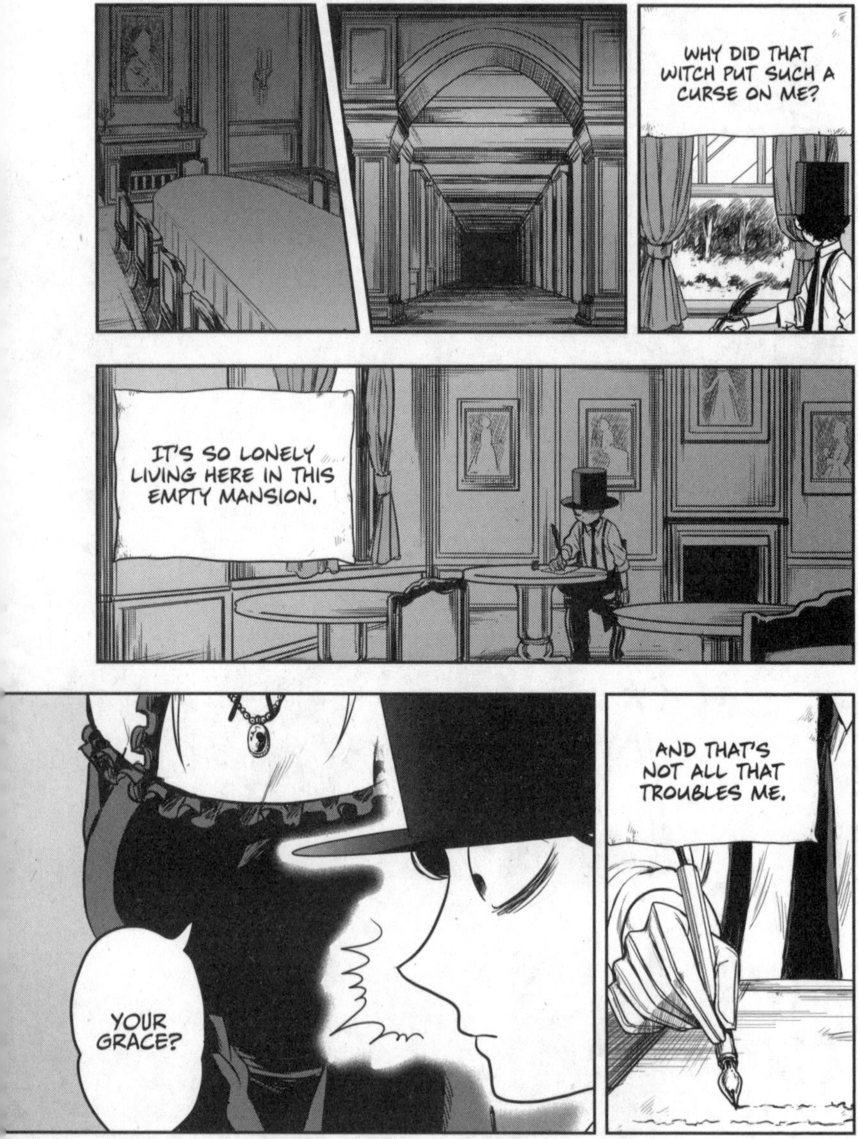
WHY DID THAT WITCH PUT SUCH A CURSE ON ME?
IT'S SO LONELY LIVING HERE IN THIS EMPTY MANSION.
AND THAT'S NOT ALL THAT TROUBLES ME.
YOUR GRACE?

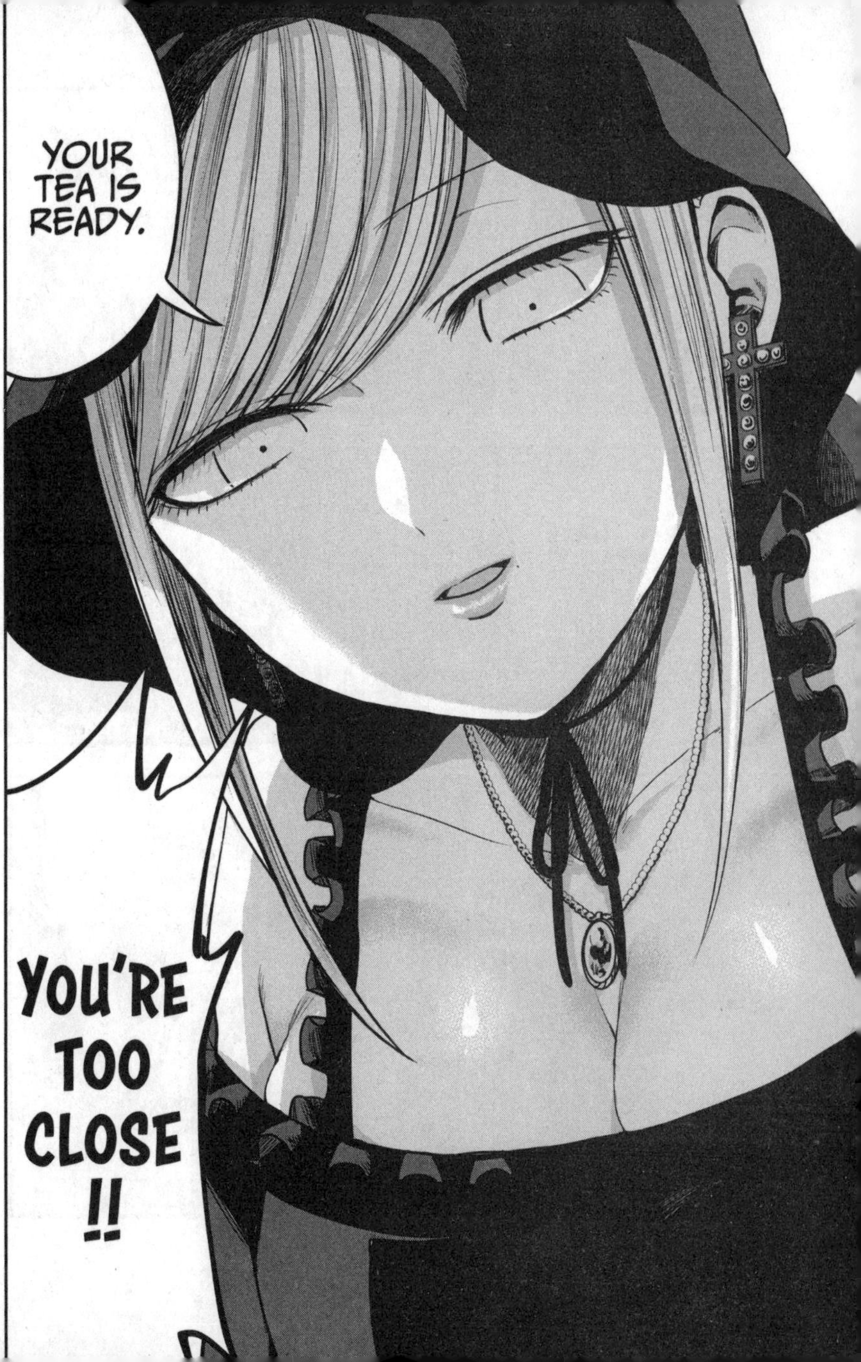
YOUR TEA IS READY.
YOU'RE TOO CLOSE !!

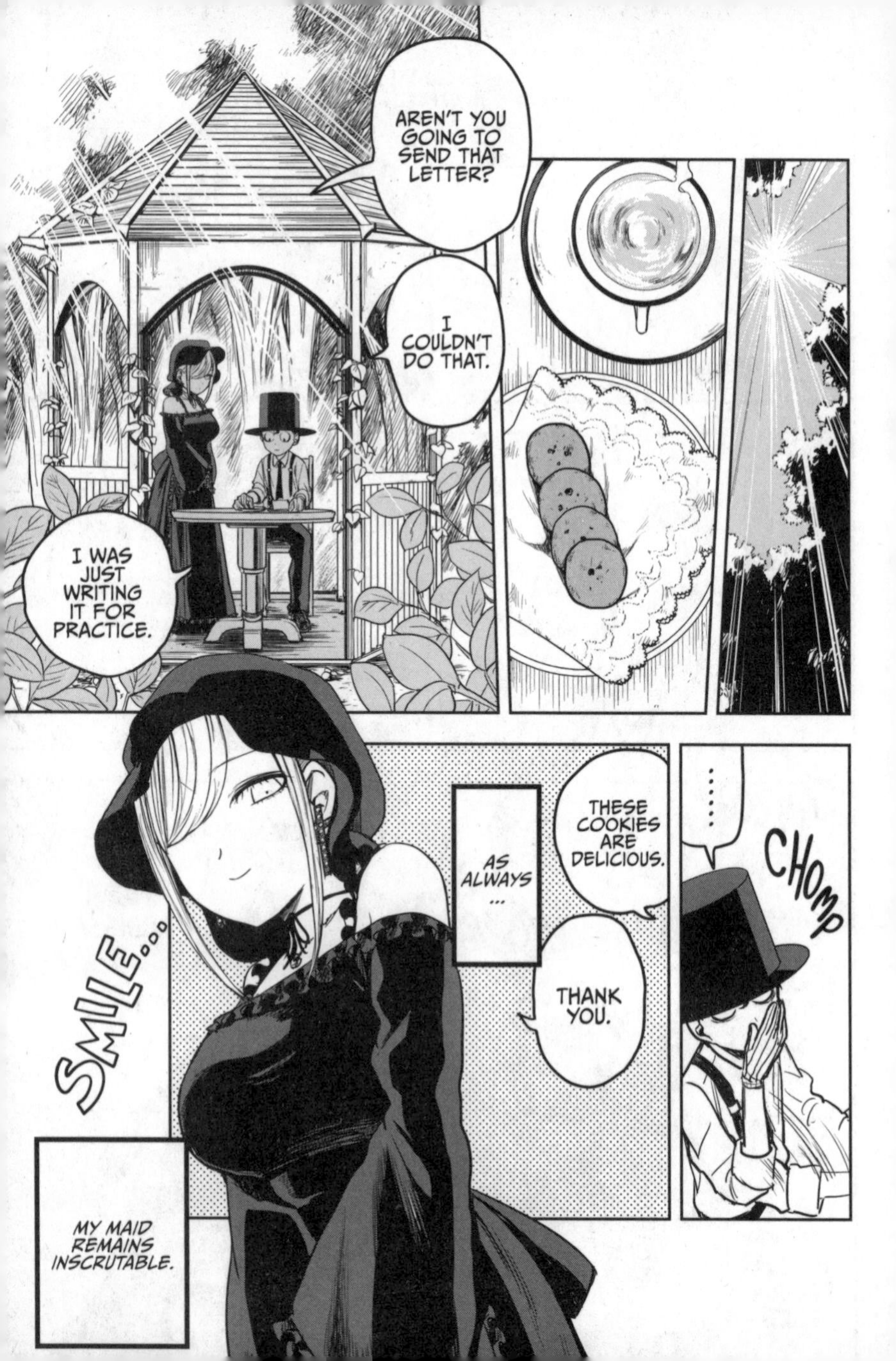

AREN'T YOU GOING TO SEND THAT LETTER?
I COULDN'T DO THAT.
I WAS JUST WRITING IT FOR PRACTICE.
......
CHOMP
THESE COOKIES ARE DELICIOUS.
AS ALWAYS...
THANK YOU.
SMILE...
MY MAID REMAINS INSCRUTABLE.

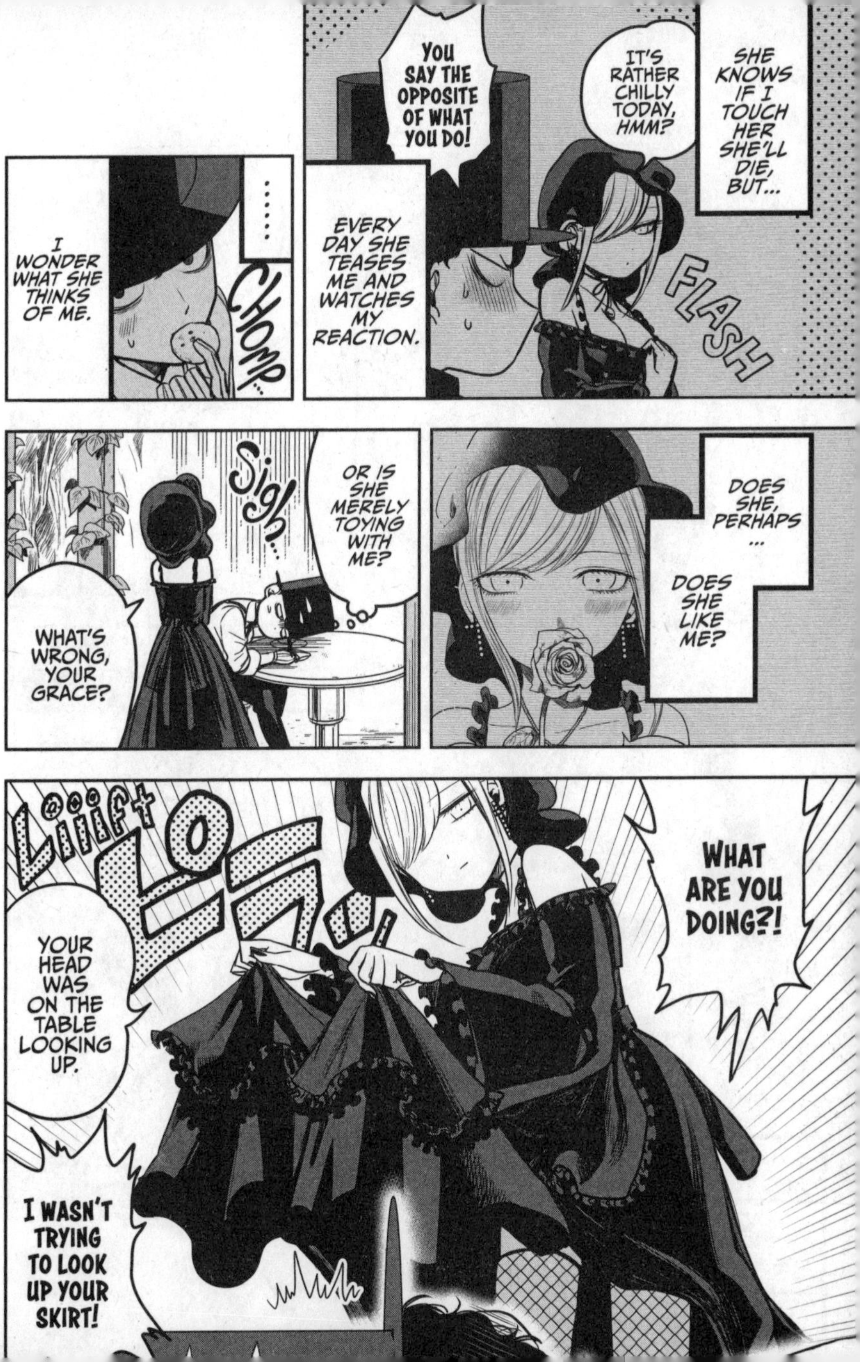
SHE KNOWS IF I TOUCH HER SHE'LL DIE, BUT...
IT'S RATHER CHILLY TODAY, HMM?
YOU SAY THE OPPOSITE OF WHAT YOU DO!
EVERY DAY SHE TEASES ME AND WATCHES MY REACTION.
FLASH
......
CHOMP...
I WONDER WHAT SHE THINKS OF ME.
DOES SHE, PERHAPS ...
DOES SHE LIKE ME?
OR IS SHE MERELY TOYING WITH ME?
Sigh...
WHAT'S WRONG, YOUR GRACE?
WHAT ARE YOU DOING?!
Liiift
YOUR HEAD WAS ON THE TABLE LOOKING UP.
I WASN'T TRYING TO LOOK UP YOUR SKIRT!

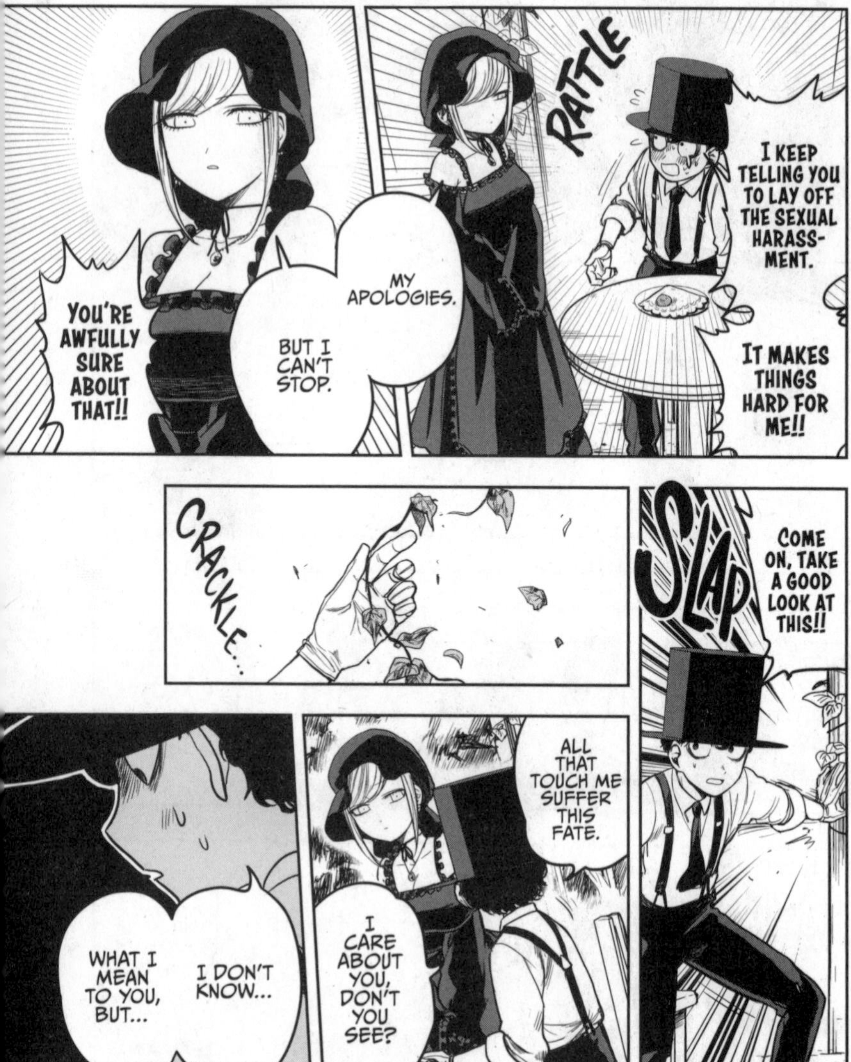
RATTLE
I KEEP TELLING YOU TO LAY OFF THE SEXUAL HARASS-MENT.
IT MAKES THINGS HARD FOR ME!!
MY APOLOGIES.
BUT I CAN'T STOP.
YOU'RE AWFULLY SURE ABOUT THAT!!
SLAP
COME ON, TAKE A GOOD LOOK AT THIS!!
CRACKLE...
ALL THAT TOUCH ME SUFFER THIS FATE.
I CARE ABOUT YOU, DON'T YOU SEE?
I DON'T KNOW...
WHAT I MEAN TO YOU, BUT...

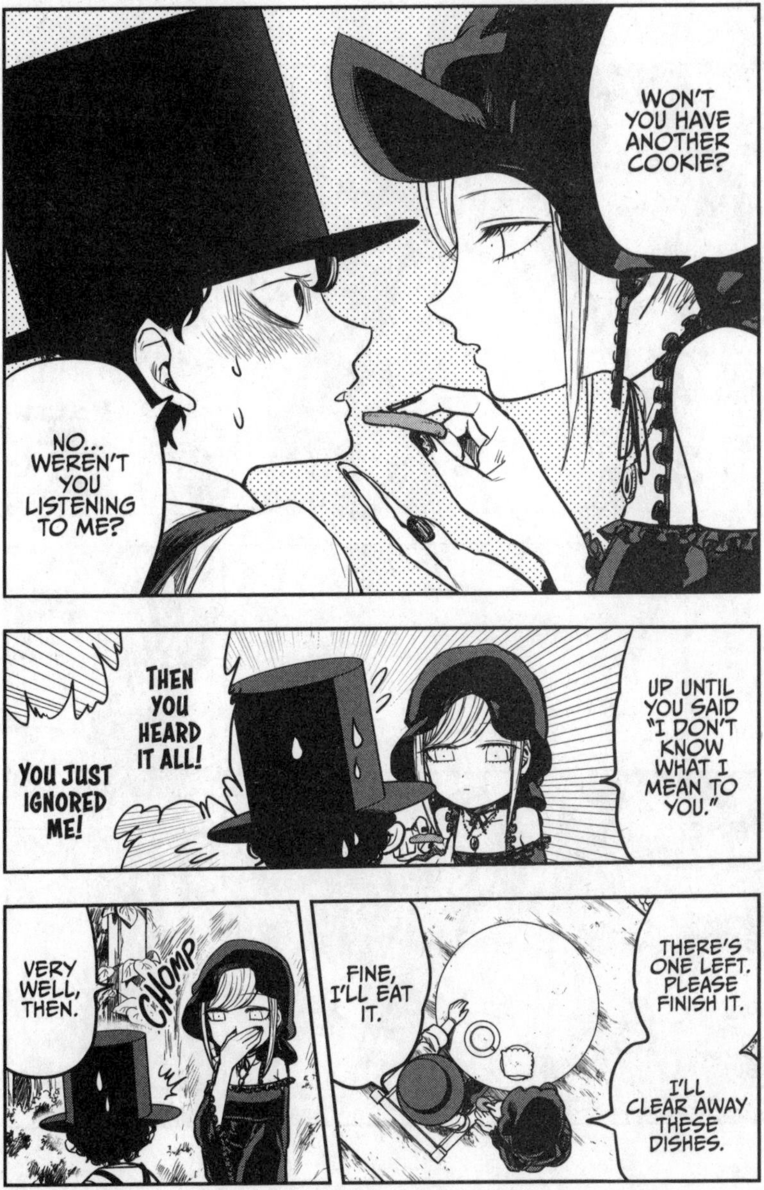
WON'T YOU HAVE ANOTHER COOKIE?
NO... WEREN'T YOU LISTENING TO ME?
UP UNTIL YOU SAID "I DON'T KNOW WHAT I MEAN TO YOU."
THEN YOU HEARD IT ALL!
YOU JUST IGNORED ME!
THERE'S ONE LEFT. PLEASE FINISH IT.
I'LL CLEAR AWAY THESE DISHES.
FINE, I'LL EAT IT.
CHOMP
VERY WELL, THEN.

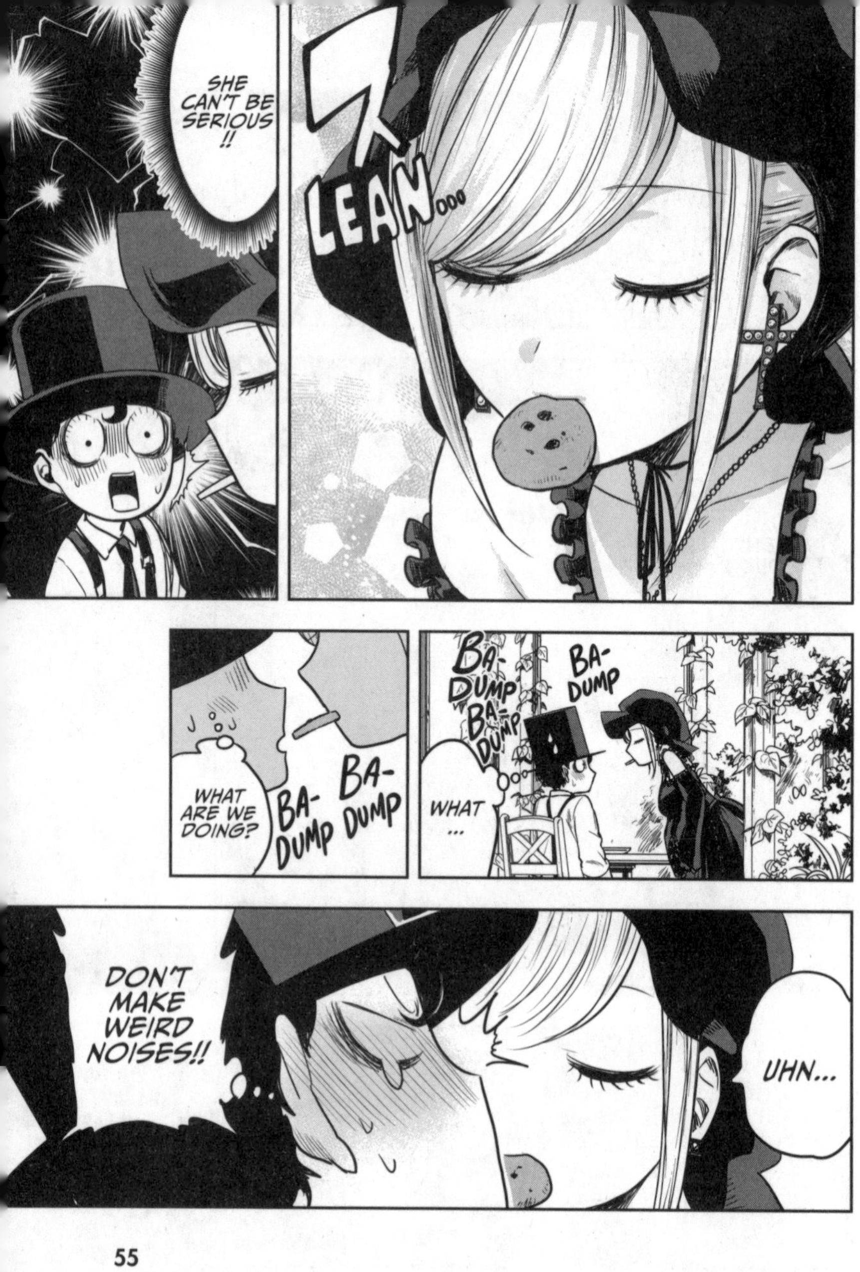
LEAN...
SHE CAN'T BE SERIOUS!!
BA-DUMP
BA-DUMP
BA-DUMP
WHAT...
BA-DUMP
BA-DUMP
WHAT ARE WE DOING?
UHN...
DON'T MAKE WEIRD NOISES!!

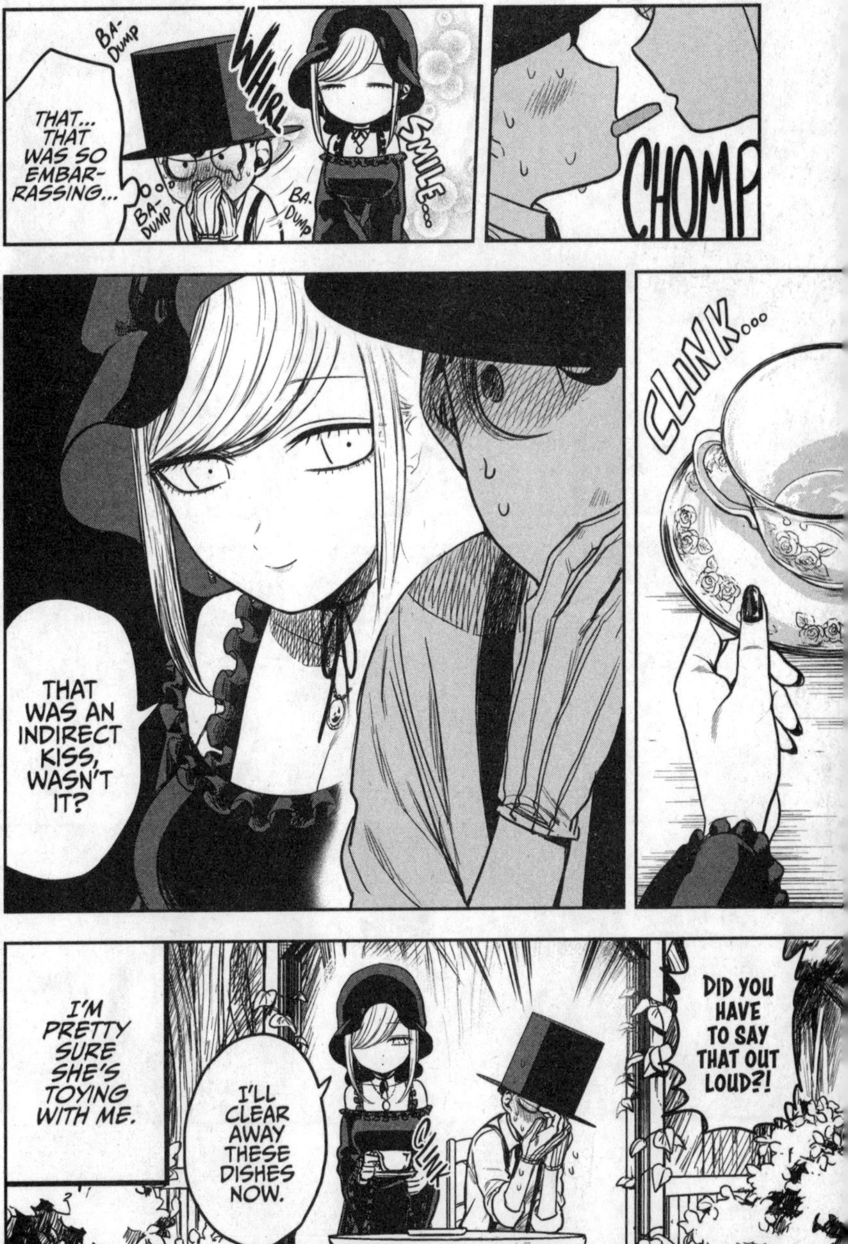
CHOMP
WHIRL
SMILE...
BA-DUMP
THAT... THAT WAS SO EMBARRASSING...
BA-DUMP
BA-DUMP
CLINK...
THAT WAS AN INDIRECT KISS, WASN'T IT?
DID YOU HAVE TO SAY THAT OUT LOUD?!
CLINK
I'LL CLEAR AWAY THESE DISHES NOW.
I'M PRETTY SURE SHE'S TOYING WITH ME.

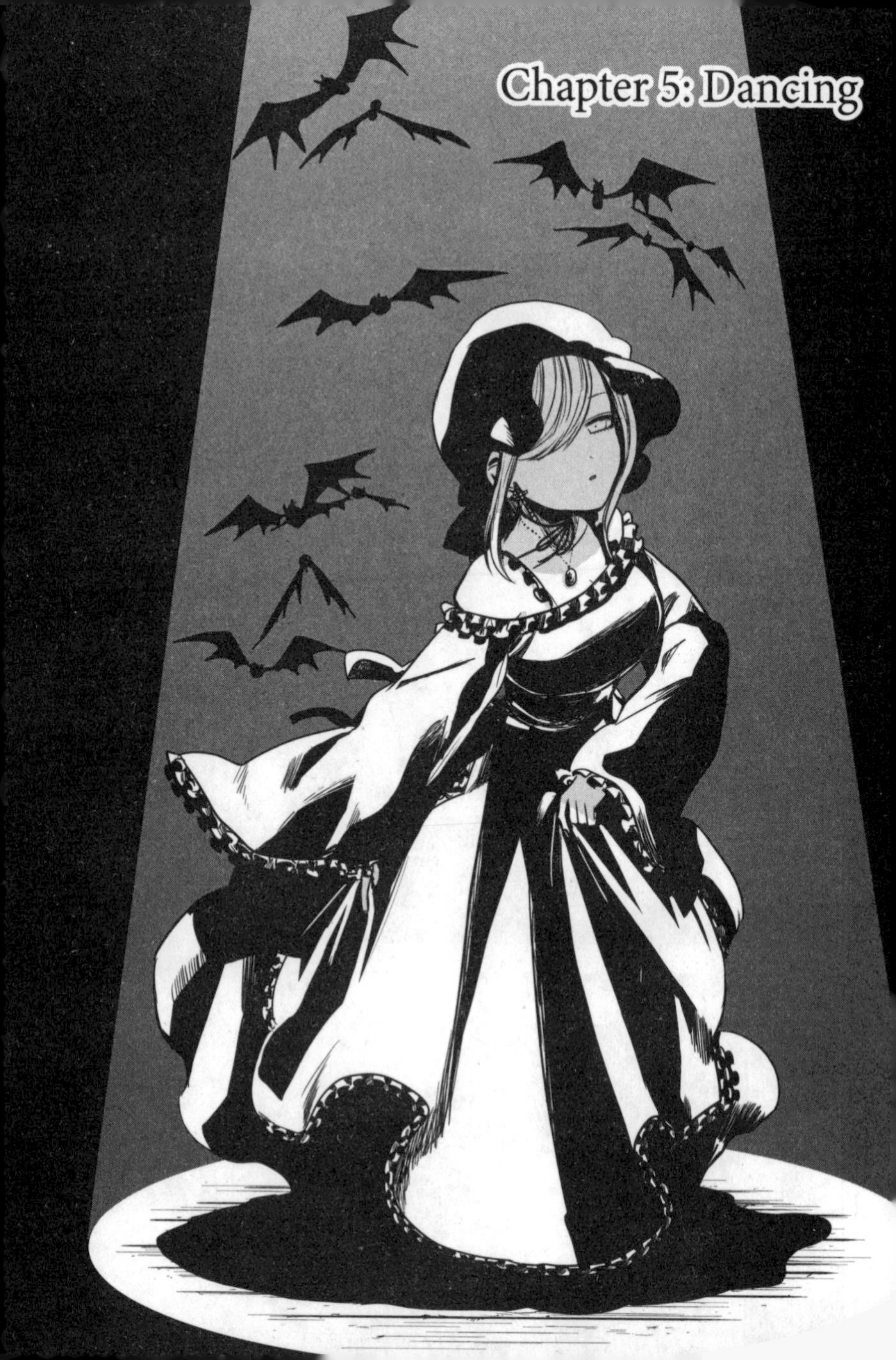
Chapter 5: Dancing

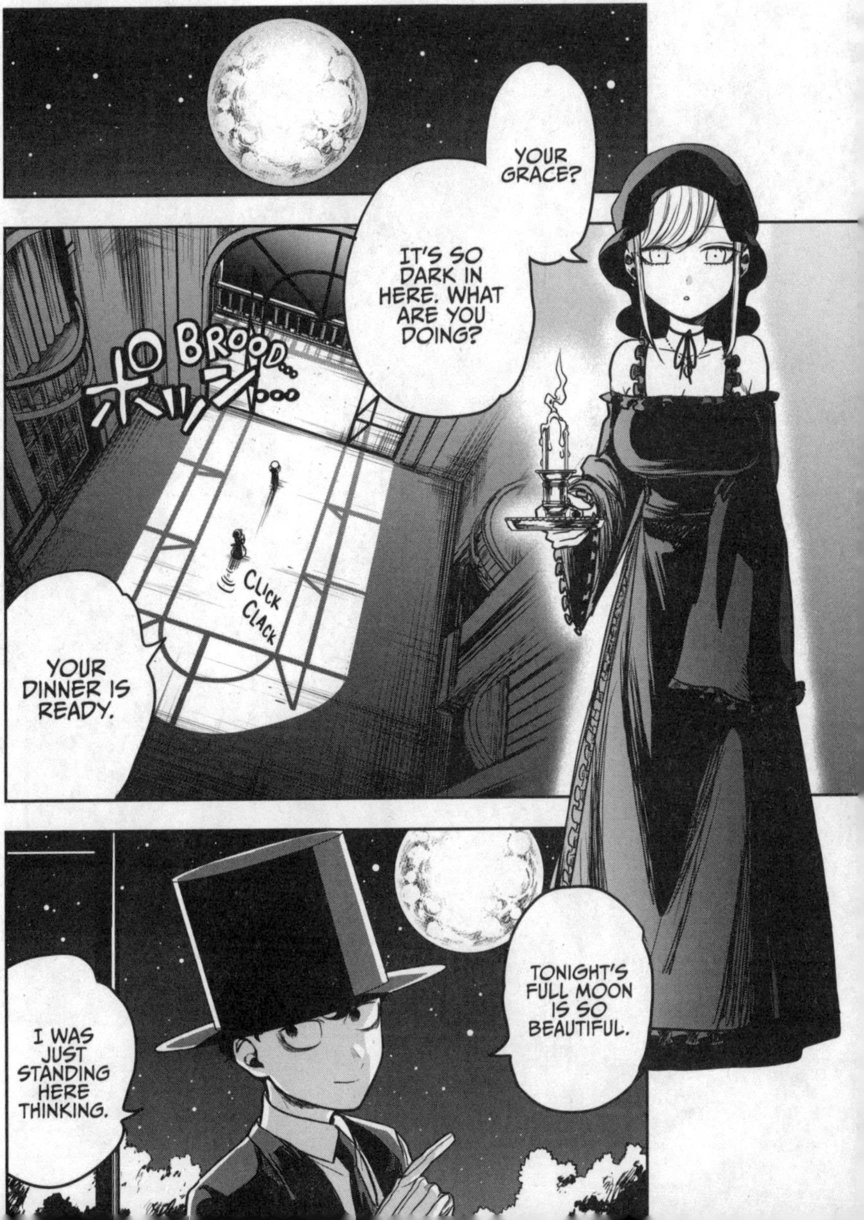
YOUR GRACE?
IT'S SO DARK IN HERE. WHAT ARE YOU DOING?
BROOD...
CLICK CLACK
YOUR DINNER IS READY.
TONIGHT'S FULL MOON IS SO BEAUTIFUL.
I WAS JUST STANDING HERE THINKING.

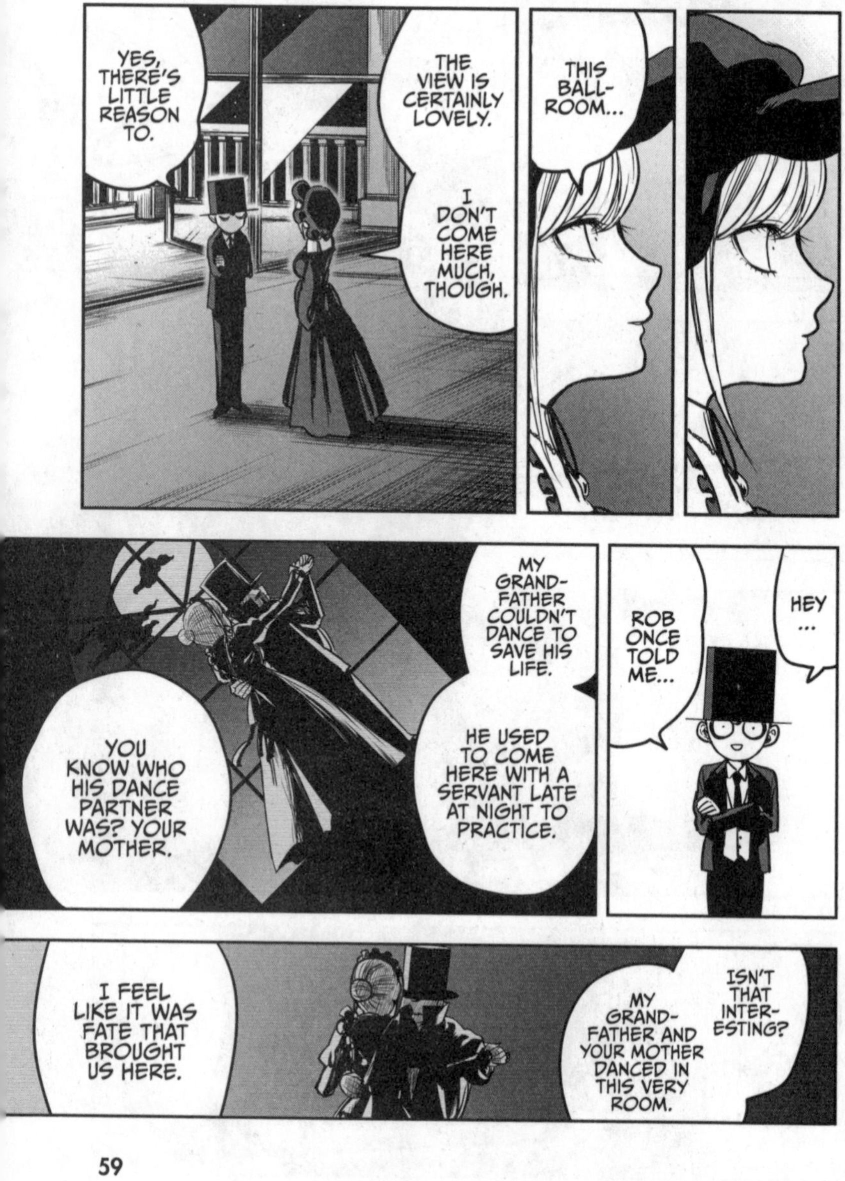
THIS BALLROOM...
THE VIEW IS CERTAINLY LOVELY.
I DON'T COME HERE MUCH, THOUGH.
YES, THERE'S LITTLE REASON TO.
HEY ...
ROB ONCE TOLD ME...
MY GRANDFATHER COULDN'T DANCE TO SAVE HIS LIFE.
HE USED TO COME HERE WITH A SERVANT LATE AT NIGHT TO PRACTICE.
YOU KNOW WHO HIS DANCE PARTNER WAS? YOUR MOTHER.
ISN'T THAT INTERESTING?
MY GRANDFATHER AND YOUR MOTHER DANCED IN THIS VERY ROOM.
I FEEL LIKE IT WAS FATE THAT BROUGHT US HERE.

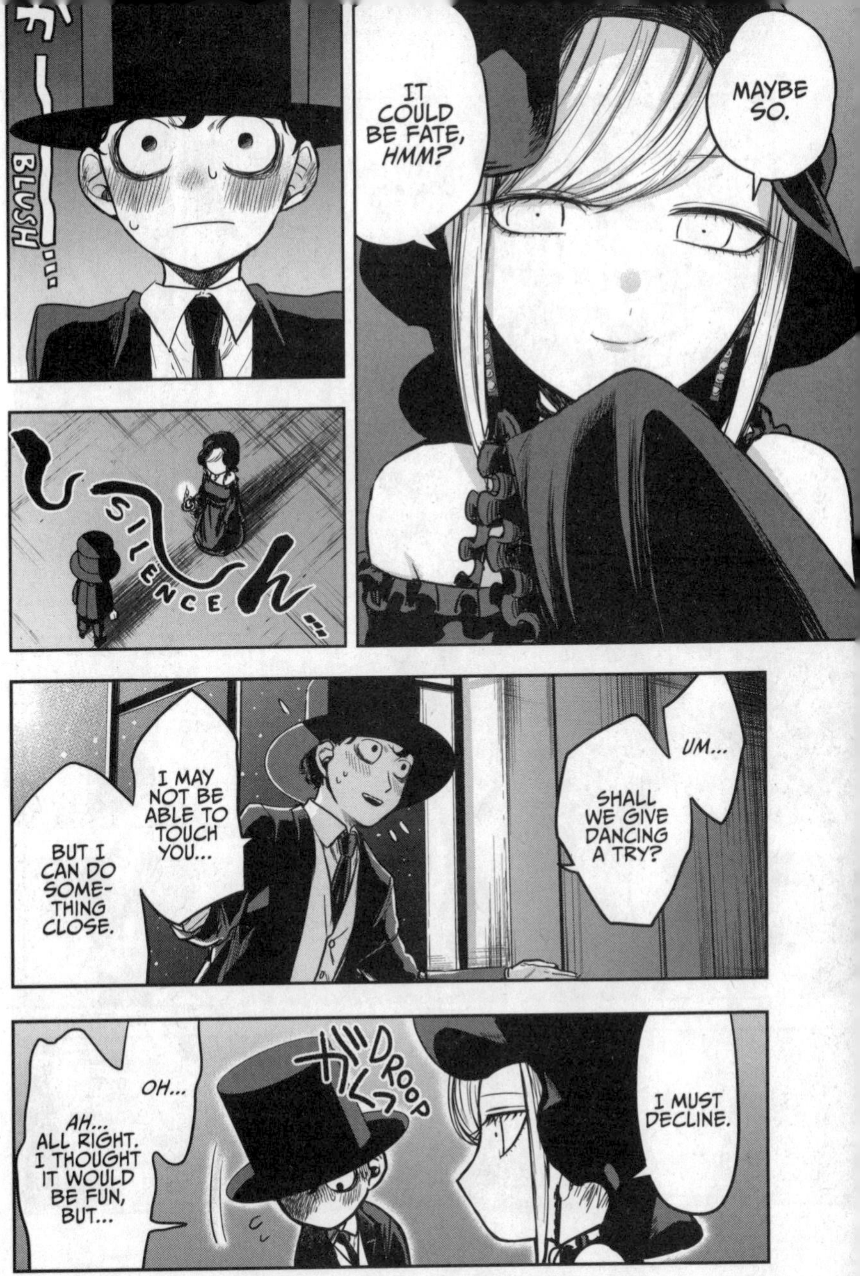
MAYBE SO.
IT COULD BE FATE, HMM?
BLUSH...
SILENCE...
UM...
SHALL WE GIVE DANCING A TRY?
I MAY NOT BE ABLE TO TOUCH YOU...
BUT I CAN DO SOME-THING CLOSE.
I MUST DECLINE.
DROOP
OH...
AH... ALL RIGHT. I THOUGHT IT WOULD BE FUN, BUT...

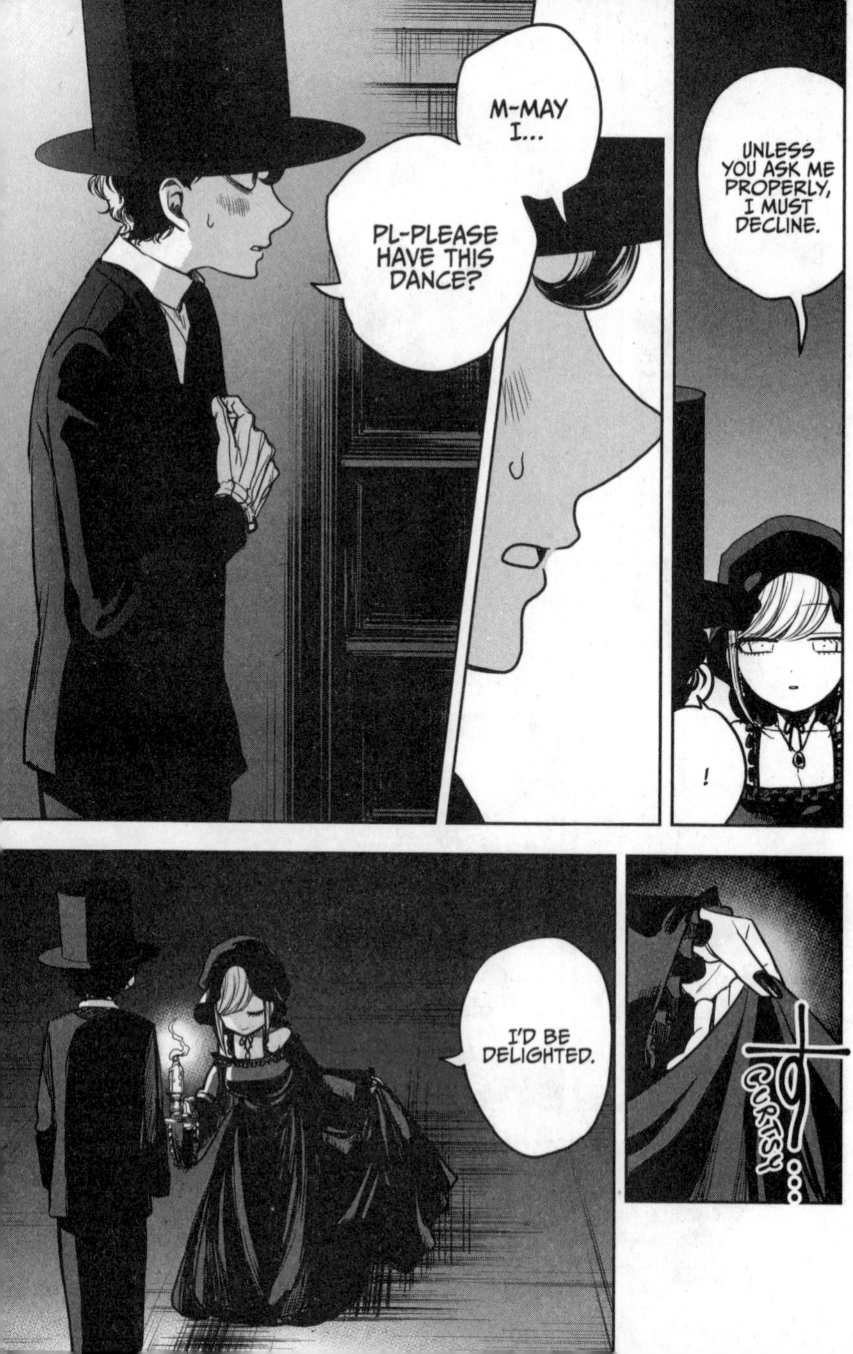
UNLESS YOU ASK ME PROPERLY, I MUST DECLINE.
!
M-MAY I...
PL-PLEASE HAVE THIS DANCE?
CURTSY...
I'D BE DELIGHTED.

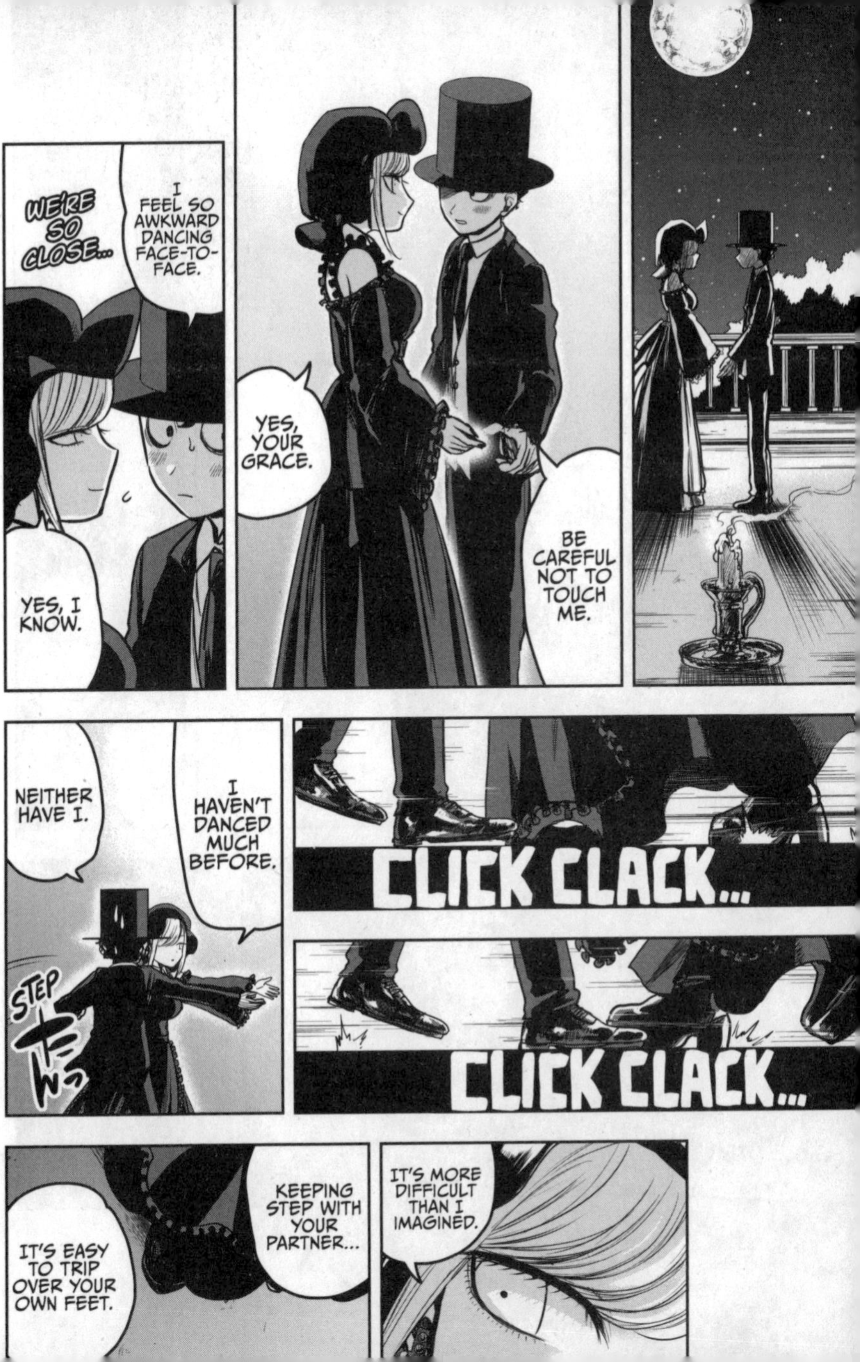
BE CAREFUL NOT TO TOUCH ME.
YES, YOUR GRACE.
I FEEL SO AWKWARD DANCING FACE-TO-FACE.
WE'RE SO CLOSE...
YES, I KNOW.
CLICK CLACK...
CLICK CLACK...
I HAVEN'T DANCED MUCH BEFORE.
NEITHER HAVE I.
STEP
IT'S MORE DIFFICULT THAN I IMAGINED.
KEEPING STEP WITH YOUR PARTNER...
IT'S EASY TO TRIP OVER YOUR OWN FEET.

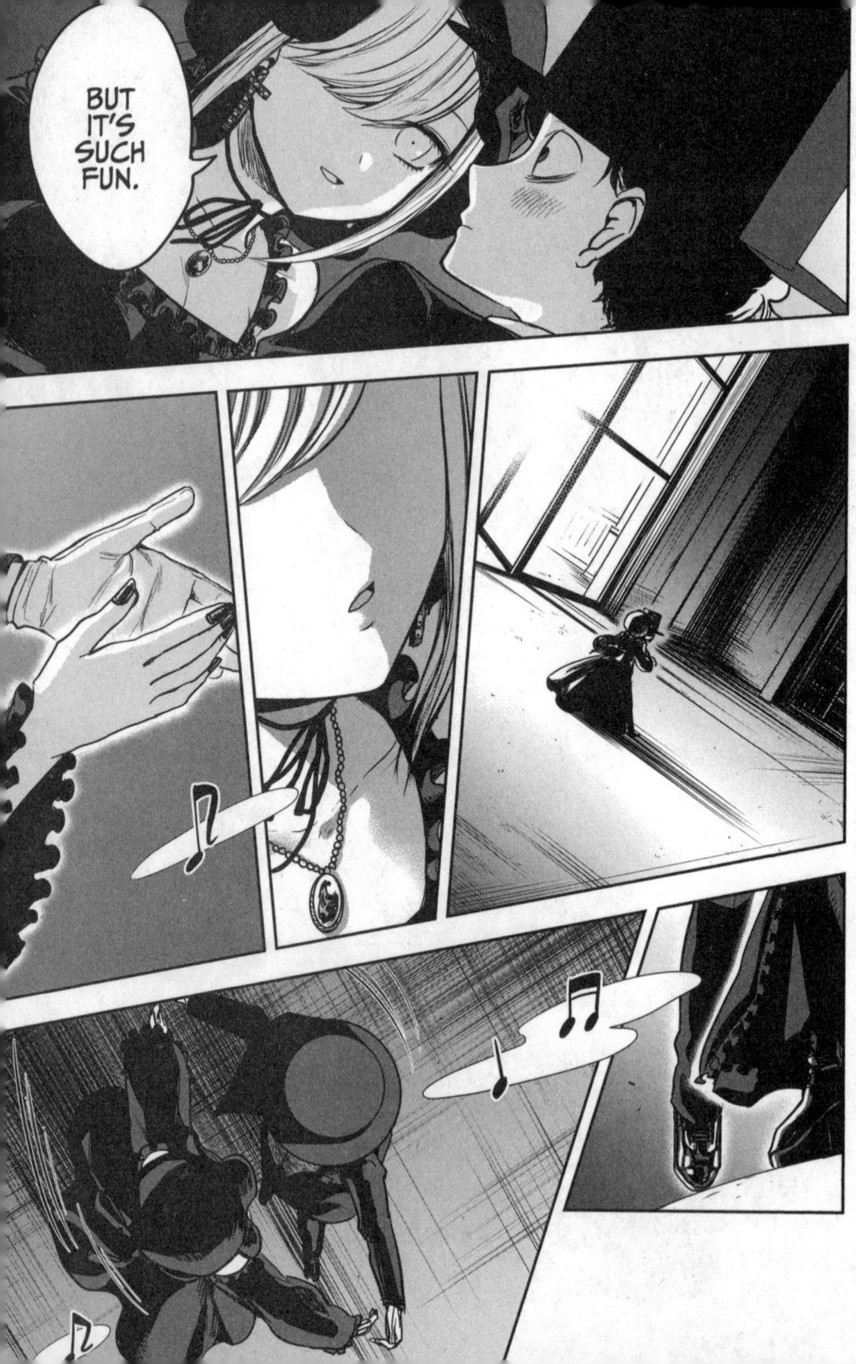
BUT IT'S SUCH FUN.

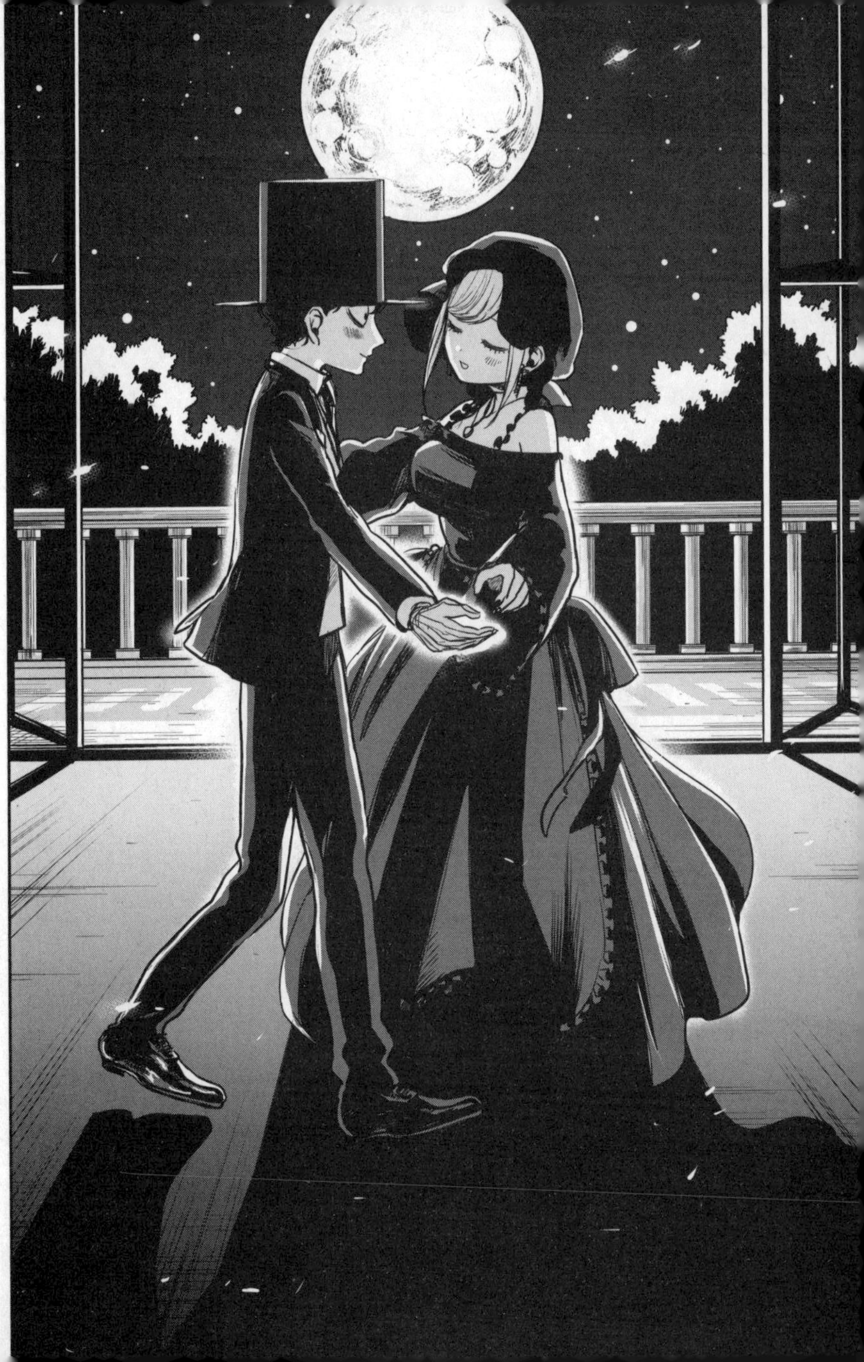

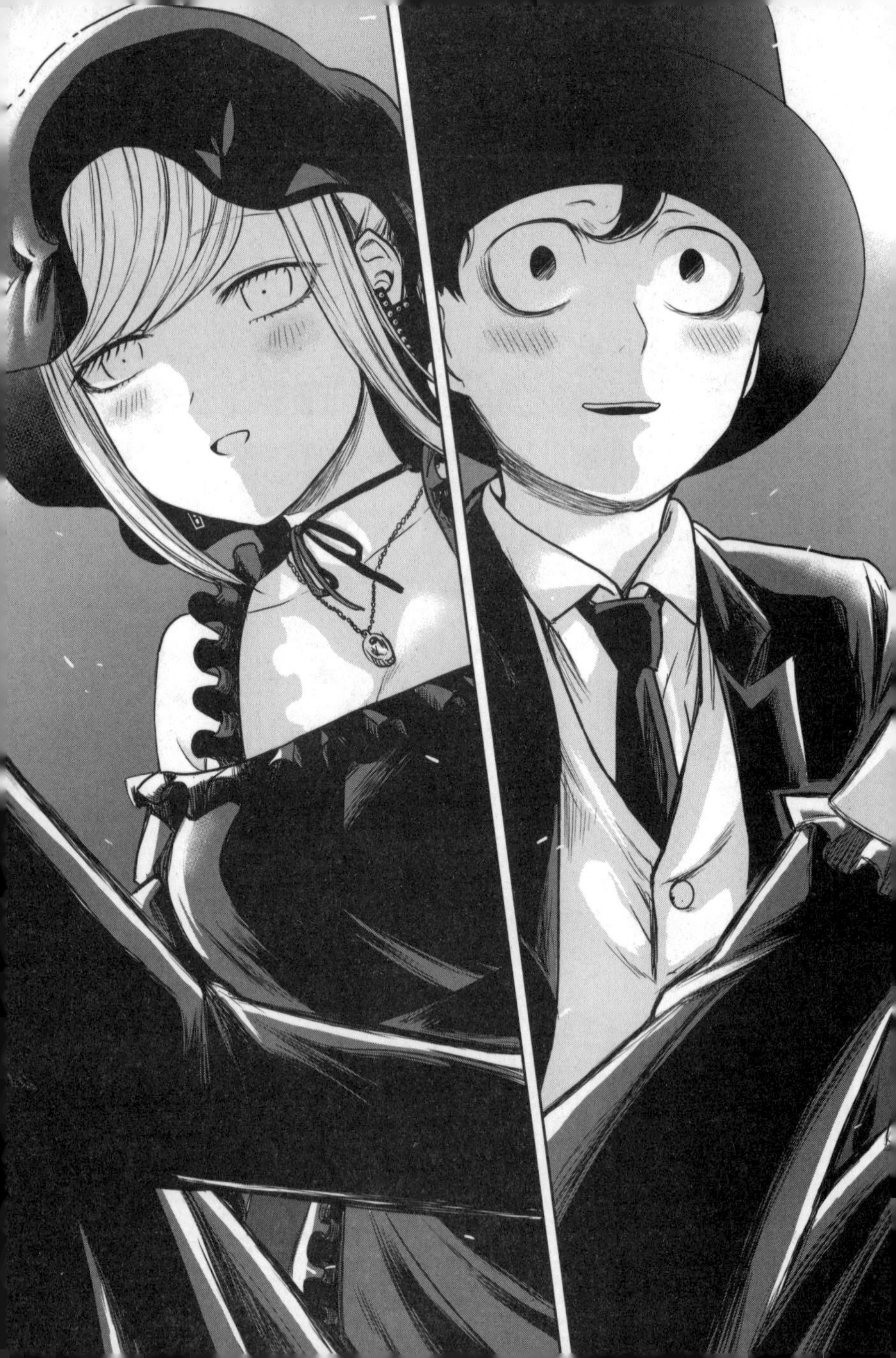

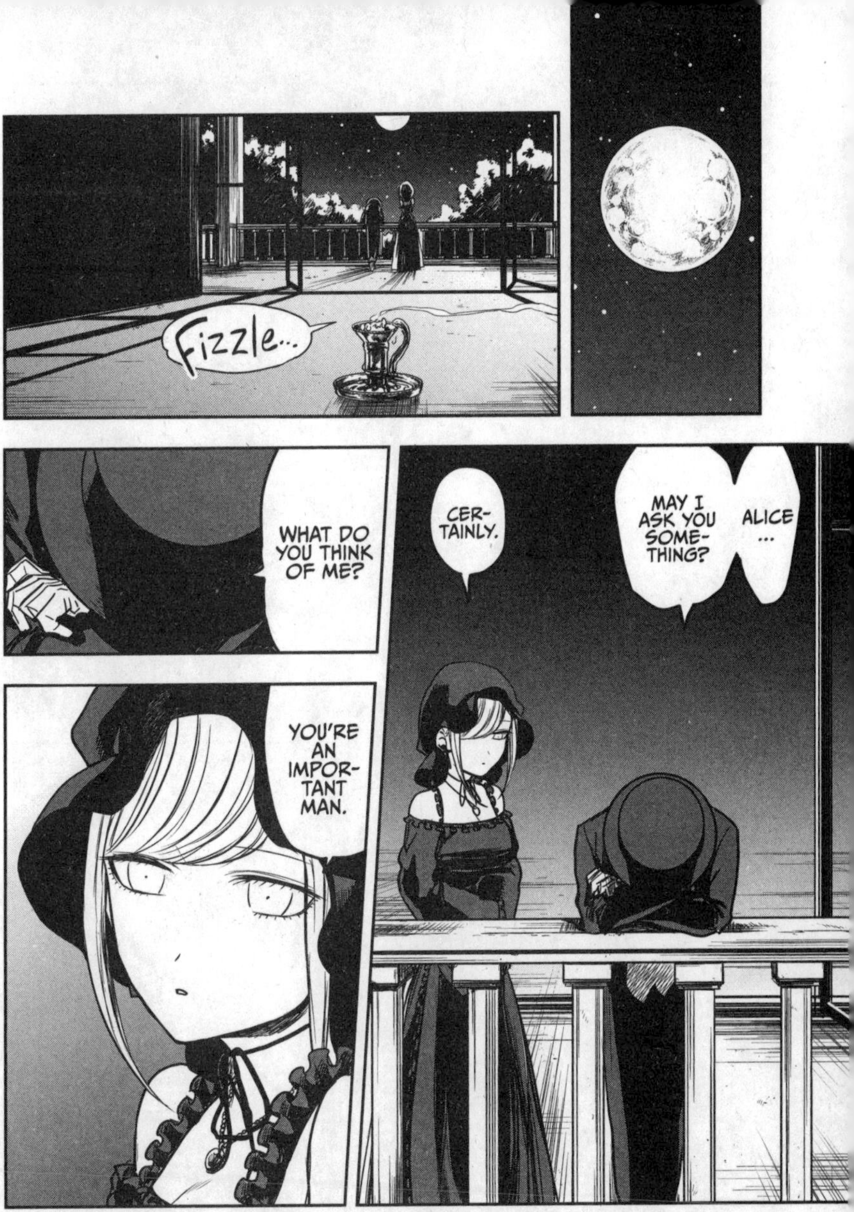
Fizzle...
ALICE ...
MAY I ASK YOU SOME-THING?
CER-TAINLY.
WHAT DO YOU THINK OF ME?
YOU'RE AN IMPOR-TANT MAN.

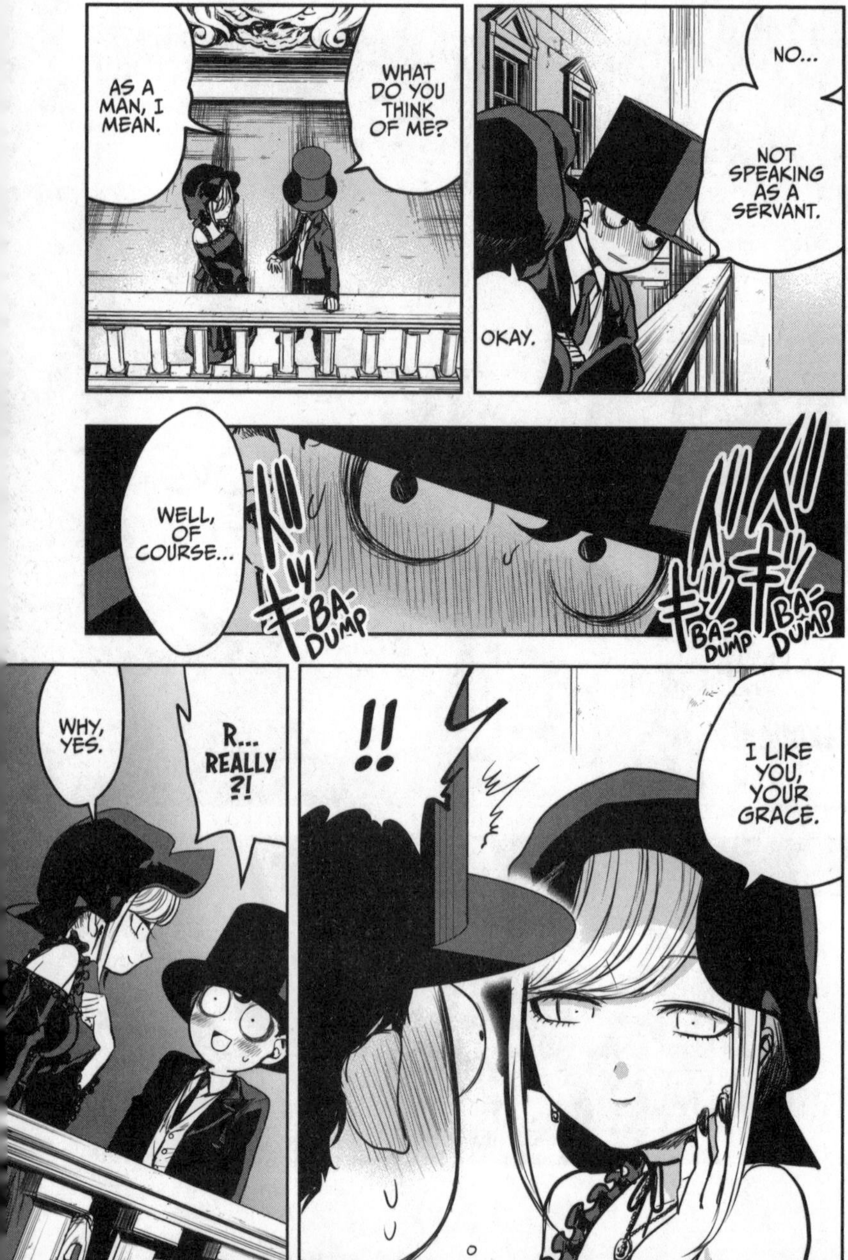
NO...
NOT SPEAKING AS A SERVANT.
OKAY.
WHAT DO YOU THINK OF ME?
AS A MAN, I MEAN.
BA-DUMP
BA-DUMP
WELL, OF COURSE...
BA-DUMP
I LIKE YOU, YOUR GRACE.
!!
R... REALLY?!
WHY, YES.

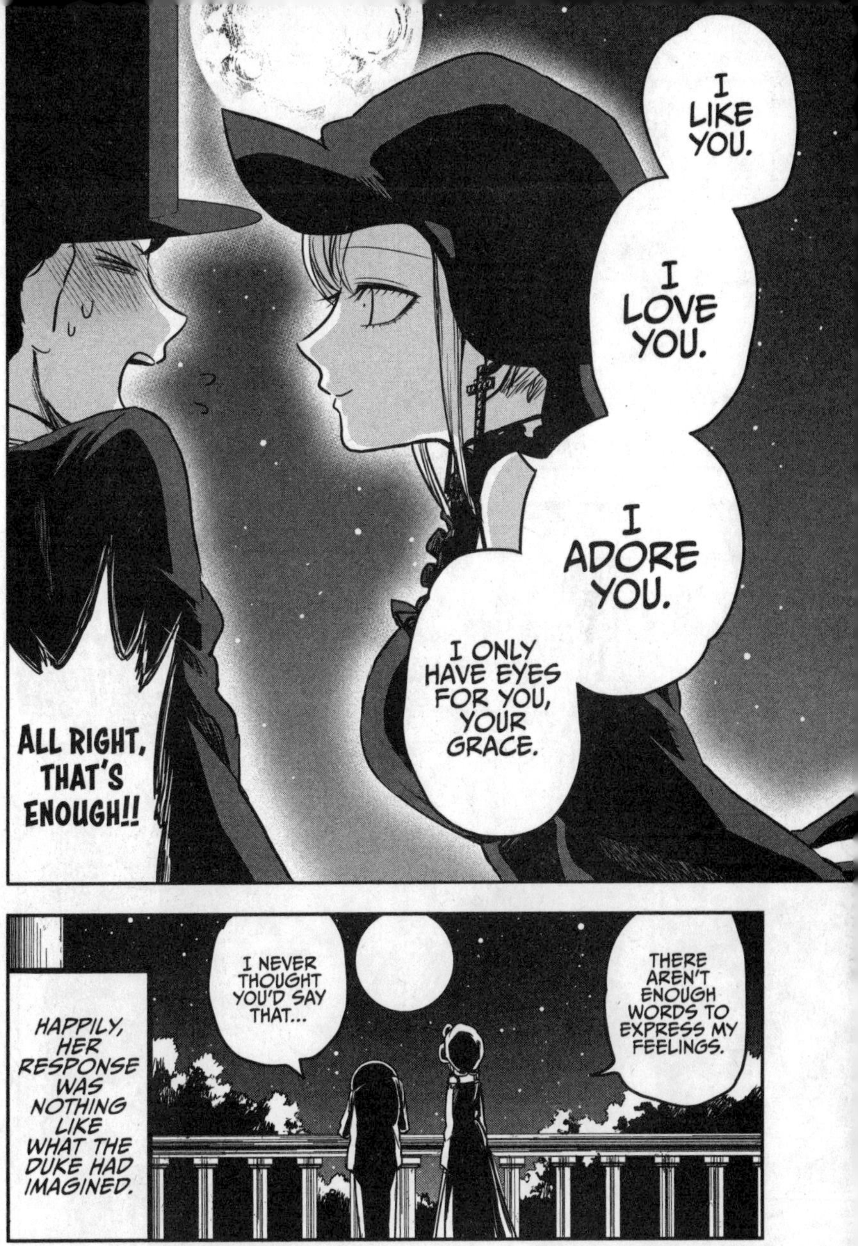
I LIKE YOU.
I LOVE YOU.
I ADORE YOU.
I ONLY HAVE EYES FOR YOU, YOUR GRACE.
ALL RIGHT, THAT'S ENOUGH!!
THERE AREN'T ENOUGH WORDS TO EXPRESS MY FEELINGS.
I NEVER THOUGHT YOU'D SAY THAT...
HAPPILY, HER RESPONSE WAS NOTHING LIKE WHAT THE DUKE HAD IMAGINED.

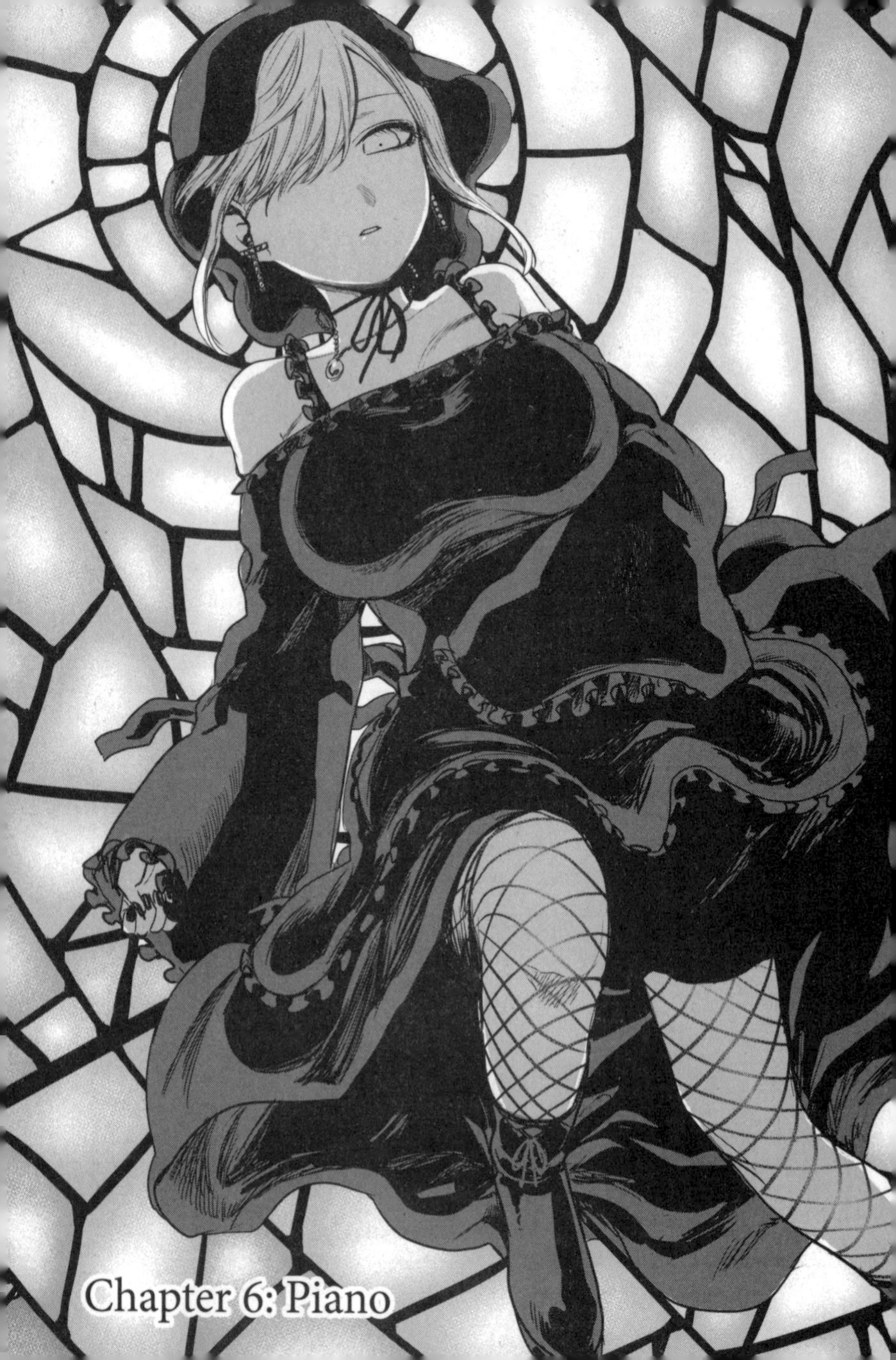

Chapter 6: Piano

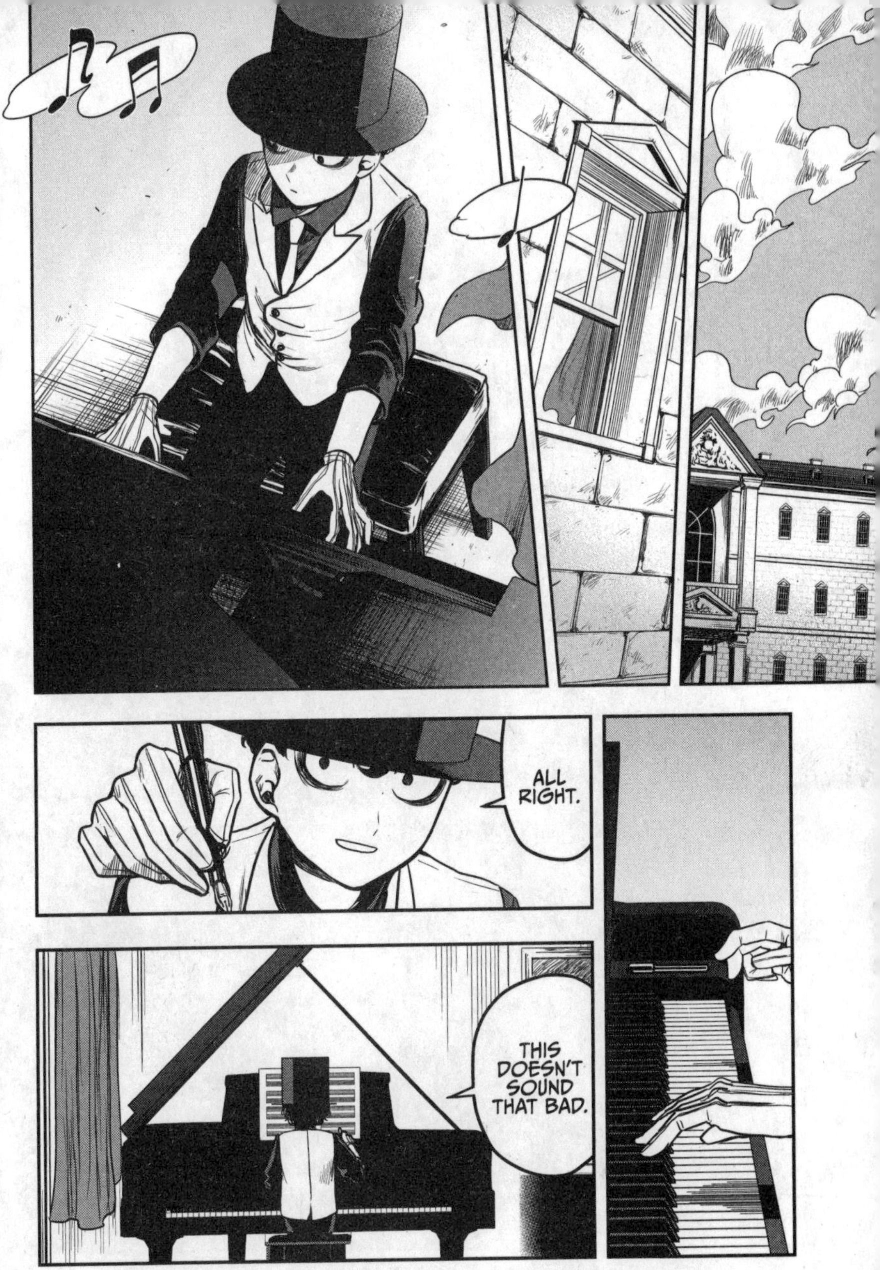

ALL RIGHT.
THIS DOESN'T SOUND THAT BAD.

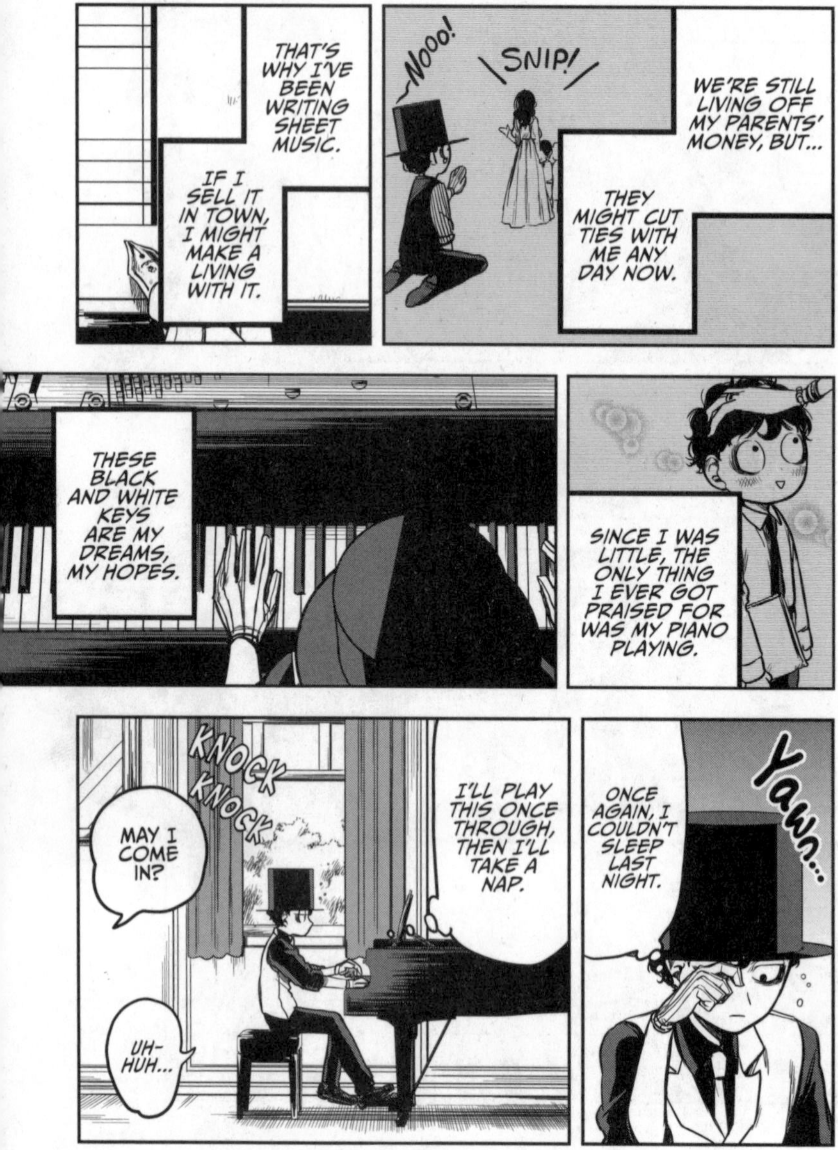
WE'RE STILL LIVING OFF MY PARENTS' MONEY, BUT...
THEY MIGHT CUT TIES WITH ME ANY DAY NOW.
SNIP!
Nooo!
THAT'S WHY I'VE BEEN WRITING SHEET MUSIC.
IF I SELL IT IN TOWN, I MIGHT MAKE A LIVING WITH IT.
SINCE I WAS LITTLE, THE ONLY THING I EVER GOT PRAISED FOR WAS MY PIANO PLAYING.
THESE BLACK AND WHITE KEYS ARE MY DREAMS, MY HOPES.
Yawn...
ONCE AGAIN, I COULDN'T SLEEP LAST NIGHT.
I'LL PLAY THIS ONCE THROUGH, THEN I'LL TAKE A NAP.
KNOCK KNOCK
MAY I COME IN?
UH-HUH...

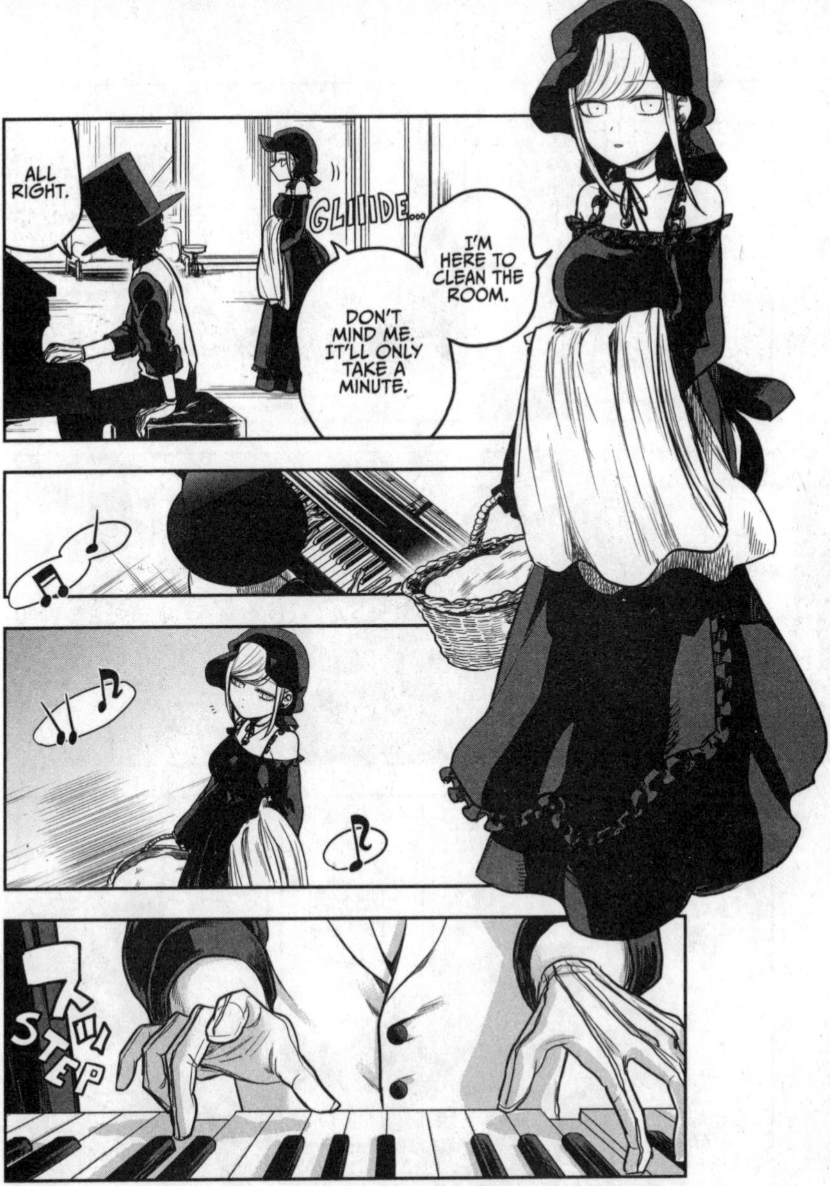
GLIIIDE...
I'M HERE TO CLEAN THE ROOM.
DON'T MIND ME. IT'LL ONLY TAKE A MINUTE.
ALL RIGHT.
STEP

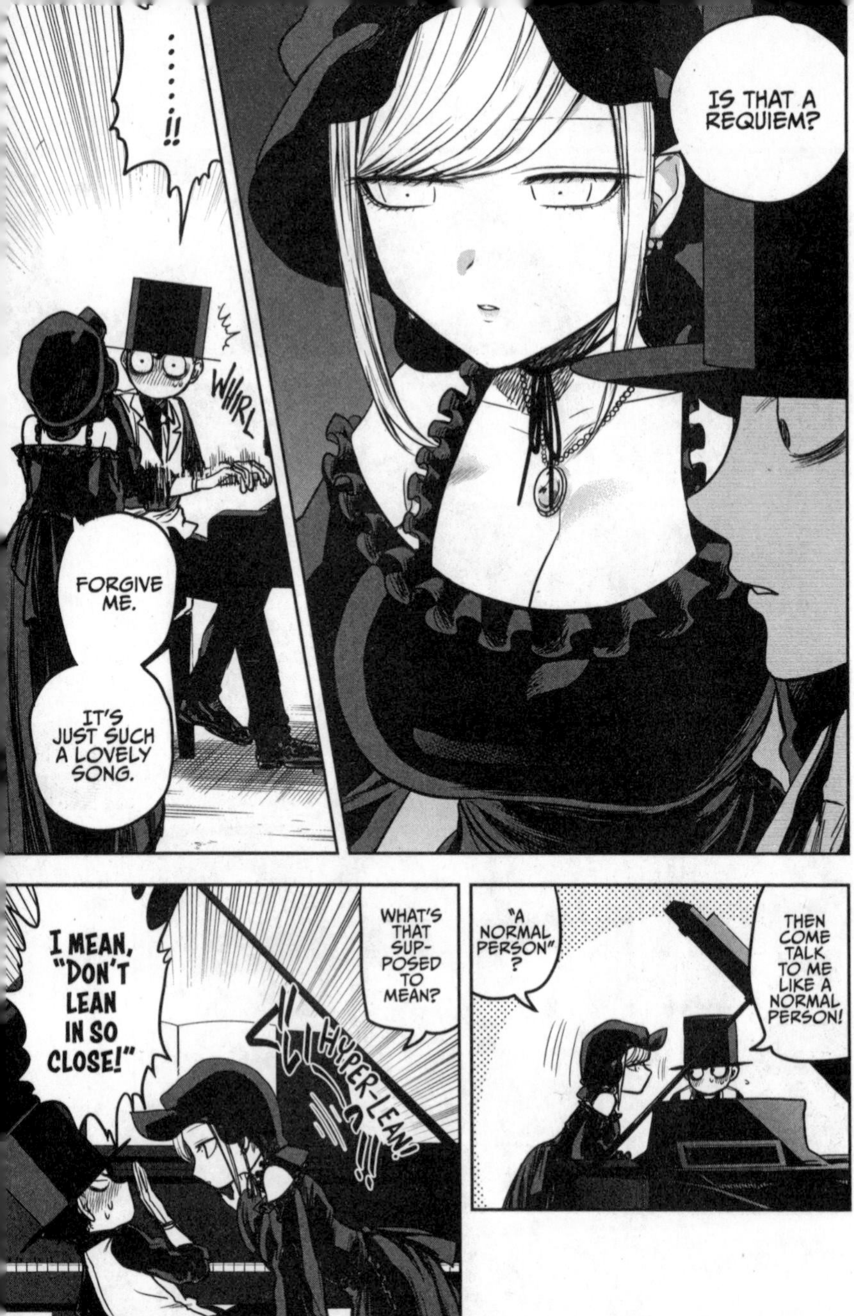
IS THAT A REQUIEM?
......!!
WHIRL
FORGIVE ME.
IT'S JUST SUCH A LOVELY SONG.
THEN COME TALK TO ME LIKE A NORMAL PERSON!
"A NORMAL PERSON"?
WHAT'S THAT SUP-POSED TO MEAN?
HYPER-LEAN!
I MEAN, "DON'T LEAN IN SO CLOSE!"

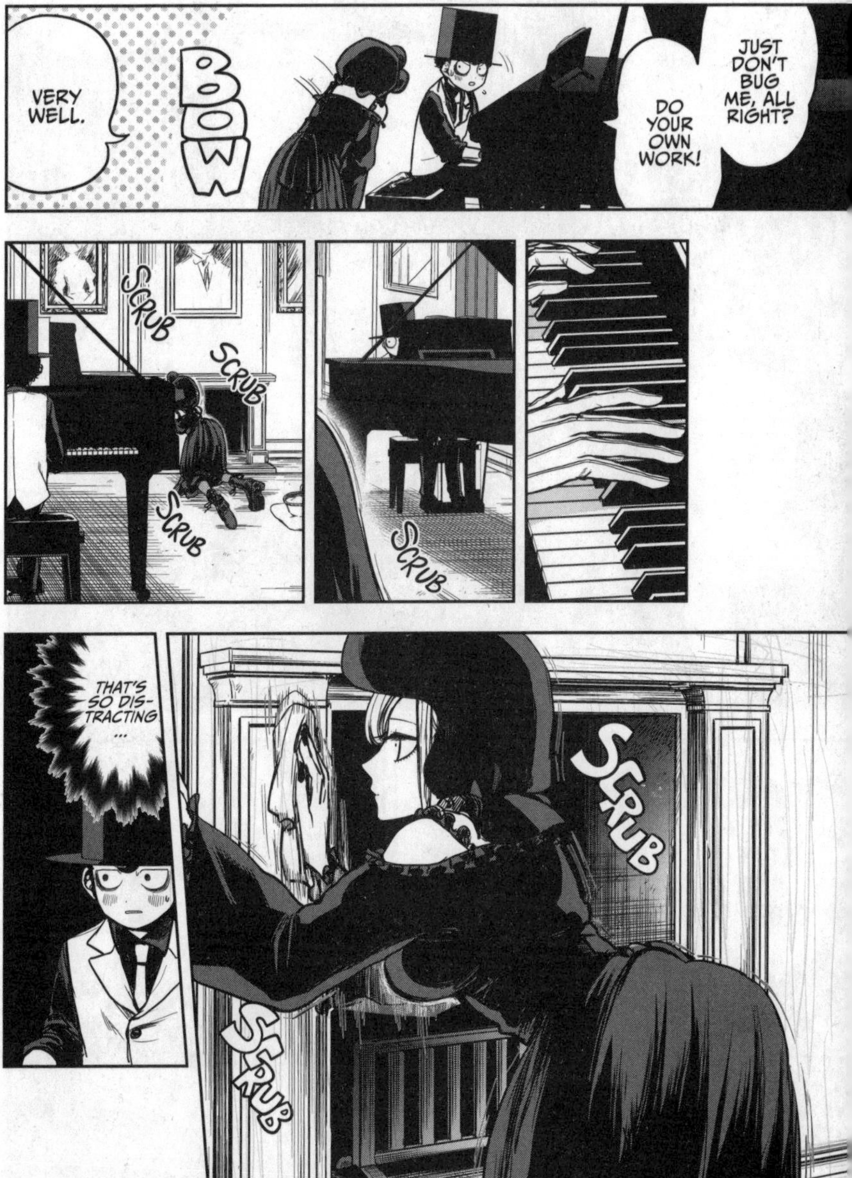
JUST DON'T BUG ME, ALL RIGHT?
DO YOUR OWN WORK!
BOW
VERY WELL.
SCRUB
SCRUB
SCRUB
SCRUB
SCRUB
SCRUB
THAT'S SO DIS-TRACTING...

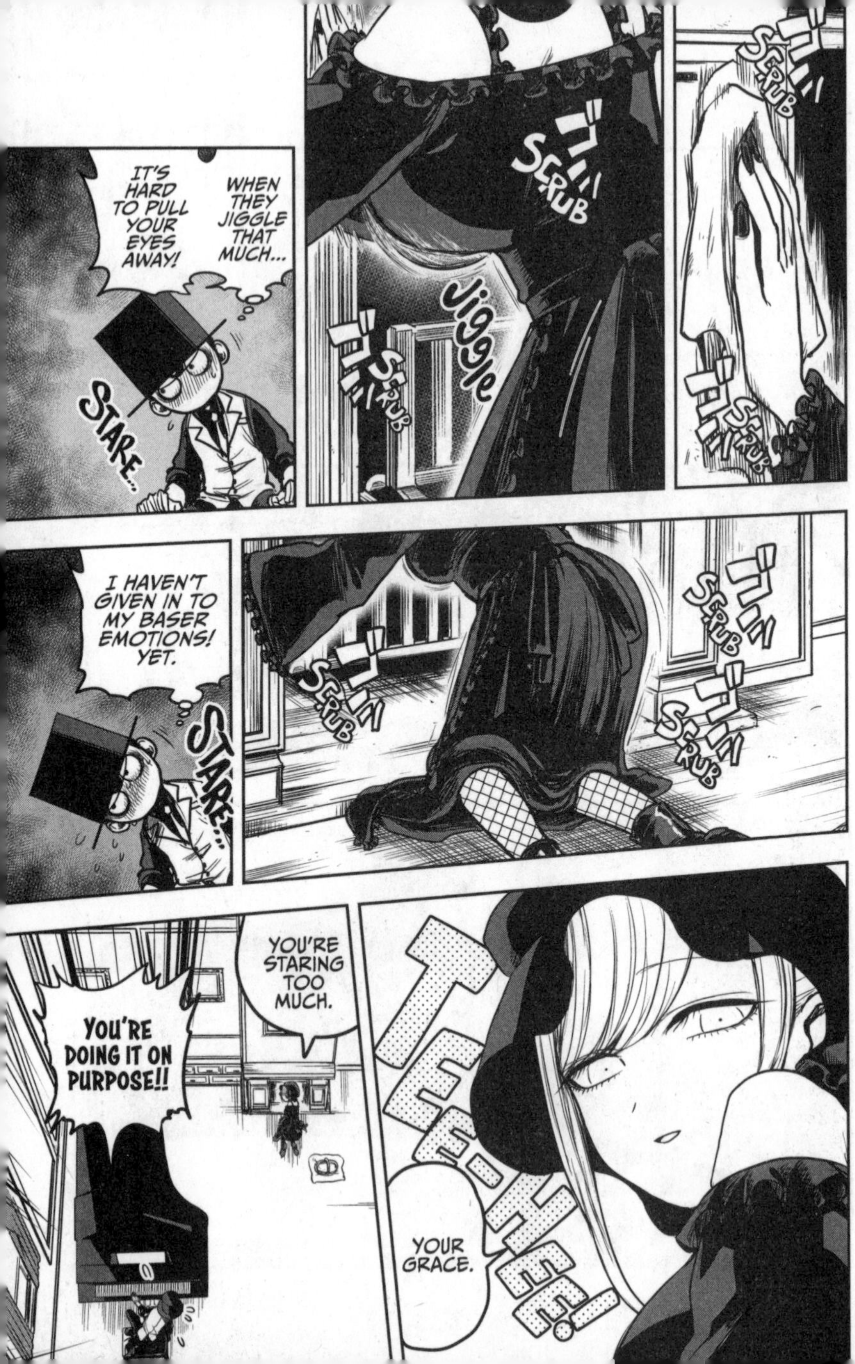
SCRUB
SCRUB
SCRUB
SCRUB
JIGGLE
SCRUB
WHEN THEY JIGGLE THAT MUCH...
IT'S HARD TO PULL YOUR EYES AWAY!
STARE...
SCRUB
SCRUB
SCRUB
I HAVEN'T GIVEN IN TO MY BASER EMOTIONS! YET.
STARE...
TEE-HEE!
YOUR GRACE.
YOU'RE STARING TOO MUCH.
YOU'RE DOING IT ON PURPOSE!!

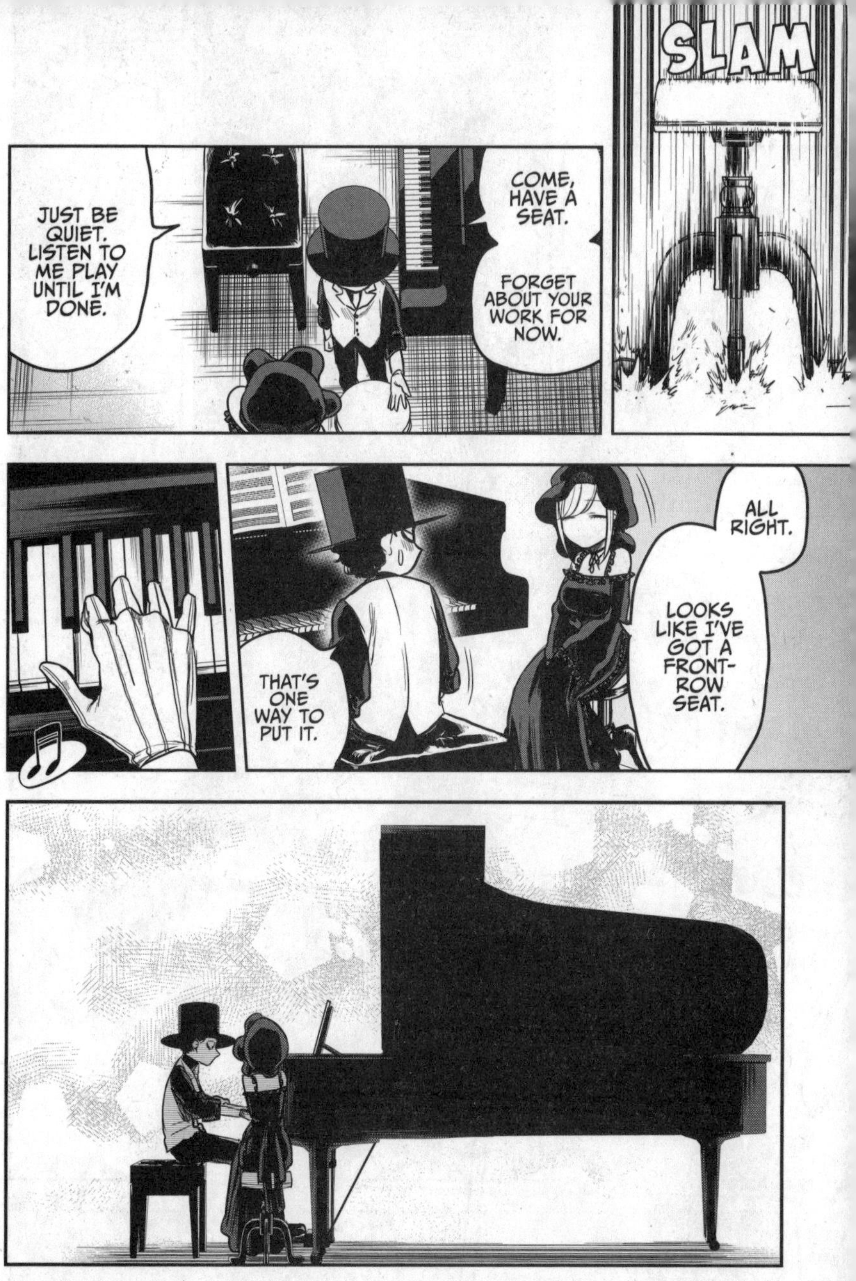
SLAM
COME, HAVE A SEAT.
FORGET ABOUT YOUR WORK FOR NOW.
JUST BE QUIET. LISTEN TO ME PLAY UNTIL I'M DONE.
ALL RIGHT.
LOOKS LIKE I'VE GOT A FRONT-ROW SEAT.
THAT'S ONE WAY TO PUT IT.

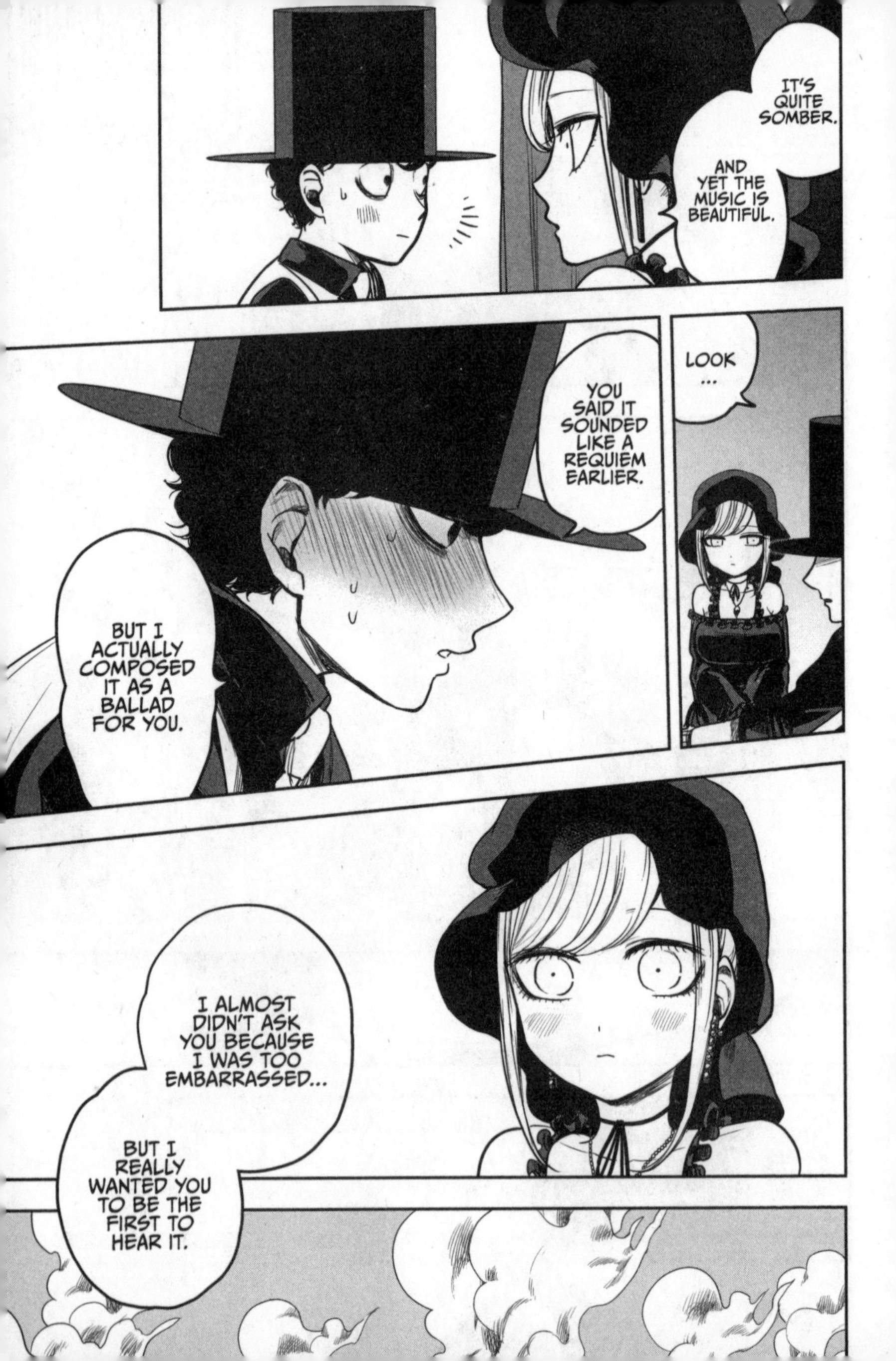
IT'S QUITE SOMBER.
AND YET THE MUSIC IS BEAUTIFUL.
LOOK ...
YOU SAID IT SOUNDED LIKE A REQUIEM EARLIER.
BUT I ACTUALLY COMPOSED IT AS A BALLAD FOR YOU.
I ALMOST DIDN'T ASK YOU BECAUSE I WAS TOO EMBARRASSED...
BUT I REALLY WANTED YOU TO BE THE FIRST TO HEAR IT.

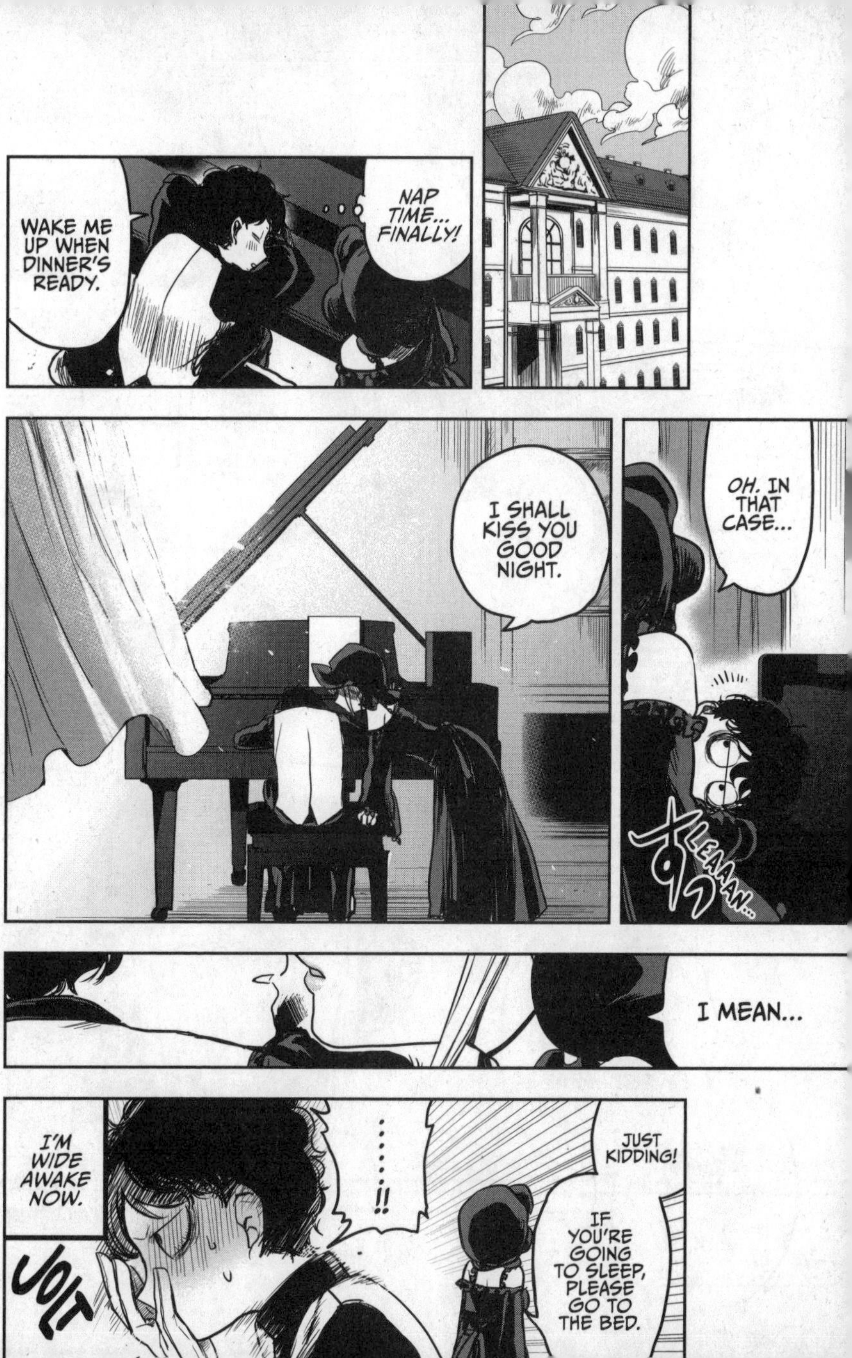
NAP TIME... FINALLY!
WAKE ME UP WHEN DINNER'S READY.
OH. IN THAT CASE...
LEAAAAN...
I SHALL KISS YOU GOOD NIGHT.
I MEAN...
JUST KIDDING!
IF YOU'RE GOING TO SLEEP, PLEASE GO TO THE BED.
......!!
I'M WIDE AWAKE NOW.
JOLT

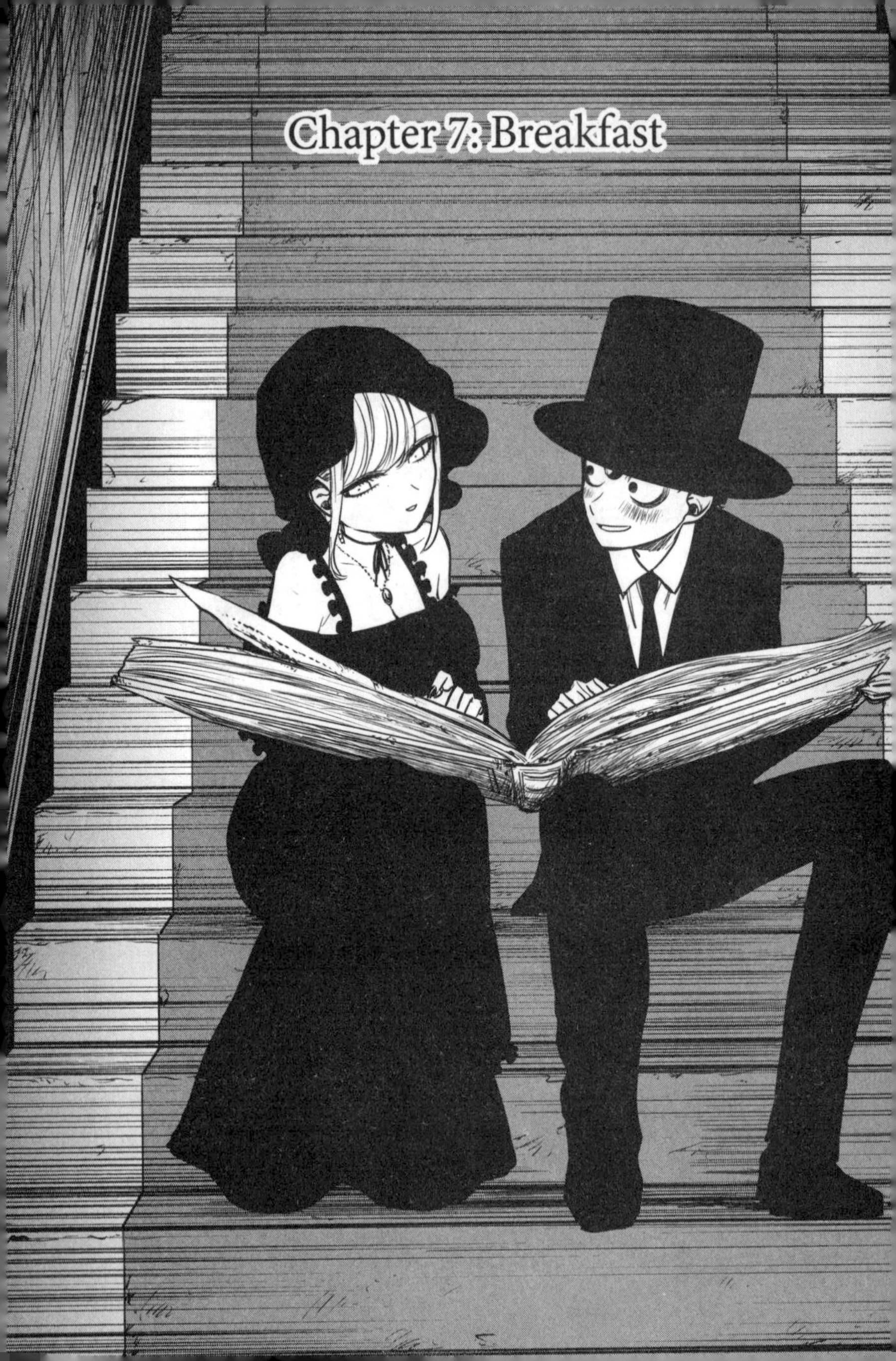
Chapter 7: Breakfast

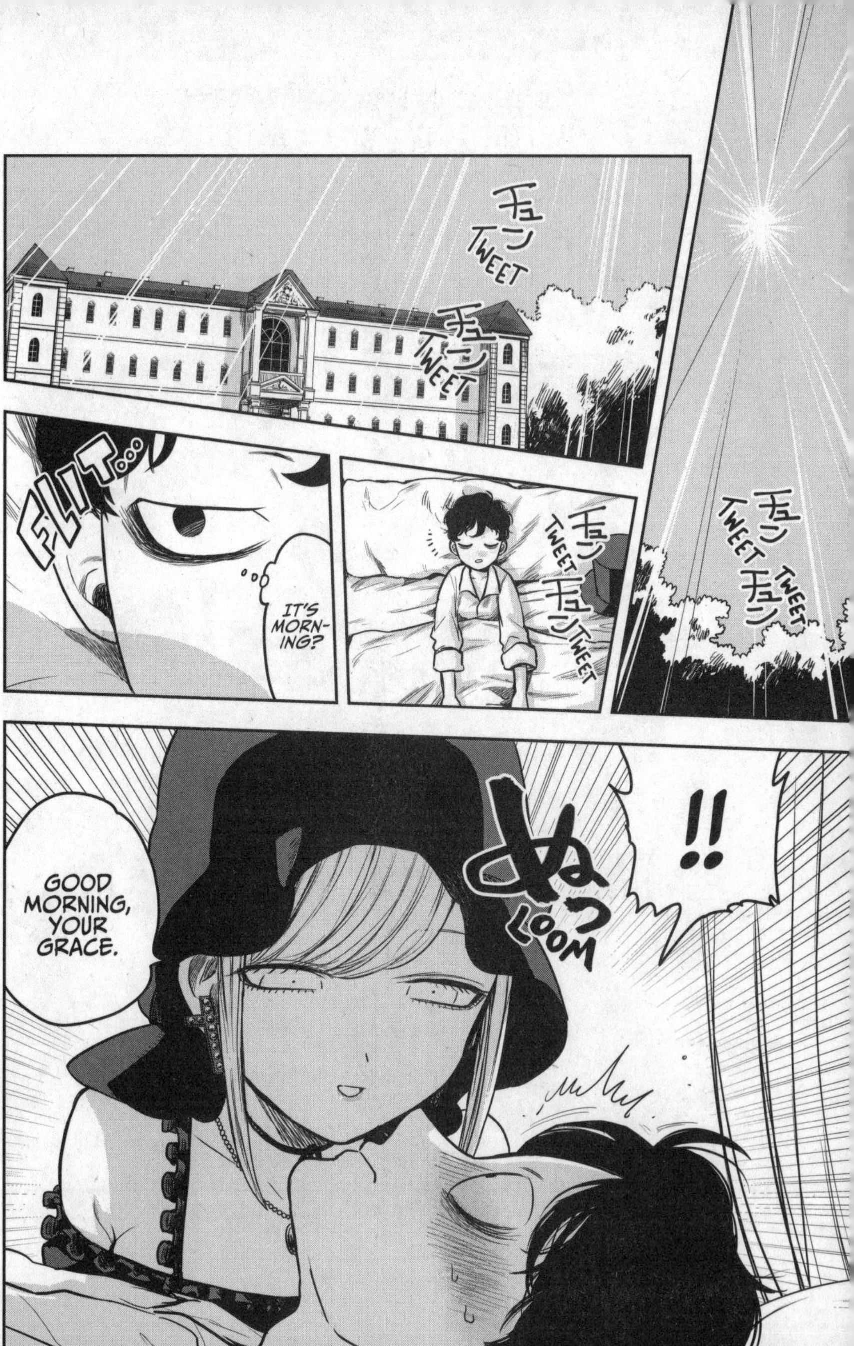

チュン TWEET
チュン TWEET
チュン TWEET
チュン TWEET
チュン TWEET
チュン TWEET
FLIT...
IT'S MORNING?
!!
ぬっ LOOM
GOOD MORNING, YOUR GRACE.

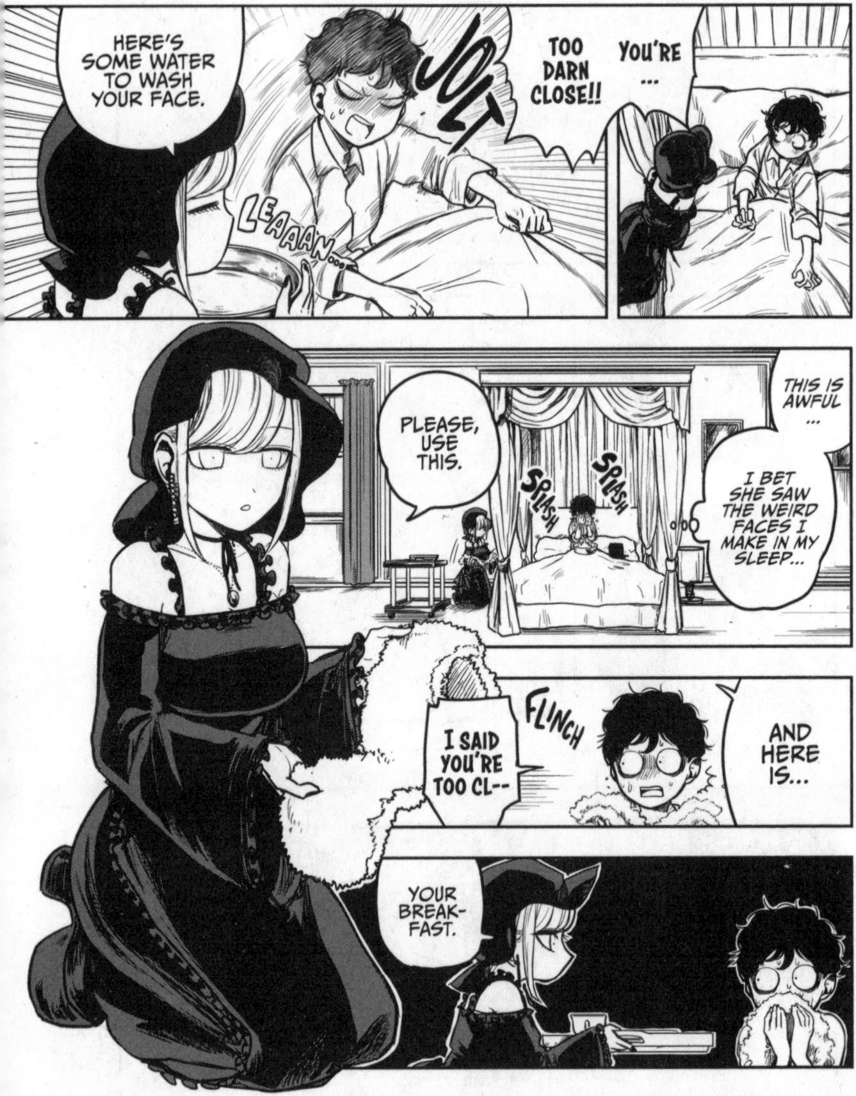
YOU'RE ...
TOO DARN CLOSE!!
JOLT
HERE'S SOME WATER TO WASH YOUR FACE.
LEAAAAN...
THIS IS AWFUL ...
I BET SHE SAW THE WEIRD FACES I MAKE IN MY SLEEP...
SPLASH
SPLASH
PLEASE, USE THIS.
AND HERE IS...
FLINCH
I SAID YOU'RE TOO CL--
YOUR BREAK-FAST.

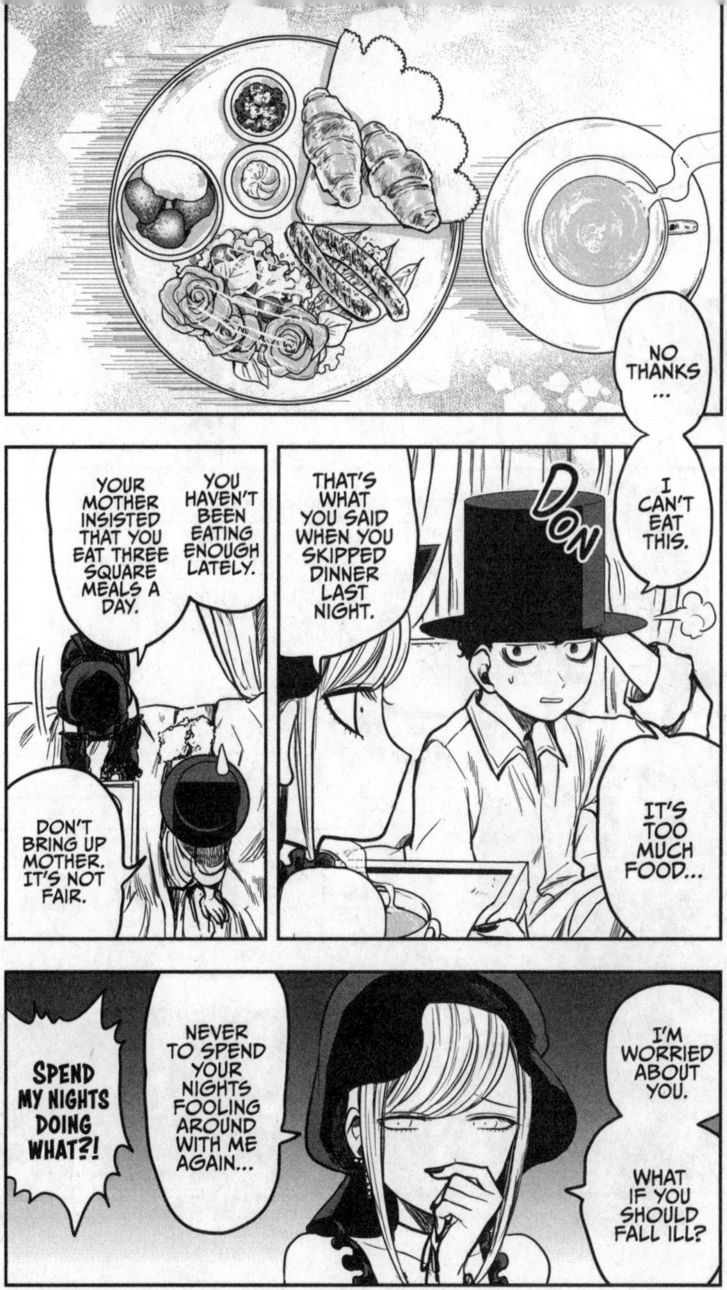
NO THANKS ...
I CAN'T EAT THIS.
DON
IT'S TOO MUCH FOOD...
THAT'S WHAT YOU SAID WHEN YOU SKIPPED DINNER LAST NIGHT.
YOU HAVEN'T BEEN EATING ENOUGH LATELY.
YOUR MOTHER INSISTED THAT YOU EAT THREE SQUARE MEALS A DAY.
DON'T BRING UP MOTHER. IT'S NOT FAIR.
I'M WORRIED ABOUT YOU.
WHAT IF YOU SHOULD FALL ILL?
NEVER TO SPEND YOUR NIGHTS FOOLING AROUND WITH ME AGAIN...
SPEND MY NIGHTS DOING WHAT?!

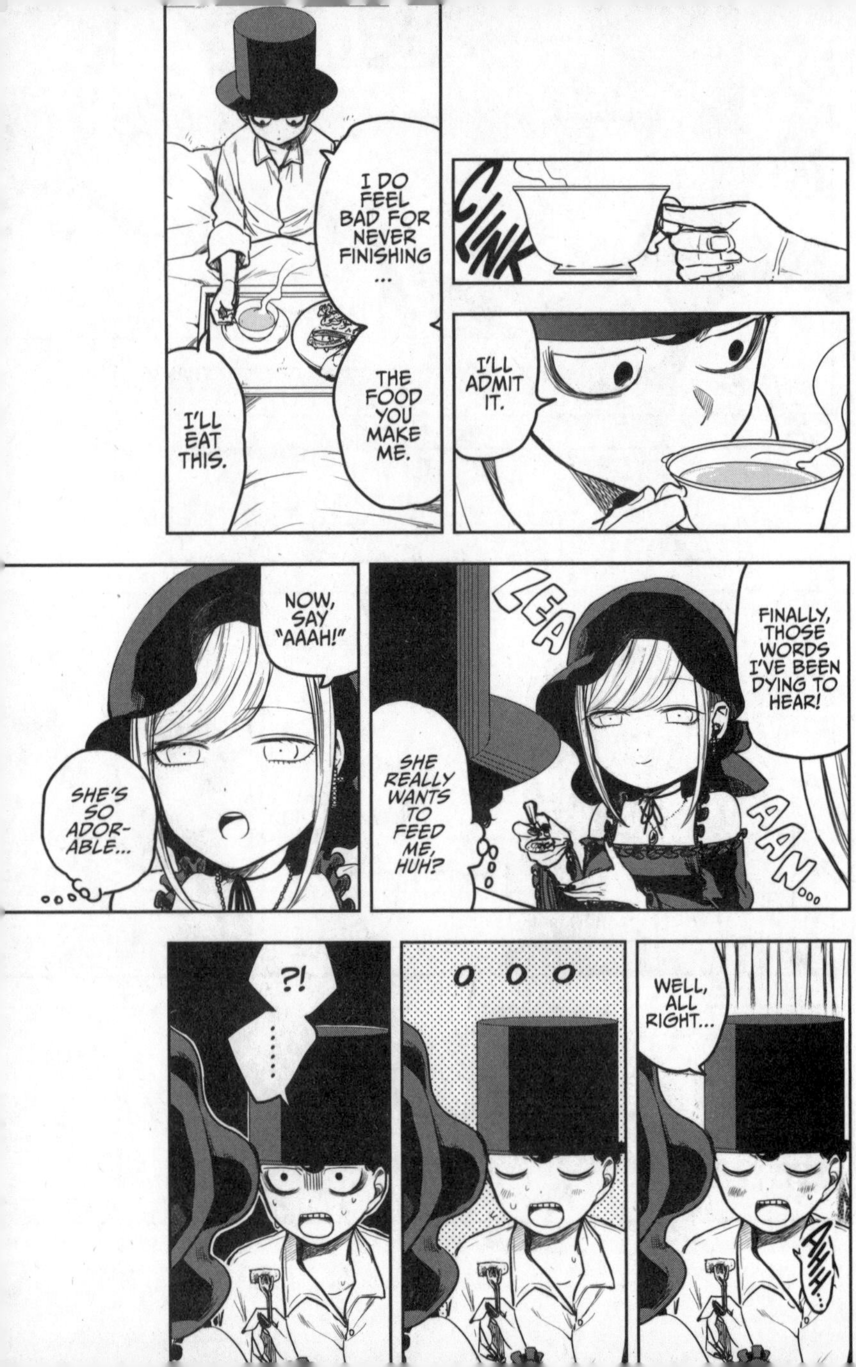
CLINK
I'LL ADMIT IT.
I DO FEEL BAD FOR NEVER FINISHING...
THE FOOD YOU MAKE ME.
I'LL EAT THIS.
LEA
FINALLY, THOSE WORDS I'VE BEEN DYING TO HEAR!
AAN...
SHE REALLY WANTS TO FEED ME, HUH?
NOW, SAY "AAAH!"
SHE'S SO ADORABLE...
WELL, ALL RIGHT...
AHH...
?!
......

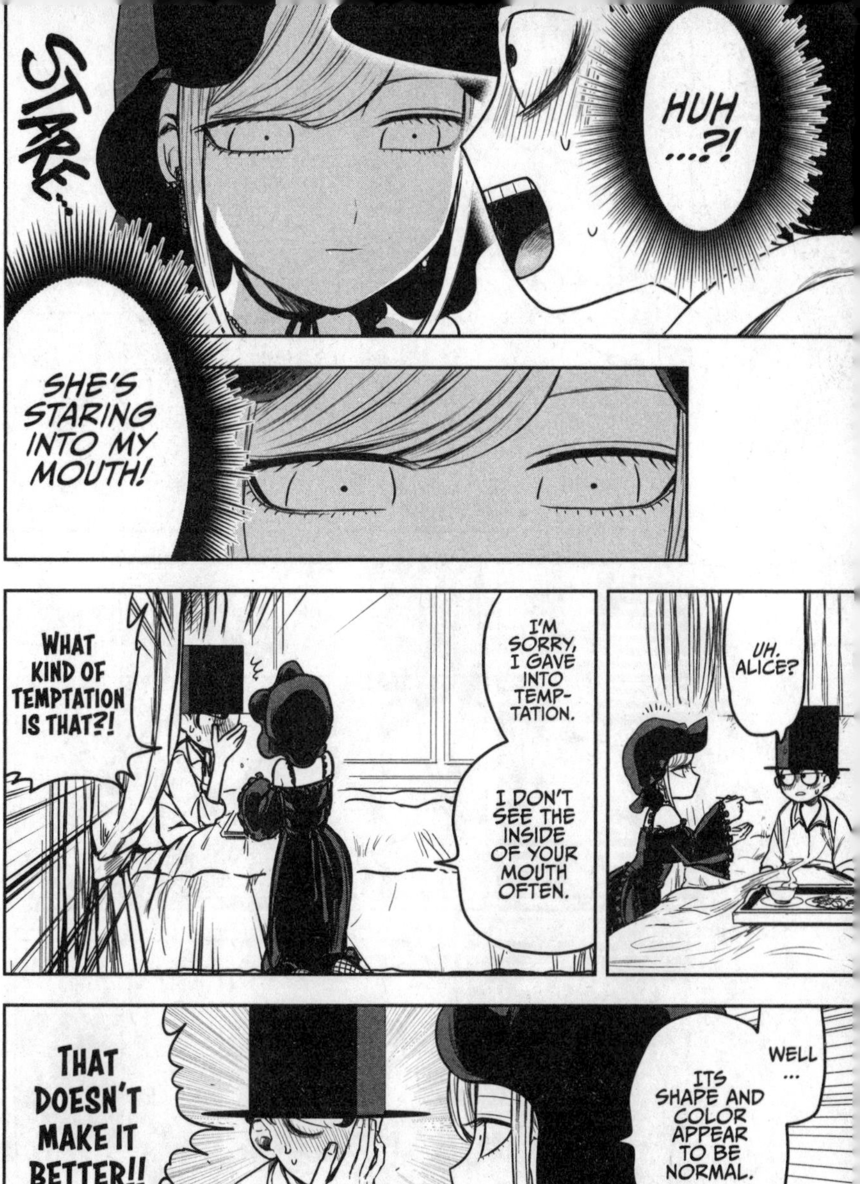
HUH ...?!
STARE...
SHE'S STARING INTO MY MOUTH!
UH. ALICE?
I'M SORRY, I GAVE INTO TEMP-TATION.
I DON'T SEE THE INSIDE OF YOUR MOUTH OFTEN.
WHAT KIND OF TEMPTATION IS THAT?!
WELL ...
ITS SHAPE AND COLOR APPEAR TO BE NORMAL.
THAT DOESN'T MAKE IT BETTER!!

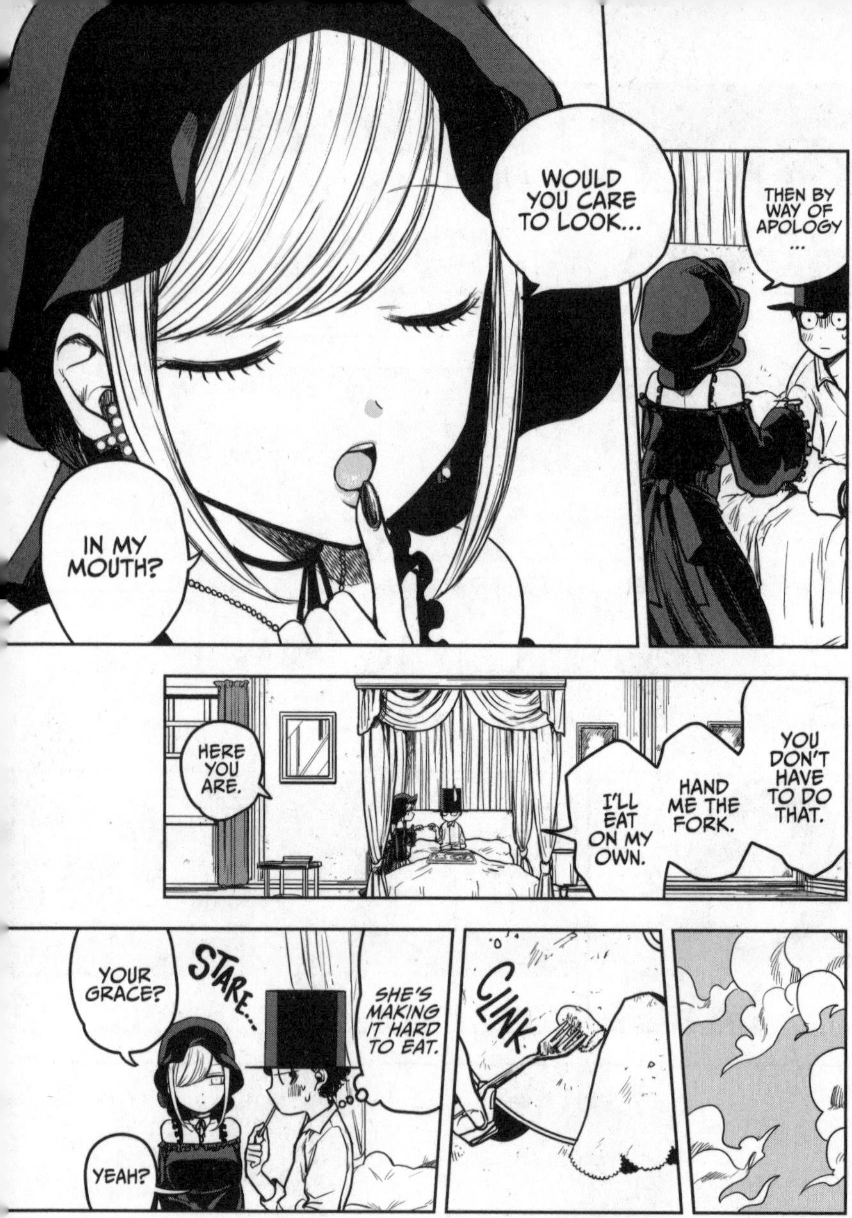
THEN BY WAY OF APOLOGY ...
WOULD YOU CARE TO LOOK...
IN MY MOUTH?
YOU DON'T HAVE TO DO THAT.
HAND ME THE FORK.
I'LL EAT ON MY OWN.
HERE YOU ARE.
CLINK
SHE'S MAKING IT HARD TO EAT.
STARE...
YOUR GRACE?
YEAH?

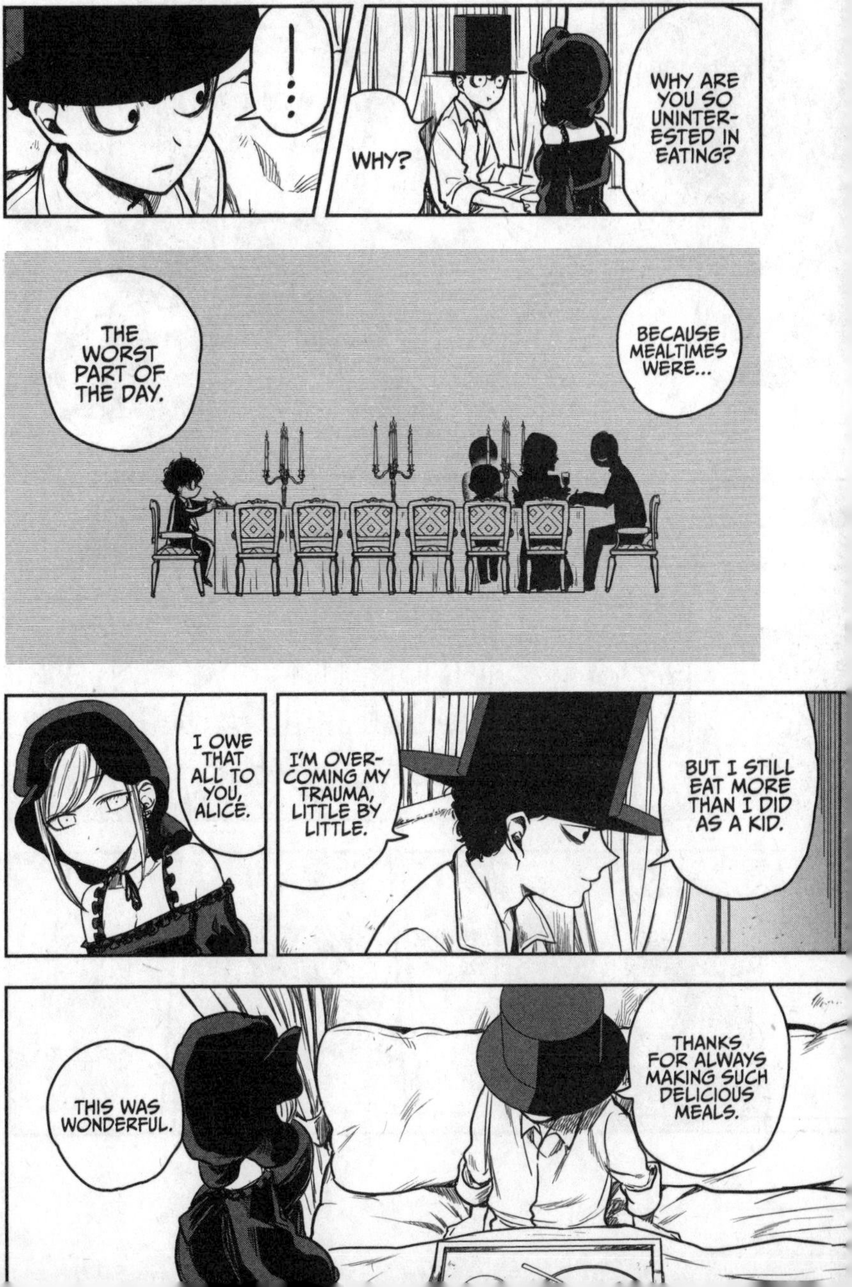
WHY ARE YOU SO UNINTER-ESTED IN EATING?
WHY?
!...
BECAUSE MEALTIMES WERE...
THE WORST PART OF THE DAY.
BUT I STILL EAT MORE THAN I DID AS A KID.
I'M OVER-COMING MY TRAUMA, LITTLE BY LITTLE.
I OWE THAT ALL TO YOU, ALICE.
THANKS FOR ALWAYS MAKING SUCH DELICIOUS MEALS.
THIS WAS WONDERFUL.

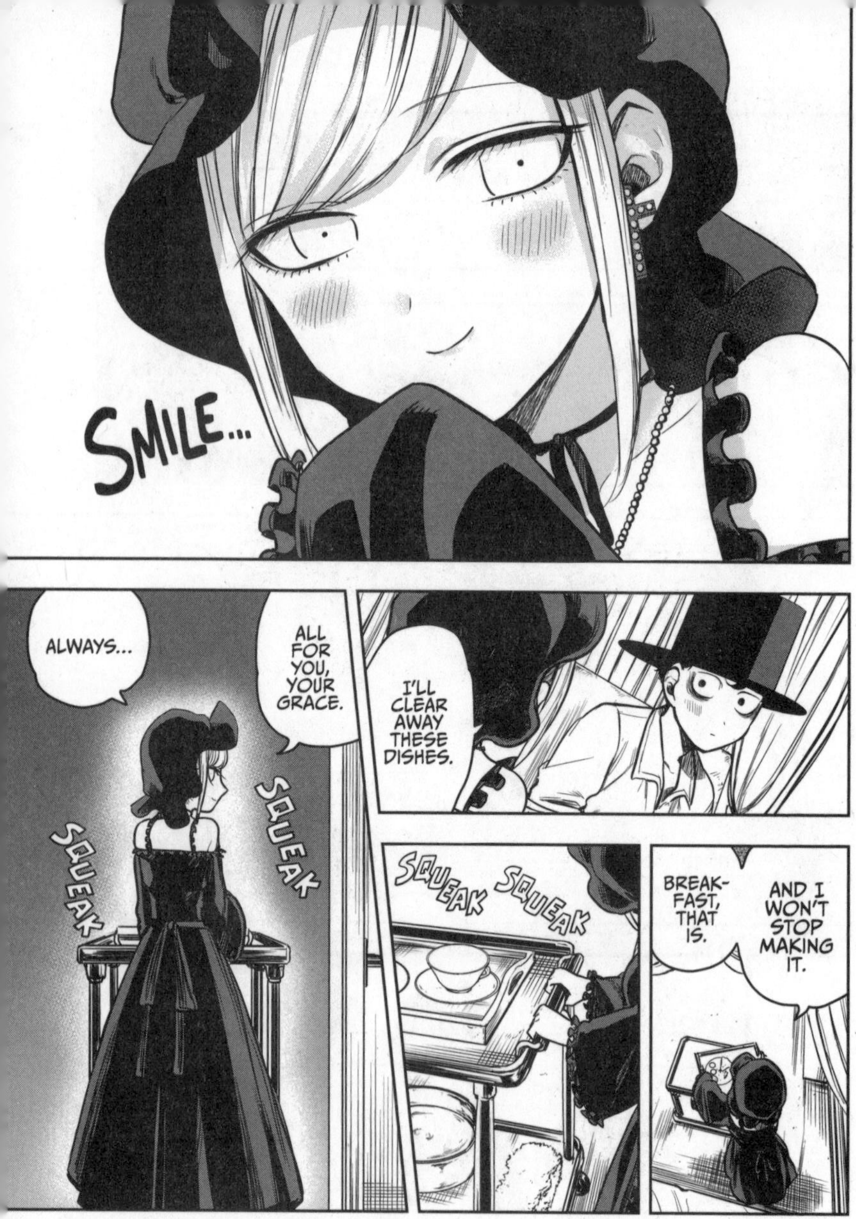
SMILE...
I'LL CLEAR AWAY THESE DISHES.
AND I WON'T STOP MAKING IT.
BREAKFAST, THAT IS.
SQUEAK SQUEAK
ALL FOR YOU, YOUR GRACE.
ALWAYS...
SQUEAK SQUEAK

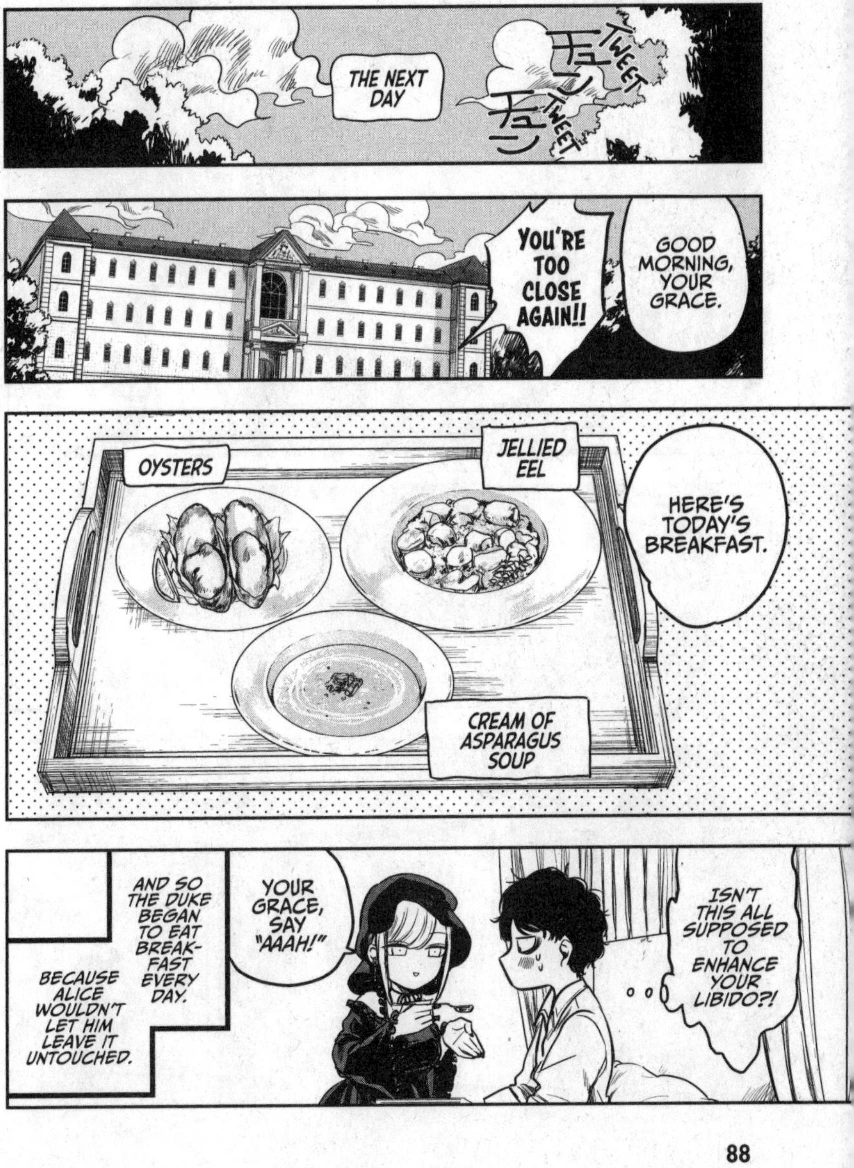
チュン TWEET
チュン TWEET
THE NEXT DAY
GOOD MORNING, YOUR GRACE.
YOU'RE TOO CLOSE AGAIN!!
HERE'S TODAY'S BREAKFAST.
JELLIED EEL
OYSTERS
CREAM OF ASPARAGUS SOUP
ISN'T THIS ALL SUPPOSED TO ENHANCE YOUR LIBIDO?!
YOUR GRACE, SAY "AAAH!"
AND SO THE DUKE BEGAN TO EAT BREAK-FAST EVERY DAY.
BECAUSE ALICE WOULDN'T LET HIM LEAVE IT UNTOUCHED.

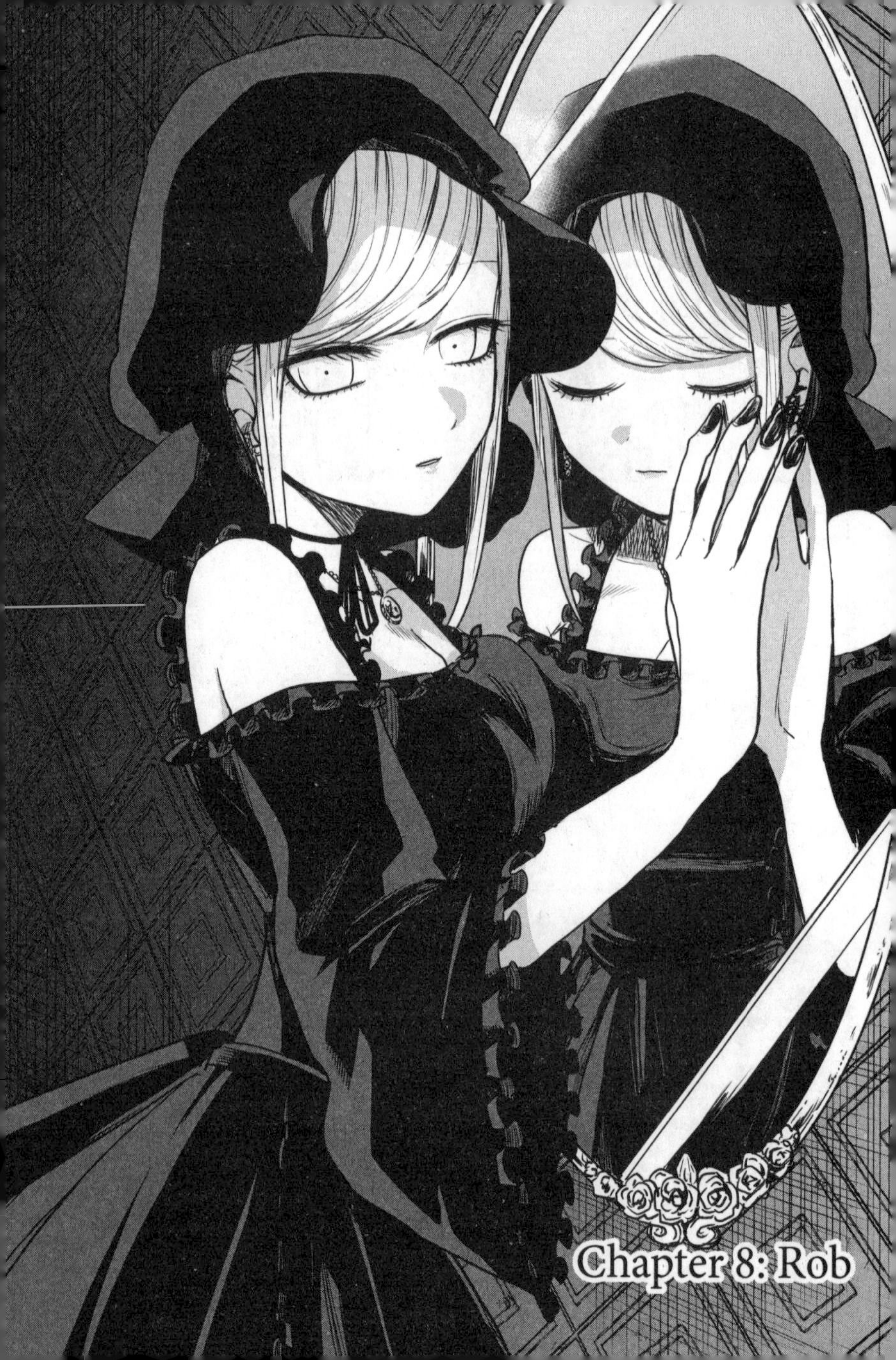
Chapter 8: Rob

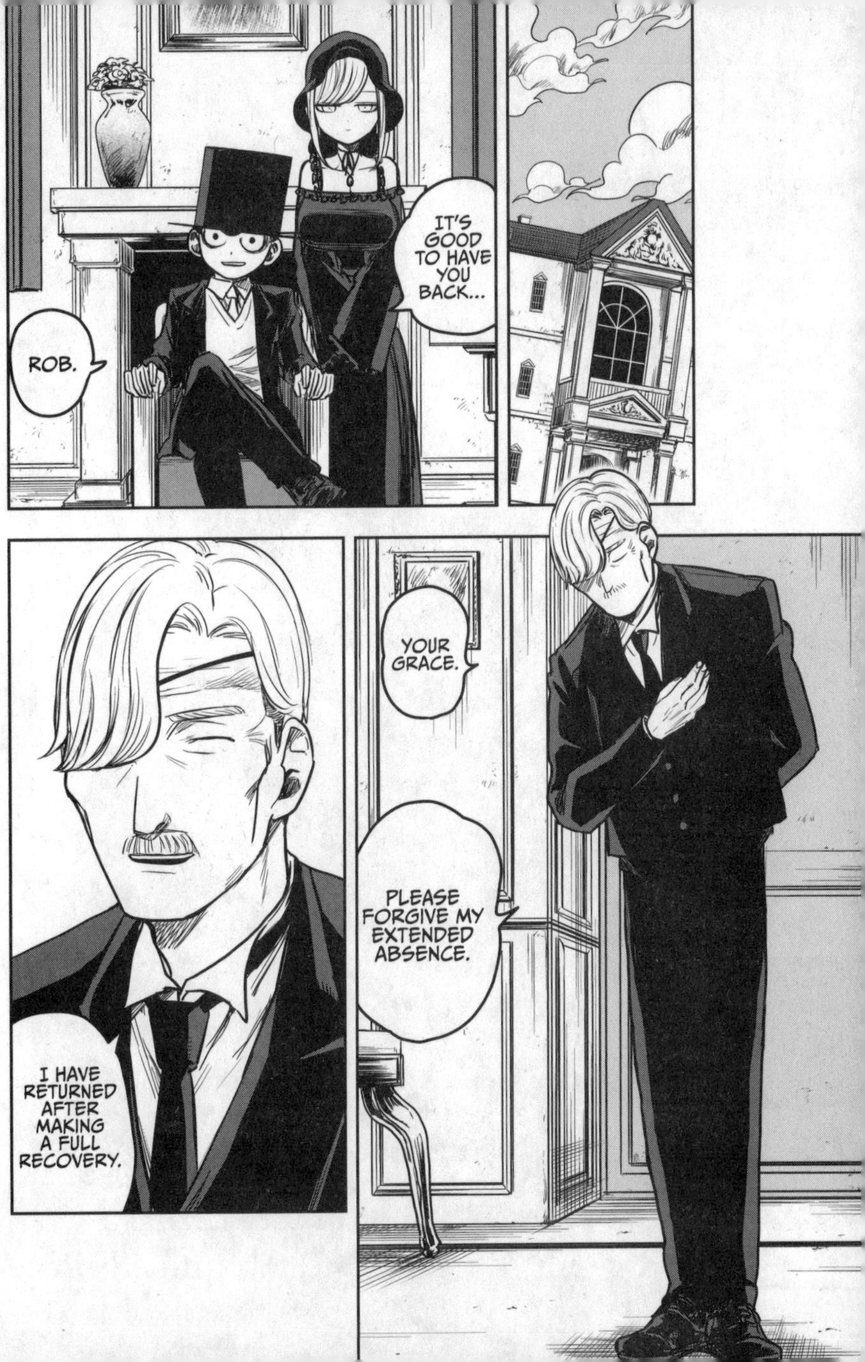
IT'S GOOD TO HAVE YOU BACK...
ROB.
YOUR GRACE.
PLEASE FORGIVE MY EXTENDED ABSENCE.
I HAVE RETURNED AFTER MAKING A FULL RECOVERY.

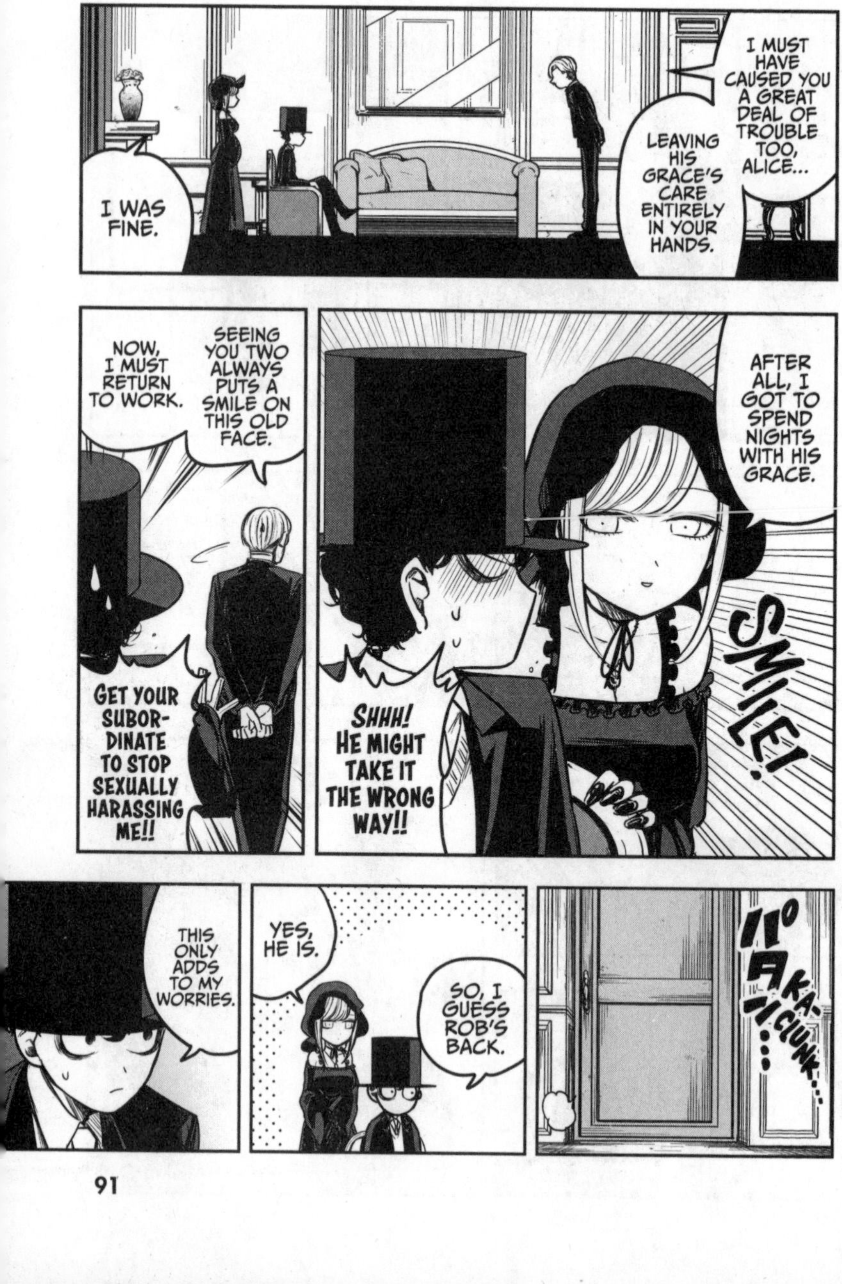
I MUST HAVE CAUSED YOU A GREAT DEAL OF TROUBLE TOO, ALICE...
LEAVING HIS GRACE'S CARE ENTIRELY IN YOUR HANDS.
I WAS FINE.
AFTER ALL, I GOT TO SPEND NIGHTS WITH HIS GRACE.
SMILE!
SHHH! HE MIGHT TAKE IT THE WRONG WAY!!
SEEING YOU TWO ALWAYS PUTS A SMILE ON THIS OLD FACE.
NOW, I MUST RETURN TO WORK.
GET YOUR SUBORDINATE TO STOP SEXUALLY HARASSING ME!!
KA-CIUNK...
SO, I GUESS ROB'S BACK.
YES, HE IS.
THIS ONLY ADDS TO MY WORRIES.

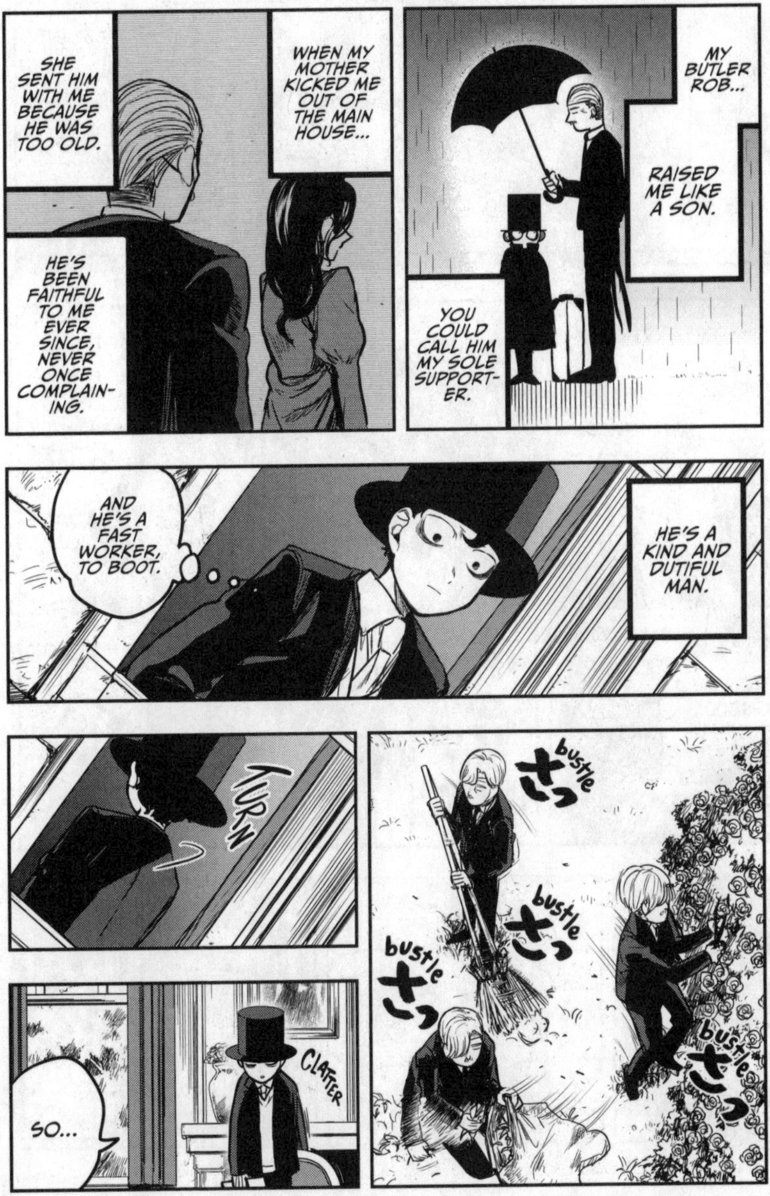
MY BUTLER ROB...
RAISED ME LIKE A SON.
YOU COULD CALL HIM MY SOLE SUPPORTER.
WHEN MY MOTHER KICKED ME OUT OF THE MAIN HOUSE...
SHE SENT HIM WITH ME BECAUSE HE WAS TOO OLD.
HE'S BEEN FAITHFUL TO ME EVER SINCE, NEVER ONCE COMPLAINING.
HE'S A KIND AND DUTIFUL MAN.
AND HE'S A FAST WORKER, TO BOOT.
bustle さっ
bustle さっ
bustle さっ
bustle さっ
TURN
CLATTER
SO...

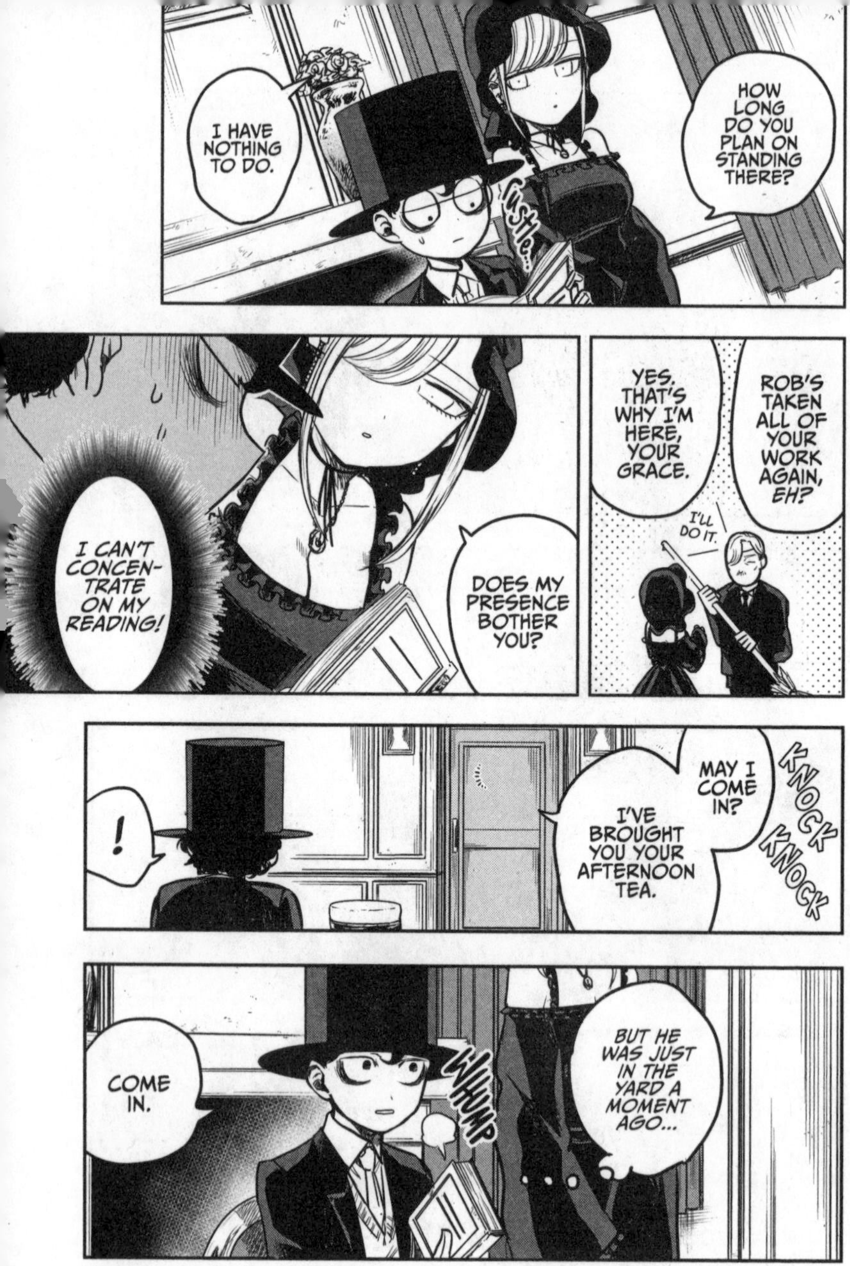
HOW LONG DO YOU PLAN ON STANDING THERE?
rustle...
I HAVE NOTHING TO DO.
ROB'S TAKEN ALL OF YOUR WORK AGAIN, EH?
YES. THAT'S WHY I'M HERE, YOUR GRACE.
I'LL DO IT.
DOES MY PRESENCE BOTHER YOU?
I CAN'T CONCENTRATE ON MY READING!
KNOCK KNOCK
MAY I COME IN?
I'VE BROUGHT YOU YOUR AFTERNOON TEA.
!
BUT HE WAS JUST IN THE YARD A MOMENT AGO...
WHUMP
COME IN.

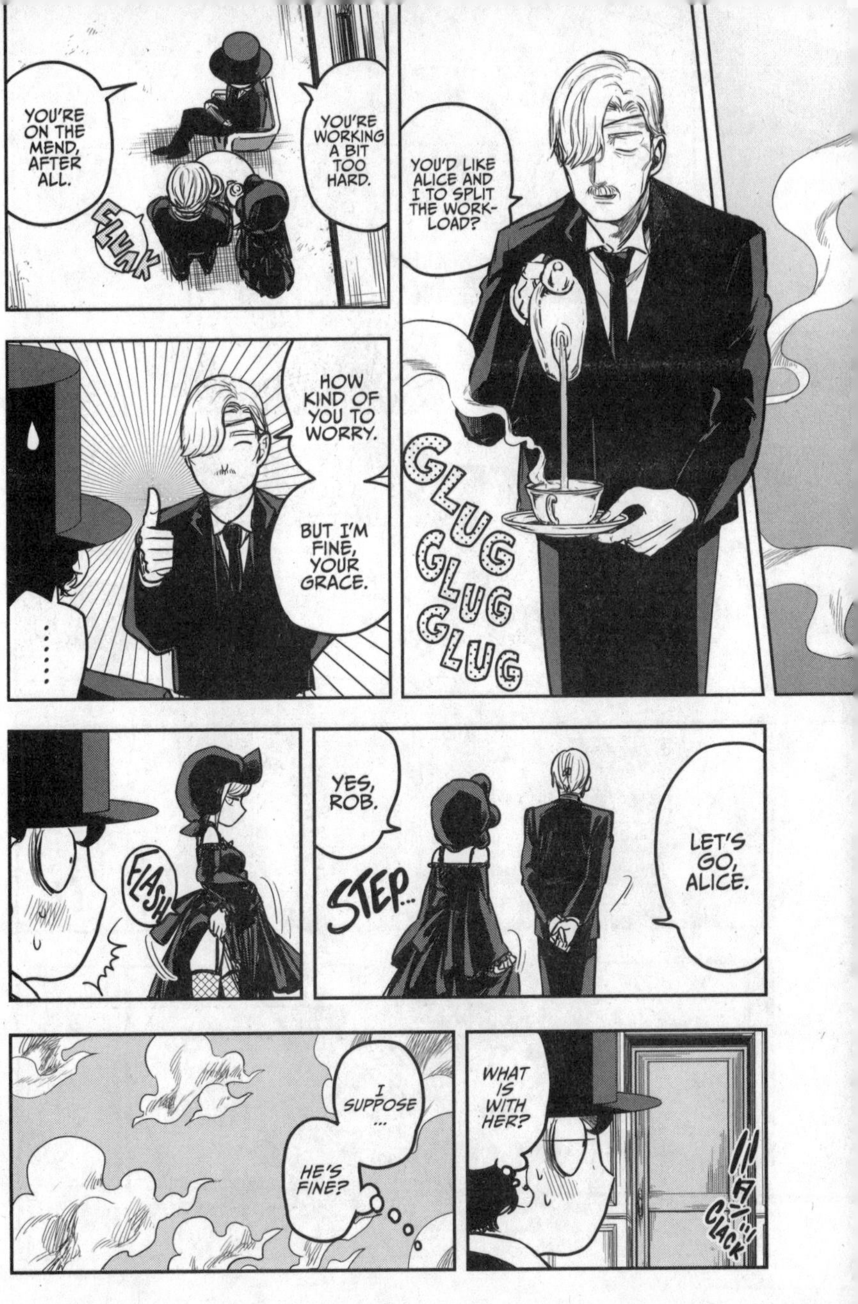
YOU'D LIKE ALICE AND I TO SPLIT THE WORK-LOAD?
GLUG GLUG GLUG GLUG
YOU'RE WORKING A BIT TOO HARD.
YOU'RE ON THE MEND, AFTER ALL.
CLINK
HOW KIND OF YOU TO WORRY.
BUT I'M FINE, YOUR GRACE.
......
LET'S GO, ALICE.
YES, ROB.
STEP...
FLASH
WHAT IS WITH HER?
CLACK
I SUPPOSE... HE'S FINE?

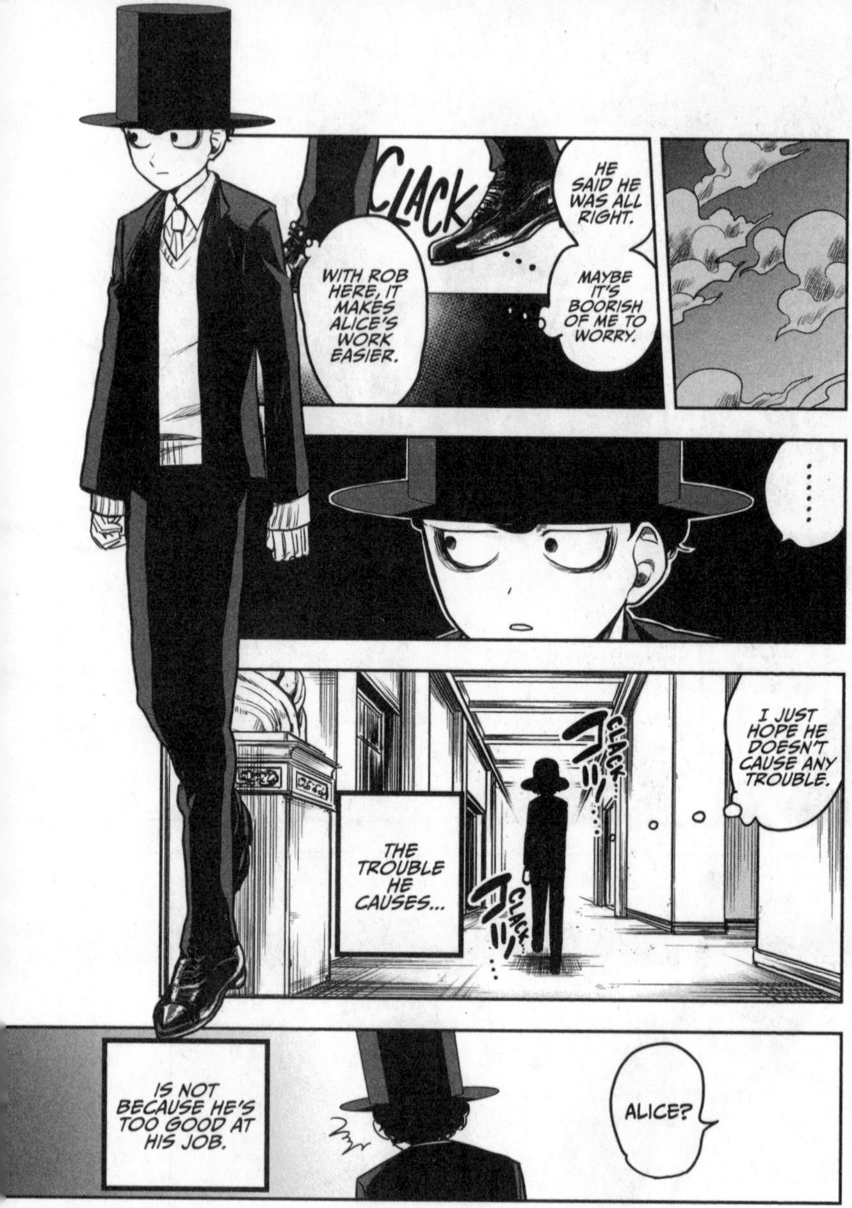
HE SAID HE WAS ALL RIGHT.
MAYBE IT'S BOORISH OF ME TO WORRY.
CLACK
WITH ROB HERE, IT MAKES ALICE'S WORK EASIER.
......
I JUST HOPE HE DOESN'T CAUSE ANY TROUBLE.
CLACK...
CLACK...
THE TROUBLE HE CAUSES...
ALICE?
IS NOT BECAUSE HE'S TOO GOOD AT HIS JOB.

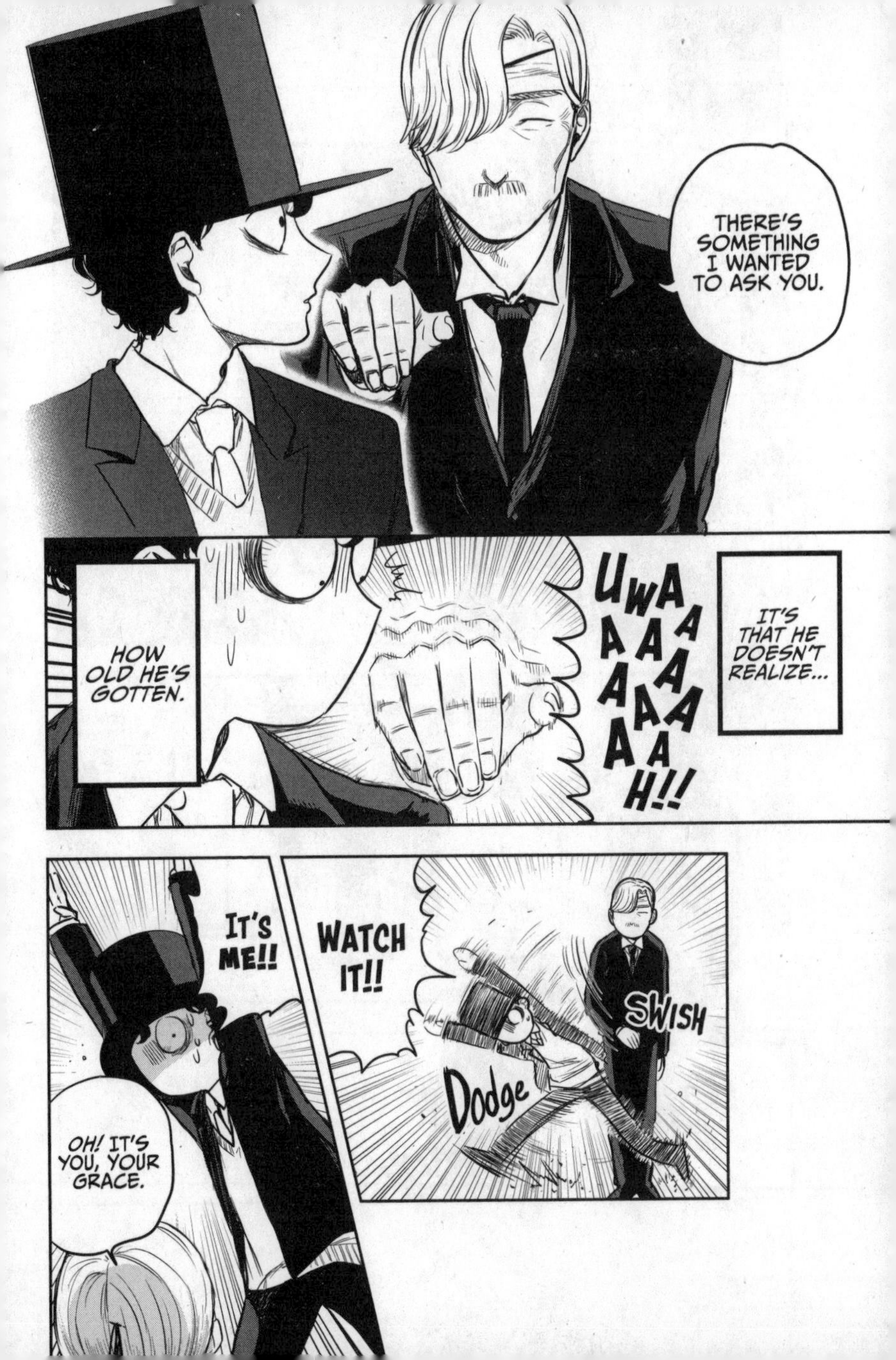
THERE'S SOMETHING I WANTED TO ASK YOU.
IT'S THAT HE DOESN'T REALIZE...
UWAAAAAAAAAAAH!!!
HOW OLD HE'S GOTTEN.
WATCH IT!!
SWISH
Dodge
IT'S ME!!
OH! IT'S YOU, YOUR GRACE.

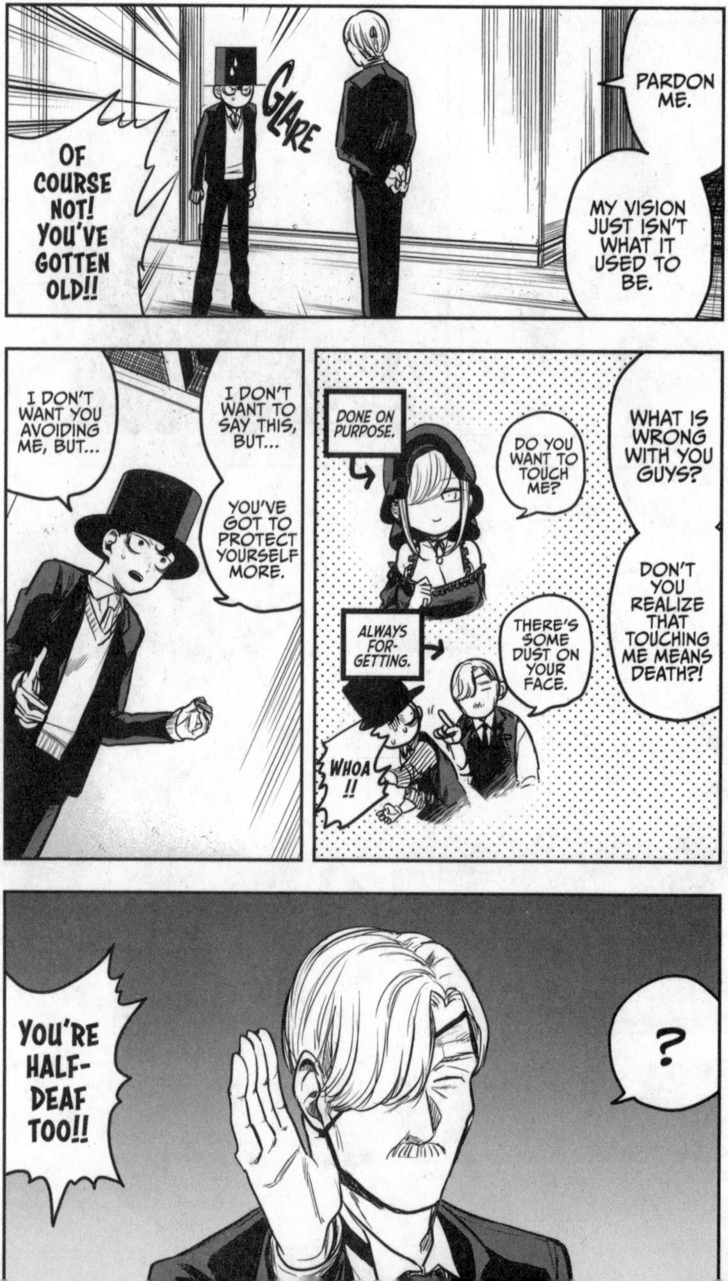
PARDON ME.
MY VISION JUST ISN'T WHAT IT USED TO BE.
GLARE
OF COURSE NOT! YOU'VE GOTTEN OLD!!
WHAT IS WRONG WITH YOU GUYS?
DON'T YOU REALIZE THAT TOUCHING ME MEANS DEATH?!
DO YOU WANT TO TOUCH ME?
DONE ON PURPOSE.
THERE'S SOME DUST ON YOUR FACE.
ALWAYS FOR-GETTING.
WHOA!!
I DON'T WANT TO SAY THIS, BUT...
YOU'VE GOT TO PROTECT YOURSELF MORE.
I DON'T WANT YOU AVOIDING ME, BUT...
?
YOU'RE HALF-DEAF TOO!!

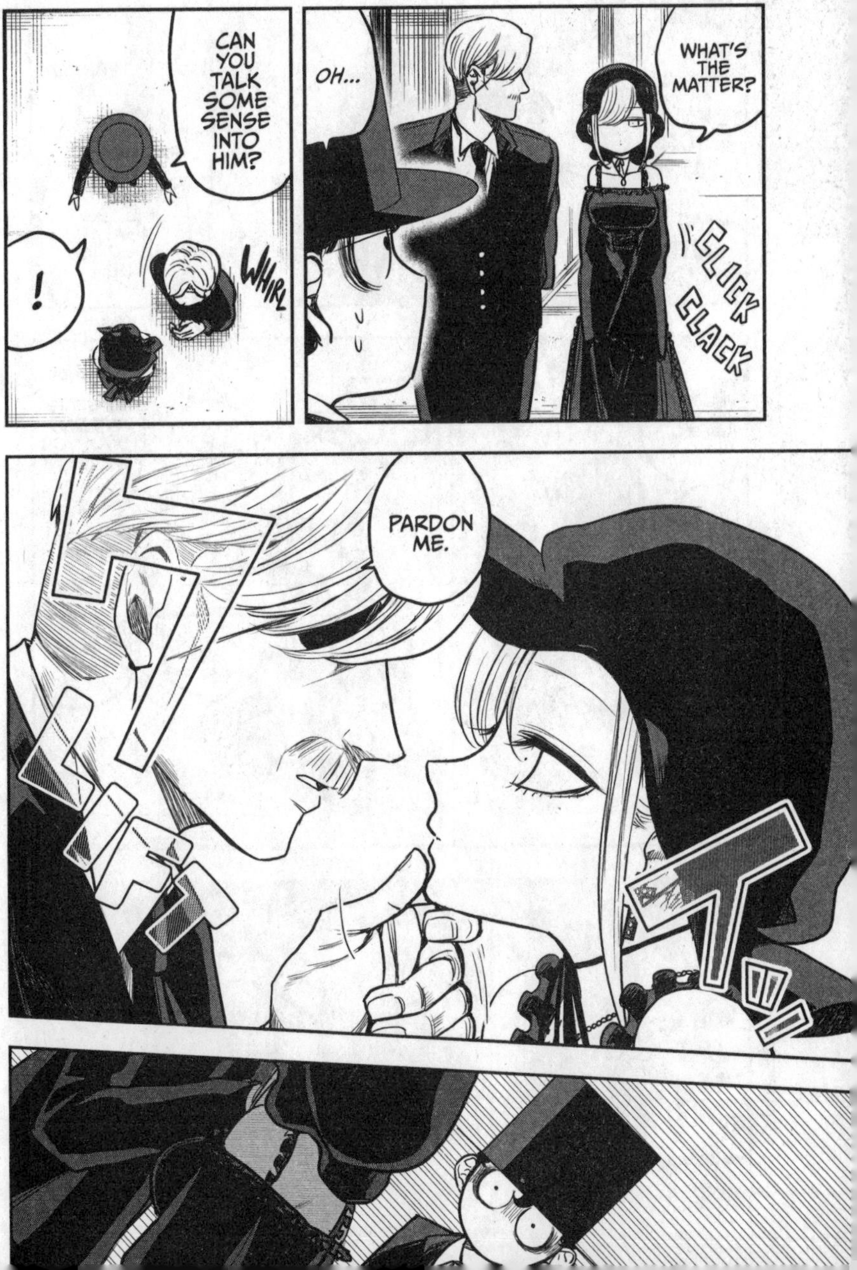
WHAT'S THE MATTER?
CLICK CLACK
OH...
CAN YOU TALK SOME SENSE INTO HIM?
WHIRL
!
PARDON ME.

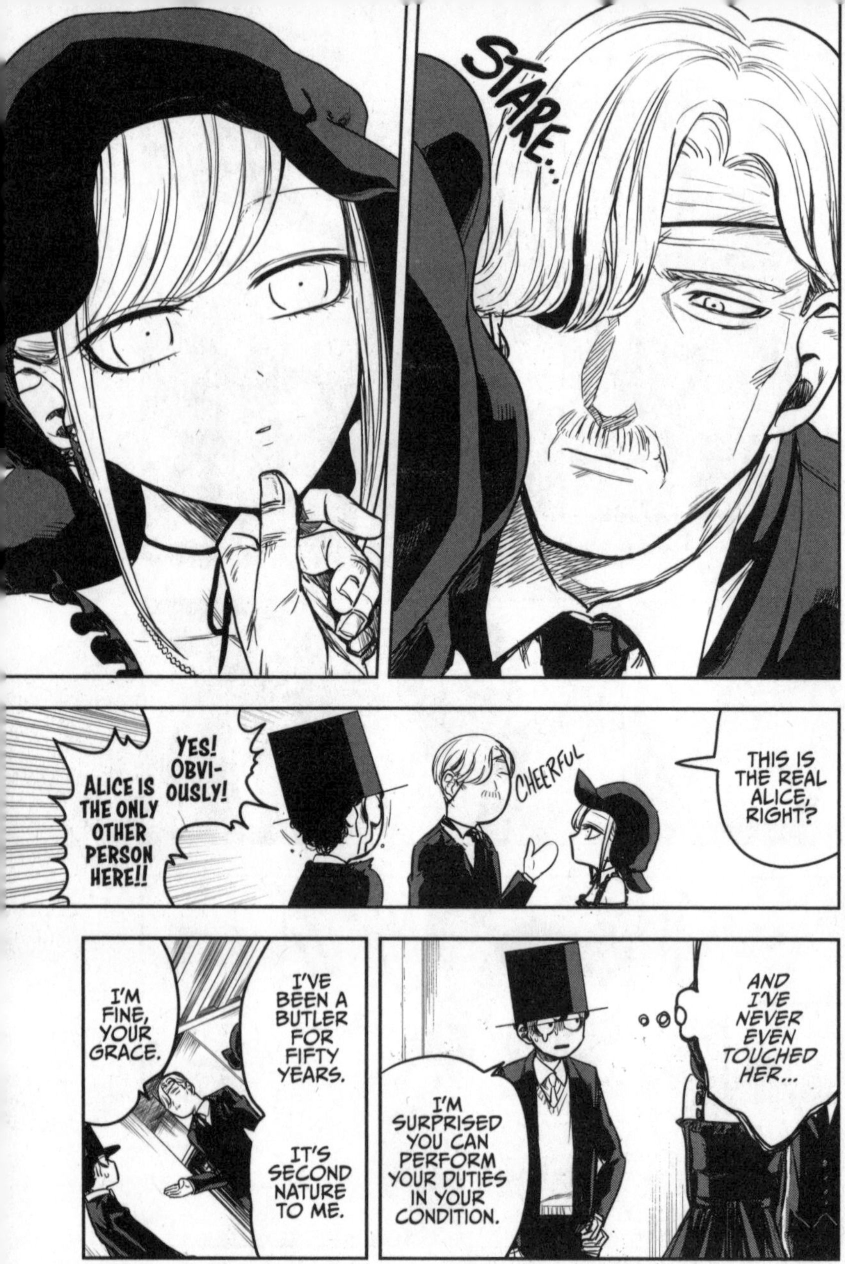
STARE...
THIS IS THE REAL ALICE, RIGHT?
CHEERFUL
YES! OBVIOUSLY!
ALICE IS THE ONLY OTHER PERSON HERE!!
AND I'VE NEVER EVEN TOUCHED HER...
...
I'M SURPRISED YOU CAN PERFORM YOUR DUTIES IN YOUR CONDITION.
I'M FINE, YOUR GRACE.
I'VE BEEN A BUTLER FOR FIFTY YEARS.
IT'S SECOND NATURE TO ME.

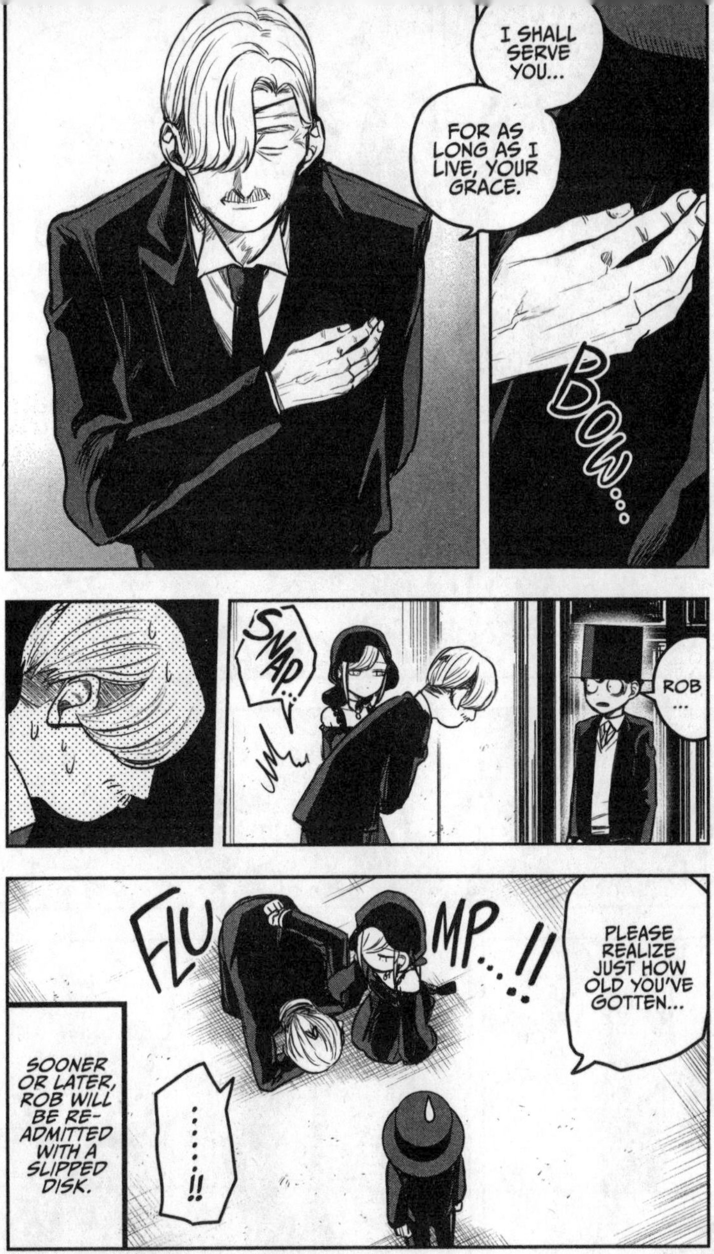
I SHALL SERVE YOU...
FOR AS LONG AS I LIVE, YOUR GRACE.
BOW...
ROB...
SNAP...
PLEASE REALIZE JUST HOW OLD YOU'VE GOTTEN...
FLUMP...!!
......!!
SOONER OR LATER, ROB WILL BE RE-ADMITTED WITH A SLIPPED DISK.

Chapter 9: Alice's Room

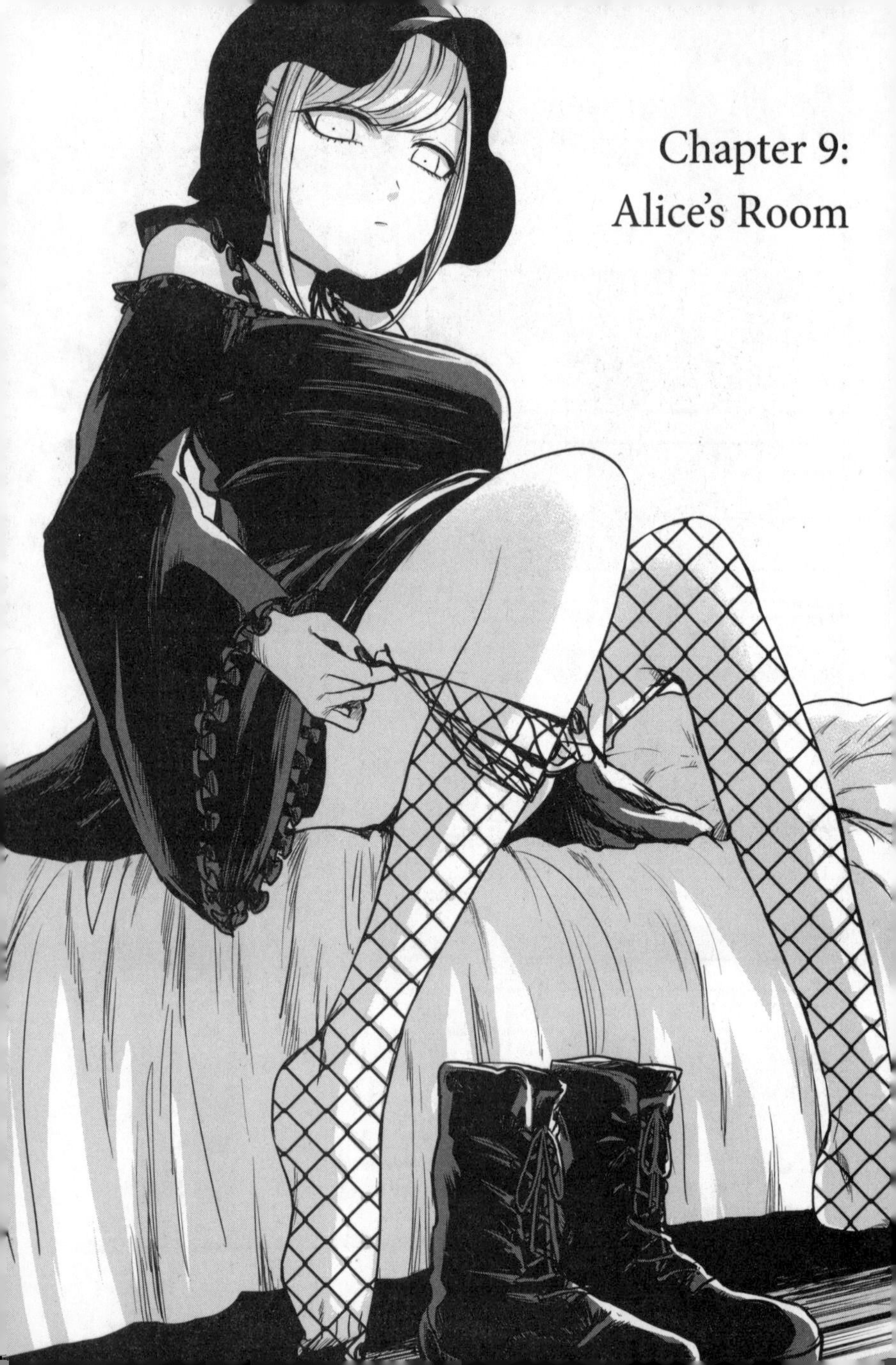

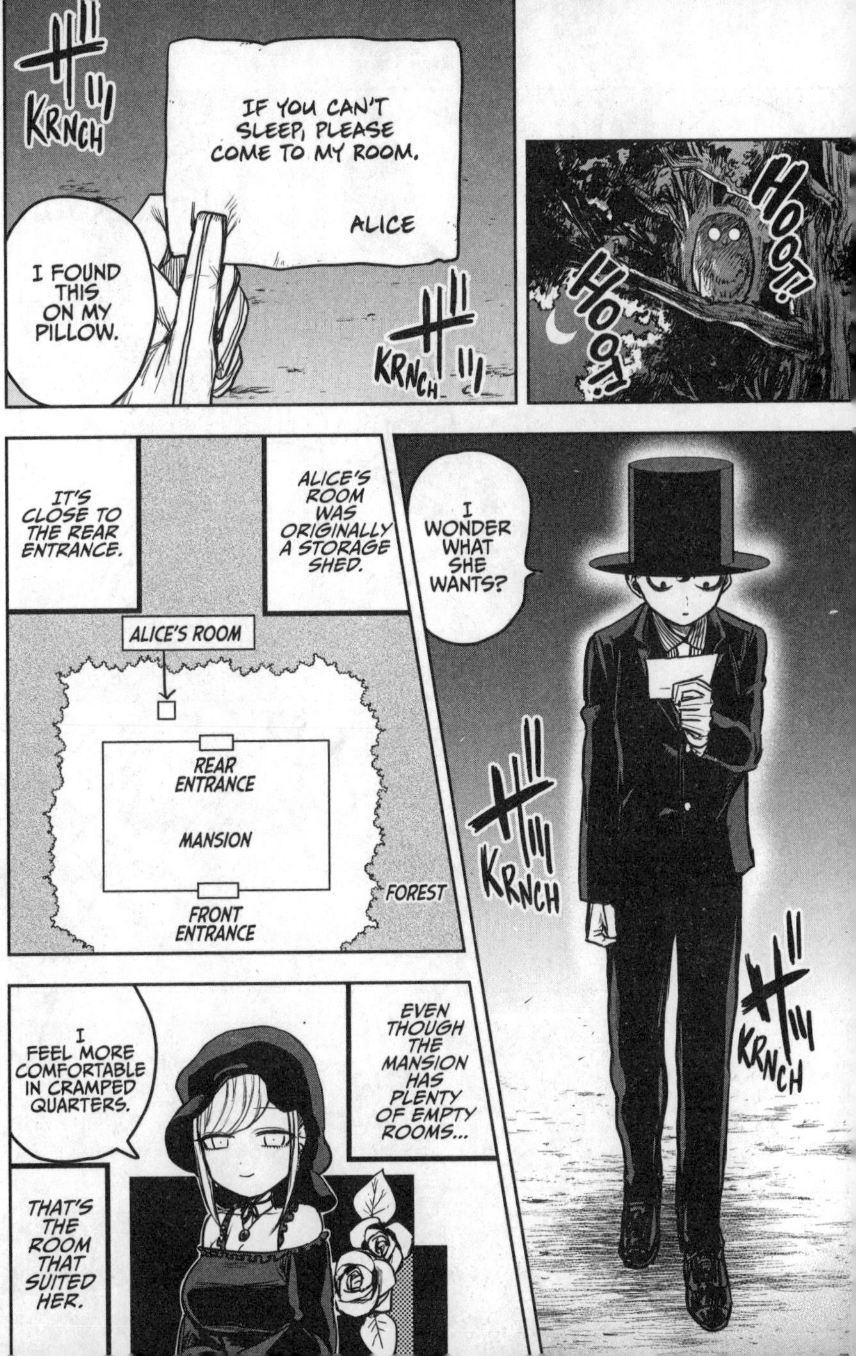
HOOT!!
HOOT!!
IF YOU CAN'T SLEEP, PLEASE COME TO MY ROOM.
ALICE
KRNCH
I FOUND THIS ON MY PILLOW.
KRNCH
I WONDER WHAT SHE WANTS?
KRNCH
KRNCH
ALICE'S ROOM WAS ORIGINALLY A STORAGE SHED.
IT'S CLOSE TO THE REAR ENTRANCE.
ALICE'S ROOM
REAR ENTRANCE
MANSION
FOREST
FRONT ENTRANCE
EVEN THOUGH THE MANSION HAS PLENTY OF EMPTY ROOMS...
I FEEL MORE COMFORTABLE IN CRAMPED QUARTERS.
THAT'S THE ROOM THAT SUITED HER.

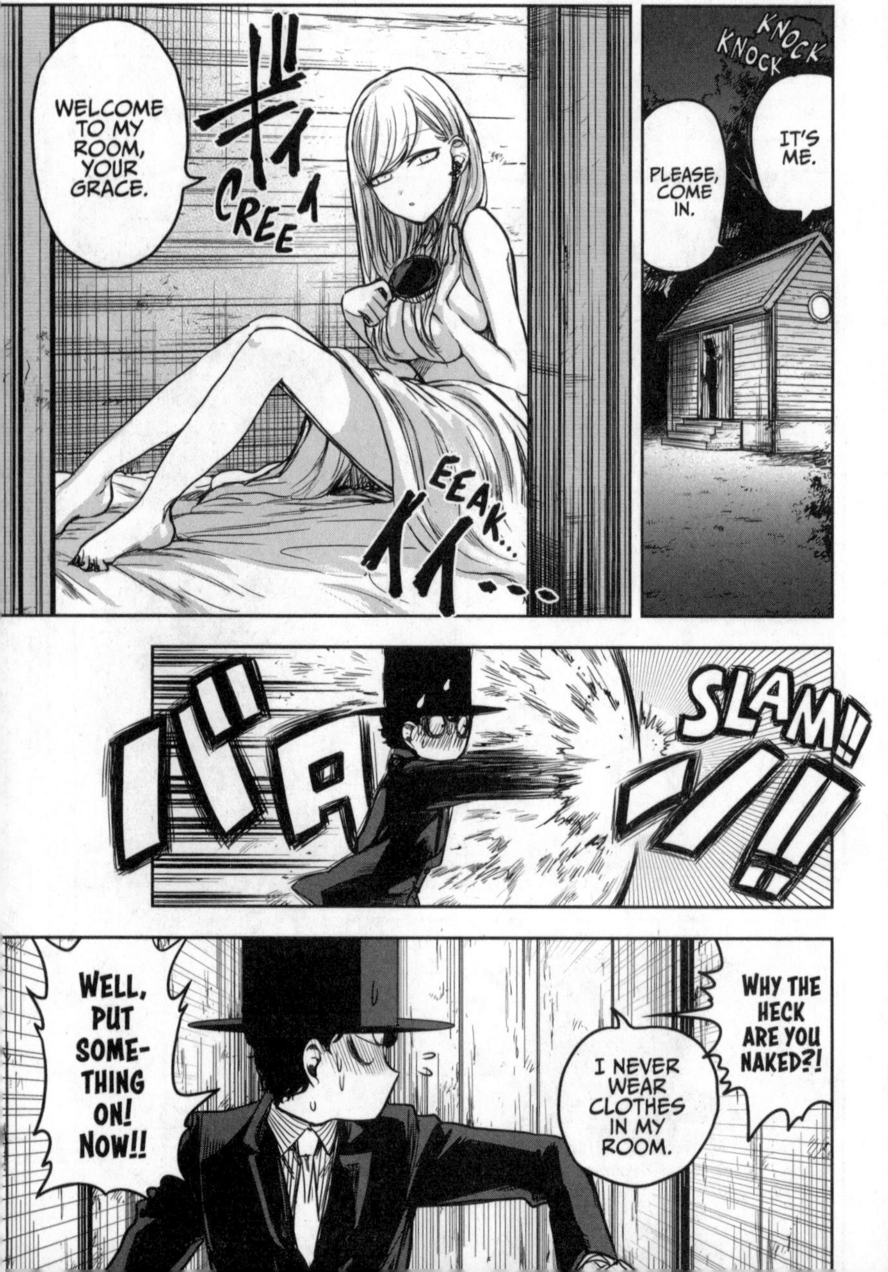
KNOCK KNOCK
IT'S ME.
PLEASE, COME IN.
CREEE
WELCOME TO MY ROOM, YOUR GRACE.
EEAK...
SLAM!!
WHY THE HECK ARE YOU NAKED?!
I NEVER WEAR CLOTHES IN MY ROOM.
WELL, PUT SOME-THING ON! NOW!!

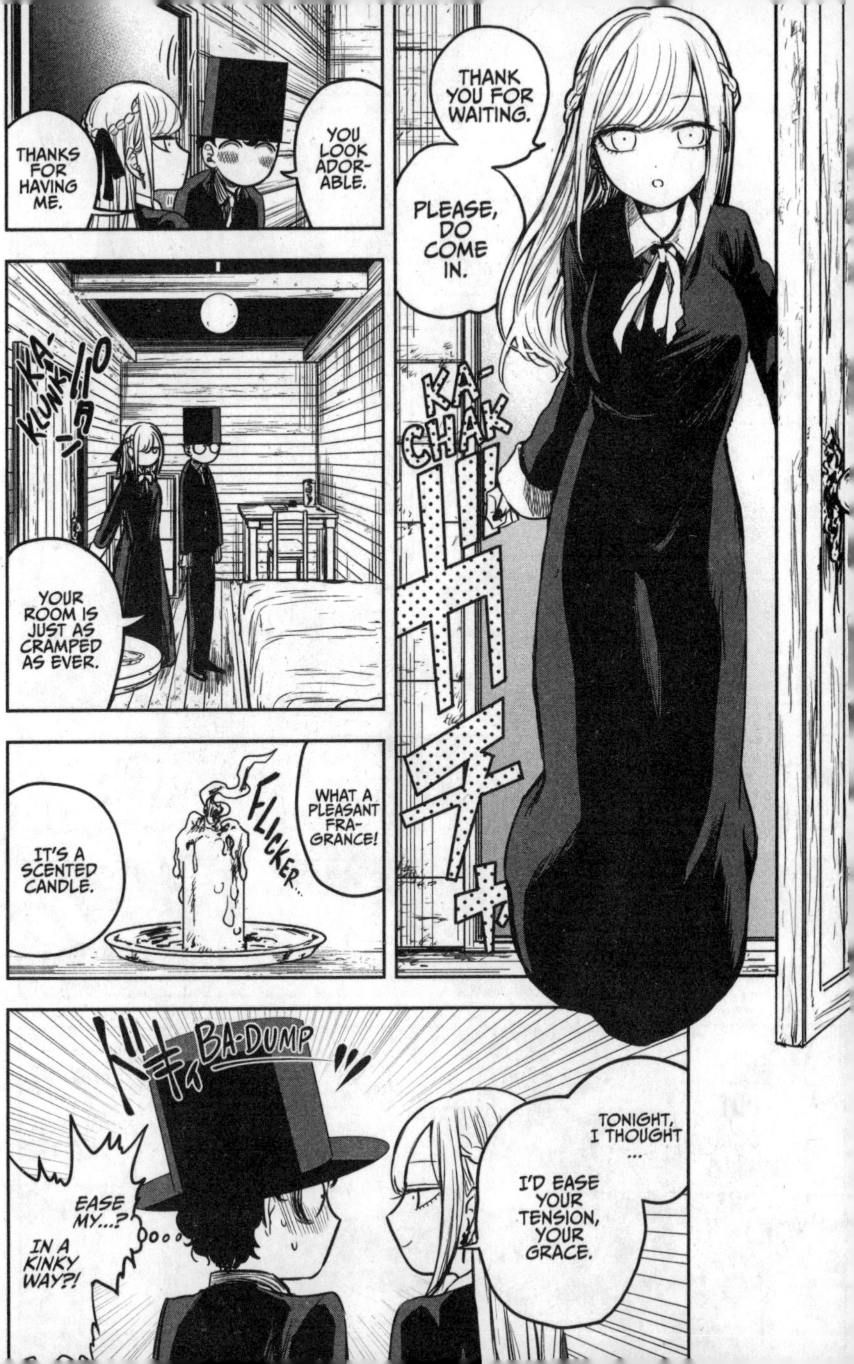
THANK YOU FOR WAITING.
PLEASE, DO COME IN.
KA-CHAK
YOU LOOK ADORABLE.
THANKS FOR HAVING ME.
KA-KLUNK
YOUR ROOM IS JUST AS CRAMPED AS EVER.
WHAT A PLEASANT FRAGRANCE!
FLICKER...
IT'S A SCENTED CANDLE.
BA-DUMP
TONIGHT, I THOUGHT ...
I'D EASE YOUR TENSION, YOUR GRACE.
EASE MY...? IN A KINKY WAY?!

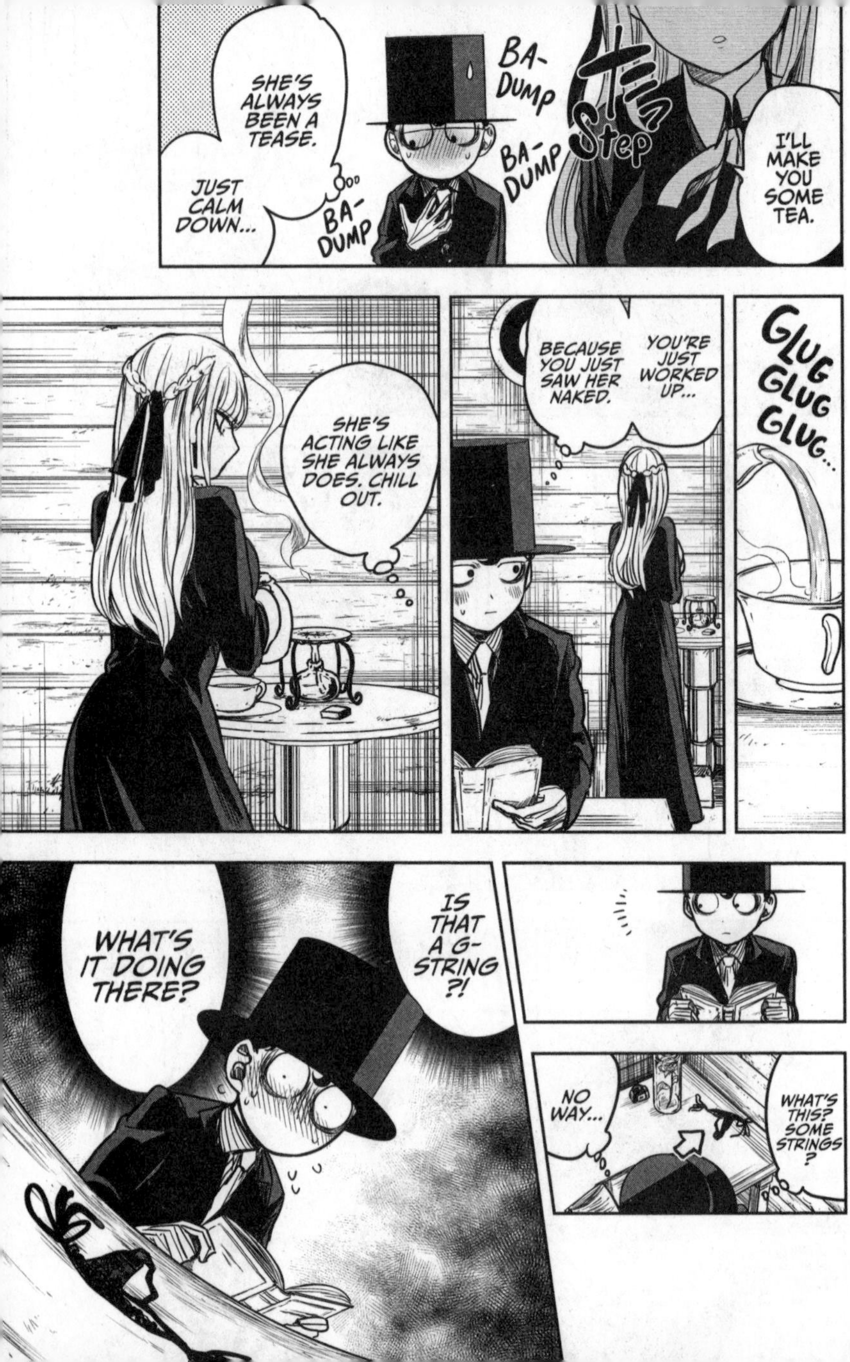

I'LL MAKE YOU SOME TEA.
Step
BA-DUMP
BA-DUMP
SHE'S ALWAYS BEEN A TEASE.
JUST CALM DOWN...
BA-DUMP
GLUG GLUG GLUG...
YOU'RE JUST WORKED UP...
BECAUSE YOU JUST SAW HER NAKED.
SHE'S ACTING LIKE SHE ALWAYS DOES. CHILL OUT.
WHAT'S THIS? SOME STRINGS?
NO WAY...
IS THAT A G-STRING?!
WHAT'S IT DOING THERE?

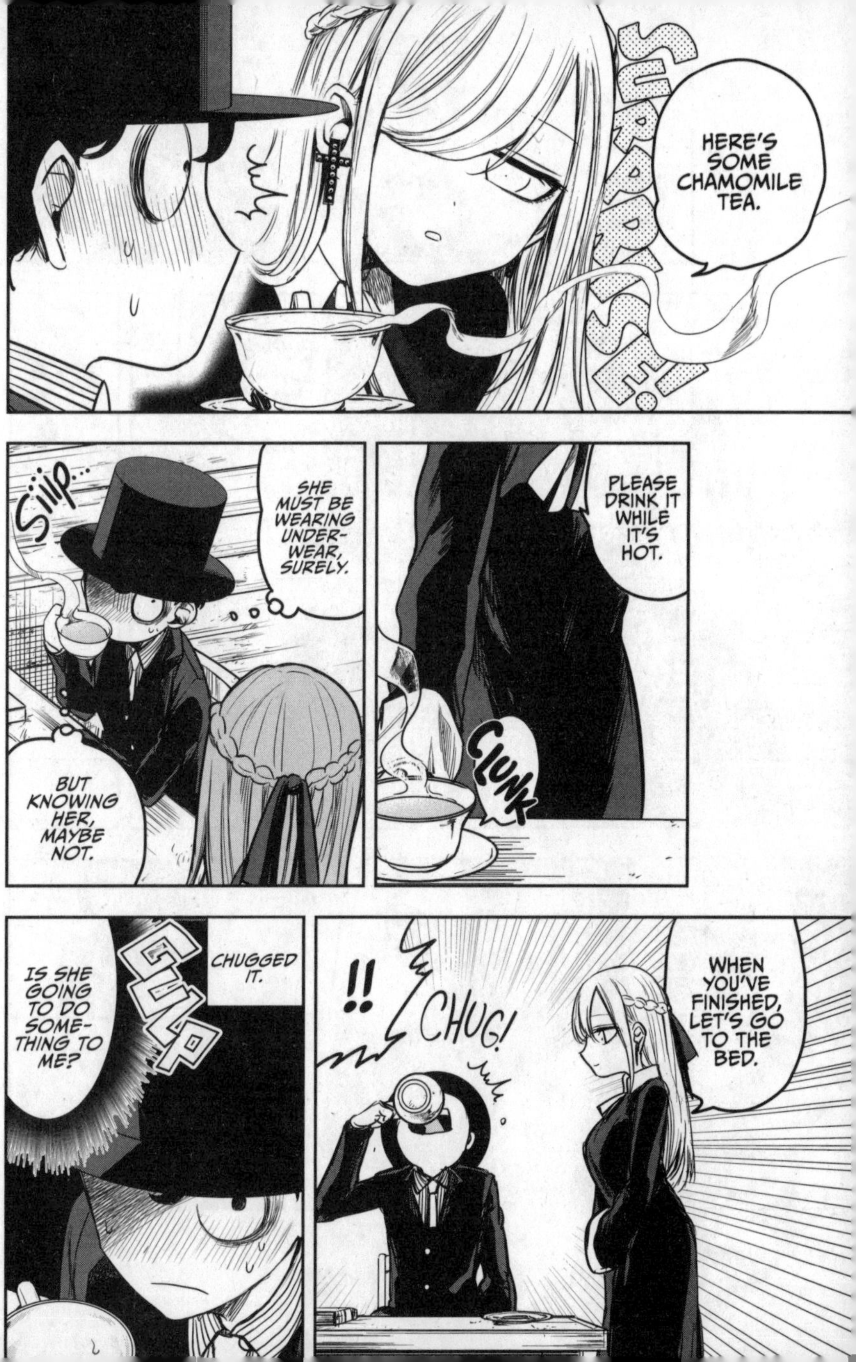
SURPRISE!
HERE'S SOME CHAMOMILE TEA.
PLEASE DRINK IT WHILE IT'S HOT.
CLUNK
SHE MUST BE WEARING UNDER-WEAR, SURELY.
Siiip...
BUT KNOWING HER, MAYBE NOT.
WHEN YOU'VE FINISHED, LET'S GO TO THE BED.
CHUG!
!!
CHUGGED IT.
GULP
IS SHE GOING TO DO SOME-THING TO ME?

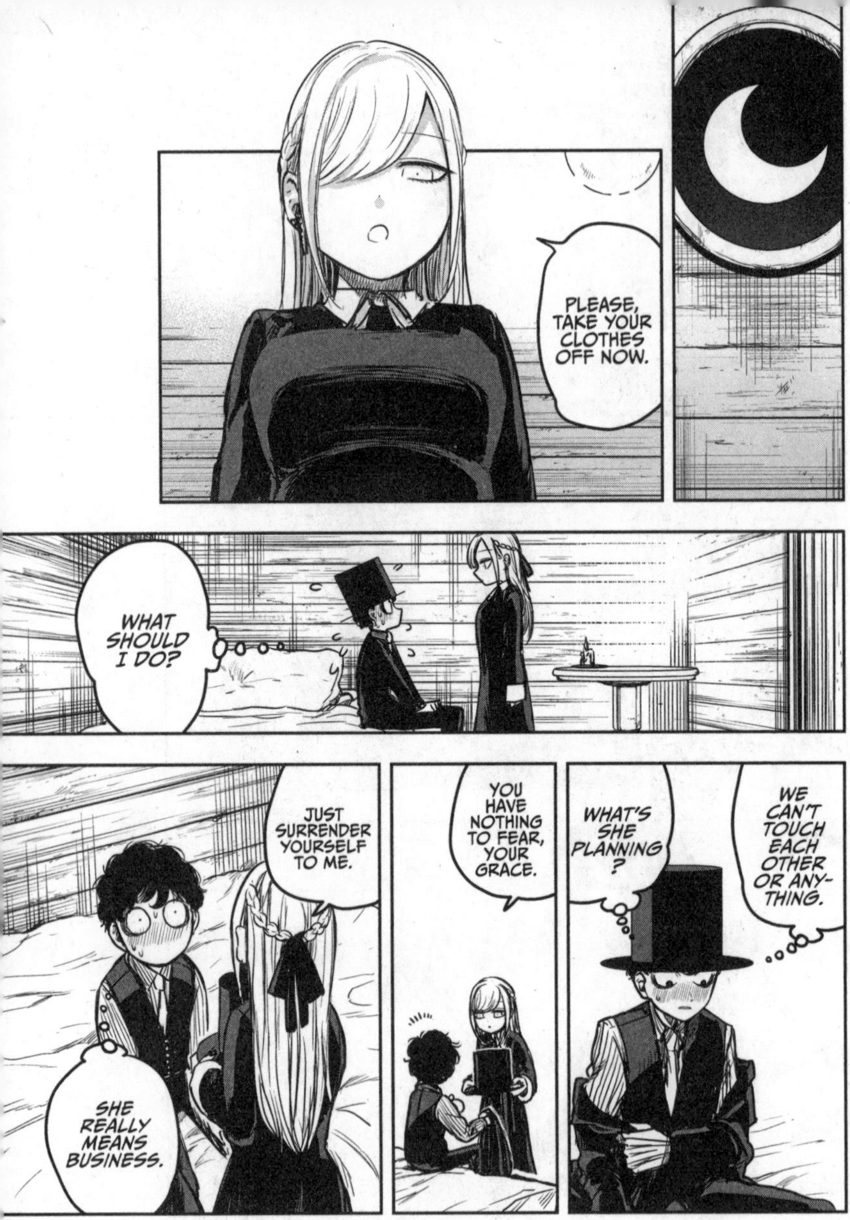
PLEASE, TAKE YOUR CLOTHES OFF NOW.
WHAT SHOULD I DO?
WE CAN'T TOUCH EACH OTHER OR ANYTHING.
WHAT'S SHE PLANNING?
YOU HAVE NOTHING TO FEAR, YOUR GRACE.
JUST SURRENDER YOURSELF TO ME.
SHE REALLY MEANS BUSINESS.

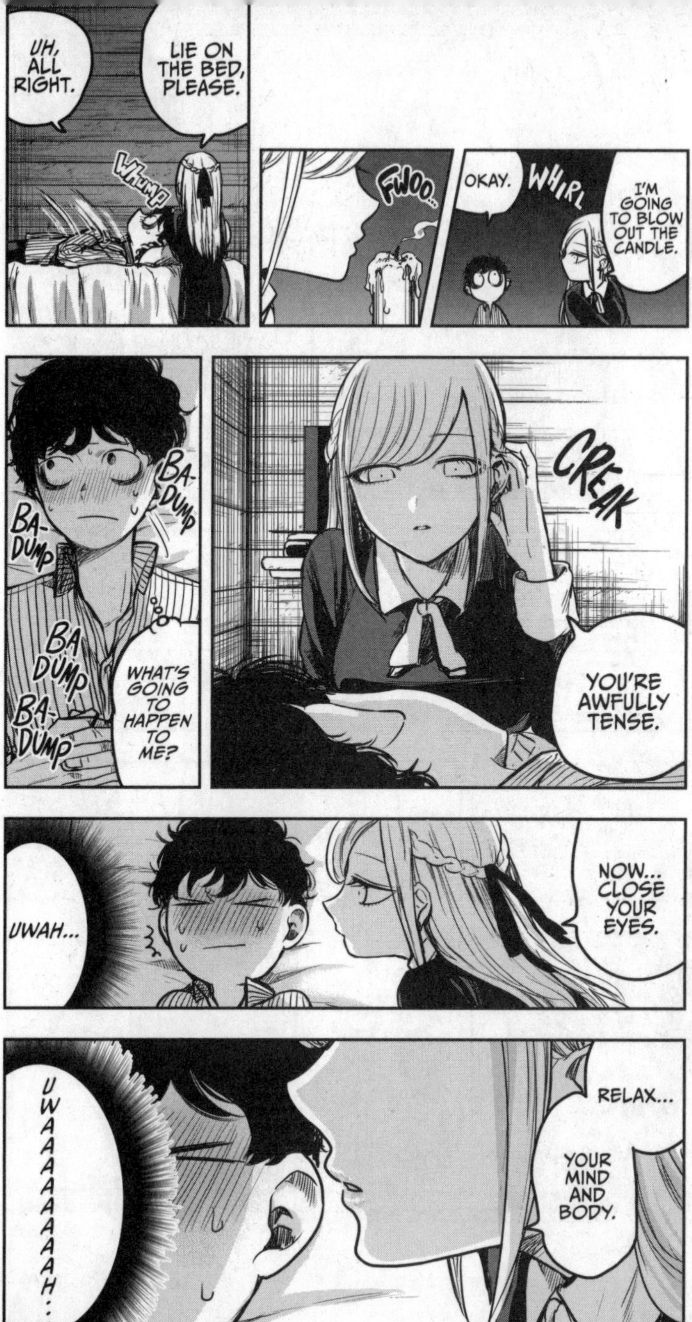
I'M GOING TO BLOW OUT THE CANDLE.
WHIRL
OKAY.
FWOO...
LIE ON THE BED, PLEASE.
WHUMP
UH, ALL RIGHT.
CREAK
YOU'RE AWFULLY TENSE.
BA-DUMP
BA-DUMP
BA DUMP
BA-DUMP
WHAT'S GOING TO HAPPEN TO ME?
NOW... CLOSE YOUR EYES.
UWAH...
RELAX...
YOUR MIND AND BODY.
UWAAAAAAAAAAAH...

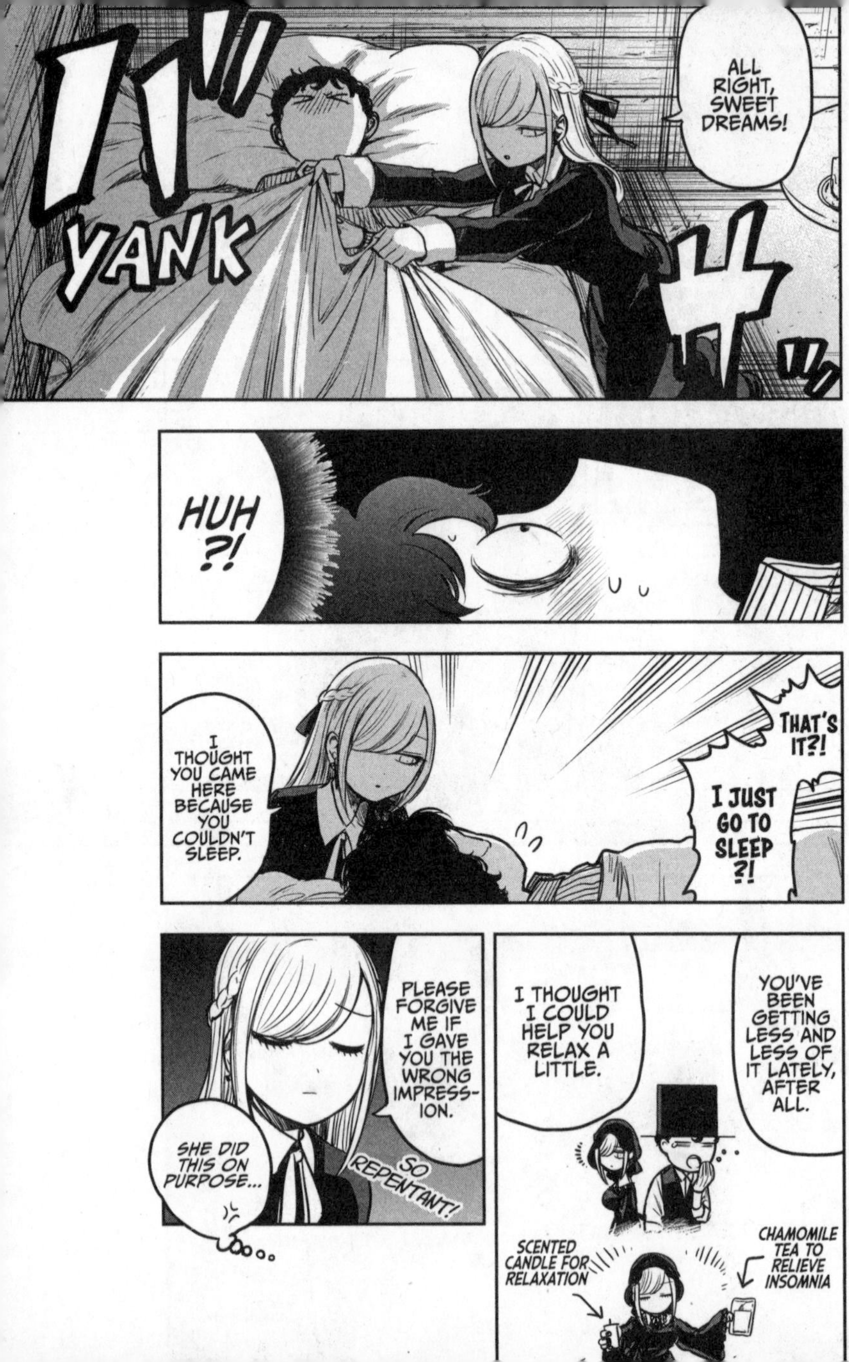
ALL RIGHT, SWEET DREAMS!
YANK
HUH ?!
THAT'S IT?!
I JUST GO TO SLEEP ?!
I THOUGHT YOU CAME HERE BECAUSE YOU COULDN'T SLEEP.
YOU'VE BEEN GETTING LESS AND LESS OF IT LATELY, AFTER ALL.
I THOUGHT I COULD HELP YOU RELAX A LITTLE.
CHAMOMILE TEA TO RELIEVE INSOMNIA
SCENTED CANDLE FOR RELAXATION
PLEASE FORGIVE ME IF I GAVE YOU THE WRONG IMPRESSION.
SO REPENTANT!
SHE DID THIS ON PURPOSE...

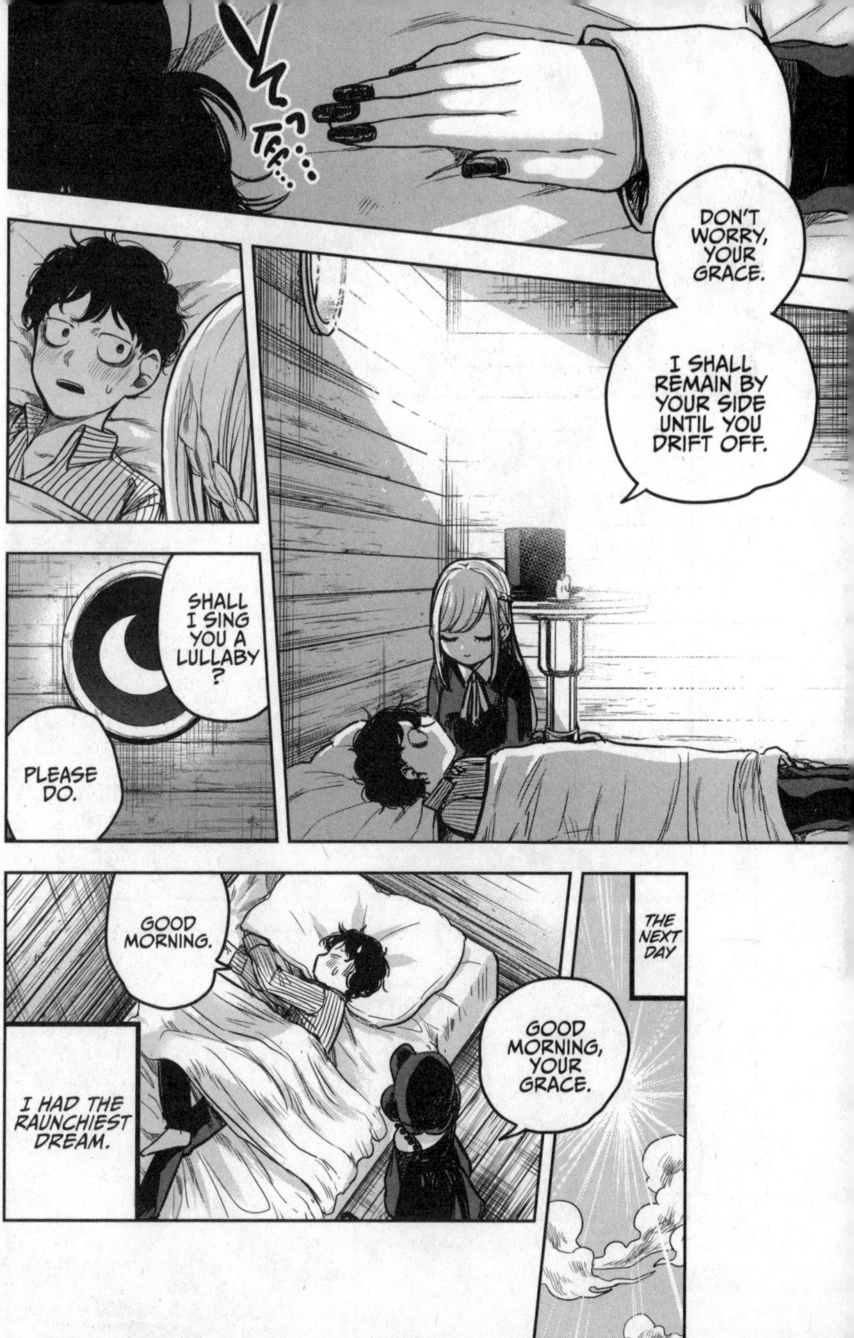
TFF...
DON'T WORRY, YOUR GRACE.
I SHALL REMAIN BY YOUR SIDE UNTIL YOU DRIFT OFF.
SHALL I SING YOU A LULLABY?
PLEASE DO.
THE NEXT DAY
GOOD MORNING, YOUR GRACE.
GOOD MORNING.
I HAD THE RAUNCHIEST DREAM.

Chapter 10: The Picnic

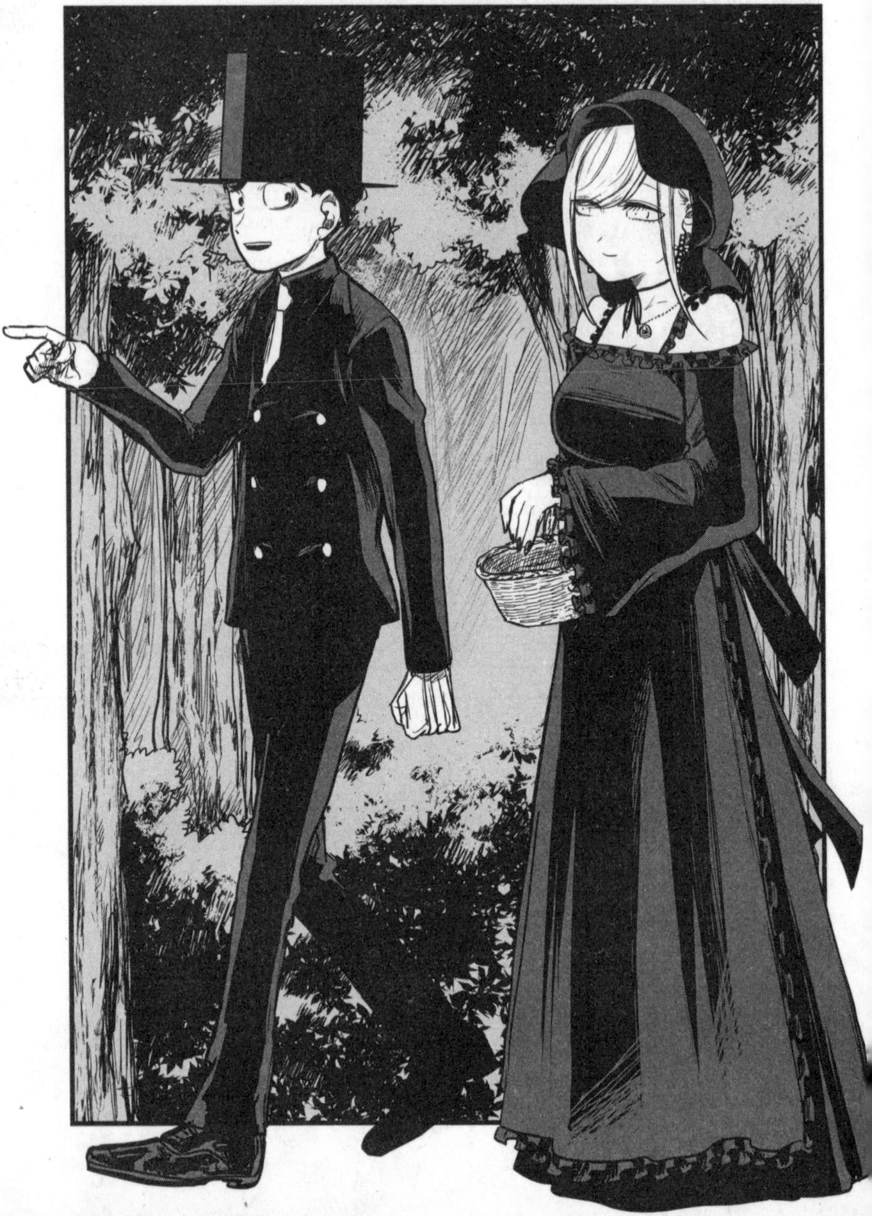

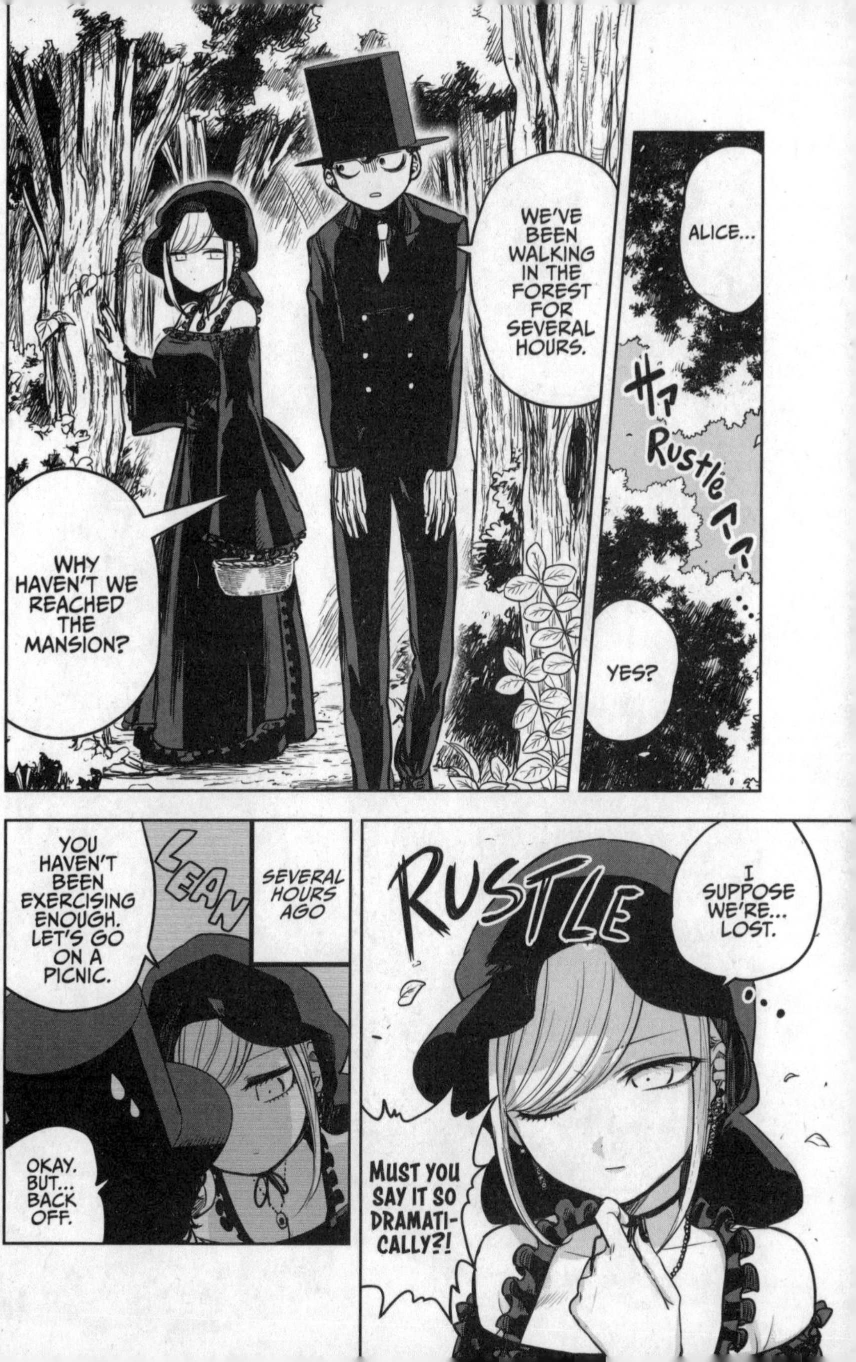
ALICE...
Rustle
YES?
WE'VE BEEN WALKING IN THE FOREST FOR SEVERAL HOURS.
WHY HAVEN'T WE REACHED THE MANSION?
RUSTLE
I SUPPOSE WE'RE... LOST.
MUST YOU SAY IT SO DRAMATI-CALLY?!
SEVERAL HOURS AGO
LEAN
YOU HAVEN'T BEEN EXERCISING ENOUGH. LET'S GO ON A PICNIC.
OKAY. BUT... BACK OFF.

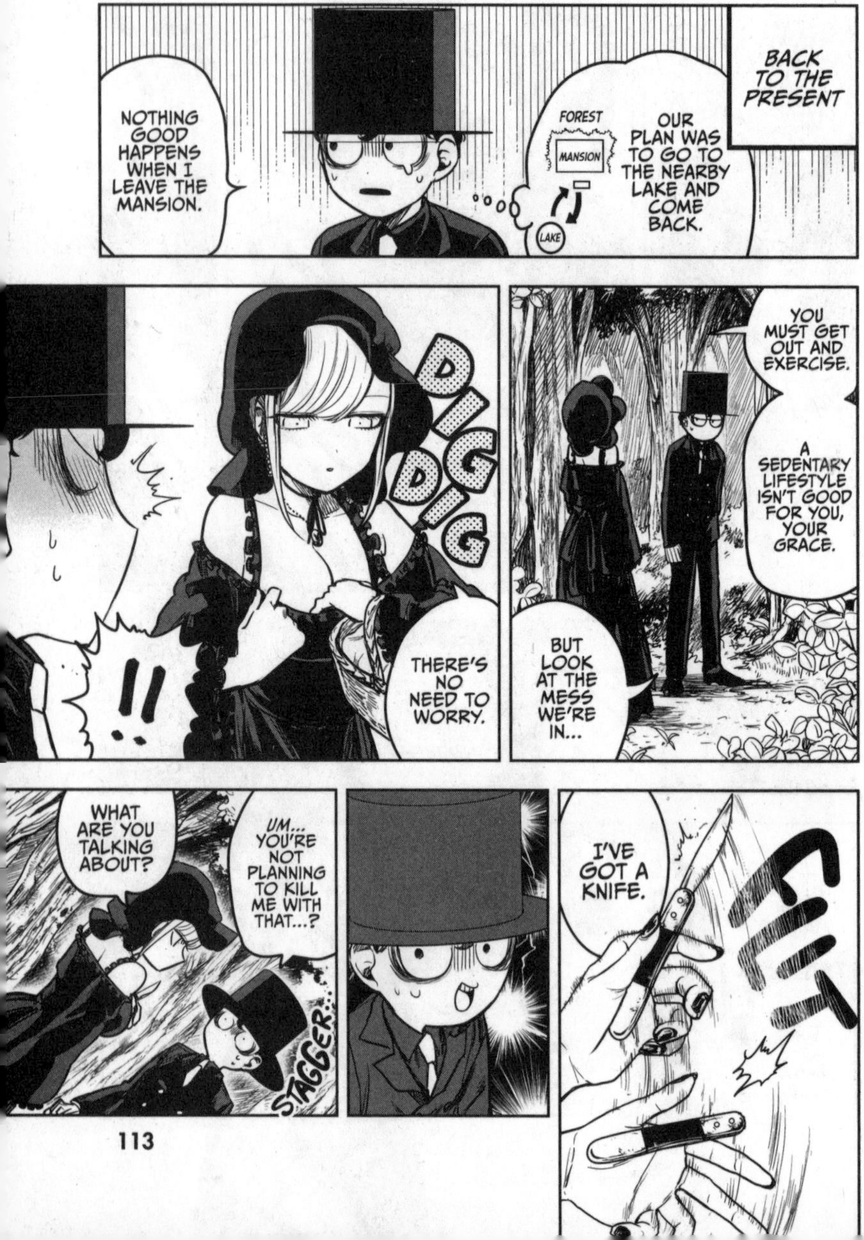
BACK TO THE PRESENT
OUR PLAN WAS TO GO TO THE NEARBY LAKE AND COME BACK.
FOREST
MANSION
LAKE
NOTHING GOOD HAPPENS WHEN I LEAVE THE MANSION.
YOU MUST GET OUT AND EXERCISE.
A SEDENTARY LIFESTYLE ISN'T GOOD FOR YOU, YOUR GRACE.
BUT LOOK AT THE MESS WE'RE IN...
THERE'S NO NEED TO WORRY.
DIG DIG
!!
I'VE GOT A KNIFE.
CUT
UM... YOU'RE NOT PLANNING TO KILL ME WITH THAT...?
WHAT ARE YOU TALKING ABOUT?
STAGGER...

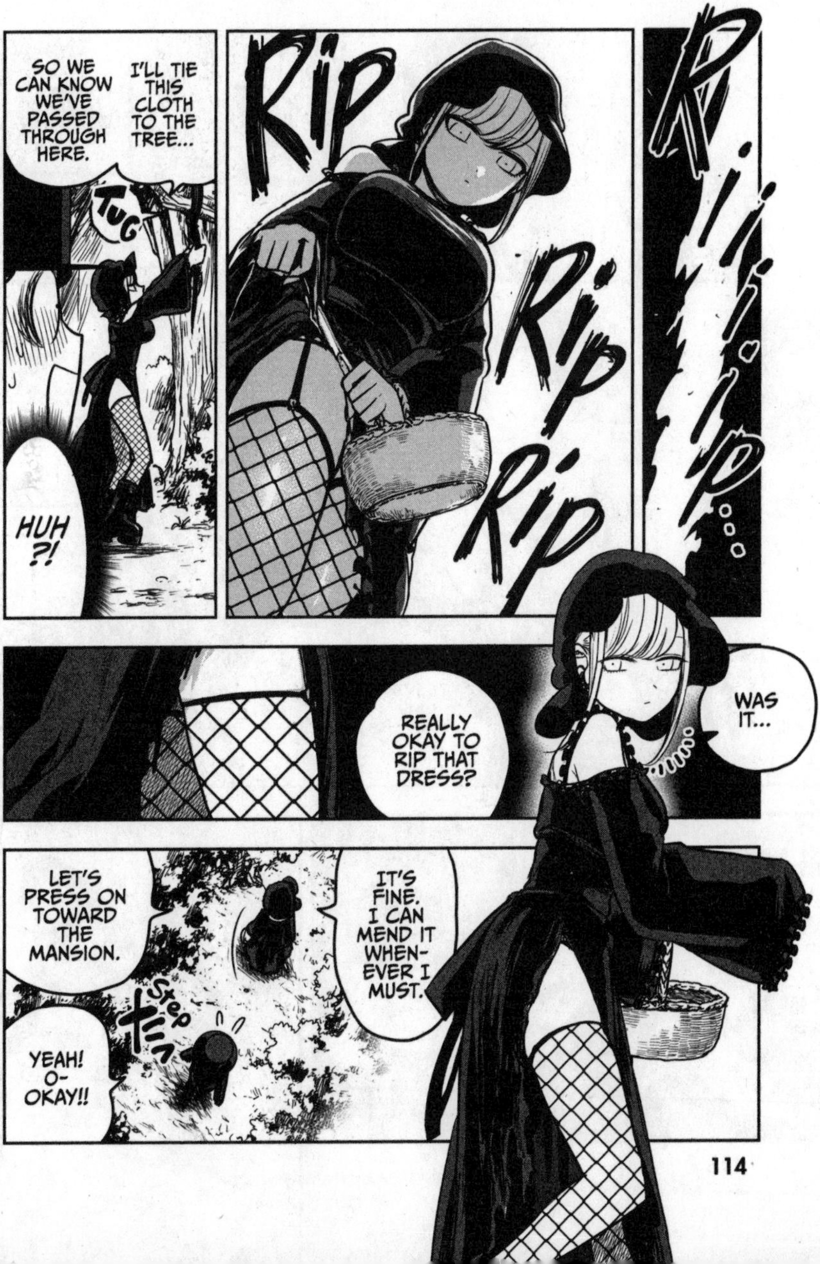
Riiiiip...
Rip
Rip
Rip
Rip
I'LL TIE THIS CLOTH TO THE TREE...
SO WE CAN KNOW WE'VE PASSED THROUGH HERE.
TUG
HUH?!
WAS IT...
REALLY OKAY TO RIP THAT DRESS?
IT'S FINE. I CAN MEND IT WHEN-EVER I MUST.
LET'S PRESS ON TOWARD THE MANSION.
Step
YEAH! O-OKAY!!

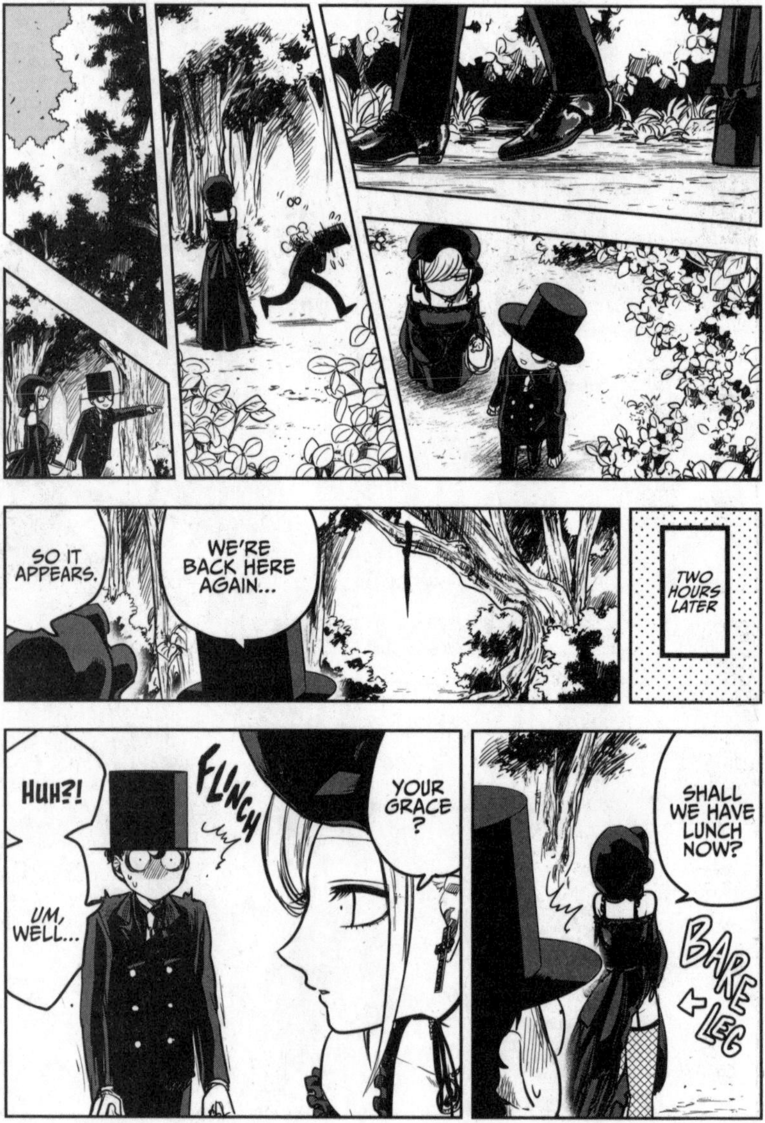
TWO HOURS LATER
WE'RE BACK HERE AGAIN...
SO IT APPEARS.
SHALL WE HAVE LUNCH NOW?
BARE LEG
YOUR GRACE?
FLINCH
HUH?!
UM, WELL...

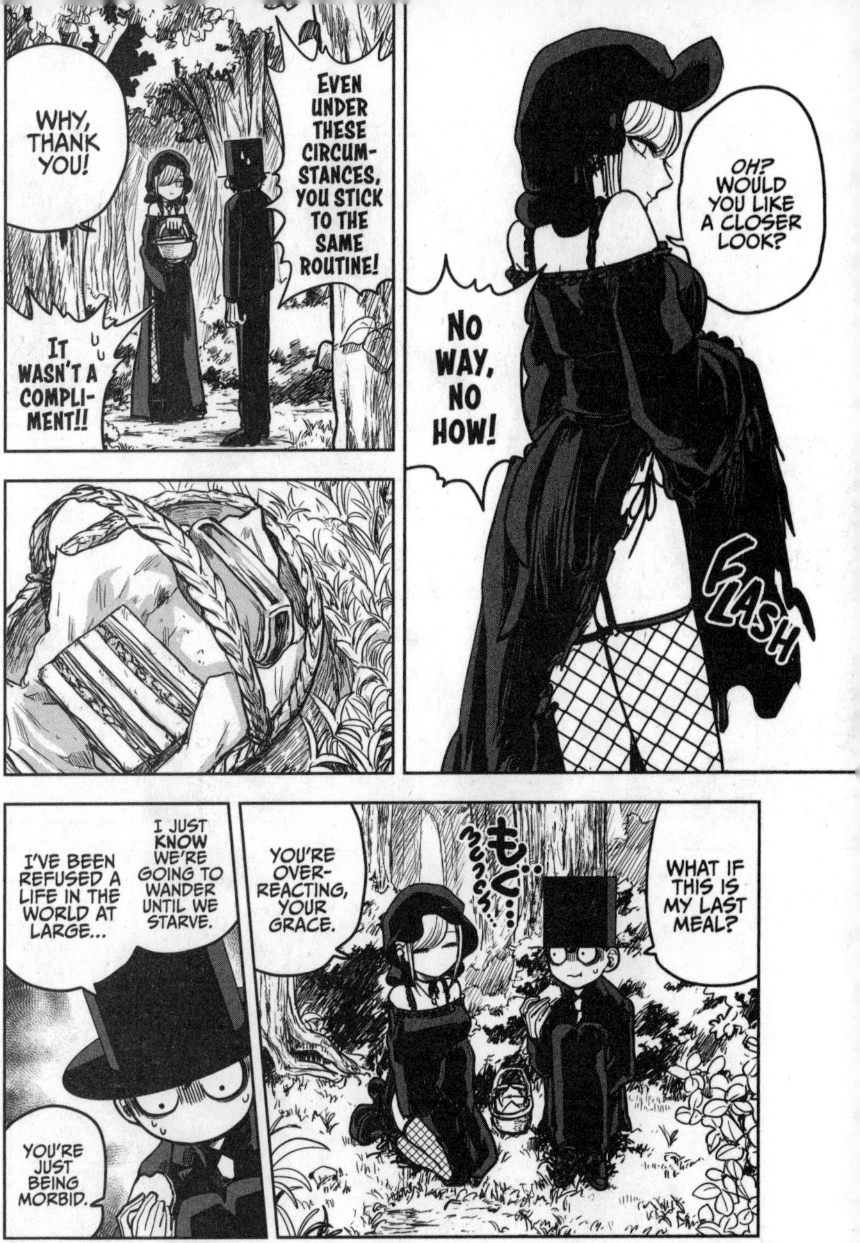
OH? WOULD YOU LIKE A CLOSER LOOK?
NO WAY, NO HOW!
FLASH
EVEN UNDER THESE CIRCUM-STANCES, YOU STICK TO THE SAME ROUTINE!
WHY, THANK YOU!
IT WASN'T A COMPLI-MENT!!
WHAT IF THIS IS MY LAST MEAL?
もぐ… munch…
YOU'RE OVER-REACTING, YOUR GRACE.
I JUST KNOW WE'RE GOING TO WANDER UNTIL WE STARVE.
I'VE BEEN REFUSED A LIFE IN THE WORLD AT LARGE...
YOU'RE JUST BEING MORBID.

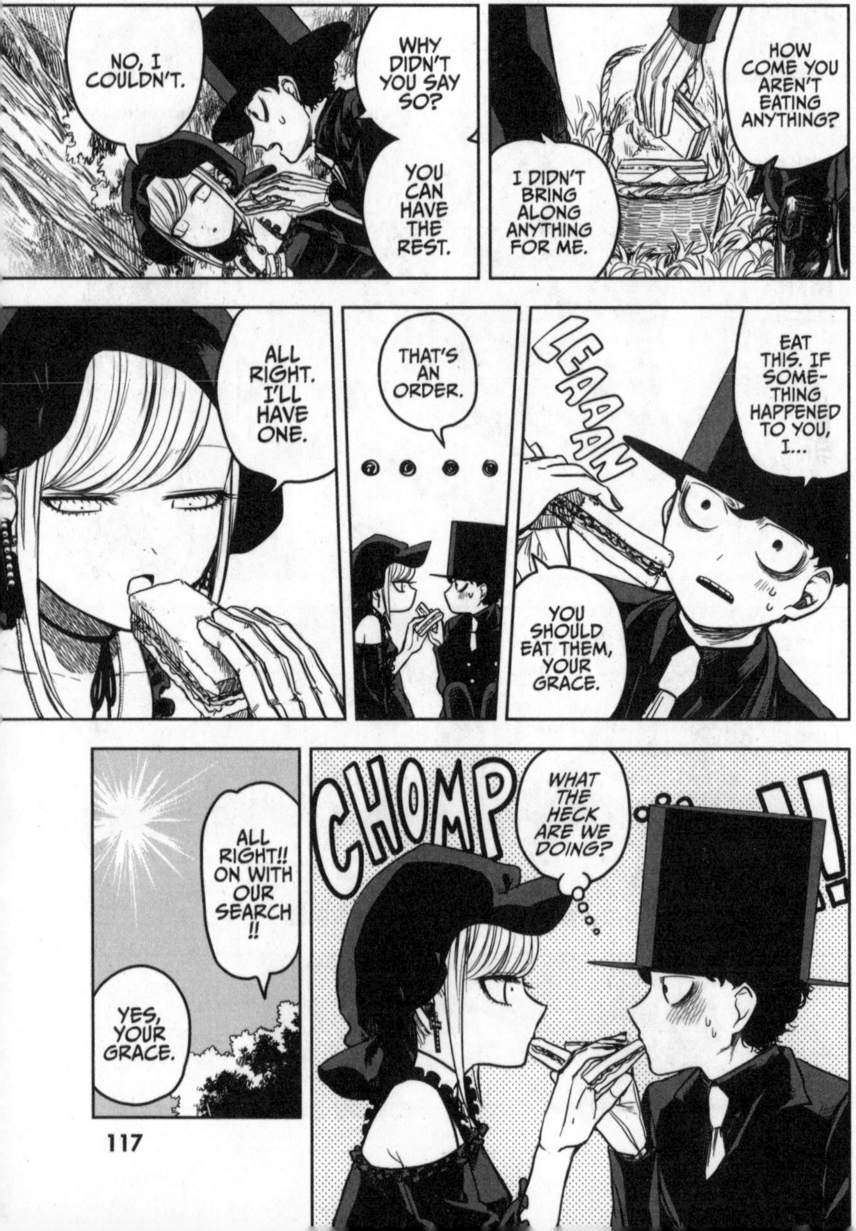
HOW COME YOU AREN'T EATING ANYTHING?
I DIDN'T BRING ALONG ANYTHING FOR ME.
WHY DIDN'T YOU SAY SO?
YOU CAN HAVE THE REST.
NO, I COULDN'T.
EAT THIS. IF SOME-THING HAPPENED TO YOU, I...
LEAAAN
YOU SHOULD EAT THEM, YOUR GRACE.
THAT'S AN ORDER.
ALL RIGHT. I'LL HAVE ONE.
CHOMP
WHAT THE HECK ARE WE DOING?
ALL RIGHT!! ON WITH OUR SEARCH!!
YES, YOUR GRACE.

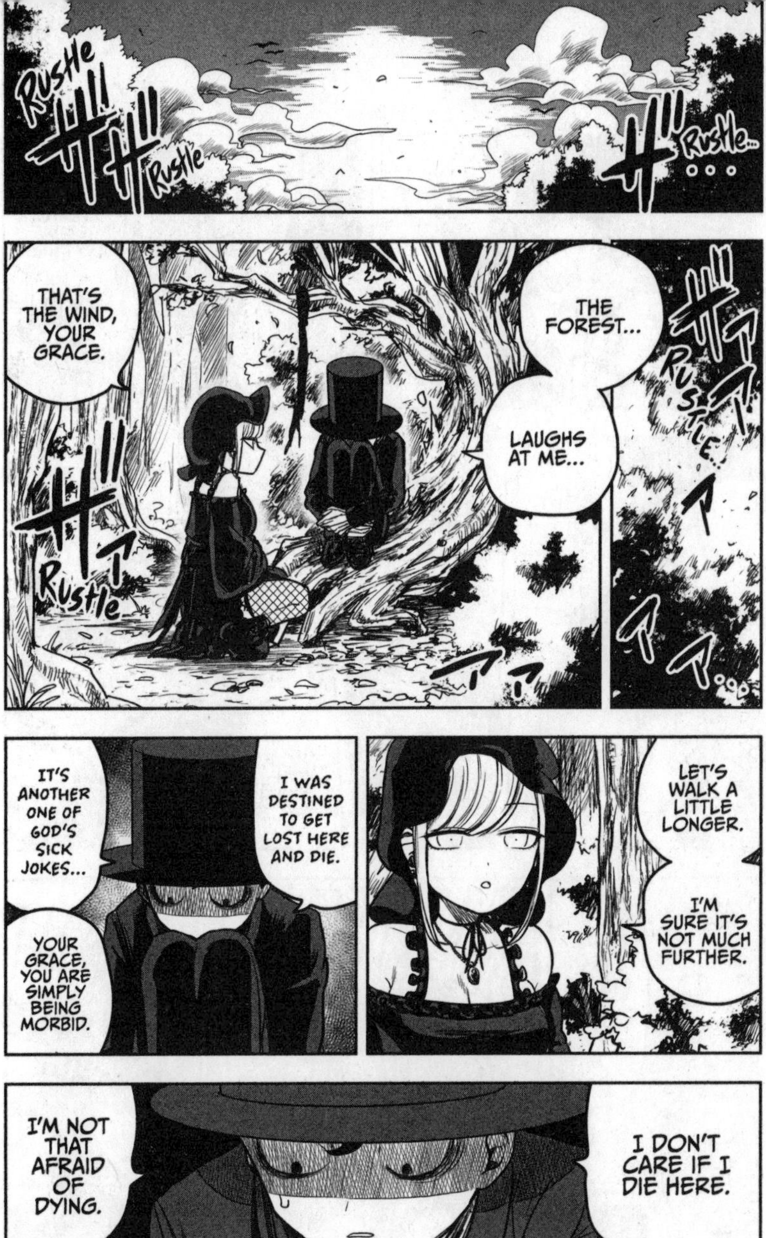
Rustle...
...
Rustle
Rustle
Rustle...
THE FOREST...
LAUGHS AT ME...
THAT'S THE WIND, YOUR GRACE.
Rustle
LET'S WALK A LITTLE LONGER.
I'M SURE IT'S NOT MUCH FURTHER.
I WAS DESTINED TO GET LOST HERE AND DIE.
IT'S ANOTHER ONE OF GOD'S SICK JOKES...
YOUR GRACE, YOU ARE SIMPLY BEING MORBID.
I DON'T CARE IF I DIE HERE.
I'M NOT THAT AFRAID OF DYING.

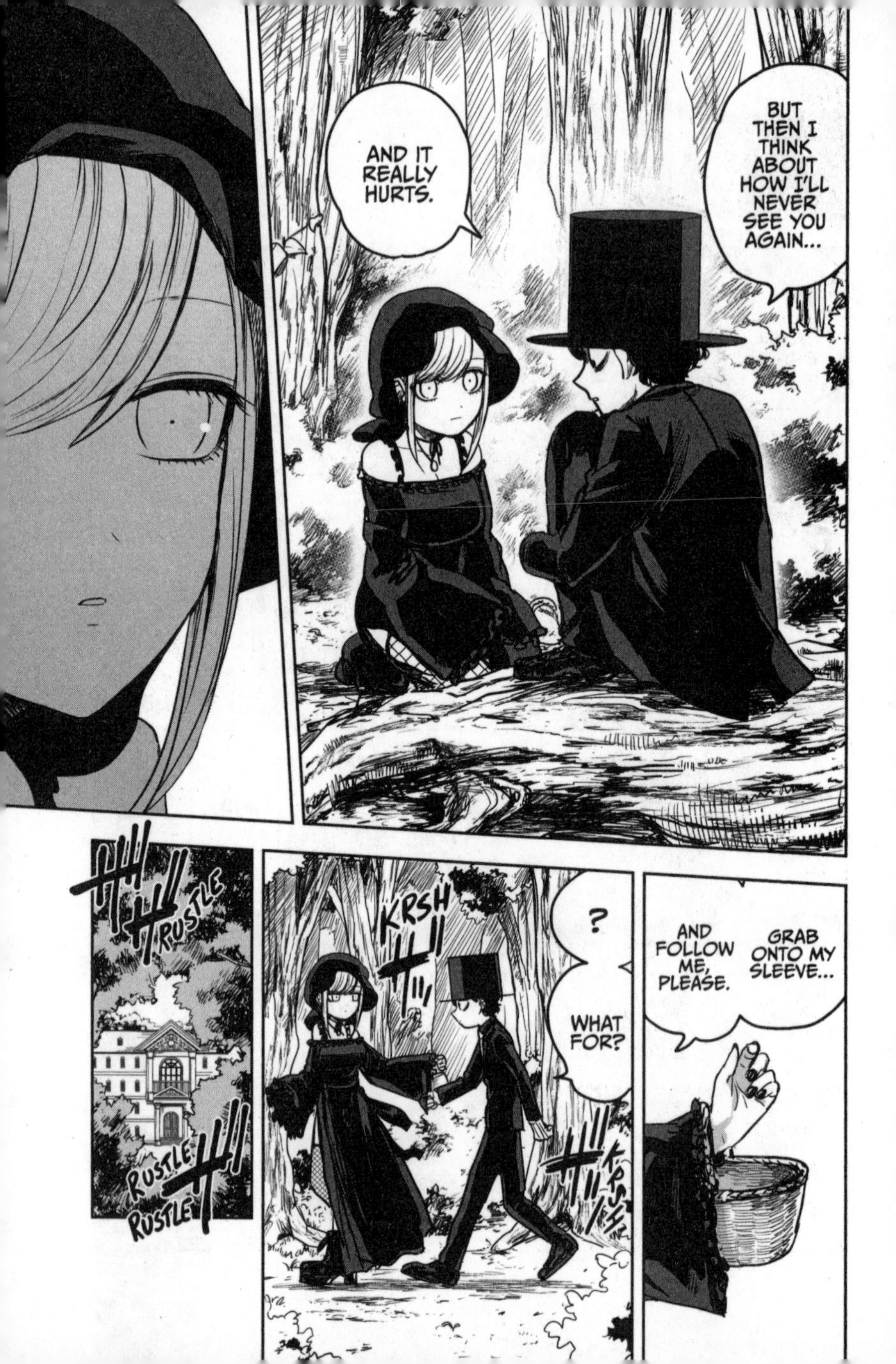
BUT THEN I THINK ABOUT HOW I'LL NEVER SEE YOU AGAIN...
AND IT REALLY HURTS.
GRAB ONTO MY SLEEVE...
AND FOLLOW ME, PLEASE.
?
WHAT FOR?
KRSH
KRSH
RUSTLE
RUSTLE
RUSTLE

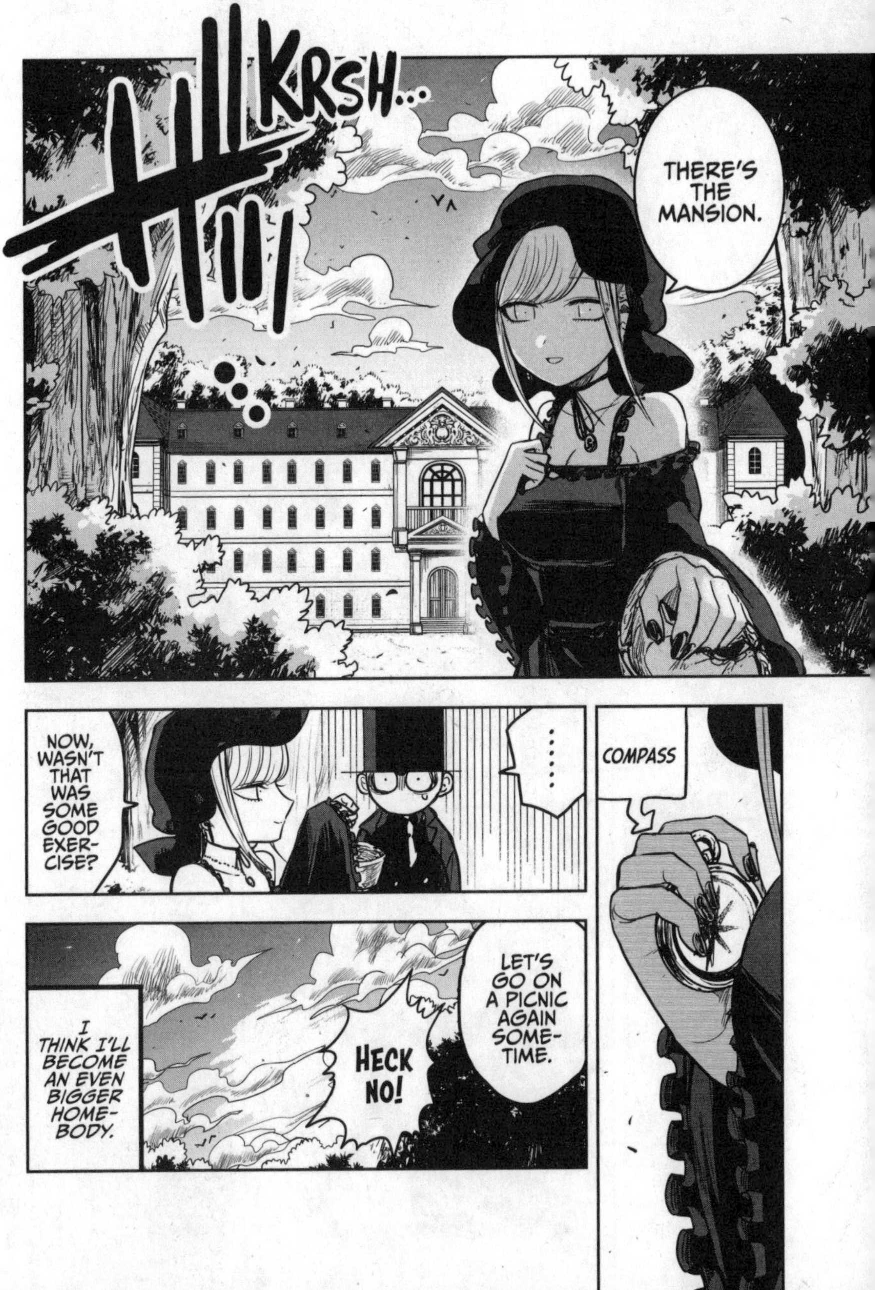
KRSH...
THERE'S THE MANSION.
COMPASS
......
NOW, WASN'T THAT WAS SOME GOOD EXERCISE?
LET'S GO ON A PICNIC AGAIN SOMETIME.
HECK NO!
I THINK I'LL BECOME AN EVEN BIGGER HOMEBODY.

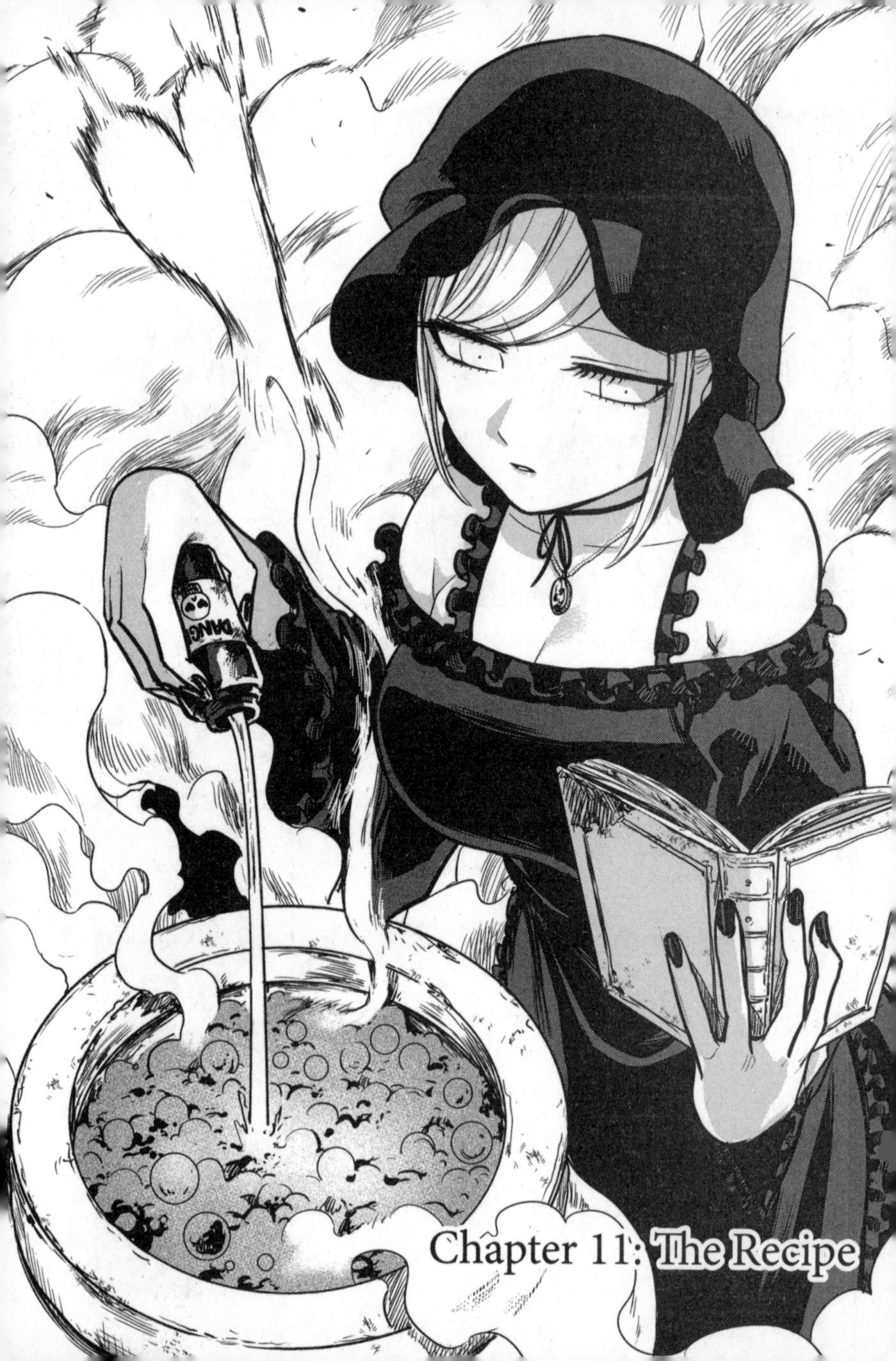
Chapter 11: The Recipe

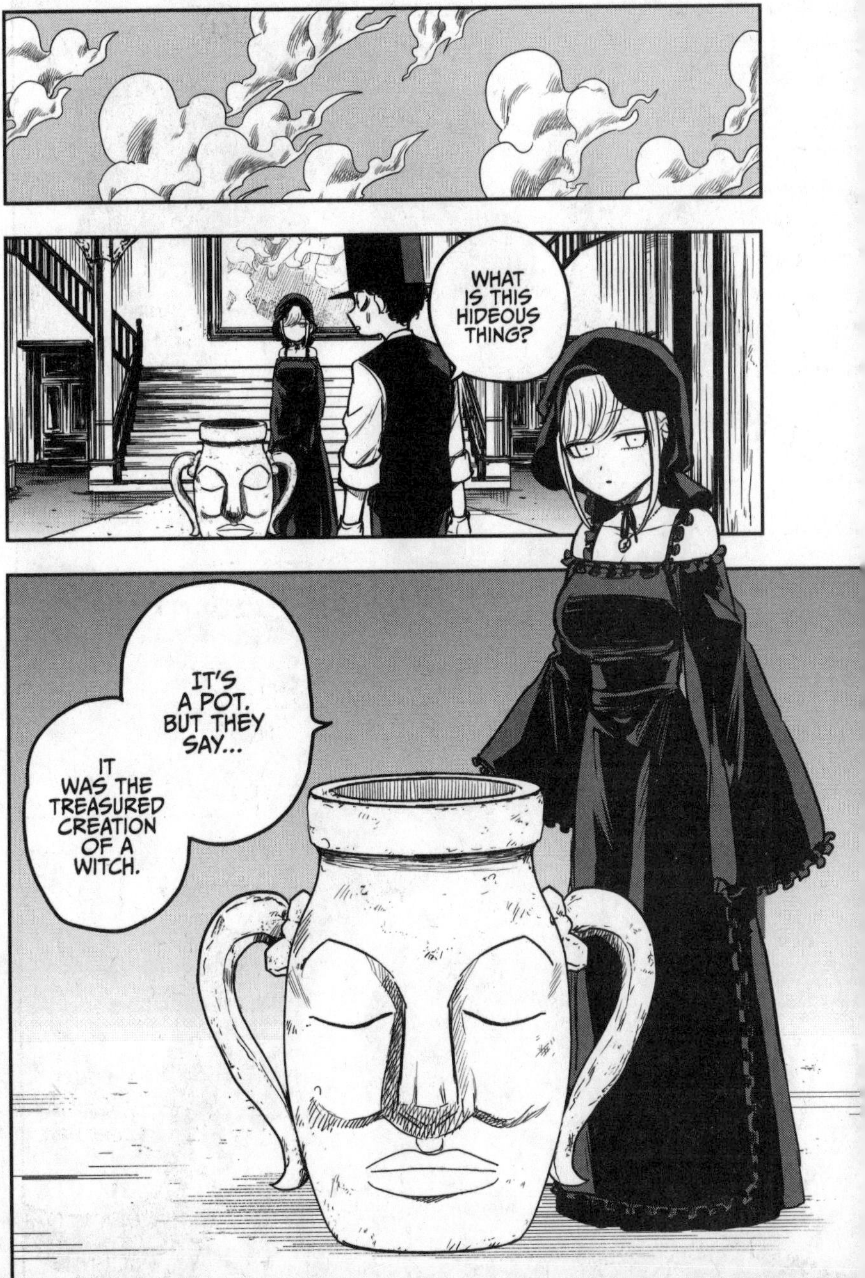
WHAT IS THIS HIDEOUS THING?
IT'S A POT. BUT THEY SAY...
IT WAS THE TREASURED CREATION OF A WITCH.

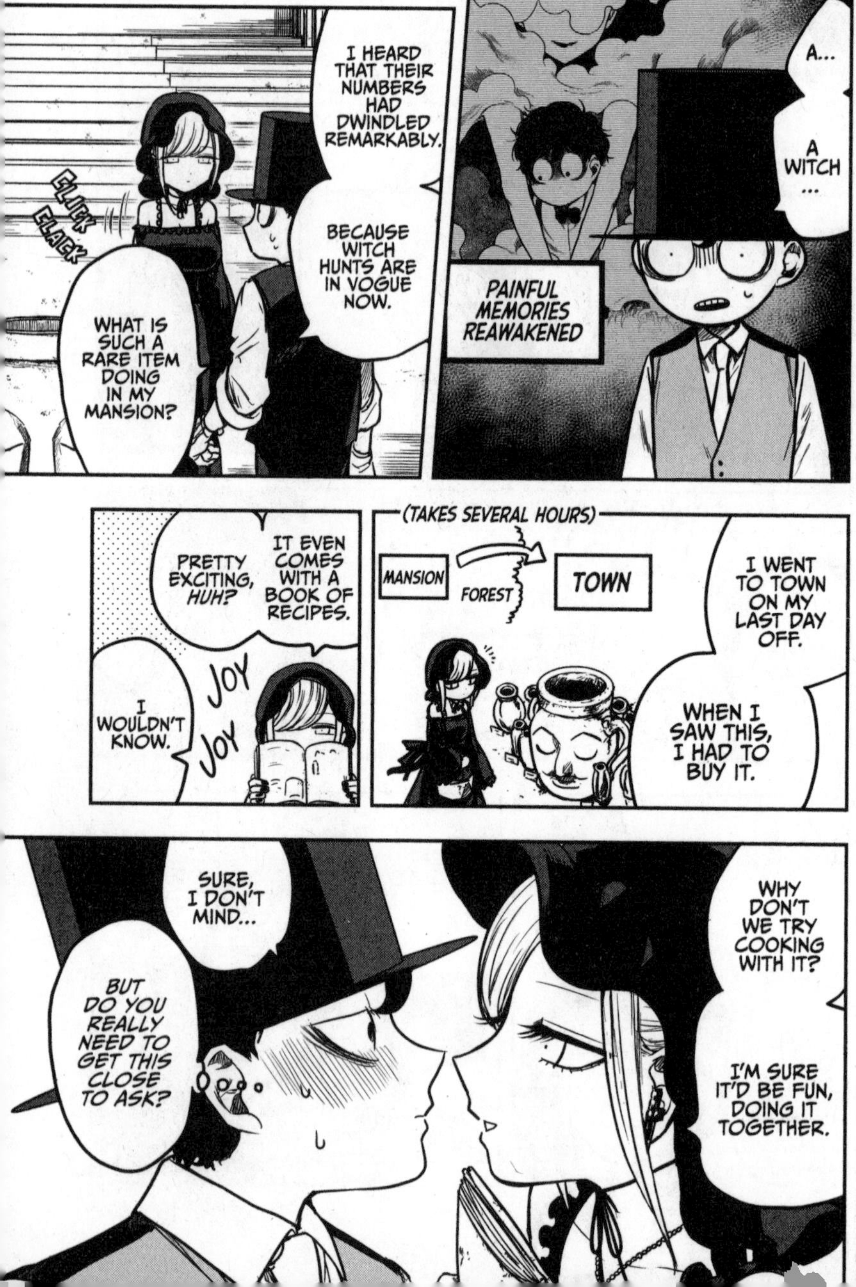
A...
A WITCH ...
PAINFUL MEMORIES REAWAKENED
I HEARD THAT THEIR NUMBERS HAD DWINDLED REMARKABLY.
BECAUSE WITCH HUNTS ARE IN VOGUE NOW.
CLICK CLACK
WHAT IS SUCH A RARE ITEM DOING IN MY MANSION?
(TAKES SEVERAL HOURS)
MANSION
FOREST
TOWN
I WENT TO TOWN ON MY LAST DAY OFF.
WHEN I SAW THIS, I HAD TO BUY IT.
IT EVEN COMES WITH A BOOK OF RECIPES.
PRETTY EXCITING, HUH?
JOY JOY
I WOULDN'T KNOW.
WHY DON'T WE TRY COOKING WITH IT?
I'M SURE IT'D BE FUN, DOING IT TOGETHER.
SURE, I DON'T MIND...
BUT DO YOU REALLY NEED TO GET THIS CLOSE TO ASK?

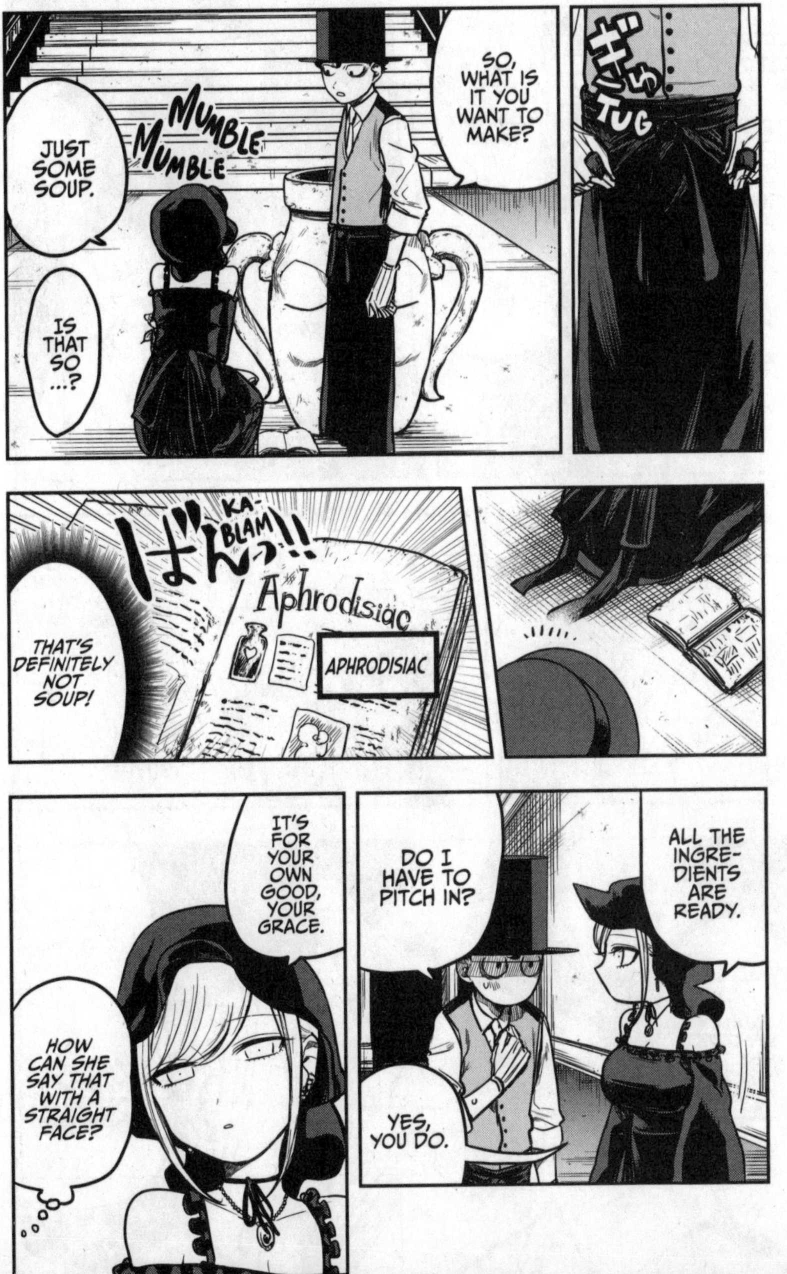

ぎゅ
TUG
SO, WHAT IS IT YOU WANT TO MAKE?
MUMBLE MUMBLE
JUST SOME SOUP.
IS THAT SO ...?
ばんっ!!
KA-BLAM
Aphrodisiac
APHRODISIAC
THAT'S DEFINITELY NOT SOUP!
ALL THE INGRE-DIENTS ARE READY.
DO I HAVE TO PITCH IN?
YES, YOU DO.
IT'S FOR YOUR OWN GOOD, YOUR GRACE.
HOW CAN SHE SAY THAT WITH A STRAIGHT FACE?

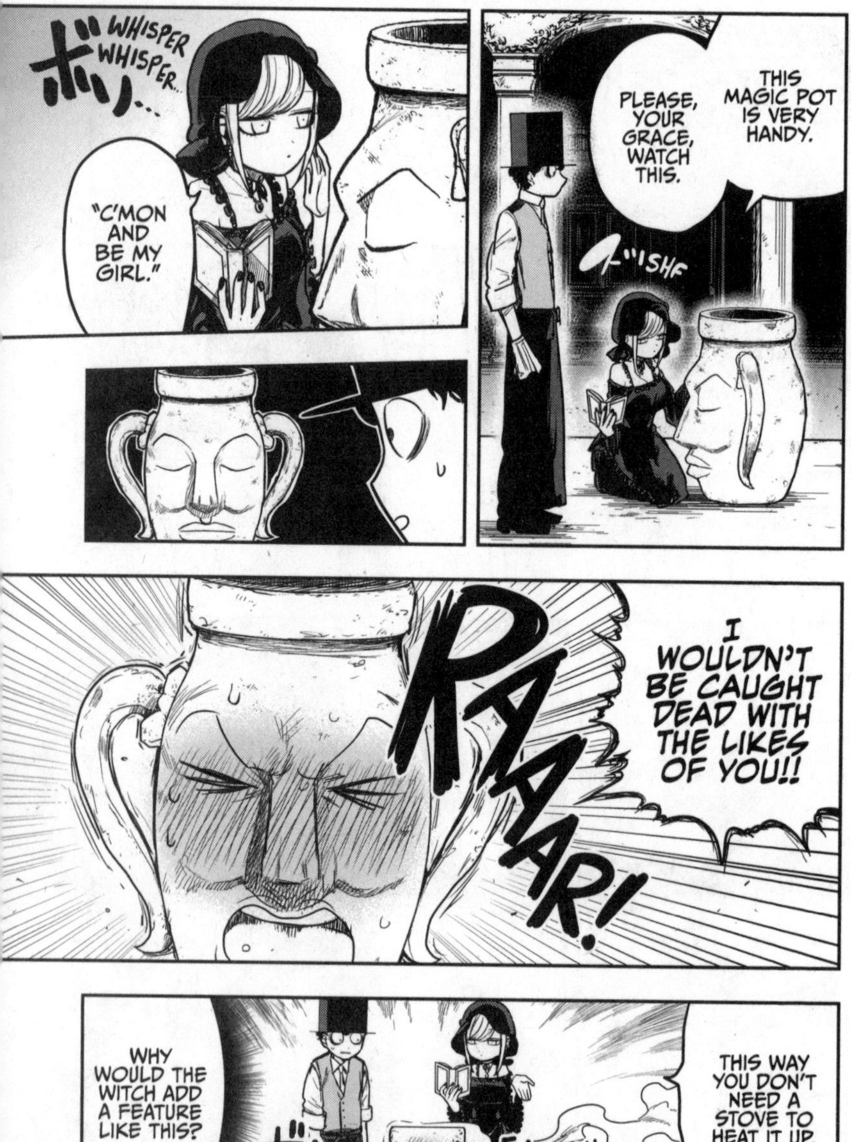
THIS MAGIC POT IS VERY HANDY.
PLEASE, YOUR GRACE, WATCH THIS.
SHF
WHISPER WHISPER...
"C'MON AND BE MY GIRL."
I WOULDN'T BE CAUGHT DEAD WITH THE LIKES OF YOU!!
RAAAR!
THIS WAY YOU DON'T NEED A STOVE TO HEAT IT UP.
FWOOOSH
WHY WOULD THE WITCH ADD A FEATURE LIKE THIS?

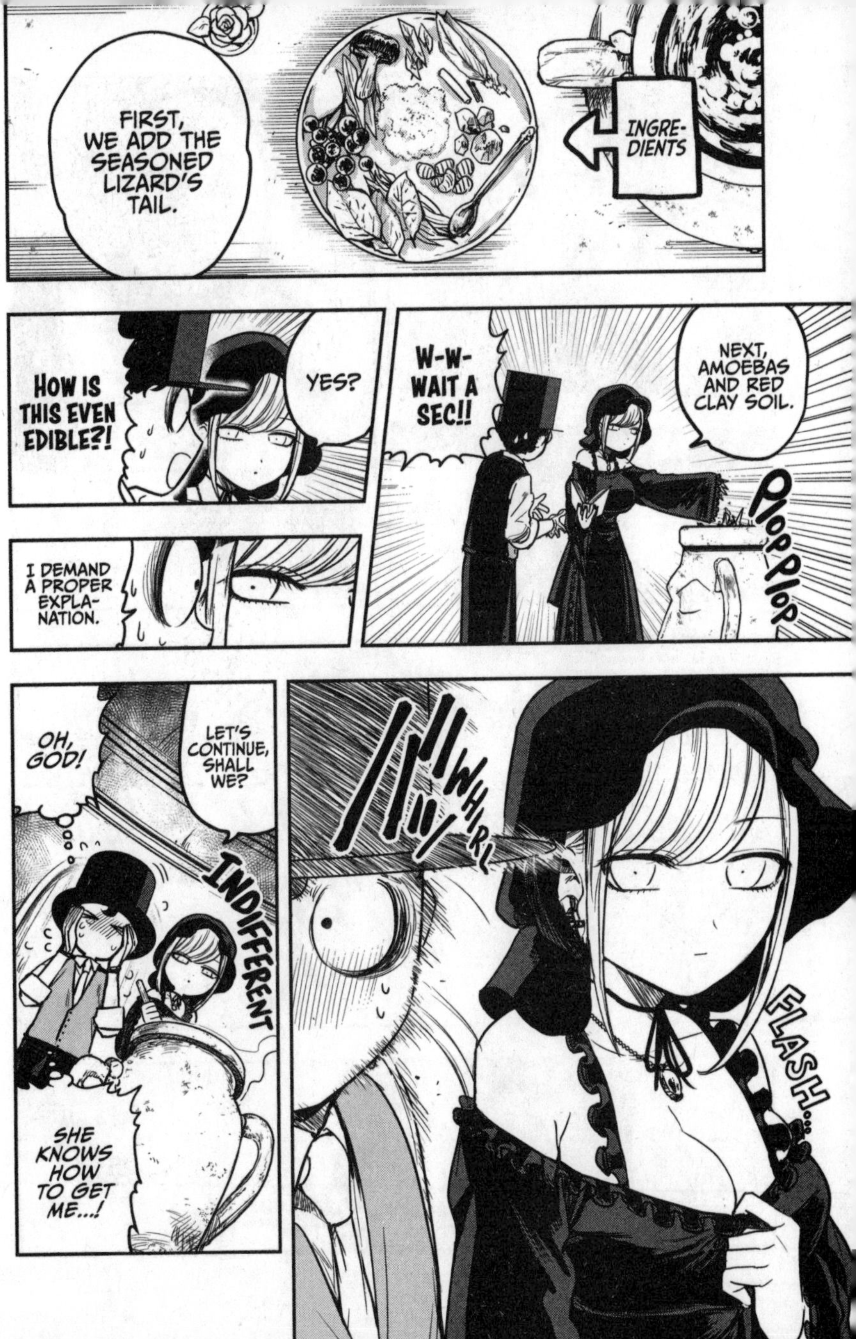
INGRE-DIENTS
FIRST, WE ADD THE SEASONED LIZARD'S TAIL.
NEXT, AMOEBAS AND RED CLAY SOIL.
PLOP PLOP
W-W-WAIT A SEC!!
YES?
HOW IS THIS EVEN EDIBLE?!
I DEMAND A PROPER EXPLA-NATION.
FLASH...
WHIRL
LET'S CONTINUE, SHALL WE?
OH, GOD!
INDIFFERENT
SHE KNOWS HOW TO GET ME...!

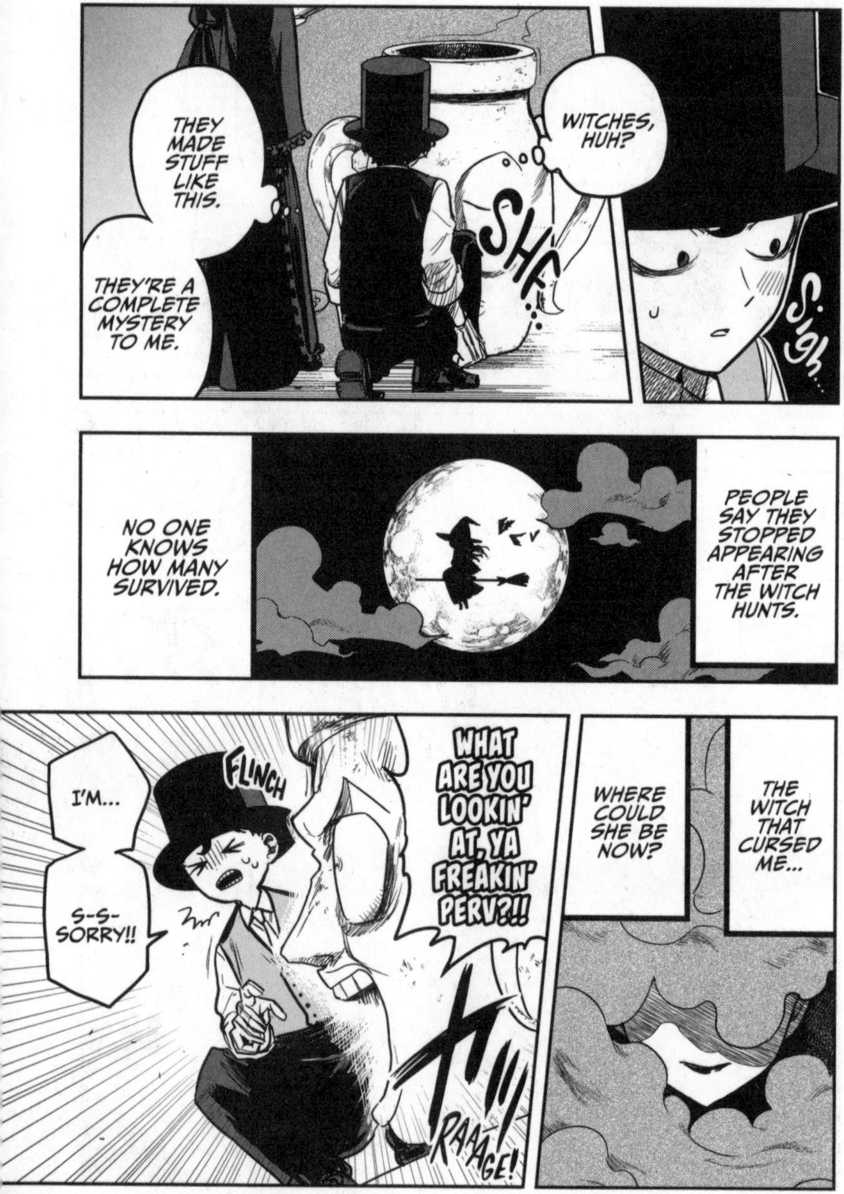

WITCHES, HUH?
Sigh...
SHF..
THEY MADE STUFF LIKE THIS.
THEY'RE A COMPLETE MYSTERY TO ME.
PEOPLE SAY THEY STOPPED APPEARING AFTER THE WITCH HUNTS.
NO ONE KNOWS HOW MANY SURVIVED.
THE WITCH THAT CURSED ME...
WHERE COULD SHE BE NOW?
WHAT ARE YOU LOOKIN' AT, YA FREAKIN' PERV?!!
FLINCH
I'M...
S-S-SORRY!!
RAAAGE!

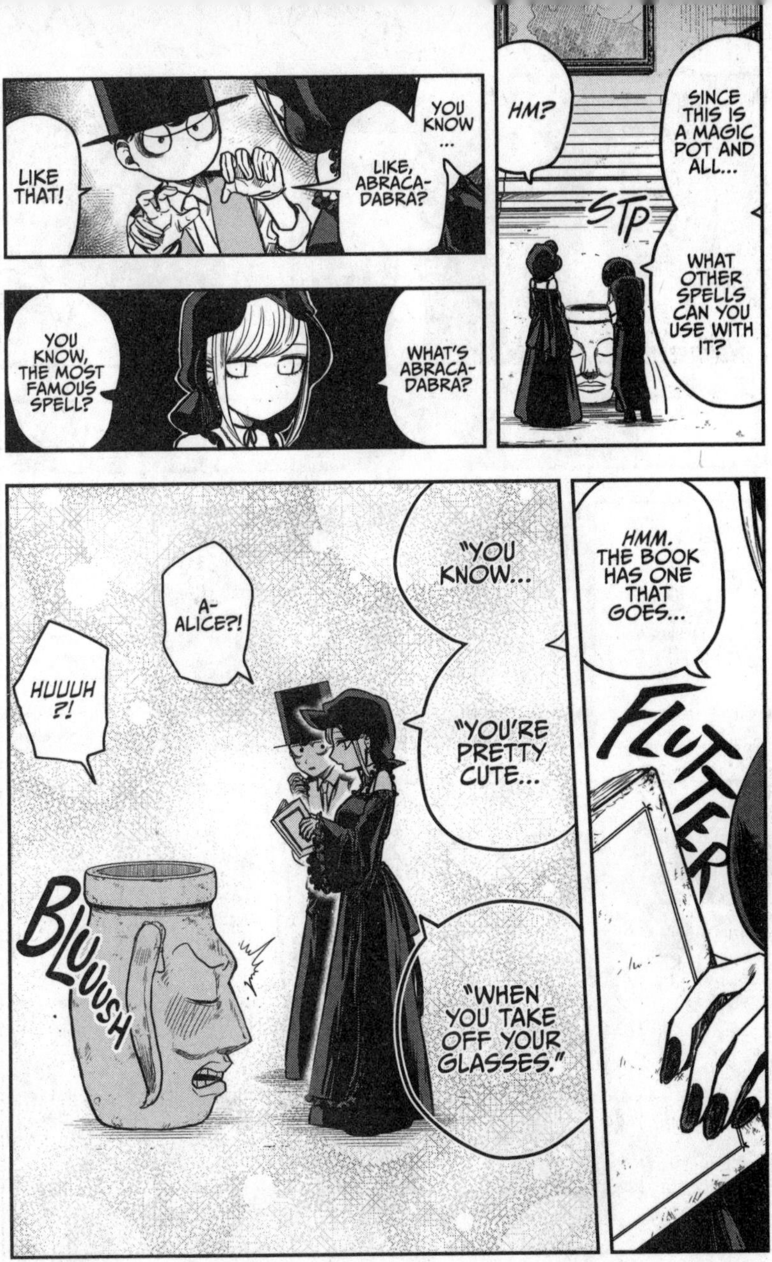
SINCE THIS IS A MAGIC POT AND ALL...
HM?
STP
WHAT OTHER SPELLS CAN YOU USE WITH IT?
YOU KNOW ...
LIKE, ABRACA-DABRA?
LIKE THAT!
WHAT'S ABRACA-DABRA?
YOU KNOW, THE MOST FAMOUS SPELL?
HMM. THE BOOK HAS ONE THAT GOES...
FLUTTER
"YOU KNOW...
"YOU'RE PRETTY CUTE...
"WHEN YOU TAKE OFF YOUR GLASSES."
A-ALICE?!
HUUUH ?!
BLUUUSH

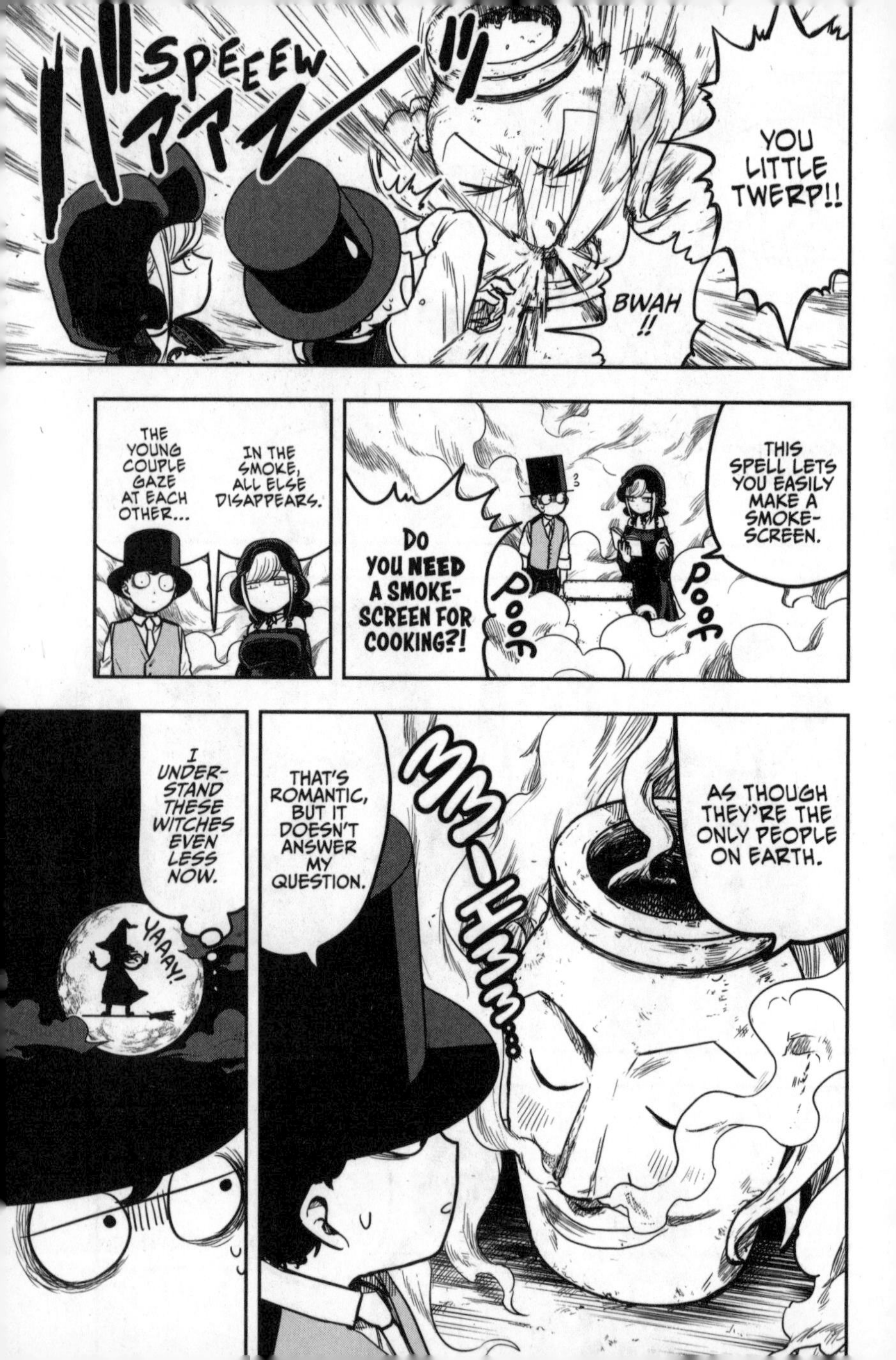
YOU LITTLE TWERP!!
BWAH !!
SPEEEW
THIS SPELL LETS YOU EASILY MAKE A SMOKE-SCREEN.
POOF
POOF
DO YOU NEED A SMOKE-SCREEN FOR COOKING?!
IN THE SMOKE, ALL ELSE DISAPPEARS.
THE YOUNG COUPLE GAZE AT EACH OTHER...
AS THOUGH THEY'RE THE ONLY PEOPLE ON EARTH.
MM-HMM...
THAT'S ROMANTIC, BUT IT DOESN'T ANSWER MY QUESTION.
I UNDERSTAND THESE WITCHES EVEN LESS NOW.
YAAAY!

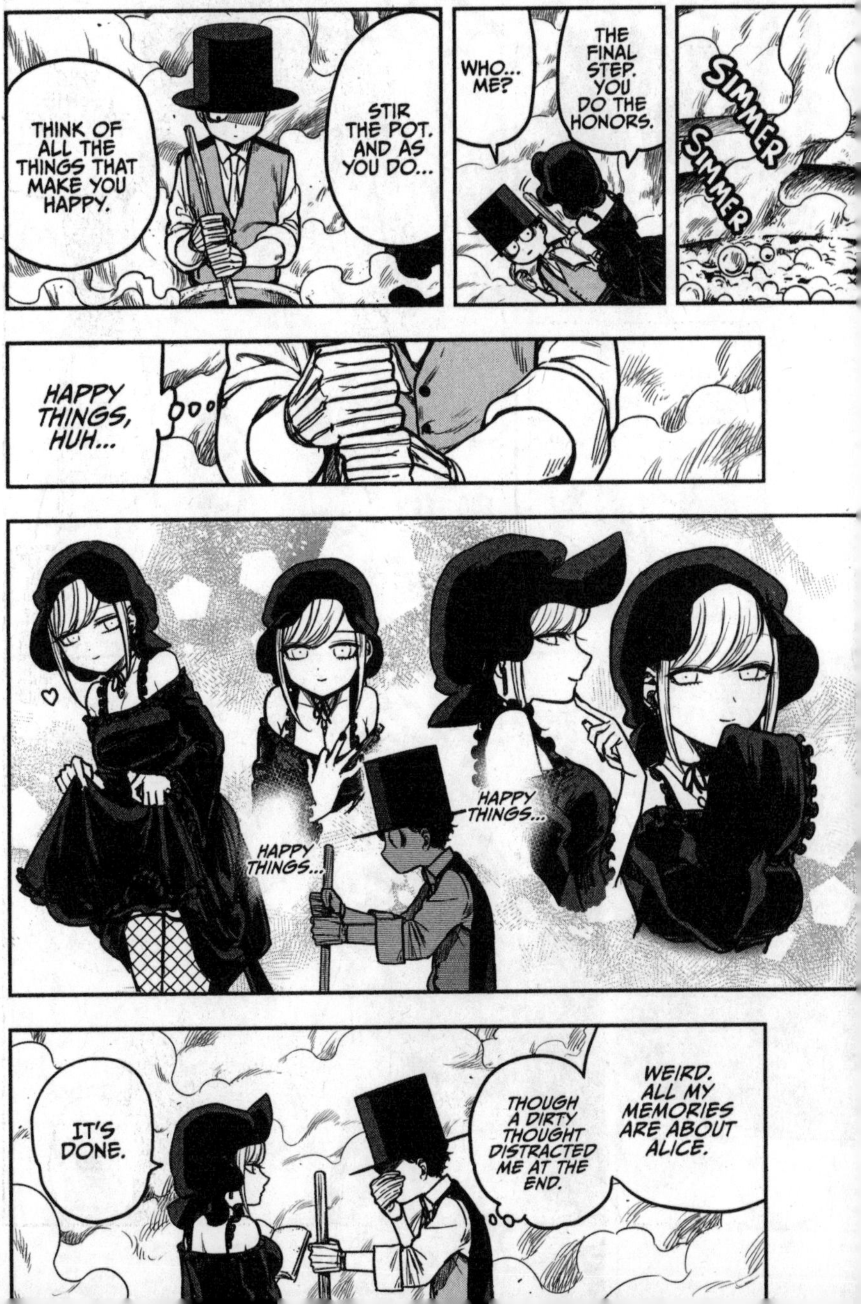
SIMMER SIMMER
THE FINAL STEP. YOU DO THE HONORS.
WHO... ME?
STIR THE POT. AND AS YOU DO...
THINK OF ALL THE THINGS THAT MAKE YOU HAPPY.
HAPPY THINGS, HUH...
HAPPY THINGS...
HAPPY THINGS...
WEIRD. ALL MY MEMORIES ARE ABOUT ALICE.
THOUGH A DIRTY THOUGHT DISTRACTED ME AT THE END.
IT'S DONE.

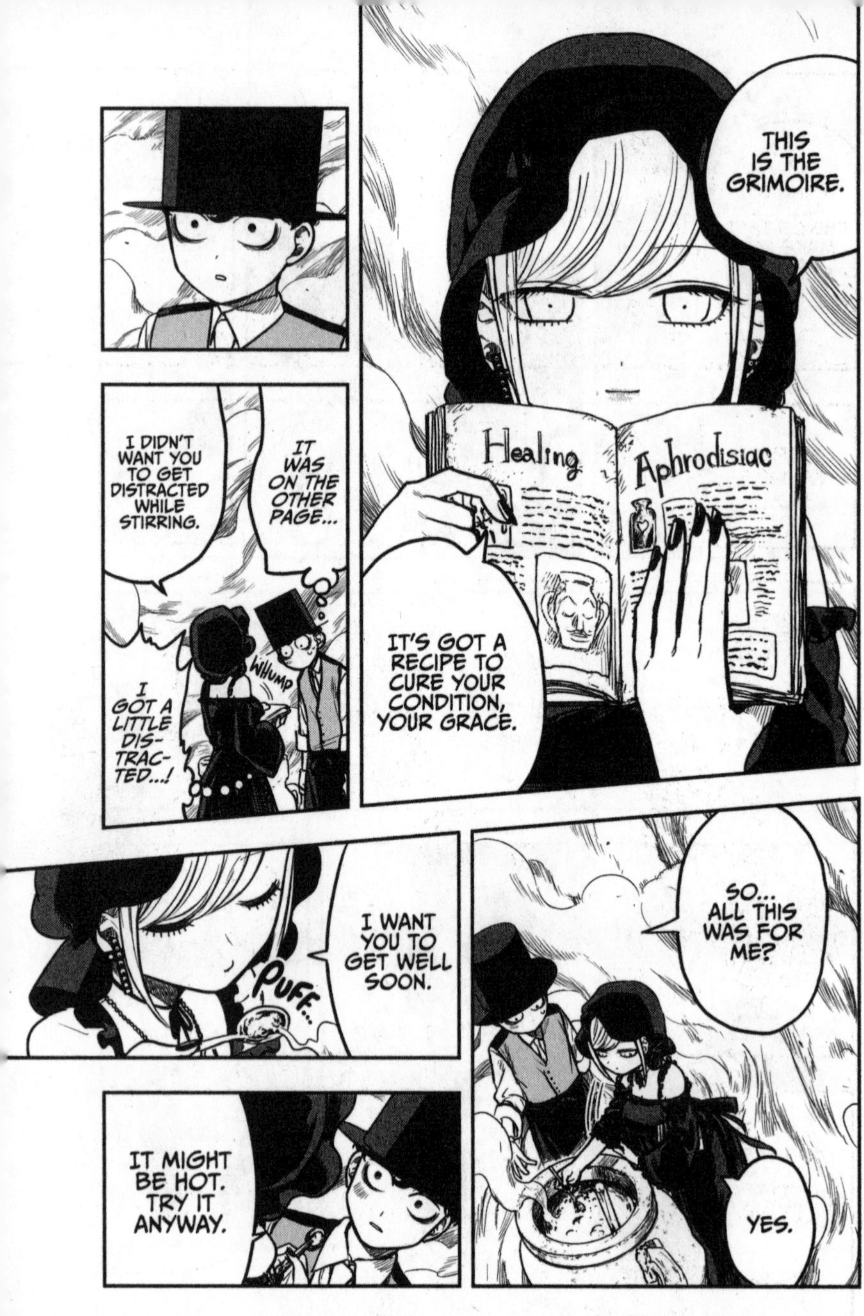
THIS IS THE GRIMOIRE.
Healing
Aphrodisiac
IT'S GOT A RECIPE TO CURE YOUR CONDITION, YOUR GRACE.
IT WAS ON THE OTHER PAGE...
I DIDN'T WANT YOU TO GET DISTRACTED WHILE STIRRING.
WHUMP
I GOT A LITTLE DIS-TRAC-TED...!
SO... ALL THIS WAS FOR ME?
YES.
I WANT YOU TO GET WELL SOON.
PUFF...
IT MIGHT BE HOT. TRY IT ANYWAY.

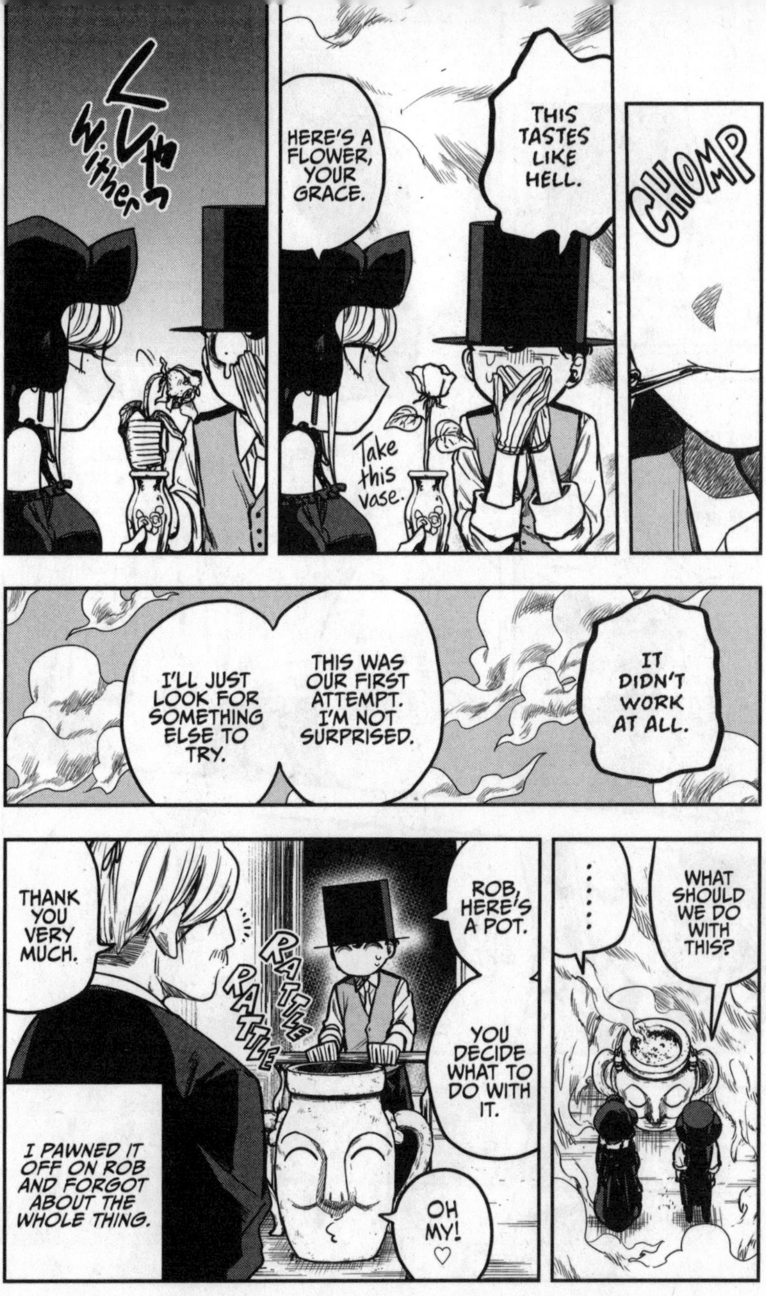
CHOMP
THIS TASTES LIKE HELL.
HERE'S A FLOWER, YOUR GRACE.
Take this vase.
Wither
IT DIDN'T WORK AT ALL.
THIS WAS OUR FIRST ATTEMPT. I'M NOT SURPRISED.
I'LL JUST LOOK FOR SOMETHING ELSE TO TRY.
WHAT SHOULD WE DO WITH THIS?
......
ROB, HERE'S A POT.
YOU DECIDE WHAT TO DO WITH IT.
RATTLE RATTLE
THANK YOU VERY MUCH.
OH MY! ♡
I PAWNED IT OFF ON ROB AND FORGOT ABOUT THE WHOLE THING.

Chapter 12: The Cat

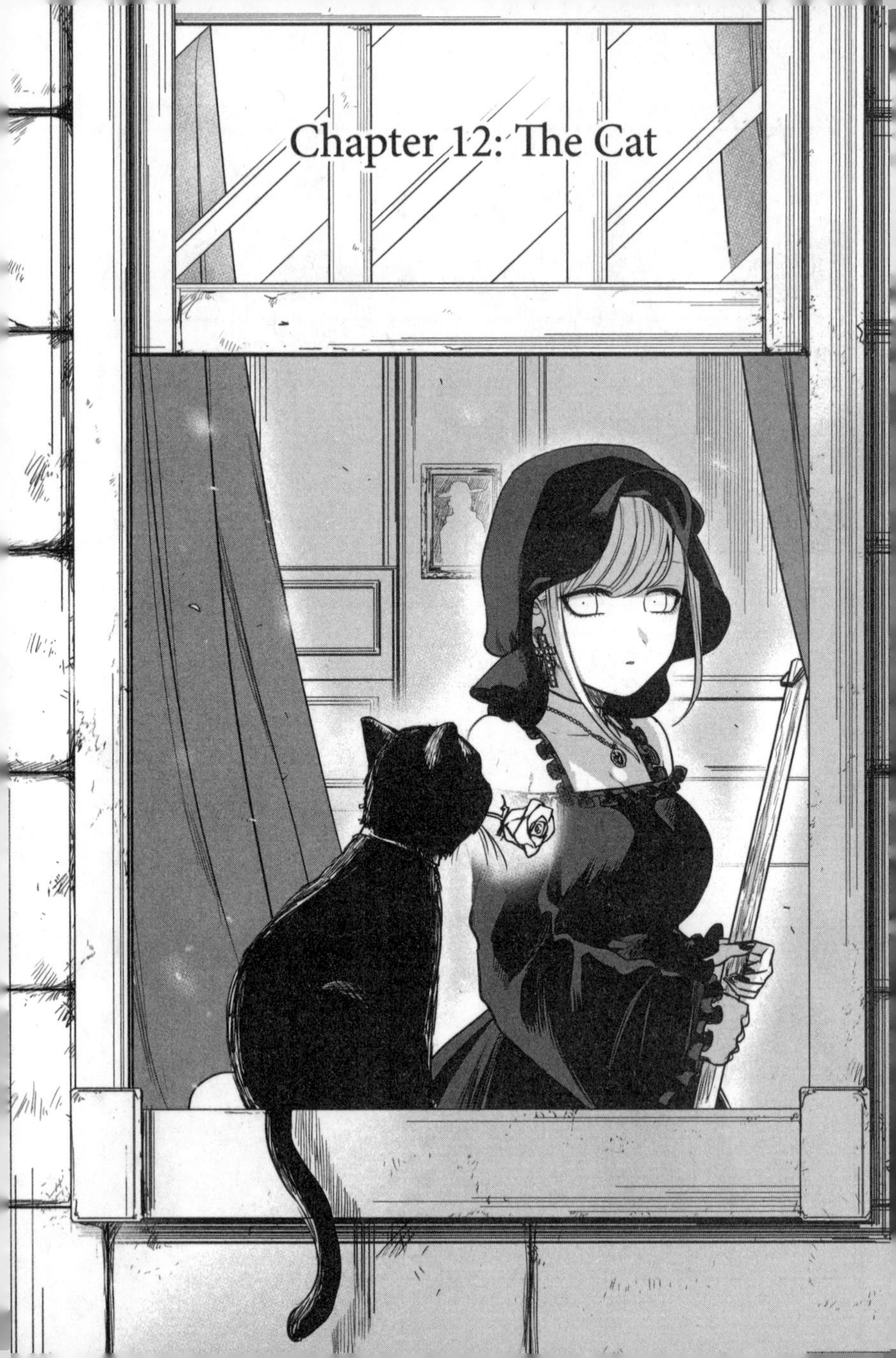

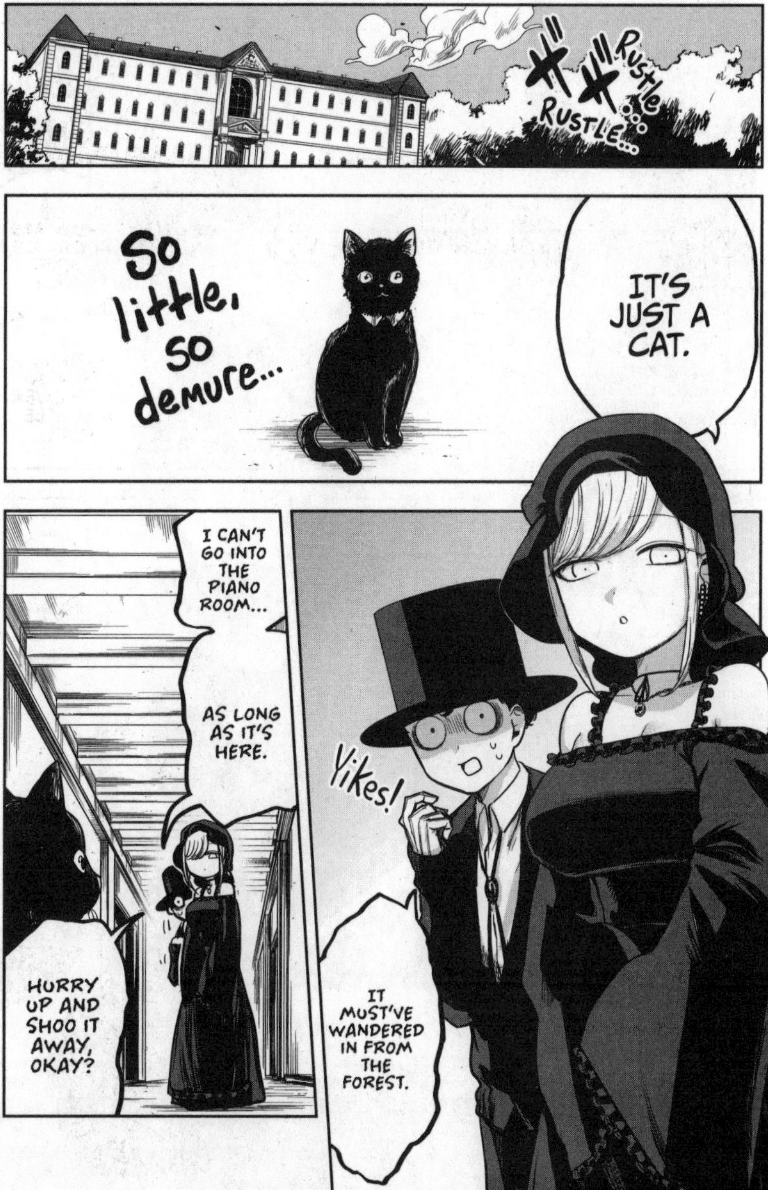
Rustle...
RUSTLE...
IT'S JUST A CAT.
So little, so demure...
Yikes!
IT MUST'VE WANDERED IN FROM THE FOREST.
I CAN'T GO INTO THE PIANO ROOM...
AS LONG AS IT'S HERE.
HURRY UP AND SHOO IT AWAY, OKAY?

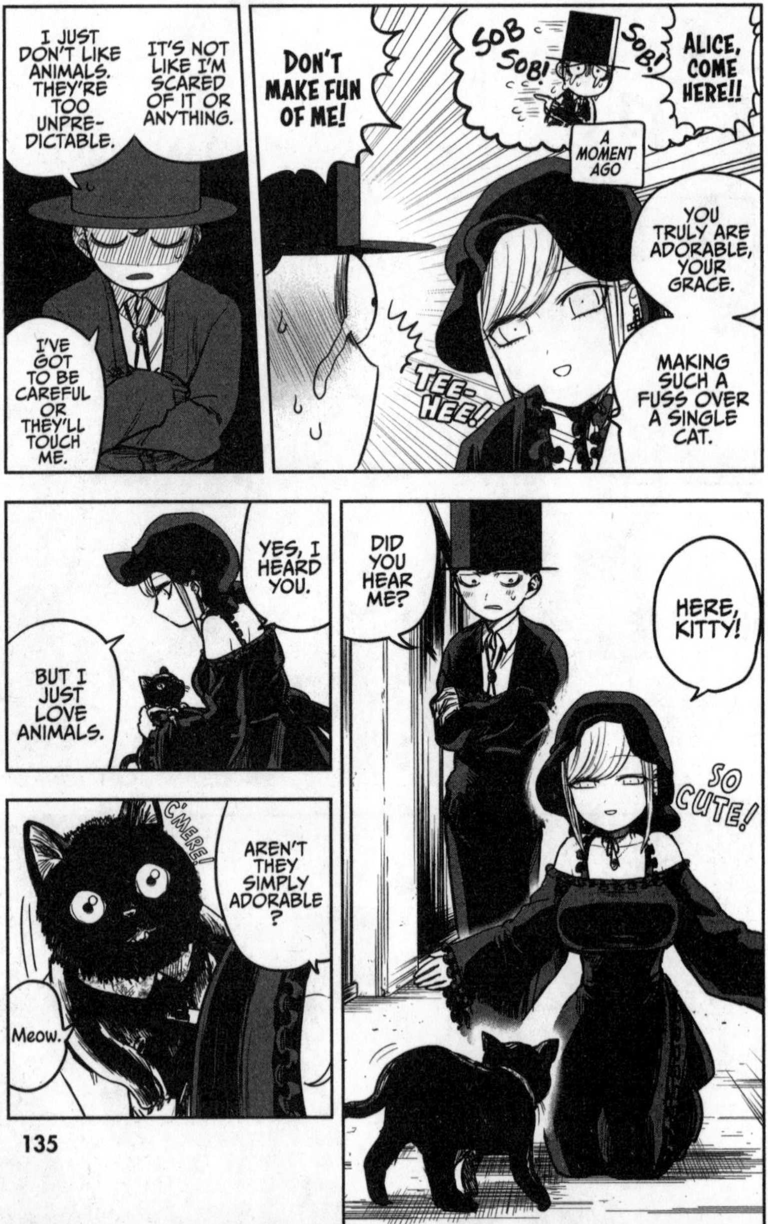
ALICE, COME HERE!!
SOB! SOB SOB!
A MOMENT AGO
YOU TRULY ARE ADORABLE, YOUR GRACE.
MAKING SUCH A FUSS OVER A SINGLE CAT.
DON'T MAKE FUN OF ME!
TEE-HEE!
IT'S NOT LIKE I'M SCARED OF IT OR ANYTHING.
I JUST DON'T LIKE ANIMALS. THEY'RE TOO UNPRE-DICTABLE.
I'VE GOT TO BE CAREFUL OR THEY'LL TOUCH ME.
HERE, KITTY!
SO CUTE!
DID YOU HEAR ME?
YES, I HEARD YOU.
BUT I JUST LOVE ANIMALS.
AREN'T THEY SIMPLY ADORABLE?
C'MERE!
Meow.

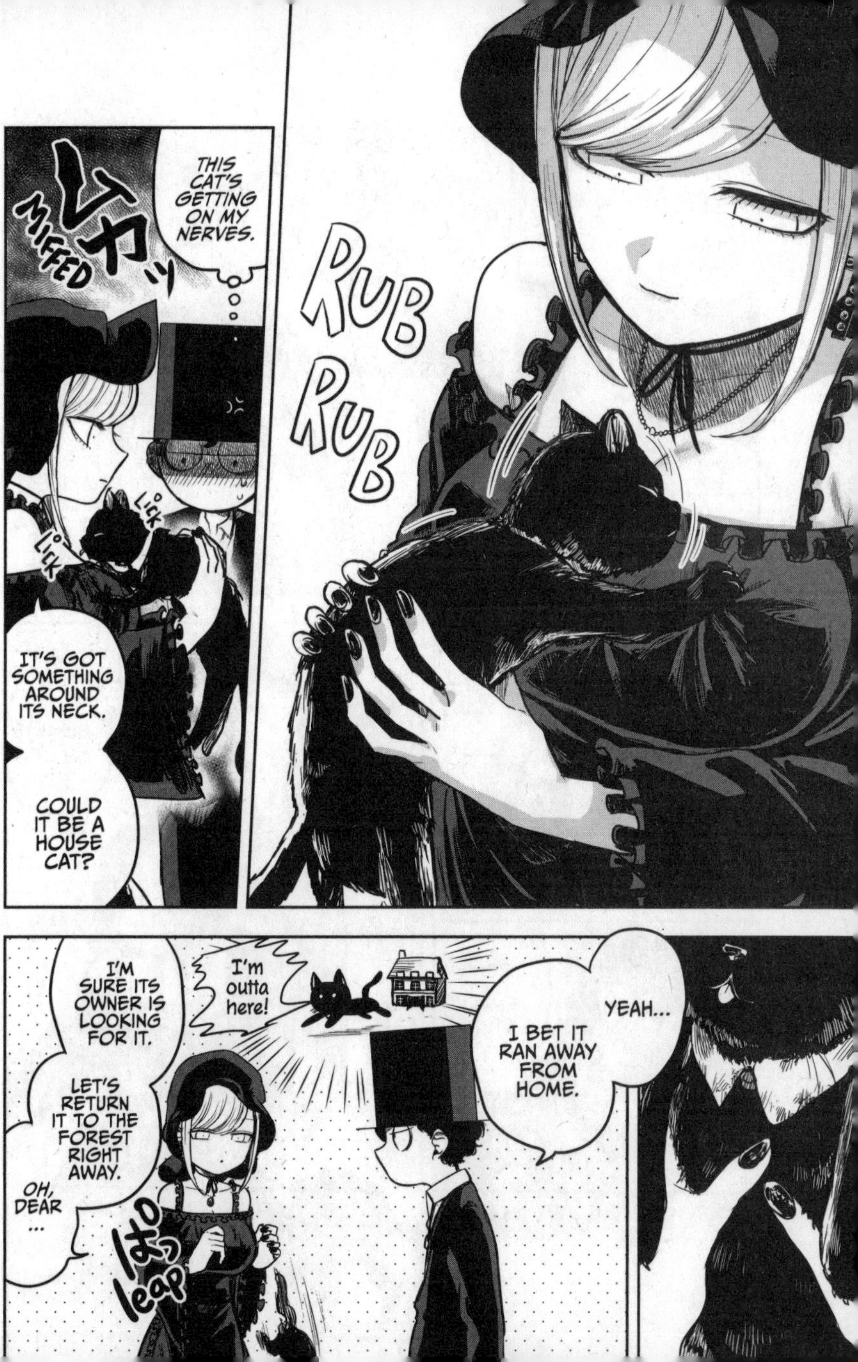
RUB RUB
ムカッ
MIFFED
THIS CAT'S GETTING ON MY NERVES.
LICK LICK
IT'S GOT SOMETHING AROUND ITS NECK.
COULD IT BE A HOUSE CAT?
YEAH...
I BET IT RAN AWAY FROM HOME.
I'm outta here!
I'M SURE ITS OWNER IS LOOKING FOR IT.
LET'S RETURN IT TO THE FOREST RIGHT AWAY.
OH, DEAR ...
はっ
leap

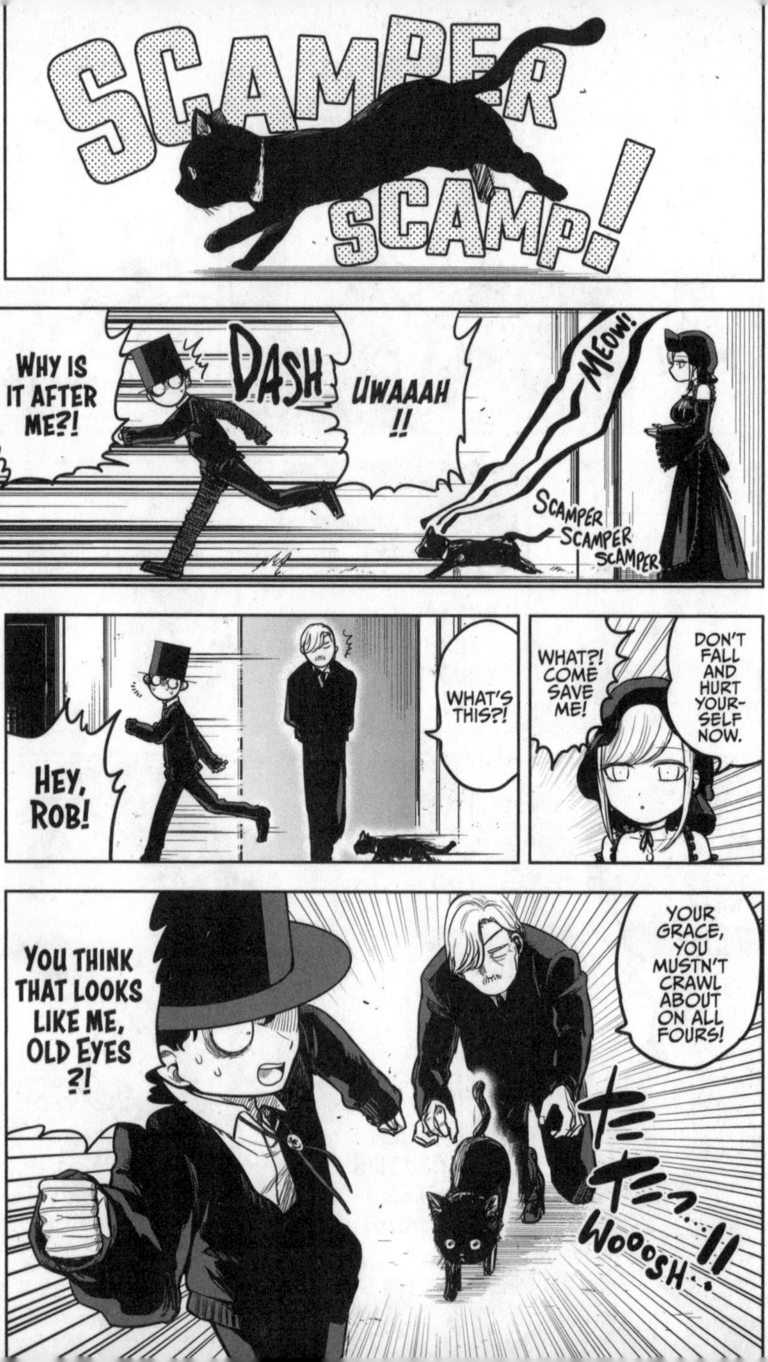
SCAMPER SCAMP!
MEOW!
SCAMPER SCAMPER SCAMPER
UWAAAH!!
DASH
WHY IS IT AFTER ME?!
DON'T FALL AND HURT YOURSELF NOW.
WHAT?! COME SAVE ME!
WHAT'S THIS?!
HEY, ROB!
YOUR GRACE, YOU MUSTN'T CRAWL ABOUT ON ALL FOURS!
WOOOSH...!!
YOU THINK THAT LOOKS LIKE ME, OLD EYES?!

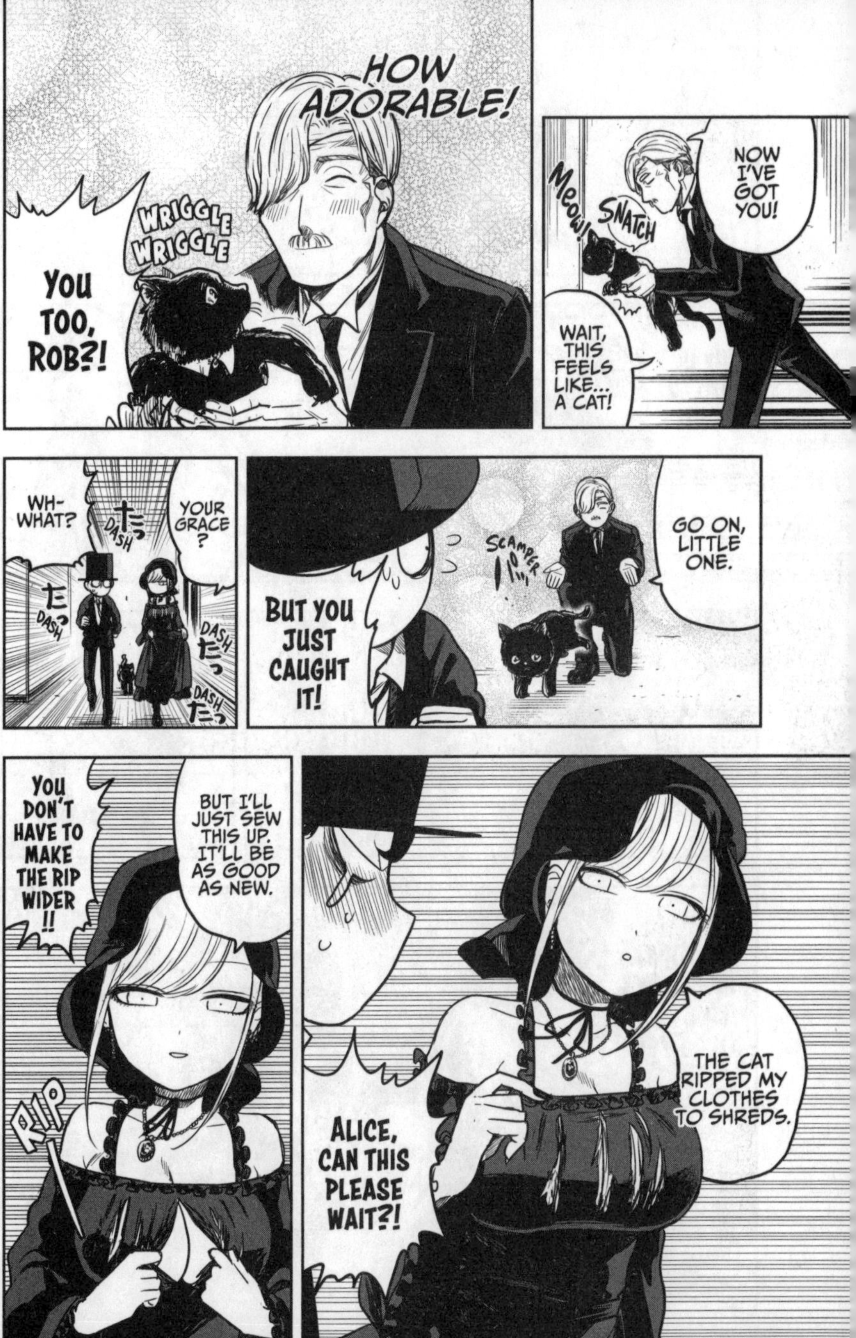
NOW I'VE GOT YOU!
SNATCH
MEOW!
WAIT, THIS FEELS LIKE... A CAT!
HOW ADORABLE!
WRIGGLE WRIGGLE
YOU TOO, ROB?!
GO ON, LITTLE ONE.
SCAMPER
BUT YOU JUST CAUGHT IT!
YOUR GRACE?
WH-WHAT?
DASH
DASH
DASH
DASH
THE CAT RIPPED MY CLOTHES TO SHREDS.
ALICE, CAN THIS PLEASE WAIT?!
BUT I'LL JUST SEW THIS UP. IT'LL BE AS GOOD AS NEW.
YOU DON'T HAVE TO MAKE THE RIP WIDER!!
RIP

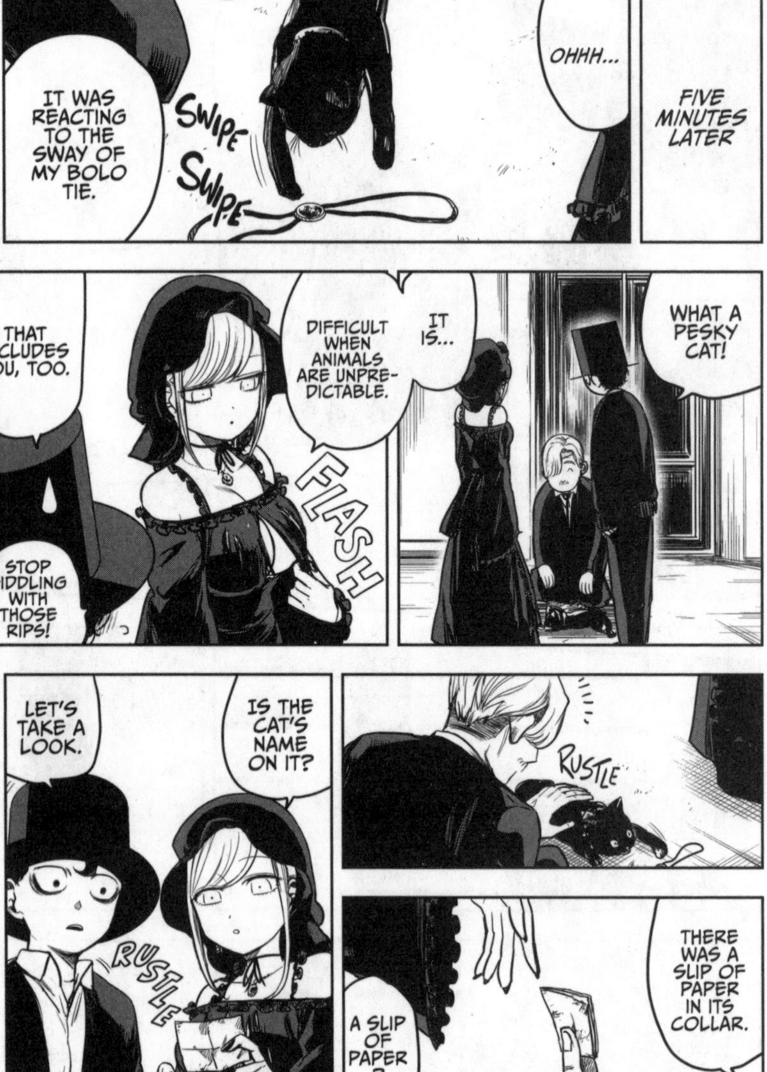
FIVE MINUTES LATER
OHHH...
IT WAS REACTING TO THE SWAY OF MY BOLO TIE.
SWIPE
SWIPE
SWIPE
WHAT A PESKY CAT!
IT IS...
DIFFICULT WHEN ANIMALS ARE UNPREDICTABLE.
FLASH
THAT INCLUDES YOU, TOO.
STOP FIDDLING WITH THOSE RIPS!
RUSTLE
THERE WAS A SLIP OF PAPER IN ITS COLLAR.
A SLIP OF PAPER?
IS THE CAT'S NAME ON IT?
LET'S TAKE A LOOK.
RUSTLE

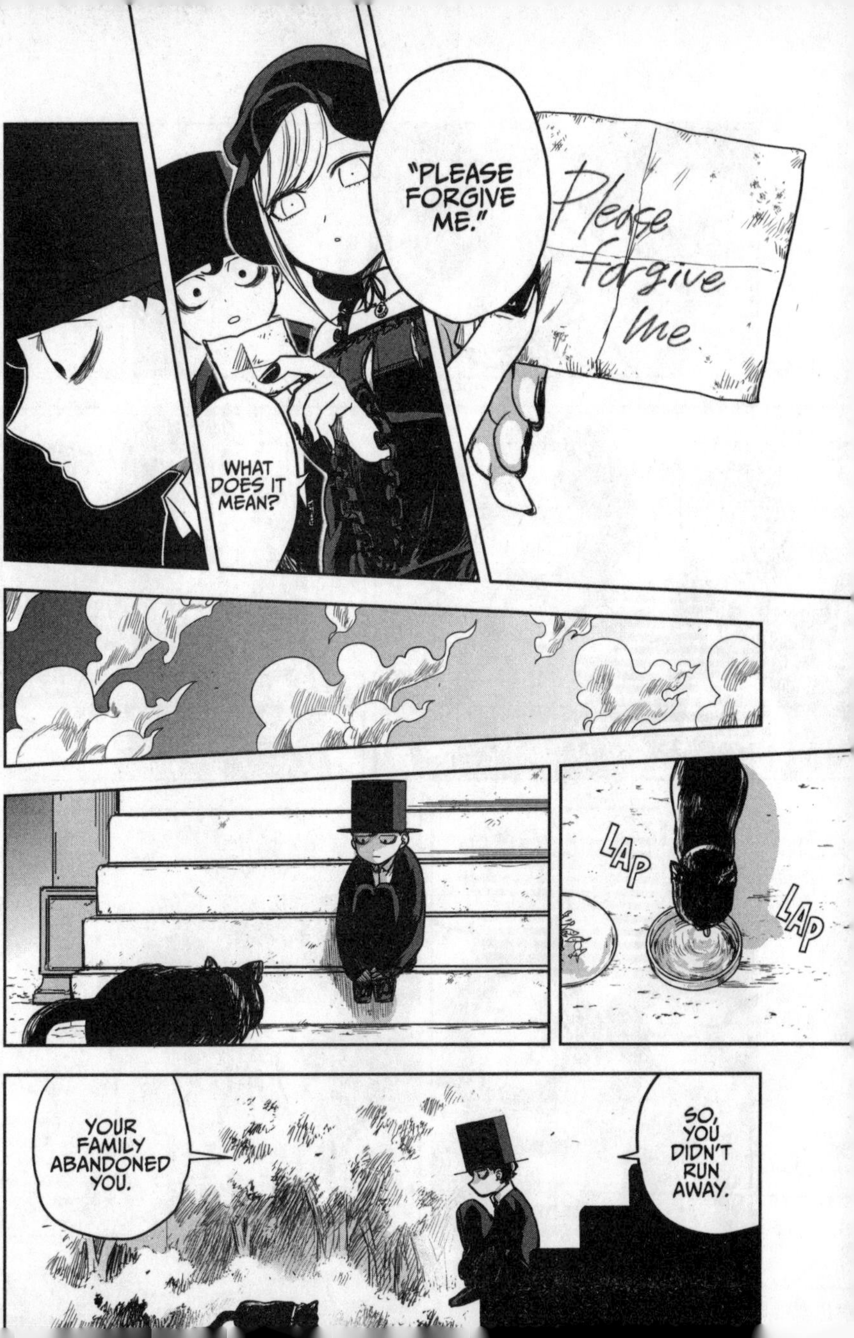
Please forgive me
"PLEASE FORGIVE ME."
WHAT DOES IT MEAN?
LAP
LAP
SO, YOU DIDN'T RUN AWAY.
YOUR FAMILY ABANDONED YOU.

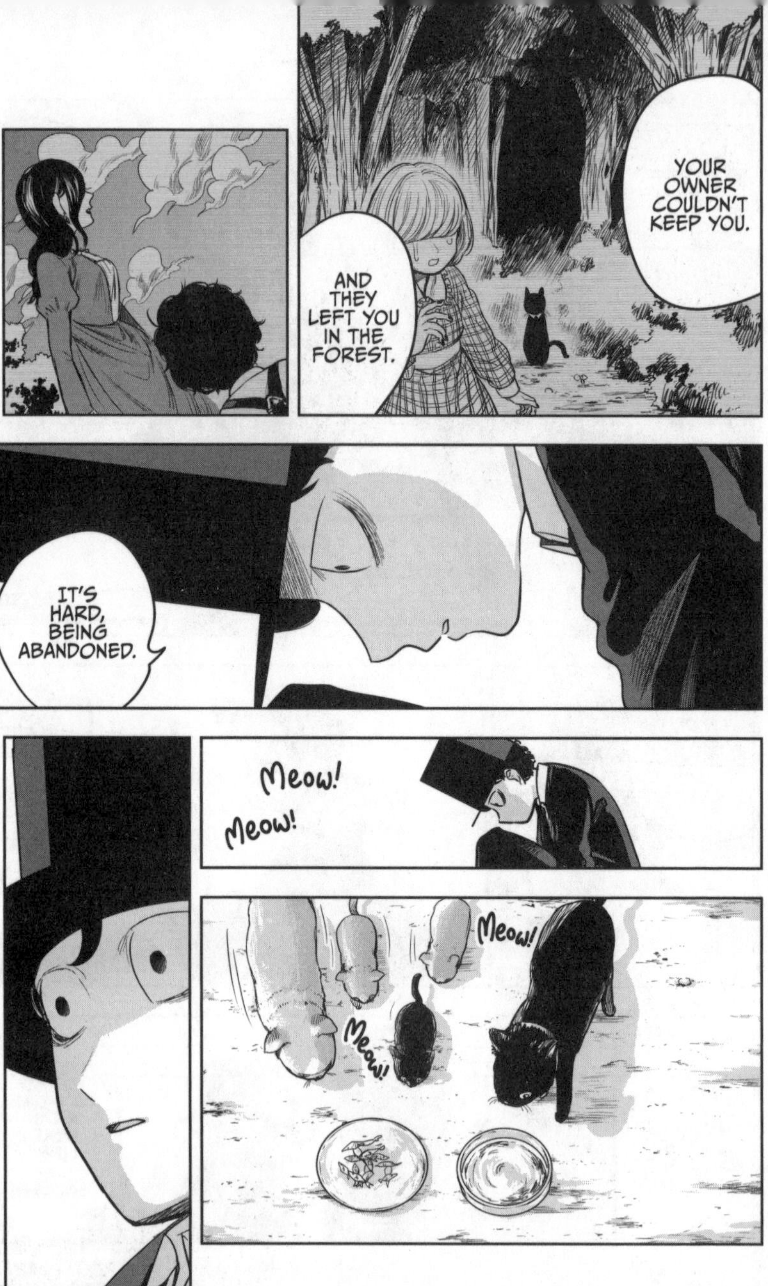
YOUR OWNER COULDN'T KEEP YOU.
AND THEY LEFT YOU IN THE FOREST.
IT'S HARD, BEING ABANDONED.
Meow!
Meow!
Meow!
Meow!

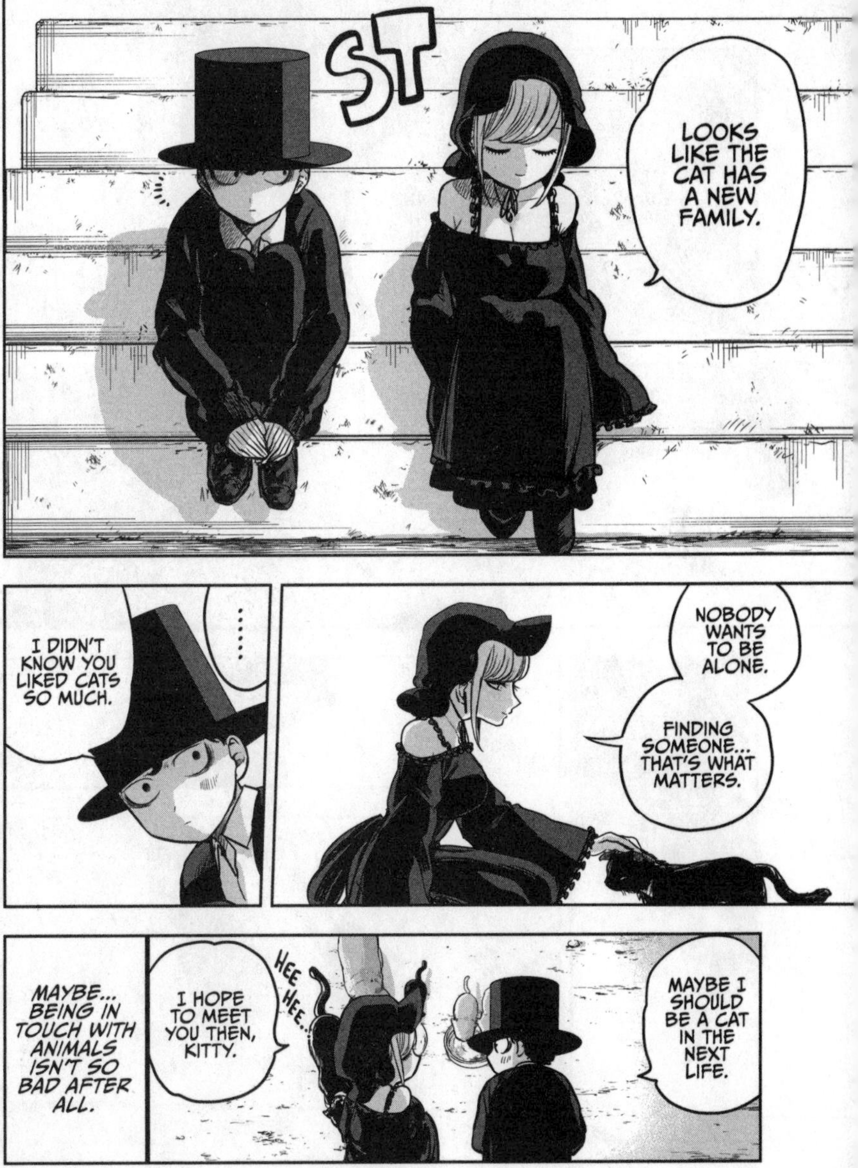
ST
LOOKS LIKE THE CAT HAS A NEW FAMILY.
NOBODY WANTS TO BE ALONE.
FINDING SOMEONE... THAT'S WHAT MATTERS.
......
I DIDN'T KNOW YOU LIKED CATS SO MUCH.
MAYBE I SHOULD BE A CAT IN THE NEXT LIFE.
HEE HEE...
I HOPE TO MEET YOU THEN, KITTY.
MAYBE... BEING IN TOUCH WITH ANIMALS ISN'T SO BAD AFTER ALL.

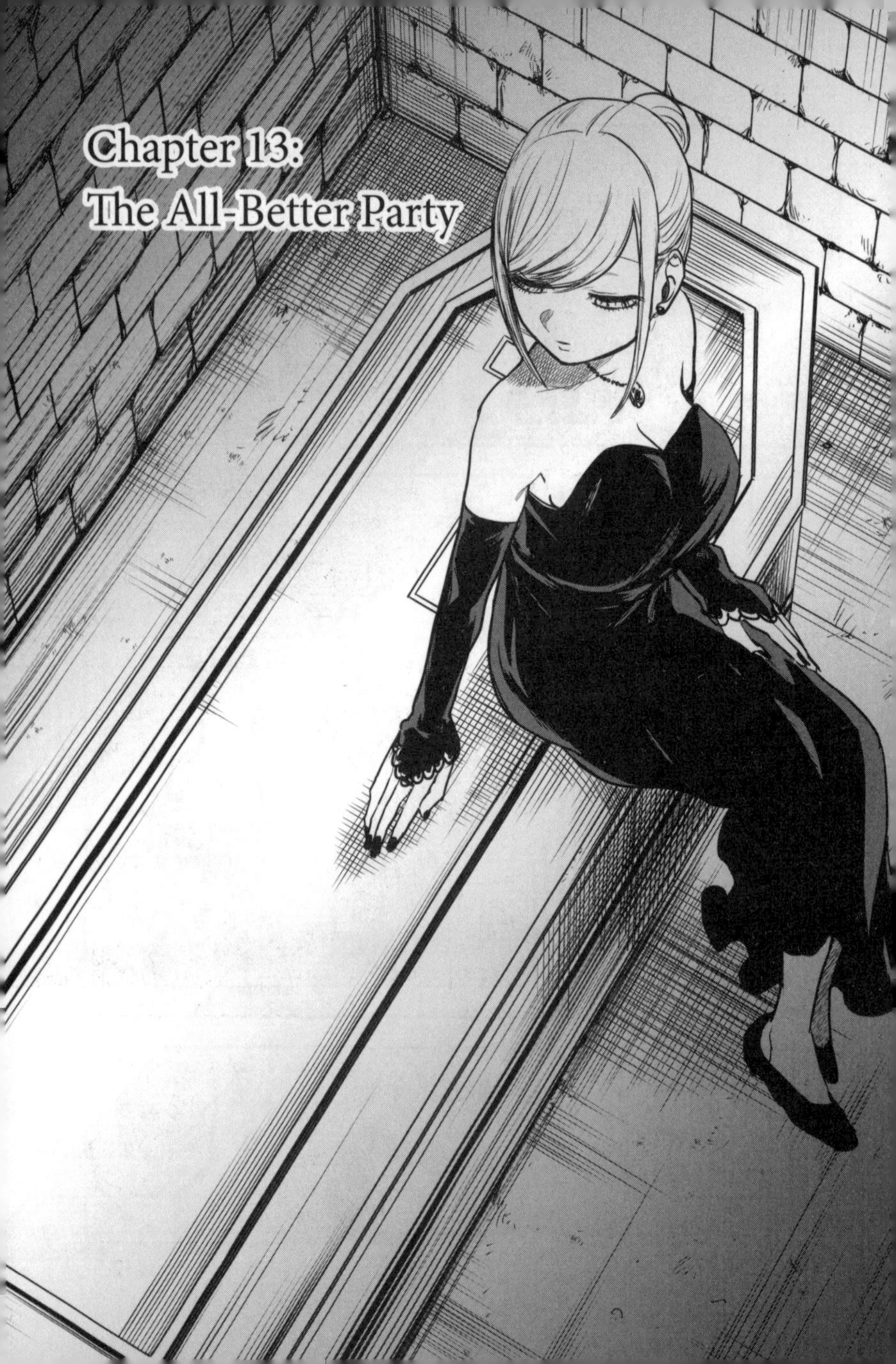
Chapter 13:
The All-Better Party

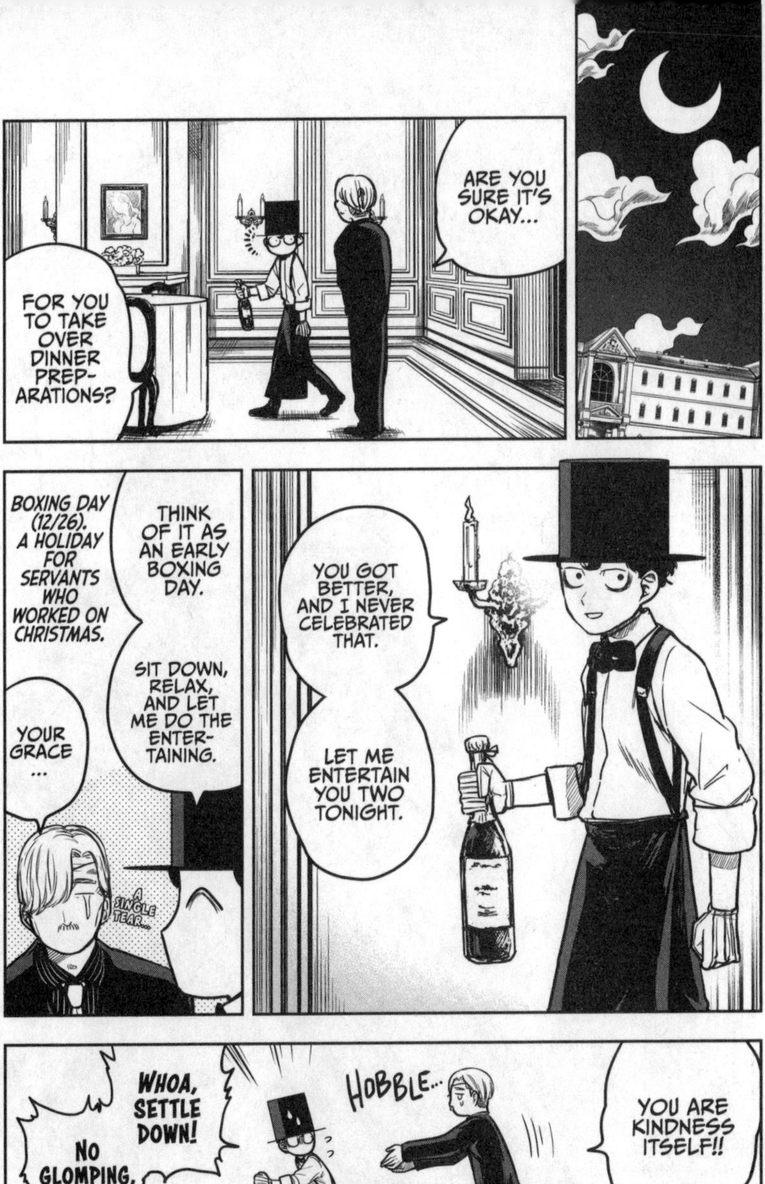
ARE YOU SURE IT'S OKAY...
FOR YOU TO TAKE OVER DINNER PREPARATIONS?
YOU GOT BETTER, AND I NEVER CELEBRATED THAT.
LET ME ENTERTAIN YOU TWO TONIGHT.
THINK OF IT AS AN EARLY BOXING DAY.
SIT DOWN, RELAX, AND LET ME DO THE ENTERTAINING.
BOXING DAY (12/26). A HOLIDAY FOR SERVANTS WHO WORKED ON CHRISTMAS.
YOUR GRACE ...
A SINGLE TEAR...
YOU ARE KINDNESS ITSELF!!
HOBBLE...
WHOA, SETTLE DOWN!
NO GLOMPING, GEEZER!!

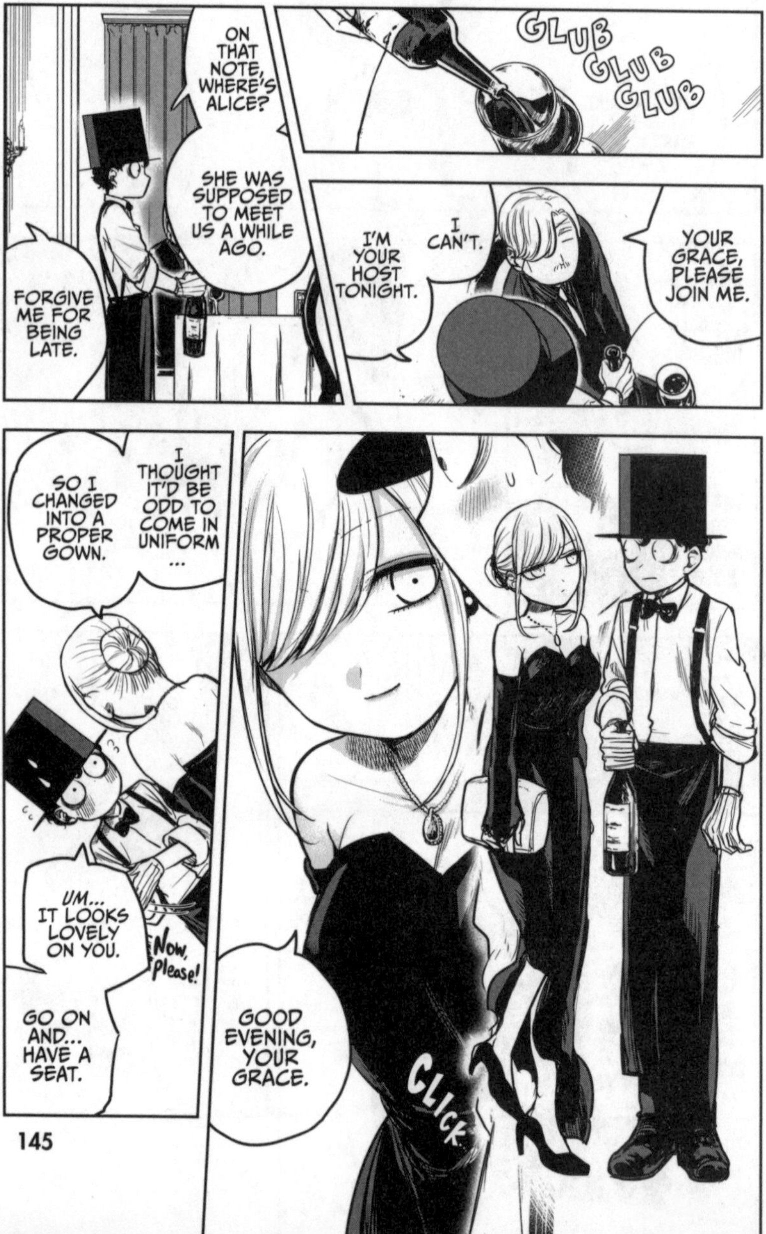
GLUB GLUB GLUB
YOUR GRACE, PLEASE JOIN ME.
I CAN'T.
I'M YOUR HOST TONIGHT.
ON THAT NOTE, WHERE'S ALICE?
SHE WAS SUPPOSED TO MEET US A WHILE AGO.
FORGIVE ME FOR BEING LATE.
GOOD EVENING, YOUR GRACE.
CLICK
I THOUGHT IT'D BE ODD TO COME IN UNIFORM ...
SO I CHANGED INTO A PROPER GOWN.
UM... IT LOOKS LOVELY ON YOU.
Now, please!
GO ON AND... HAVE A SEAT.

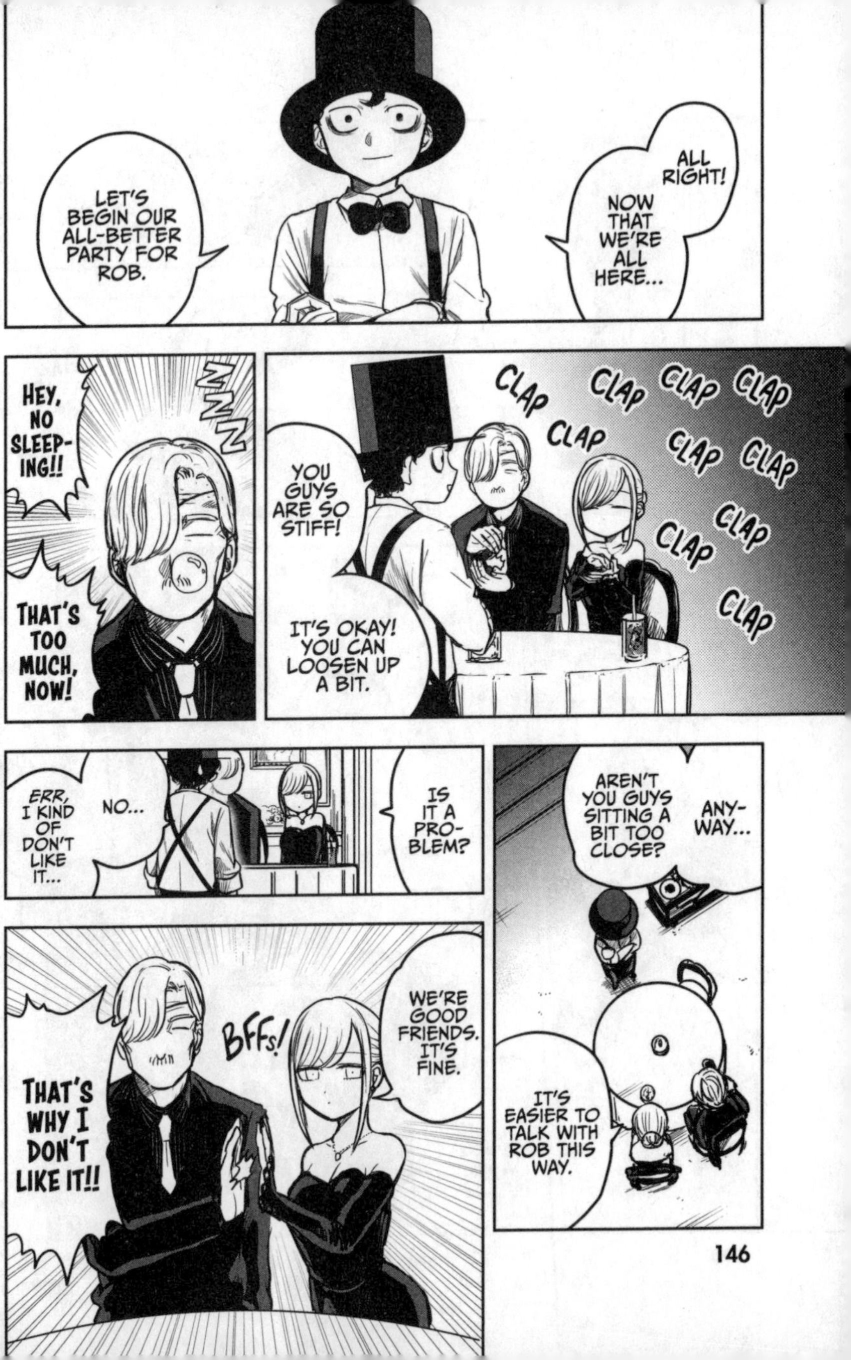

ALL RIGHT!
NOW THAT WE'RE ALL HERE...
LET'S BEGIN OUR ALL-BETTER PARTY FOR ROB.
CLAP CLAP CLAP CLAP
CLAP CLAP CLAP
CLAP CLAP
CLAP
YOU GUYS ARE SO STIFF!
IT'S OKAY! YOU CAN LOOSEN UP A BIT.
HEY, NO SLEEPING!!
THAT'S TOO MUCH, NOW!
ANY-WAY...
AREN'T YOU GUYS SITTING A BIT TOO CLOSE?
...
IT'S EASIER TO TALK WITH ROB THIS WAY.
IS IT A PRO-BLEM?
NO...
ERR, I KIND OF DON'T LIKE IT...
WE'RE GOOD FRIENDS. IT'S FINE.
BFFs!
THAT'S WHY I DON'T LIKE IT!!

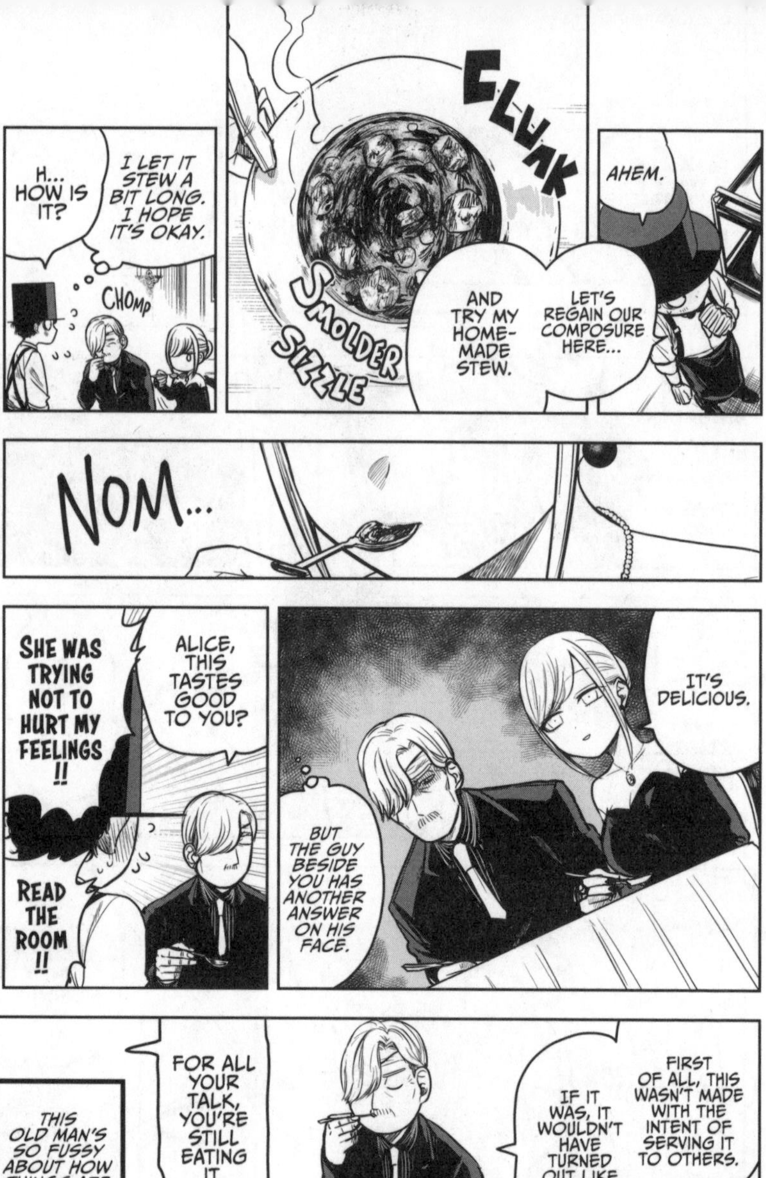
AHEM.
CLUNK
LET'S REGAIN OUR COMPOSURE HERE...
AND TRY MY HOMEMADE STEW.
SMOLDER
SIZZLE
I LET IT STEW A BIT LONG. I HOPE IT'S OKAY.
H... HOW IS IT?
CHOMP
NOM...
IT'S DELICIOUS.
BUT THE GUY BESIDE YOU HAS ANOTHER ANSWER ON HIS FACE.
ALICE, THIS TASTES GOOD TO YOU?
SHE WAS TRYING NOT TO HURT MY FEELINGS!!
READ THE ROOM!!
FIRST OF ALL, THIS WASN'T MADE WITH THE INTENT OF SERVING IT TO OTHERS.
IF IT WAS, IT WOULDN'T HAVE TURNED OUT LIKE THIS.
FOR ALL YOUR TALK, YOU'RE STILL EATING IT.
THIS OLD MAN'S SO FUSSY ABOUT HOW THINGS ARE DONE.

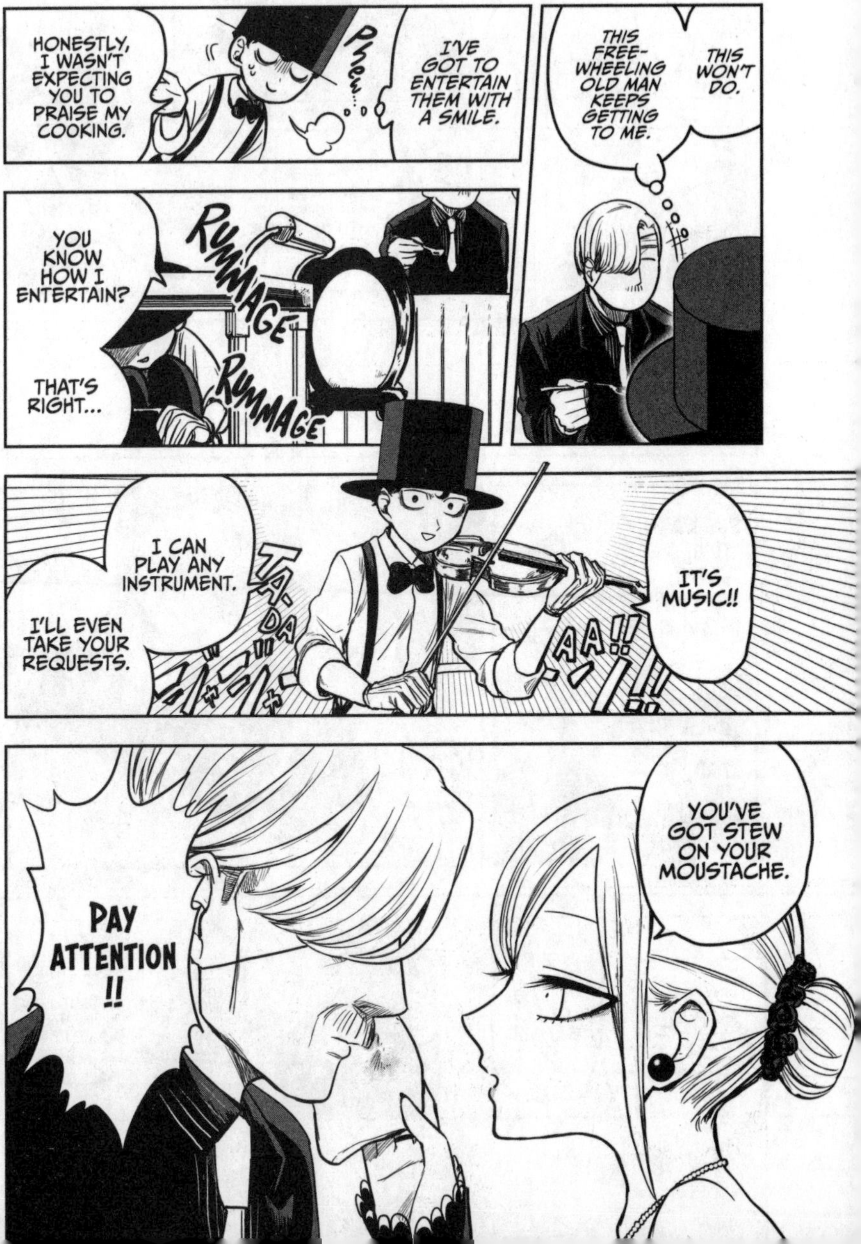
THIS WON'T DO.
THIS FREE-WHEELING OLD MAN KEEPS GETTING TO ME.
I'VE GOT TO ENTERTAIN THEM WITH A SMILE.
Phew...
HONESTLY, I WASN'T EXPECTING YOU TO PRAISE MY COOKING.
RUMMAGE
RUMMAGE
YOU KNOW HOW I ENTERTAIN?
THAT'S RIGHT...
IT'S MUSIC!!
AA!!
TA-DA!!
I CAN PLAY ANY INSTRUMENT.
I'LL EVEN TAKE YOUR REQUESTS.
YOU'VE GOT STEW ON YOUR MOUSTACHE.
PAY ATTENTION !!

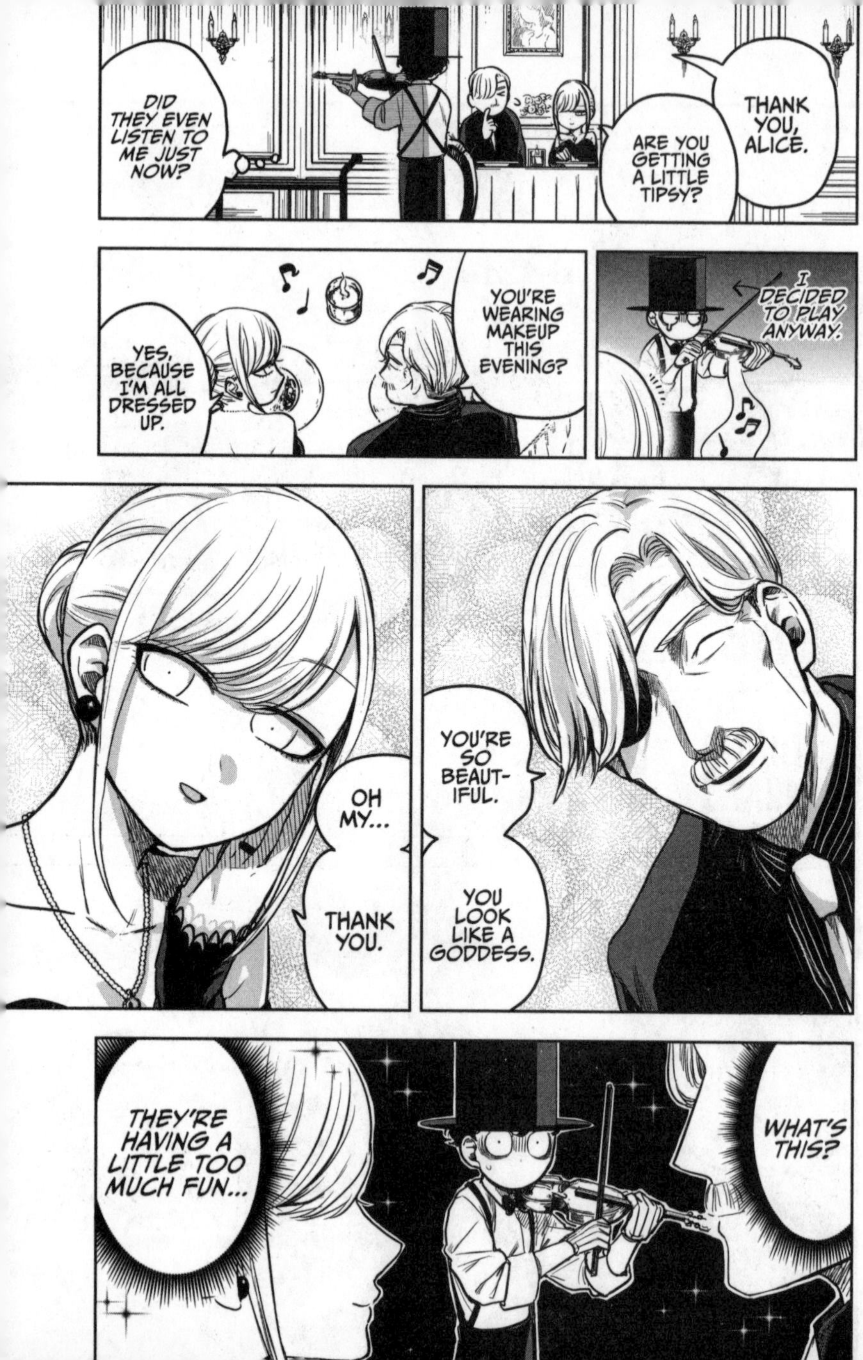

THANK YOU, ALICE.
ARE YOU GETTING A LITTLE TIPSY?
DID THEY EVEN LISTEN TO ME JUST NOW?
I DECIDED TO PLAY ANYWAY.
YOU'RE WEARING MAKEUP THIS EVENING?
YES, BECAUSE I'M ALL DRESSED UP.
YOU'RE SO BEAUTIFUL.
YOU LOOK LIKE A GODDESS.
OH MY...
THANK YOU.
WHAT'S THIS?
THEY'RE HAVING A LITTLE TOO MUCH FUN...

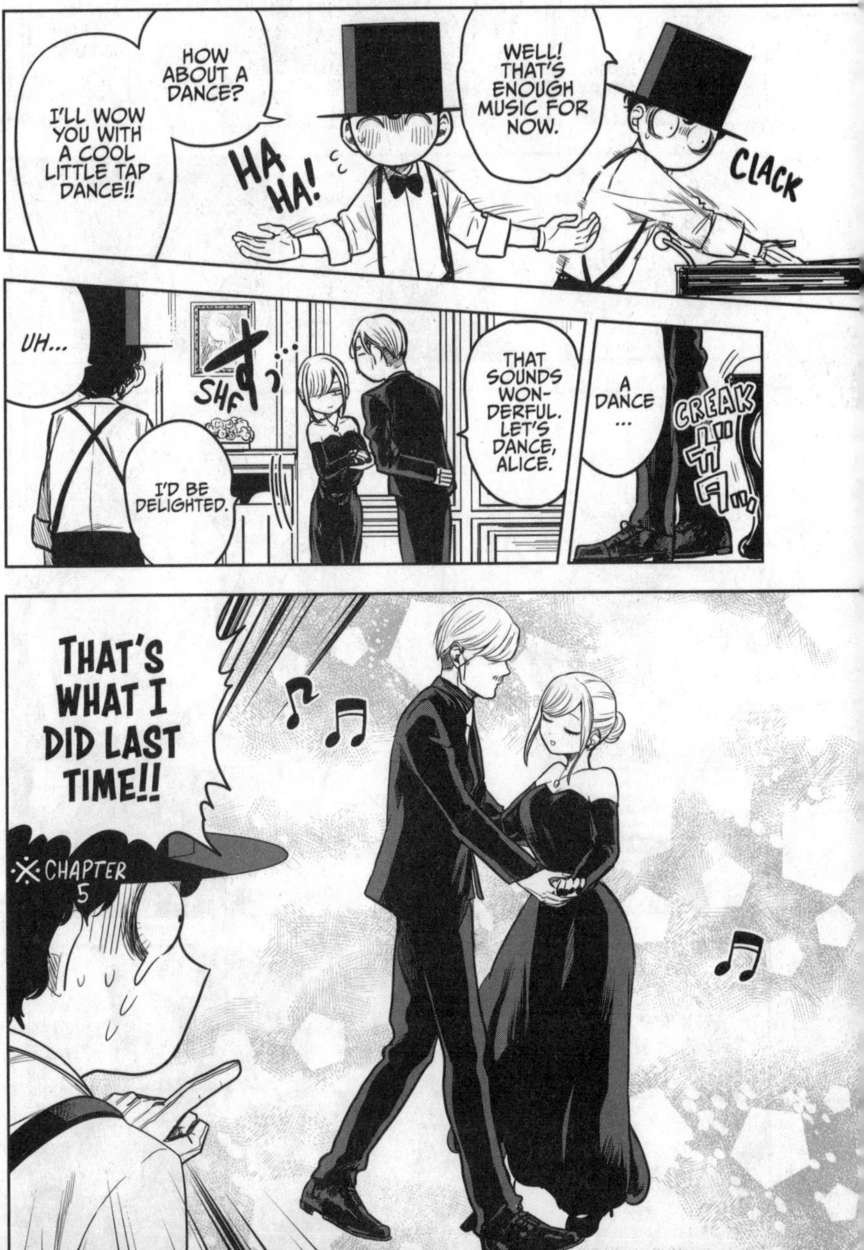
CLACK
WELL! THAT'S ENOUGH MUSIC FOR NOW.
HA HA!
HOW ABOUT A DANCE?
I'LL WOW YOU WITH A COOL LITTLE TAP DANCE!!
CREAK
A DANCE ...
THAT SOUNDS WON-DERFUL. LET'S DANCE, ALICE.
SHF
I'D BE DELIGHTED.
UH...
THAT'S WHAT I DID LAST TIME!!
※CHAPTER 5

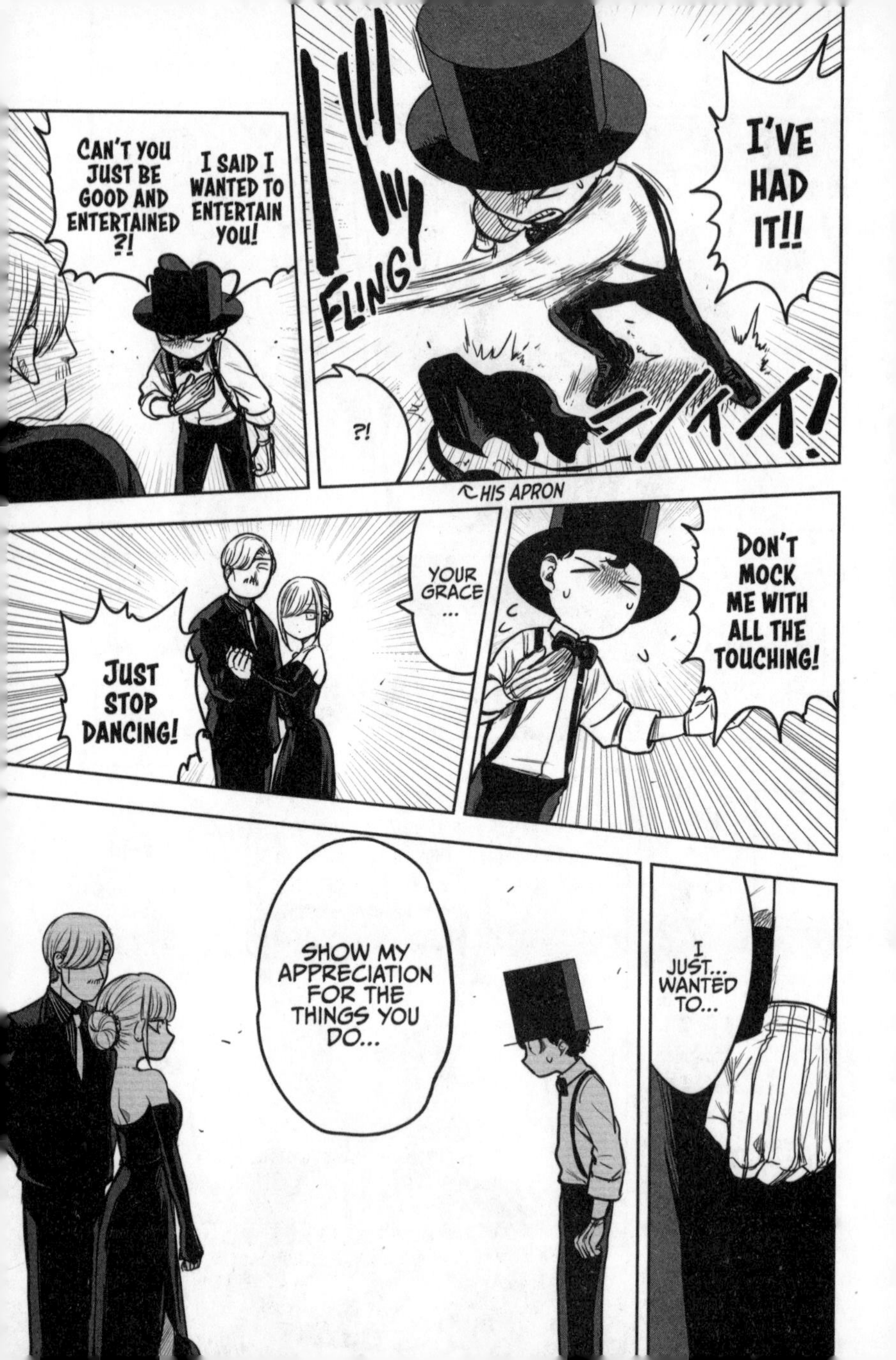
I'VE HAD IT!!
FLING
?!
HIS APRON
I SAID I WANTED TO ENTERTAIN YOU!
CAN'T YOU JUST BE GOOD AND ENTERTAINED ?!
DON'T MOCK ME WITH ALL THE TOUCHING!
YOUR GRACE ...
JUST STOP DANCING!
I JUST... WANTED TO...
SHOW MY APPRECIATION FOR THE THINGS YOU DO...

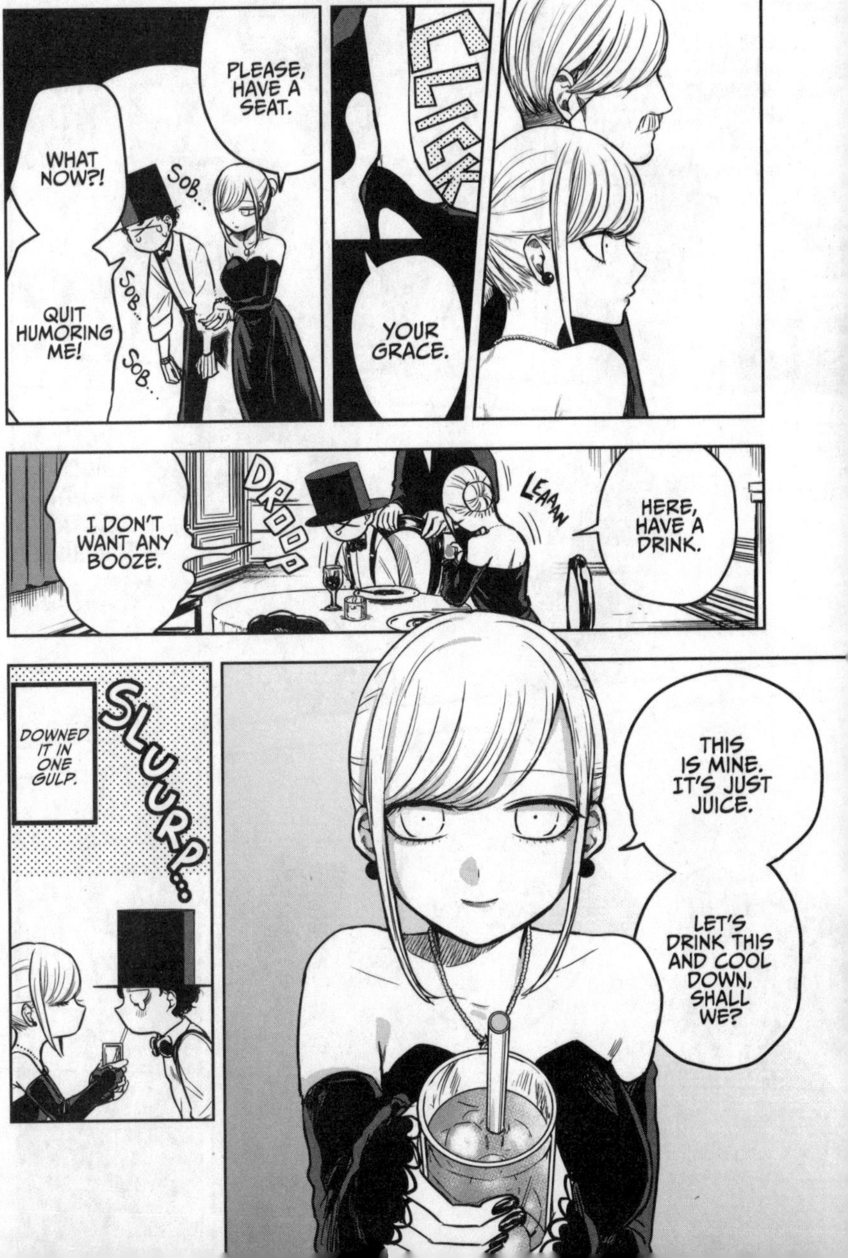
CLICK
YOUR GRACE.
PLEASE, HAVE A SEAT.
SOB...
SOB...
SOB...
WHAT NOW?!
QUIT HUMORING ME!
HERE, HAVE A DRINK.
LEAAAN
DROOP
I DON'T WANT ANY BOOZE.
THIS IS MINE. IT'S JUST JUICE.
LET'S DRINK THIS AND COOL DOWN, SHALL WE?
DOWNED IT IN ONE GULP.
SLURP...

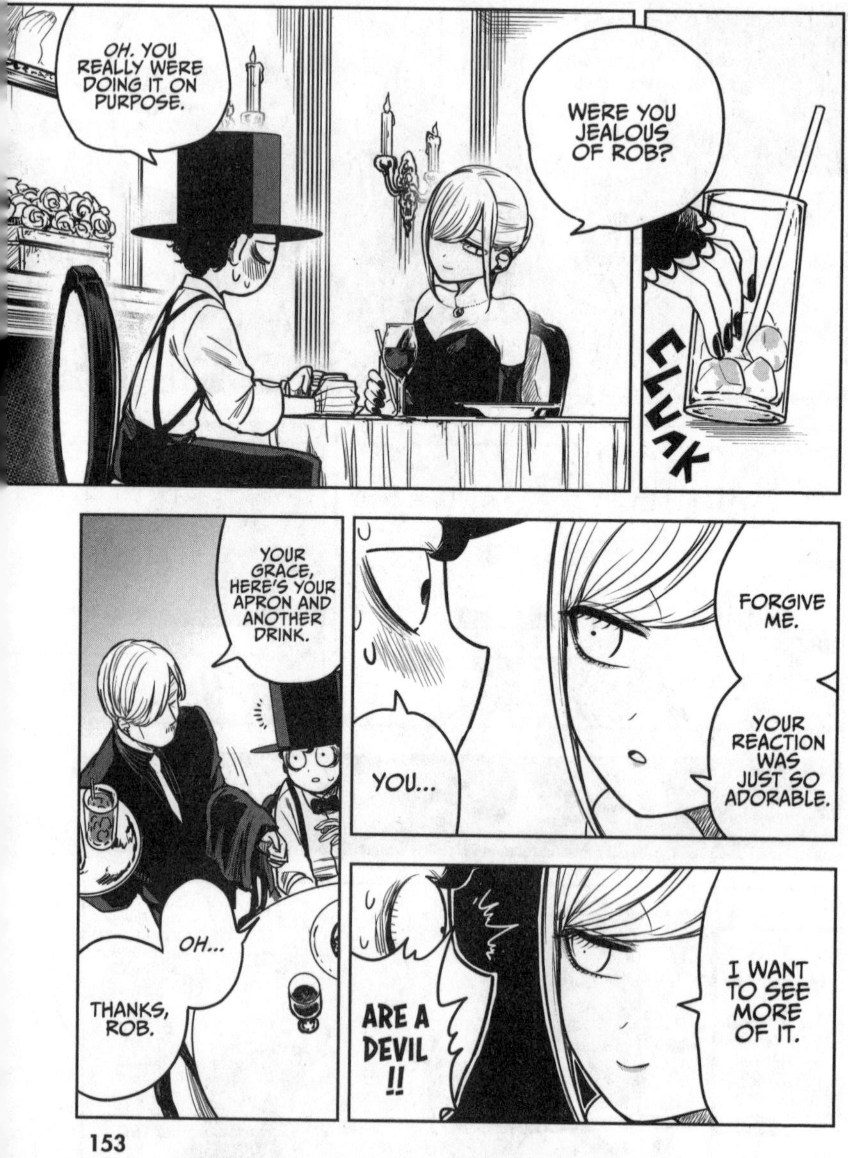
WERE YOU JEALOUS OF ROB?
CLUNK
OH. YOU REALLY WERE DOING IT ON PURPOSE.
FORGIVE ME.
YOUR REACTION WAS JUST SO ADORABLE.
YOU...
I WANT TO SEE MORE OF IT.
ARE A DEVIL !!
YOUR GRACE, HERE'S YOUR APRON AND ANOTHER DRINK.
OH...
THANKS, ROB.

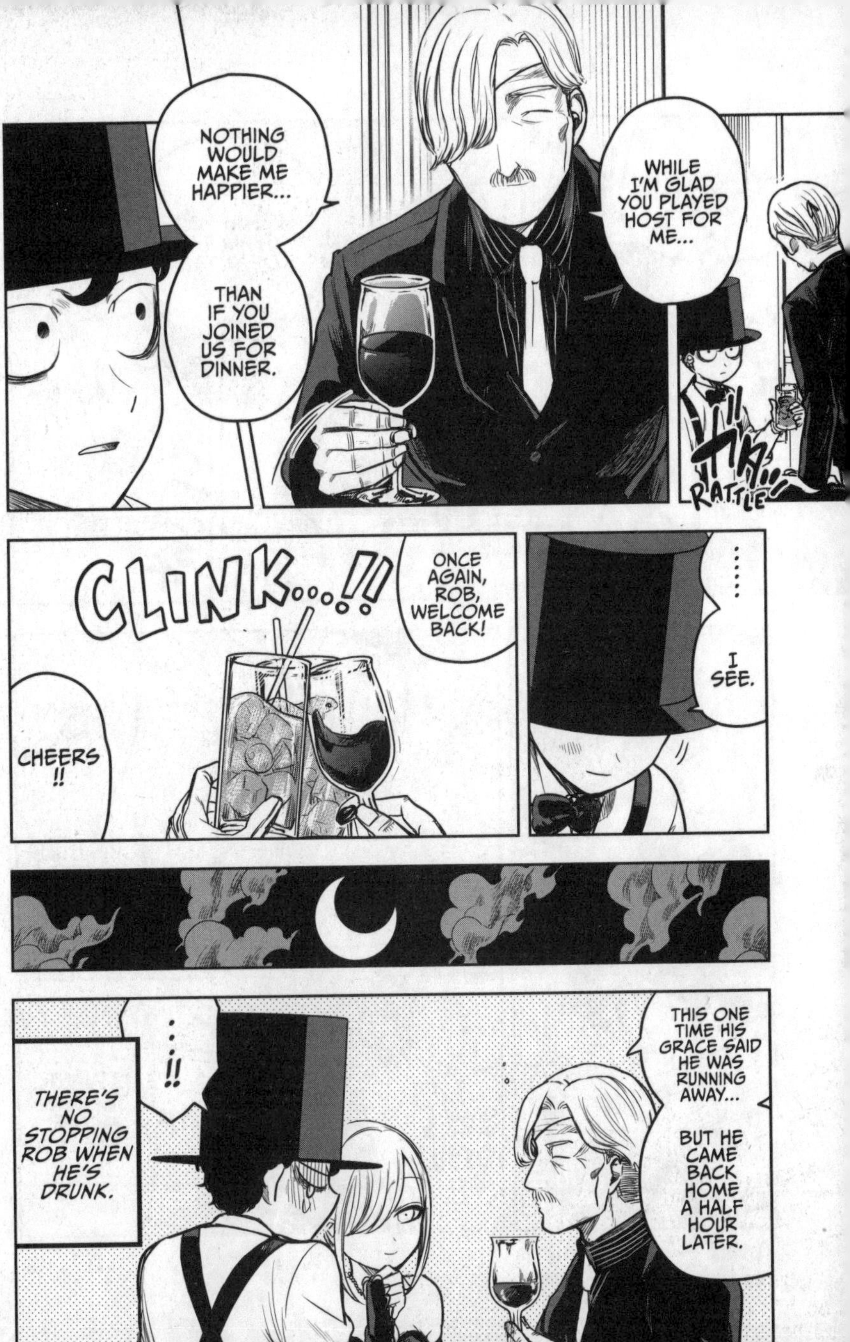
WHILE I'M GLAD YOU PLAYED HOST FOR ME...
NOTHING WOULD MAKE ME HAPPIER...
THAN IF YOU JOINED US FOR DINNER.
RATTLE
......
I SEE.
ONCE AGAIN, ROB, WELCOME BACK!
CLINK...!!
CHEERS!!
THIS ONE TIME HIS GRACE SAID HE WAS RUNNING AWAY...
BUT HE CAME BACK HOME A HALF HOUR LATER.
...!!
THERE'S NO STOPPING ROB WHEN HE'S DRUNK.

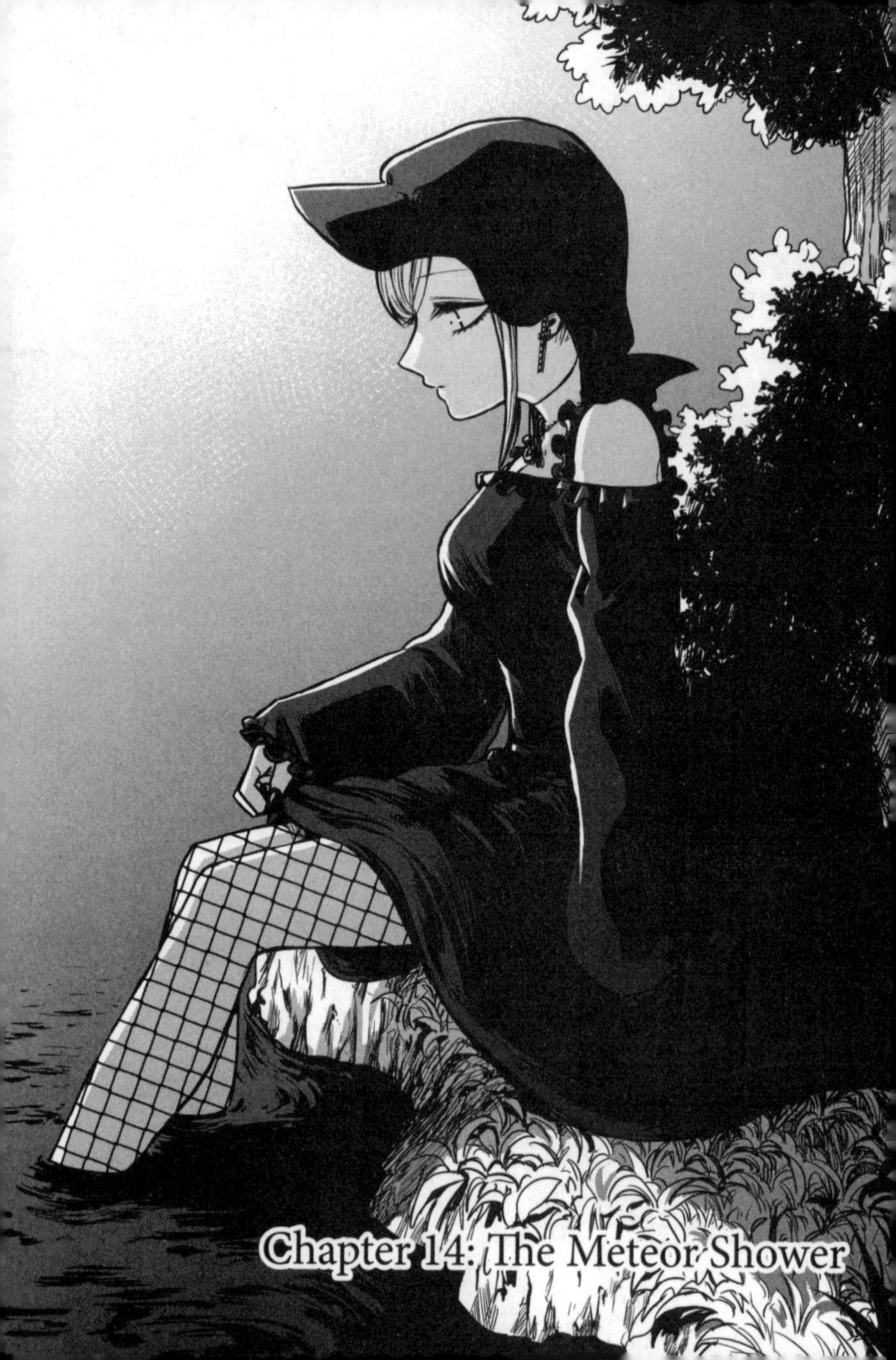
Chapter 14: The Meteor Shower

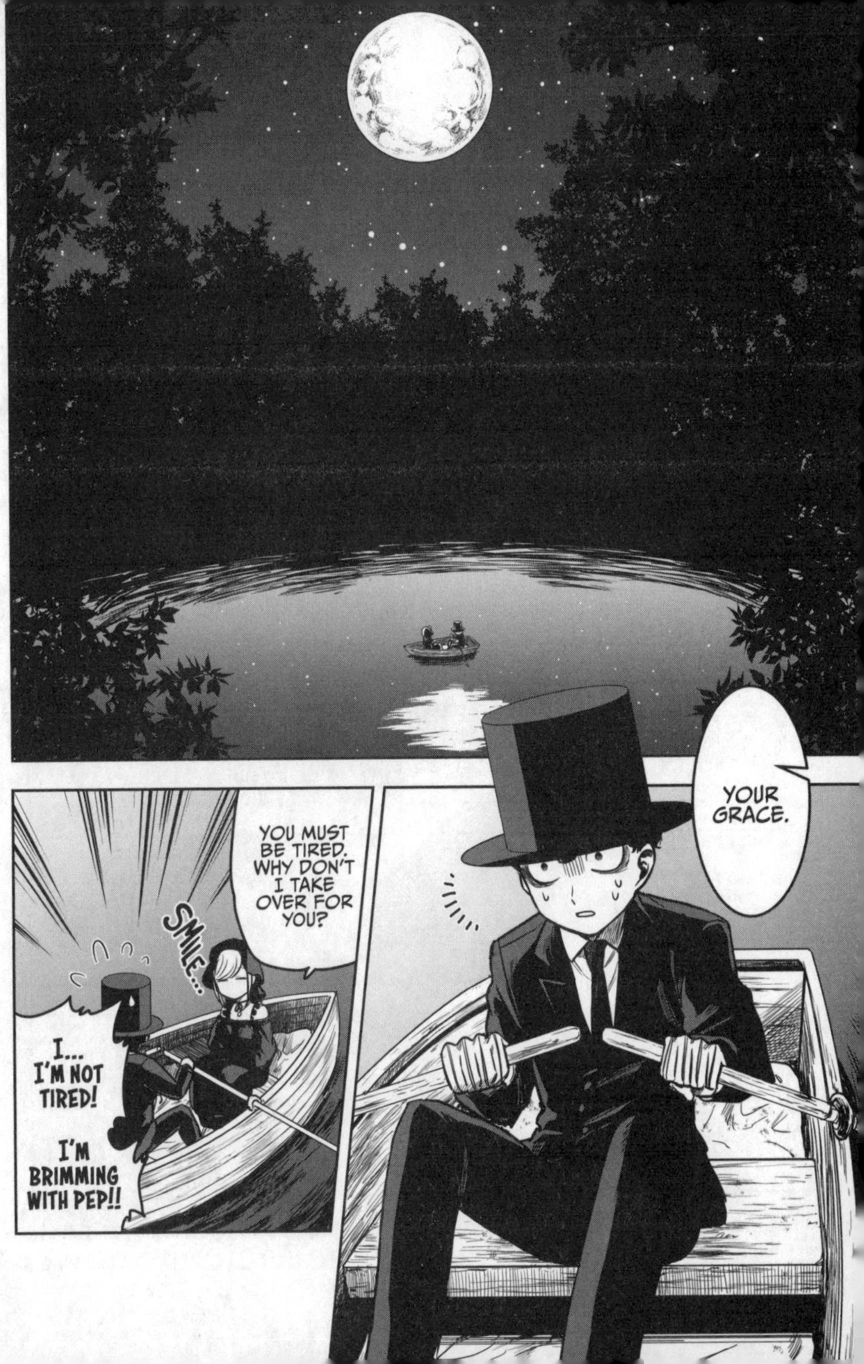
YOUR GRACE.
YOU MUST BE TIRED. WHY DON'T I TAKE OVER FOR YOU?
SMILE...
I... I'M NOT TIRED!
I'M BRIMMING WITH PEP!!

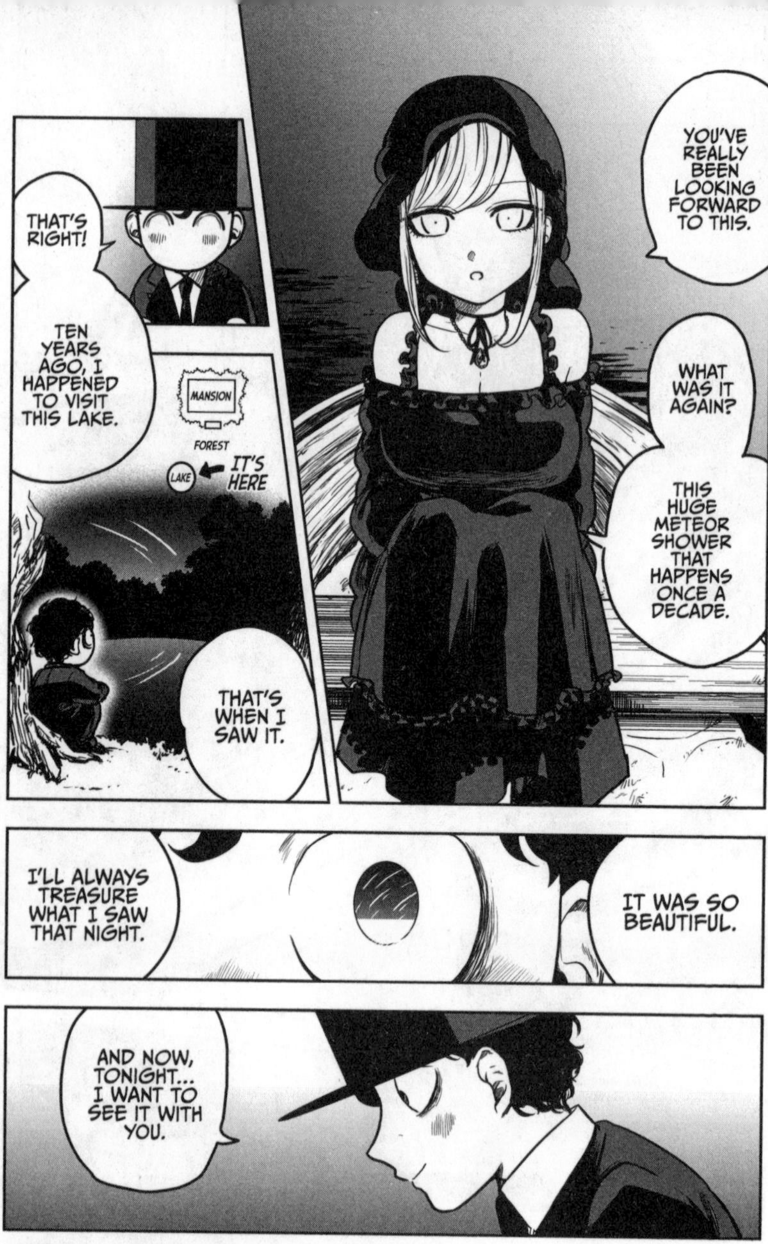
YOU'VE REALLY BEEN LOOKING FORWARD TO THIS.
WHAT WAS IT AGAIN?
THIS HUGE METEOR SHOWER THAT HAPPENS ONCE A DECADE.
THAT'S RIGHT!
TEN YEARS AGO, I HAPPENED TO VISIT THIS LAKE.
MANSION
FOREST
LAKE
IT'S HERE
THAT'S WHEN I SAW IT.
IT WAS SO BEAUTIFUL.
I'LL ALWAYS TREASURE WHAT I SAW THAT NIGHT.
AND NOW, TONIGHT... I WANT TO SEE IT WITH YOU.

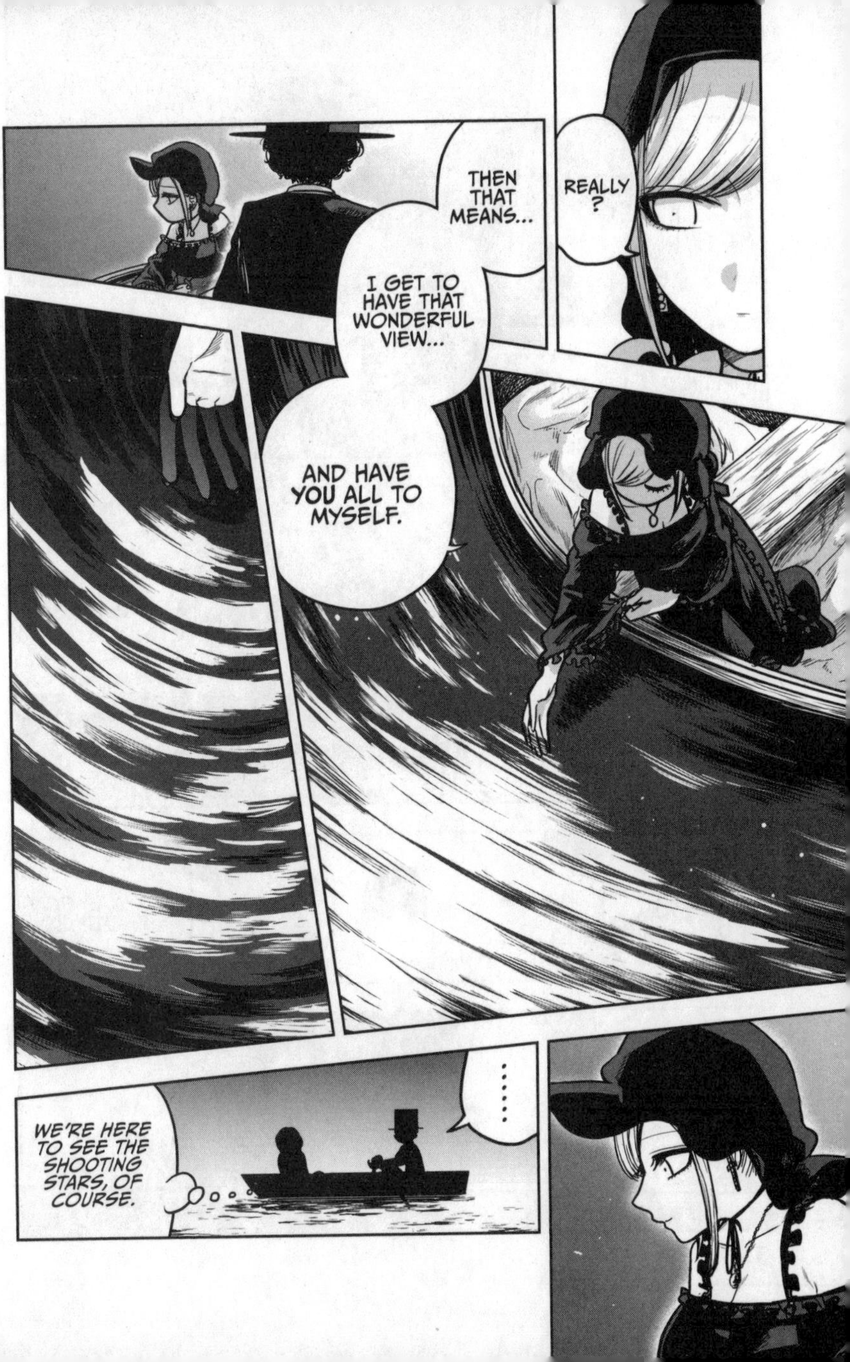
REALLY?
THEN THAT MEANS...
I GET TO HAVE THAT WONDERFUL VIEW...
AND HAVE YOU ALL TO MYSELF.
......
WE'RE HERE TO SEE THE SHOOTING STARS, OF COURSE.

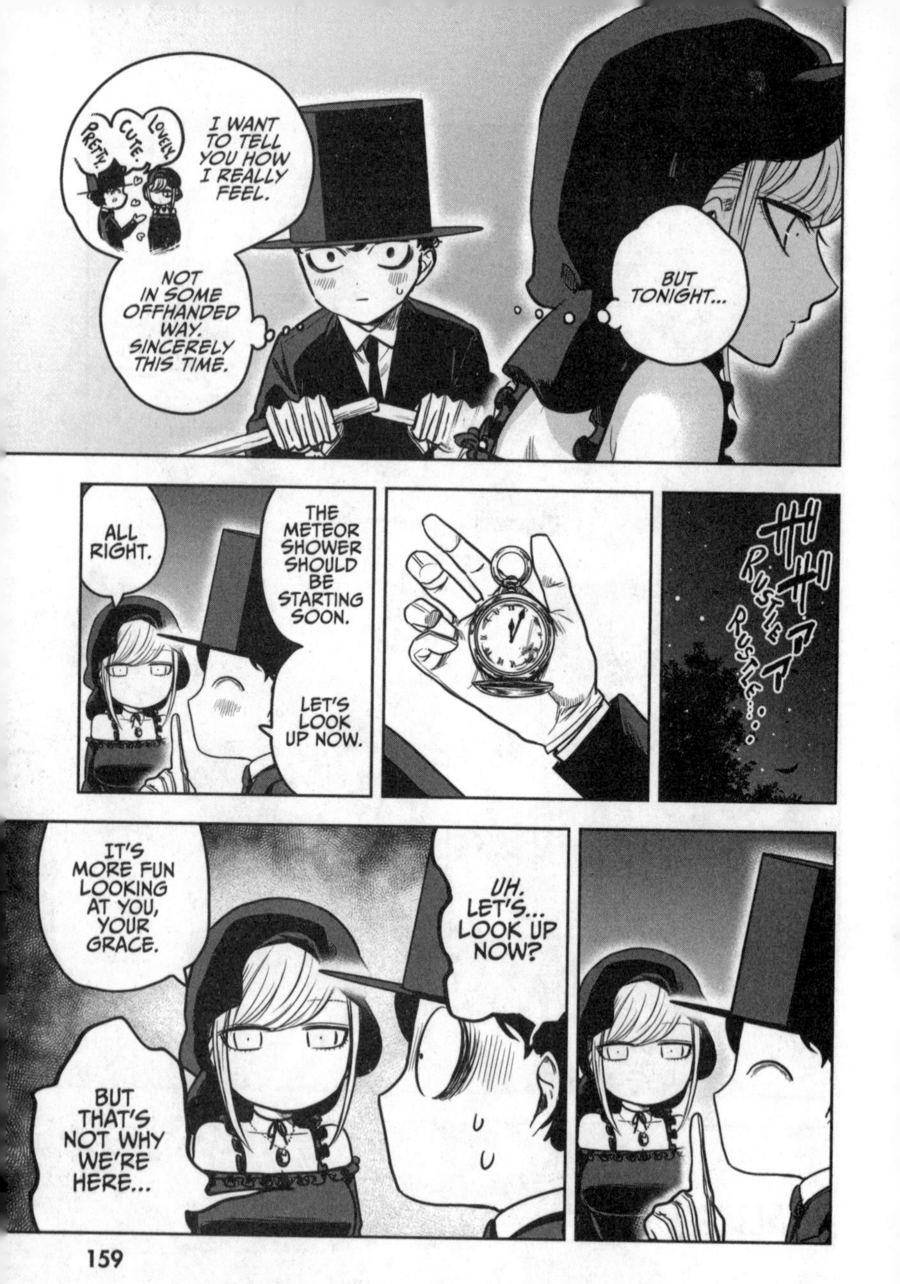
BUT TONIGHT...
I WANT TO TELL YOU HOW I REALLY FEEL.
LOVELY. CUTE. PRETTY.
NOT IN SOME OFFHANDED WAY. SINCERELY THIS TIME.
ザザァ
RUSTLE RUSTLE...
THE METEOR SHOWER SHOULD BE STARTING SOON.
LET'S LOOK UP NOW.
ALL RIGHT.
UH. LET'S... LOOK UP NOW?
IT'S MORE FUN LOOKING AT YOU, YOUR GRACE.
BUT THAT'S NOT WHY WE'RE HERE...

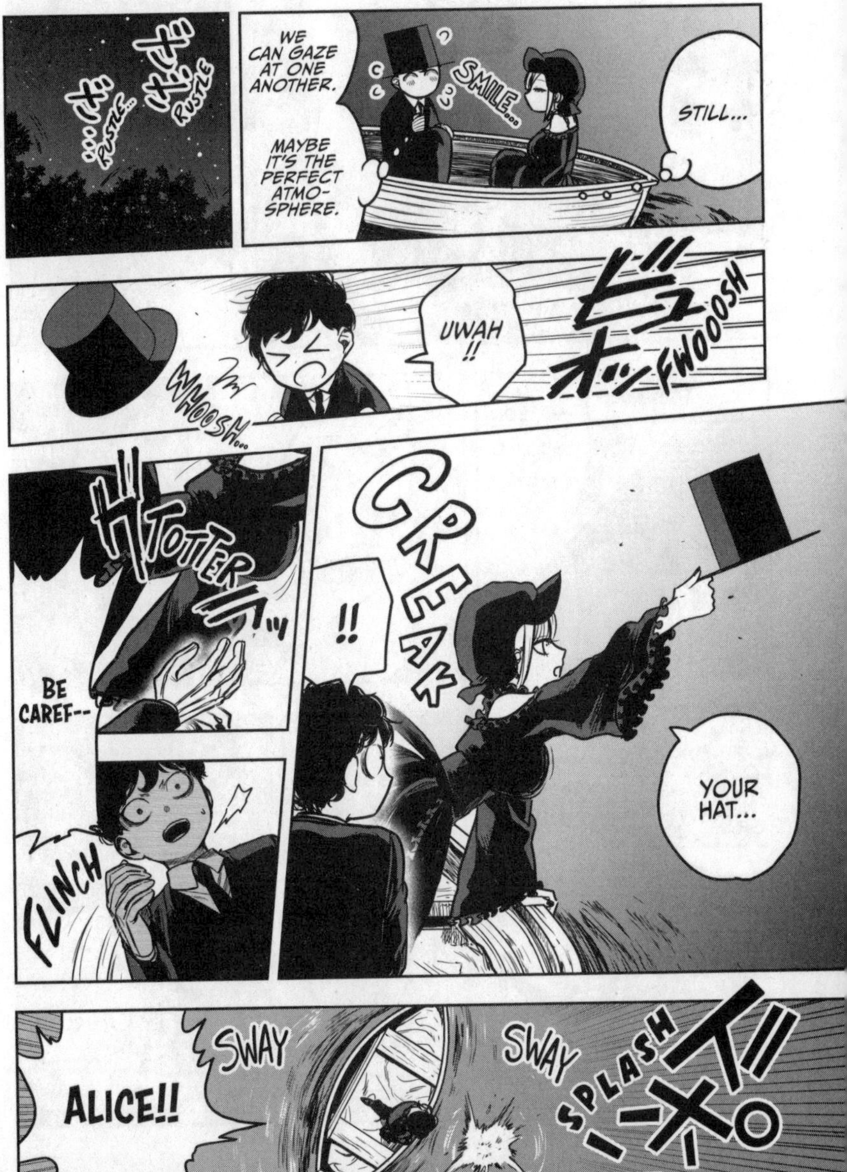
STILL...
SMILE...
WE CAN GAZE AT ONE ANOTHER.
MAYBE IT'S THE PERFECT ATMOSPHERE.
RUSTLE
...RUSTLE...
FWOOOSH
UWAH !!
WHOOSH...
CREAK
!!
YOUR HAT...
TOTTER
BE CAREF--
FLINCH
SPLASH
SWAY
SWAY
ALICE!!

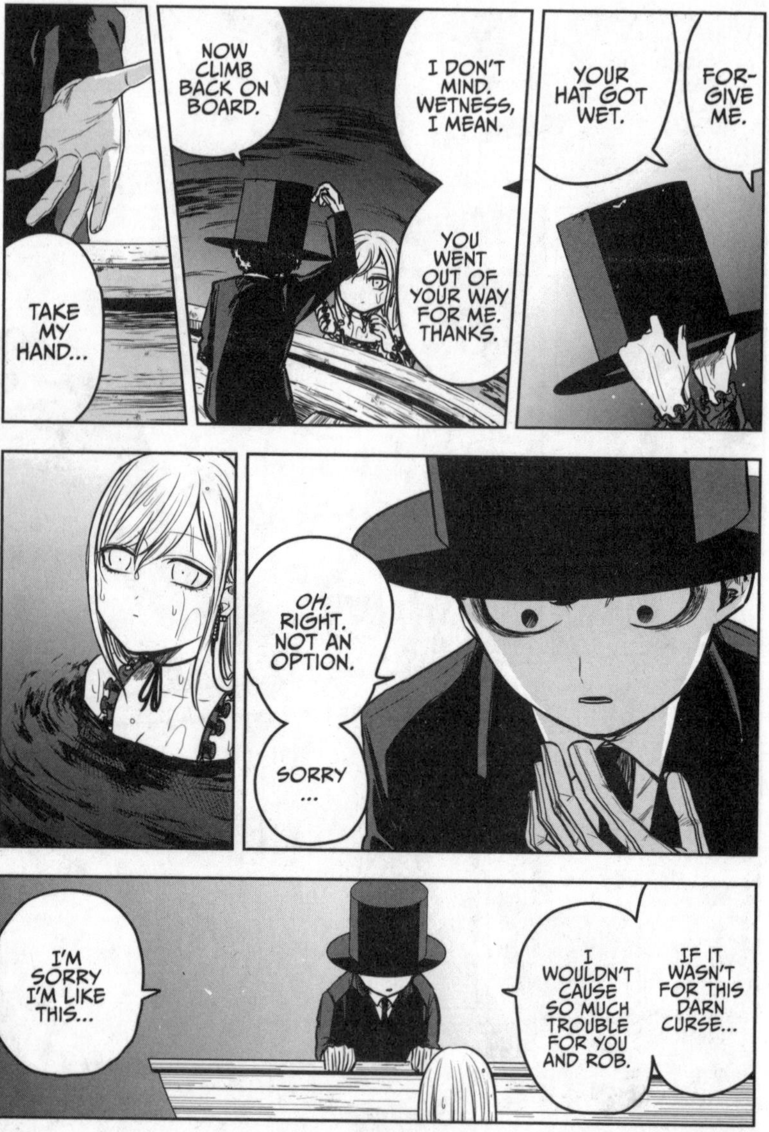
FOR-GIVE ME.
YOUR HAT GOT WET.
I DON'T MIND. WETNESS, I MEAN.
YOU WENT OUT OF YOUR WAY FOR ME. THANKS.
NOW CLIMB BACK ON BOARD.
TAKE MY HAND...
OH. RIGHT. NOT AN OPTION.
SORRY ...
IF IT WASN'T FOR THIS DARN CURSE...
I WOULDN'T CAUSE SO MUCH TROUBLE FOR YOU AND ROB.
I'M SORRY I'M LIKE THIS...

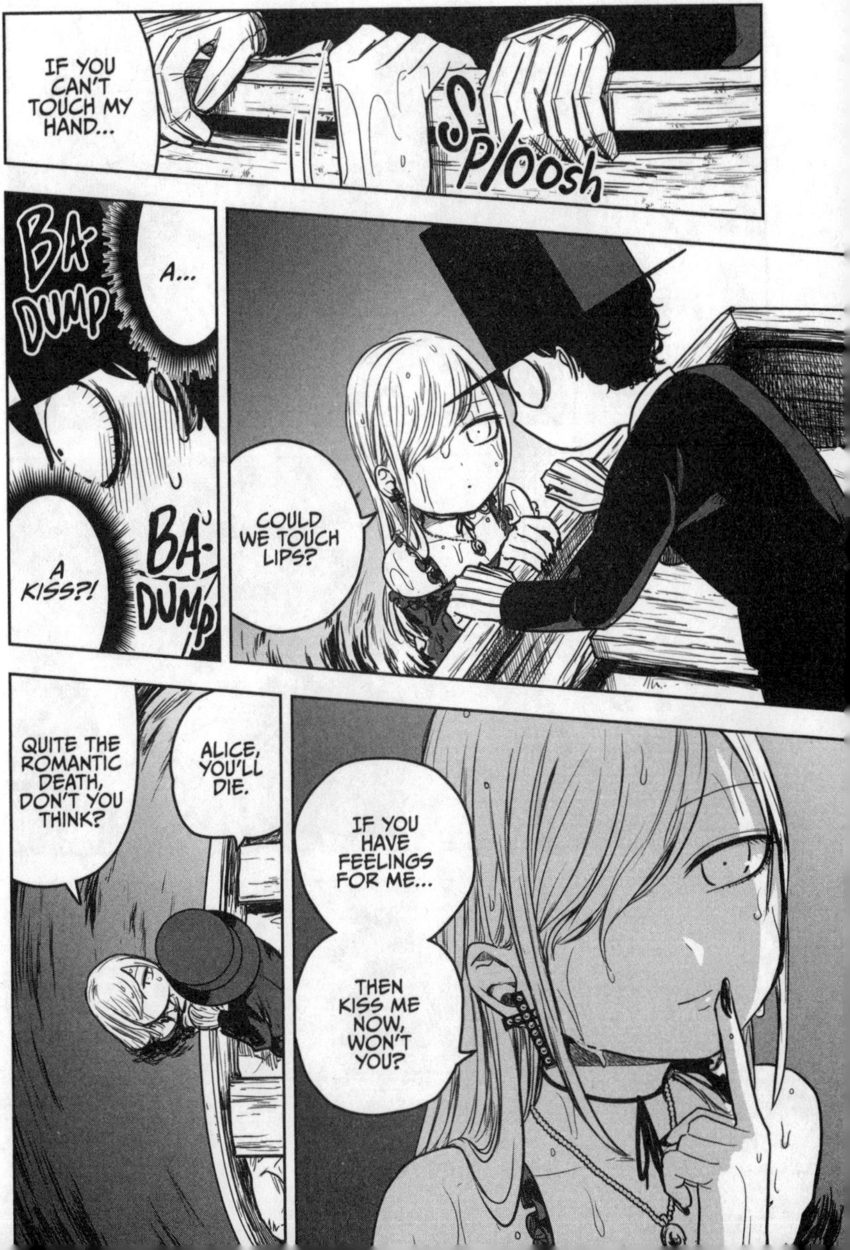
IF YOU CAN'T TOUCH MY HAND...
SPLOOSH
COULD WE TOUCH LIPS?
A...
BA-DUMP
A KISS?!
BA-DUMP
IF YOU HAVE FEELINGS FOR ME...
THEN KISS ME NOW, WON'T YOU?
ALICE, YOU'LL DIE.
QUITE THE ROMANTIC DEATH, DON'T YOU THINK?

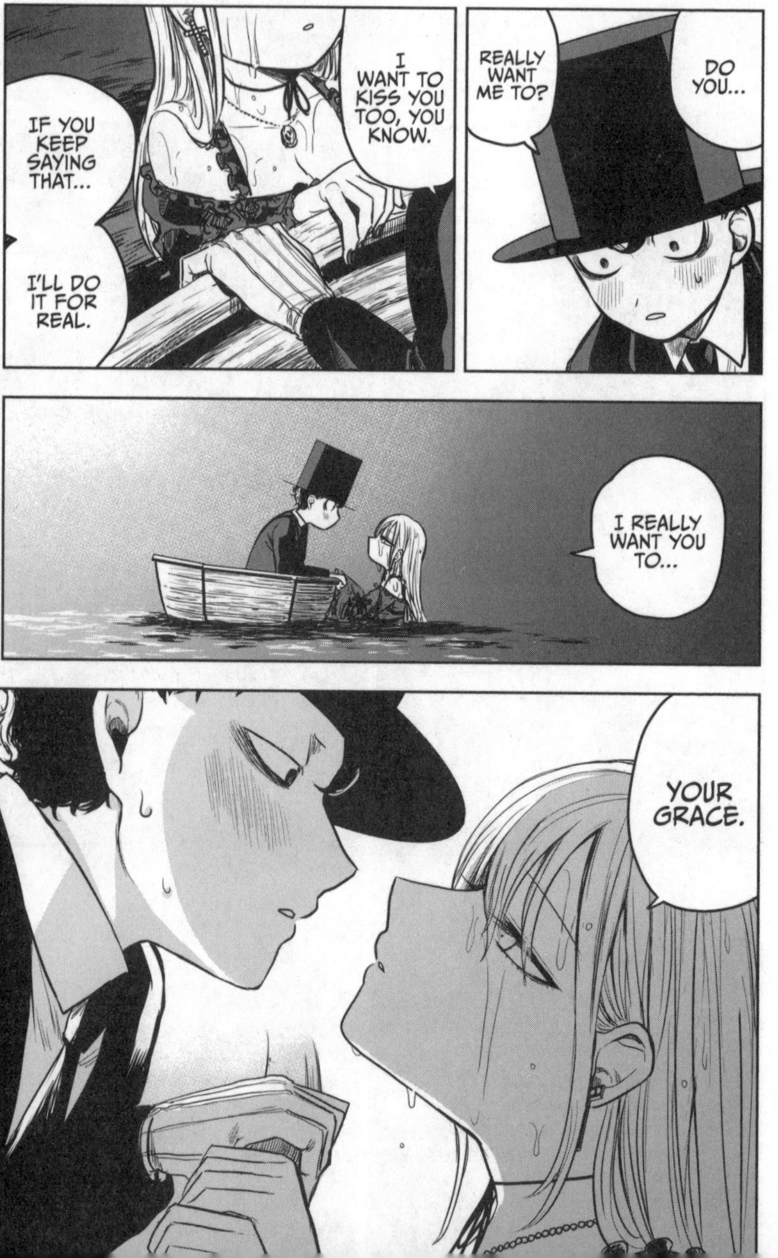
DO YOU...
REALLY WANT ME TO?
I WANT TO KISS YOU TOO, YOU KNOW.
IF YOU KEEP SAYING THAT...
I'LL DO IT FOR REAL.
I REALLY WANT YOU TO...
YOUR GRACE.

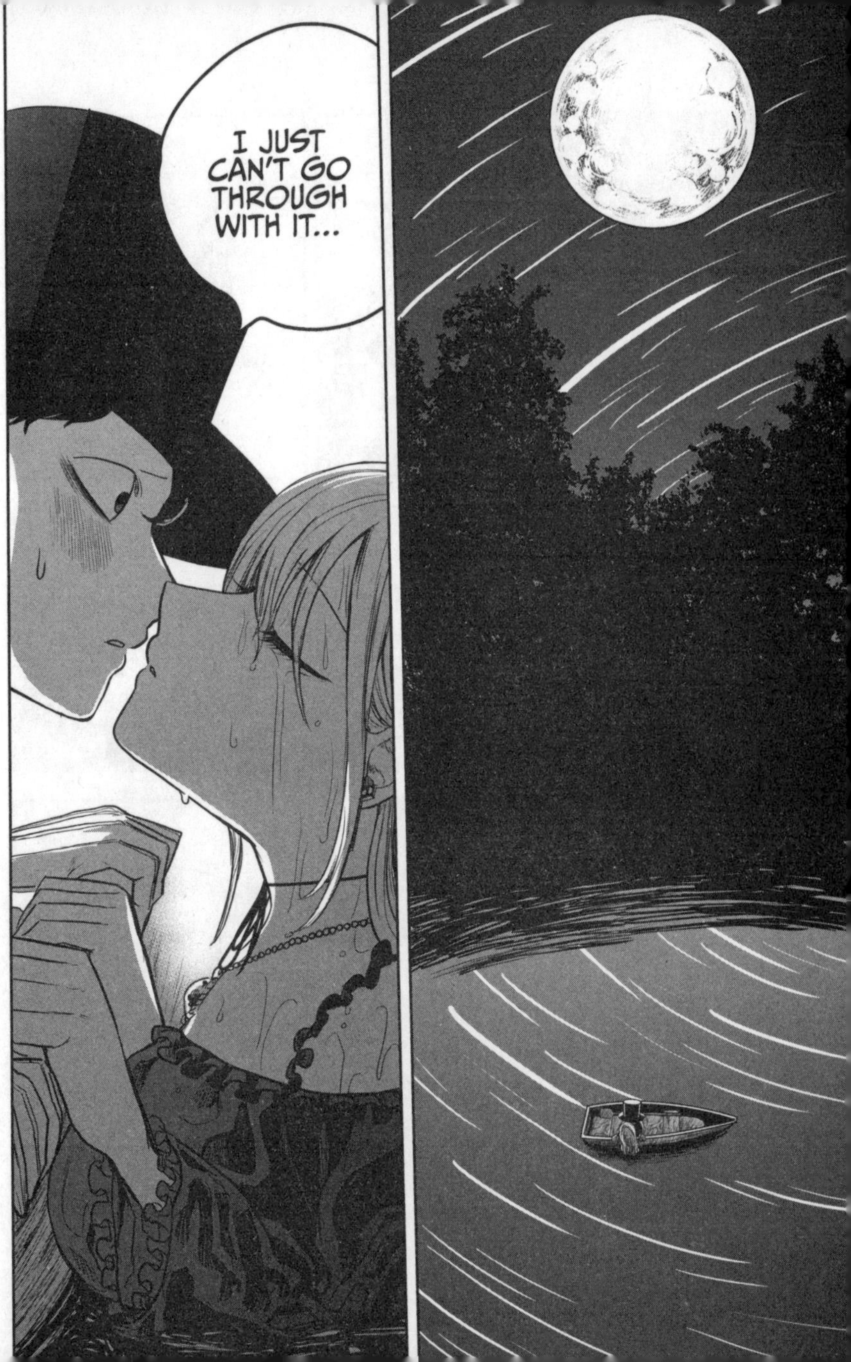
I JUST CAN'T GO THROUGH WITH IT...

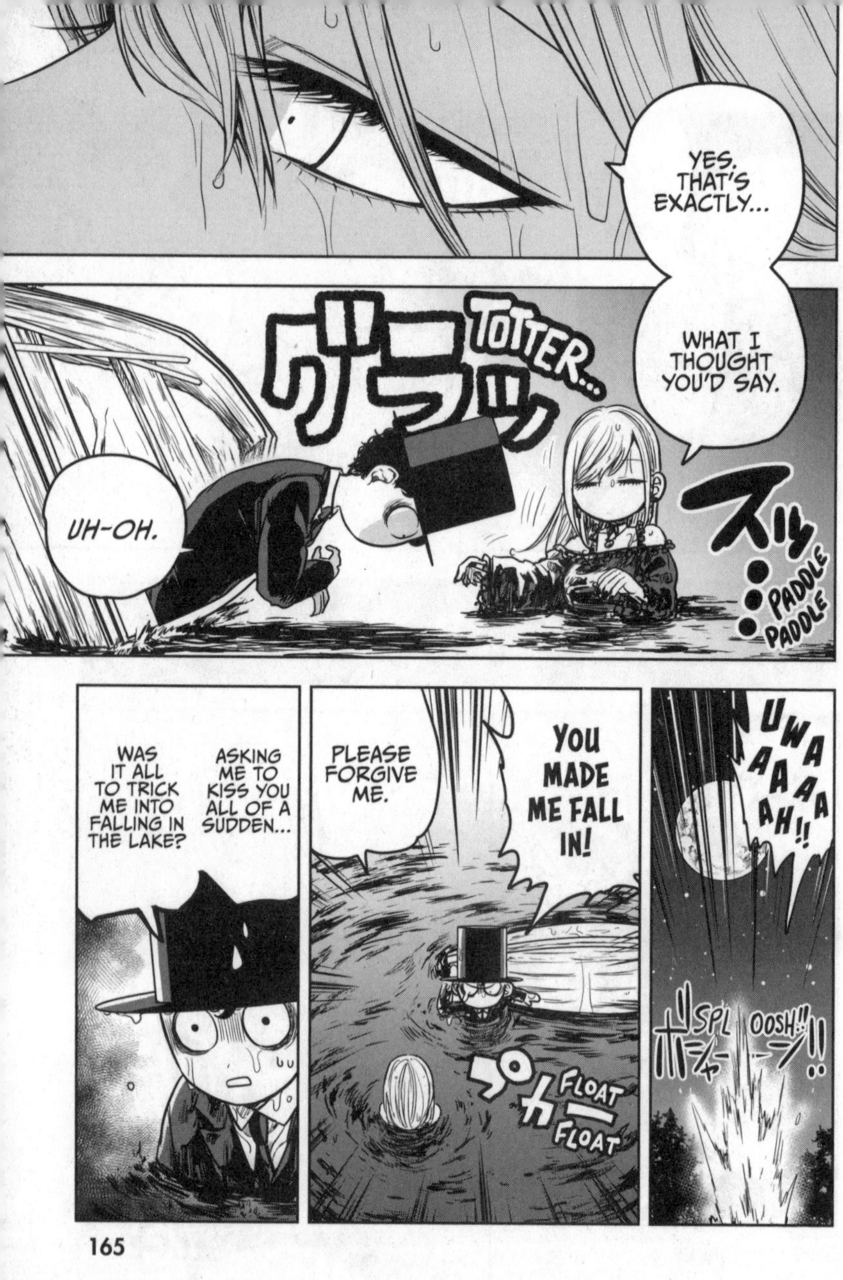

YES. THAT'S EXACTLY...
WHAT I THOUGHT YOU'D SAY.
グラッ
TOTTER...
UH-OH.
スイッ
PADDLE PADDLE
UWAAAAAAAH!!
SPLOOSH!!
YOU MADE ME FALL IN!
PLEASE FORGIVE ME.
プカー
FLOAT FLOAT
ASKING ME TO KISS YOU ALL OF A SUDDEN...
WAS IT ALL TO TRICK ME INTO FALLING IN THE LAKE?

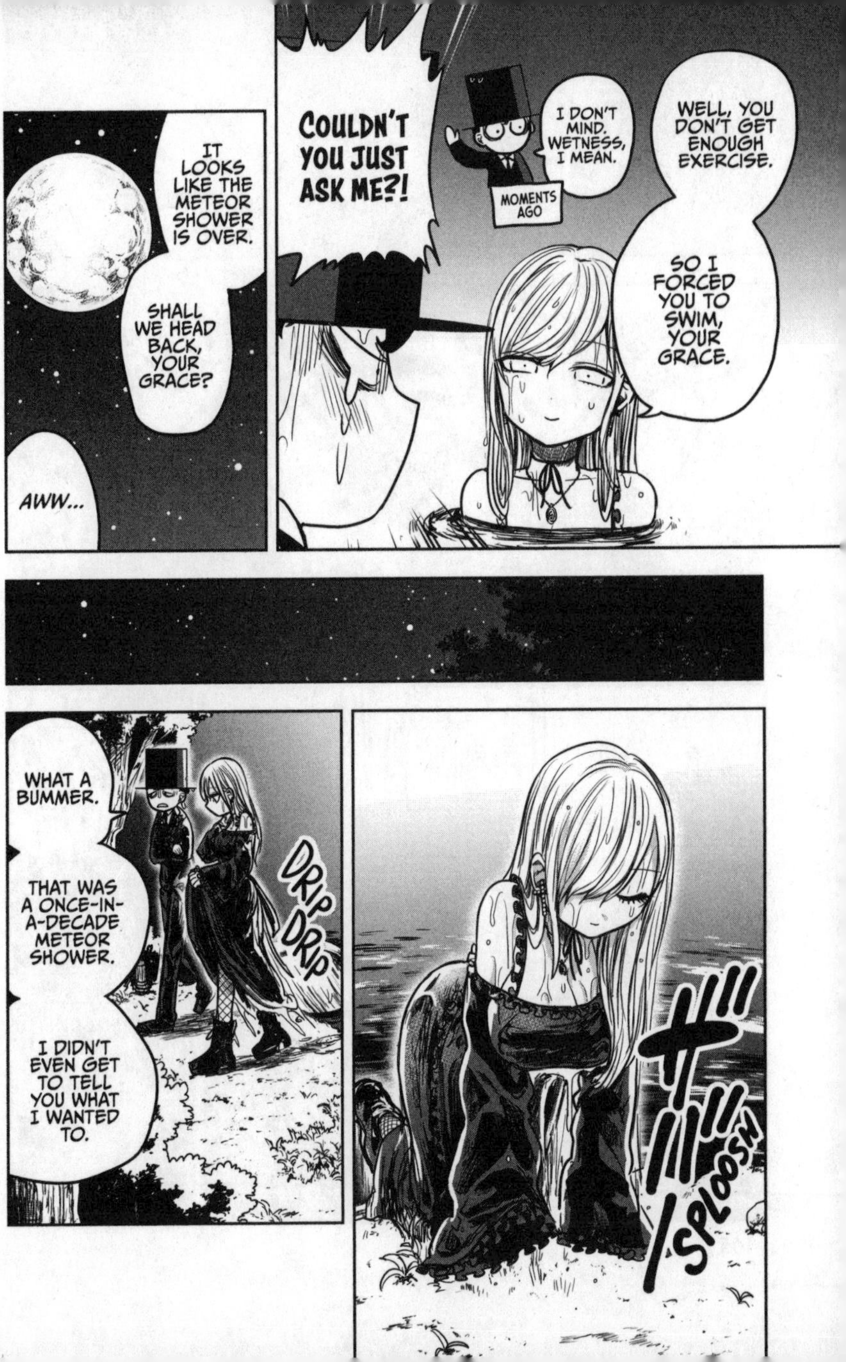
MOMENTS AGO
I DON'T MIND. WETNESS, I MEAN.
WELL, YOU DON'T GET ENOUGH EXERCISE.
SO I FORCED YOU TO SWIM, YOUR GRACE.
COULDN'T YOU JUST ASK ME?!
IT LOOKS LIKE THE METEOR SHOWER IS OVER.
SHALL WE HEAD BACK, YOUR GRACE?
AWW...
SPLOOSH
DRIP DRIP
WHAT A BUMMER.
THAT WAS A ONCE-IN-A-DECADE METEOR SHOWER.
I DIDN'T EVEN GET TO TELL YOU WHAT I WANTED TO.

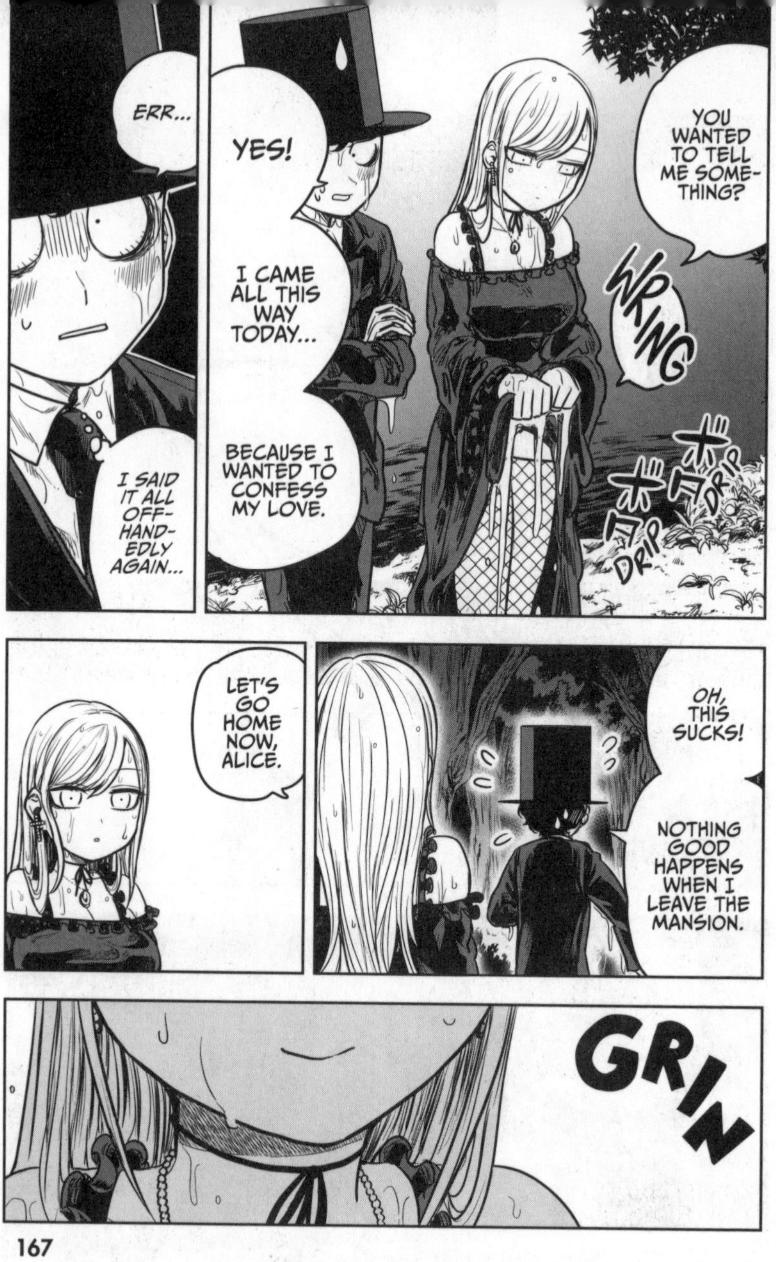
YOU WANTED TO TELL ME SOME-THING?
WRING
DRIP DRIP
YES!
I CAME ALL THIS WAY TODAY...
BECAUSE I WANTED TO CONFESS MY LOVE.
ERR...
I SAID IT ALL OFF-HAND-EDLY AGAIN...
OH, THIS SUCKS!
NOTHING GOOD HAPPENS WHEN I LEAVE THE MANSION.
LET'S GO HOME NOW, ALICE.
GRIN

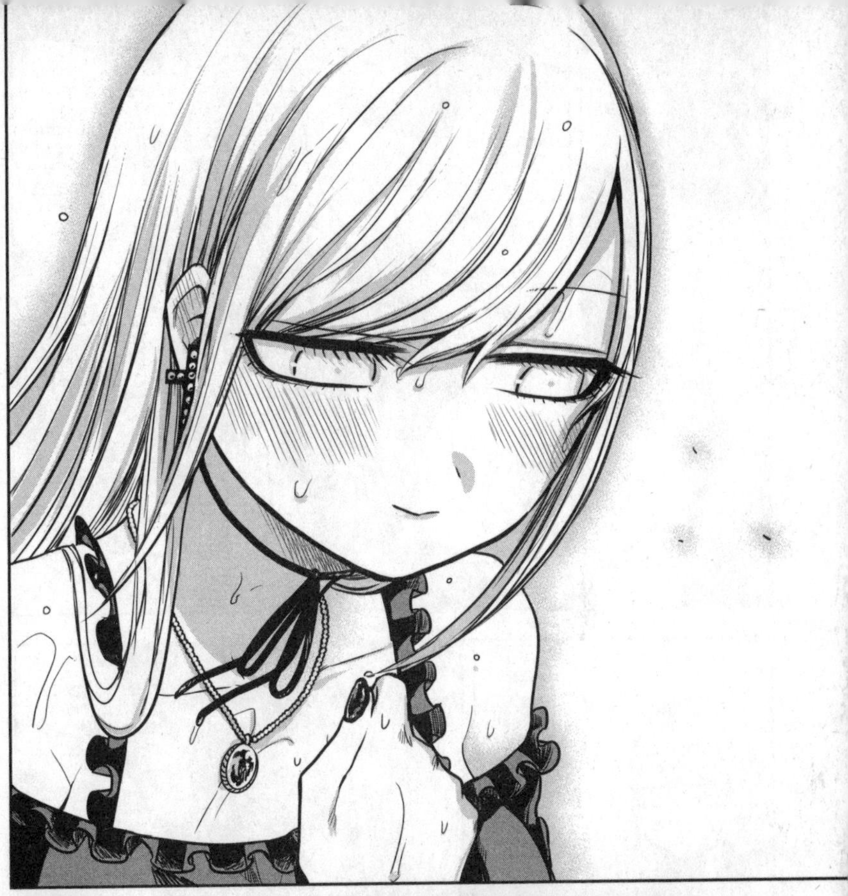

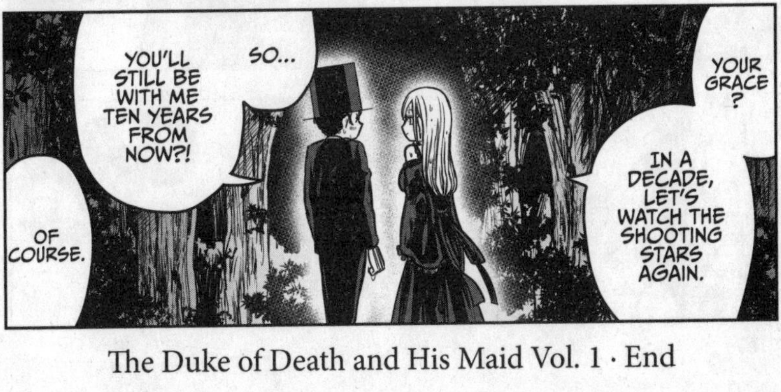
YOUR GRACE?
SO...
YOU'LL STILL BE WITH ME TEN YEARS FROM NOW?!
IN A DECADE, LET'S WATCH THE SHOOTING STARS AGAIN.
OF COURSE.

The Duke of Death and His Maid Vol. 1 · End

THE DUKE OF DEATH AND HIS MAID

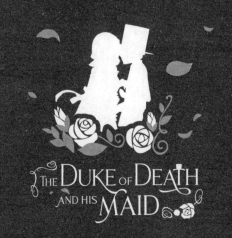

THE DUKE OF DEATH AND HIS MAID

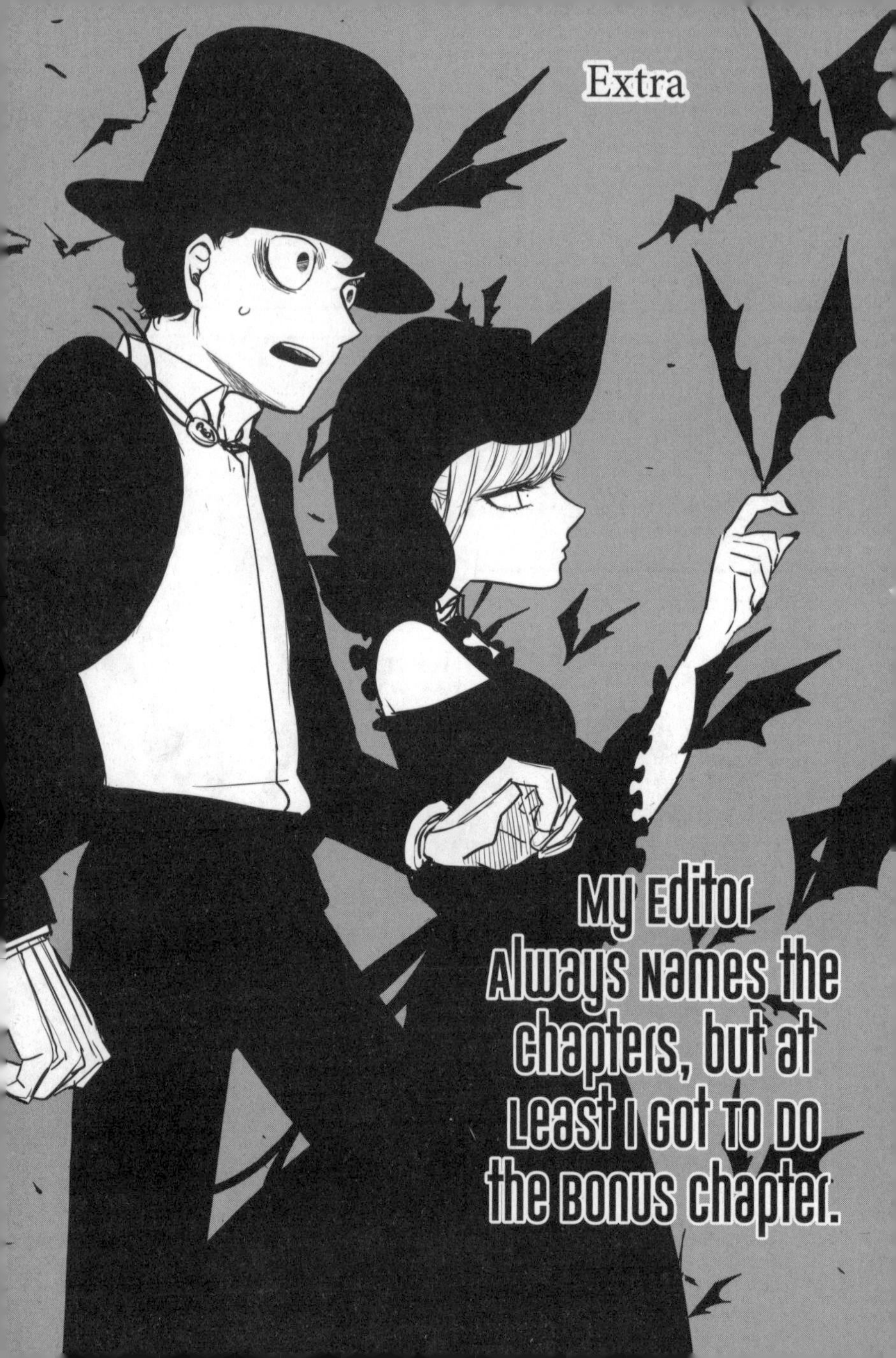
Extra
My Editor Always Names the chapters, but at Least I Got To Do the Bonus chapter.

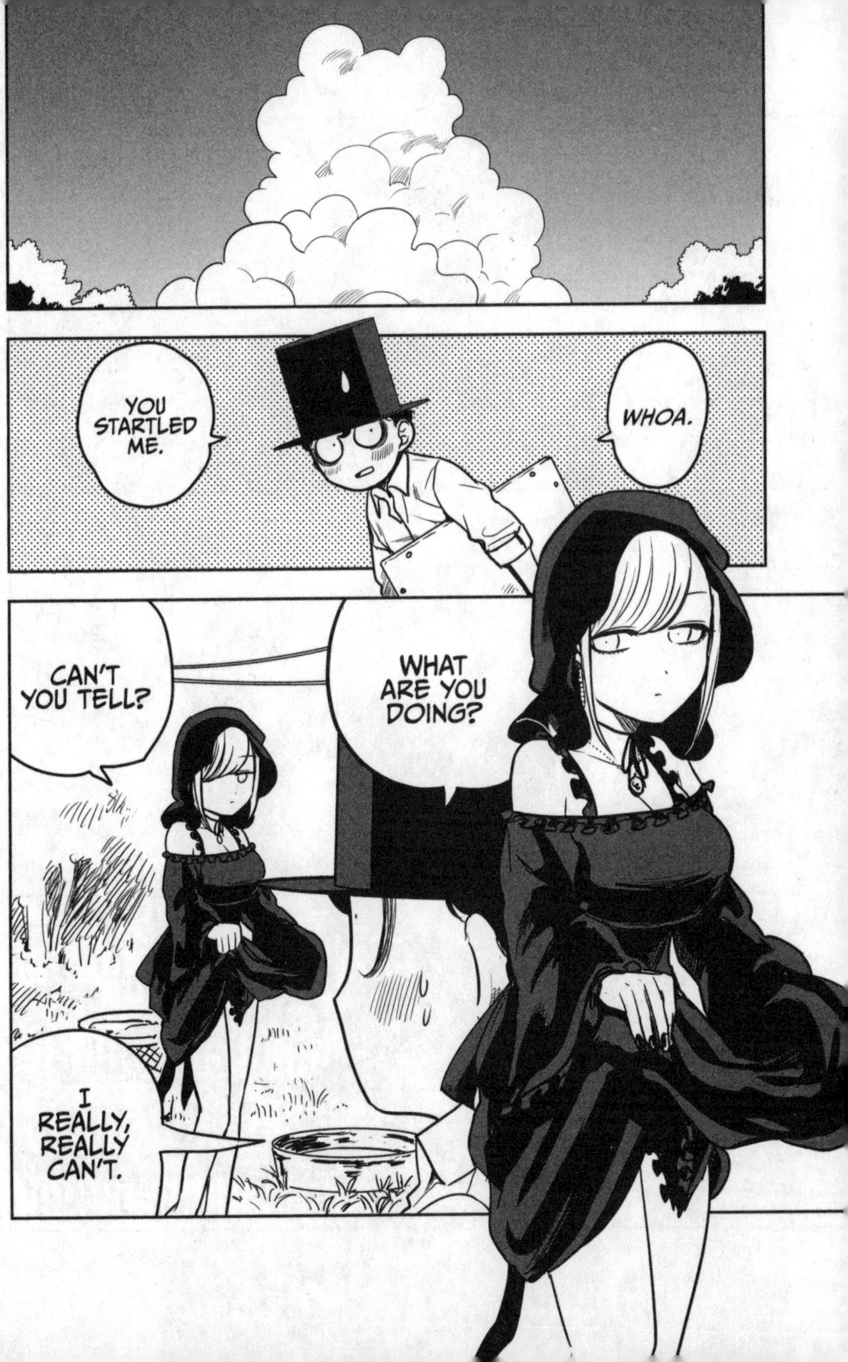
WHOA.
YOU STARTLED ME.
WHAT ARE YOU DOING?
CAN'T YOU TELL?
I REALLY, REALLY CAN'T.

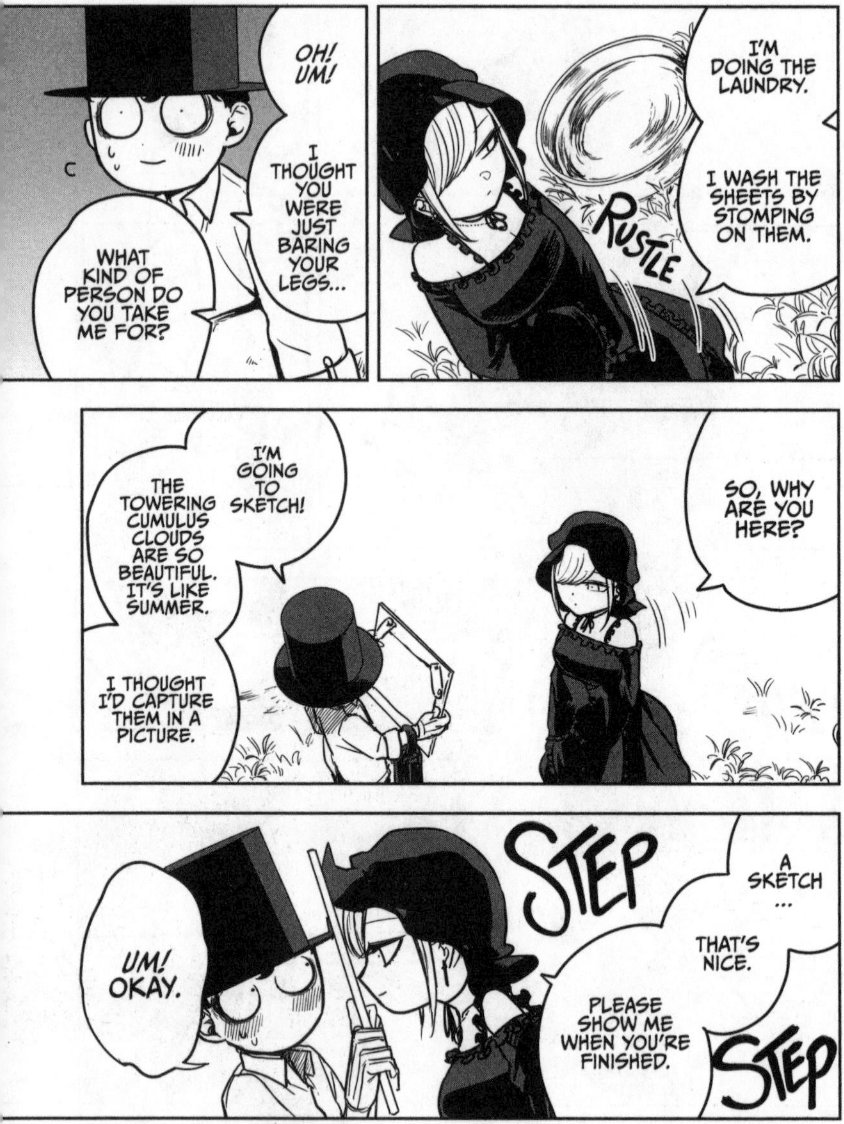
I'M DOING THE LAUNDRY.
I WASH THE SHEETS BY STOMPING ON THEM.
RUSTLE
OH! UM!
I THOUGHT YOU WERE JUST BARING YOUR LEGS...
WHAT KIND OF PERSON DO YOU TAKE ME FOR?
SO, WHY ARE YOU HERE?
I'M GOING TO SKETCH!
THE TOWERING CUMULUS CLOUDS ARE SO BEAUTIFUL. IT'S LIKE SUMMER.
I THOUGHT I'D CAPTURE THEM IN A PICTURE.
A SKETCH...
THAT'S NICE.
STEP
PLEASE SHOW ME WHEN YOU'RE FINISHED.
STEP
UM! OKAY.

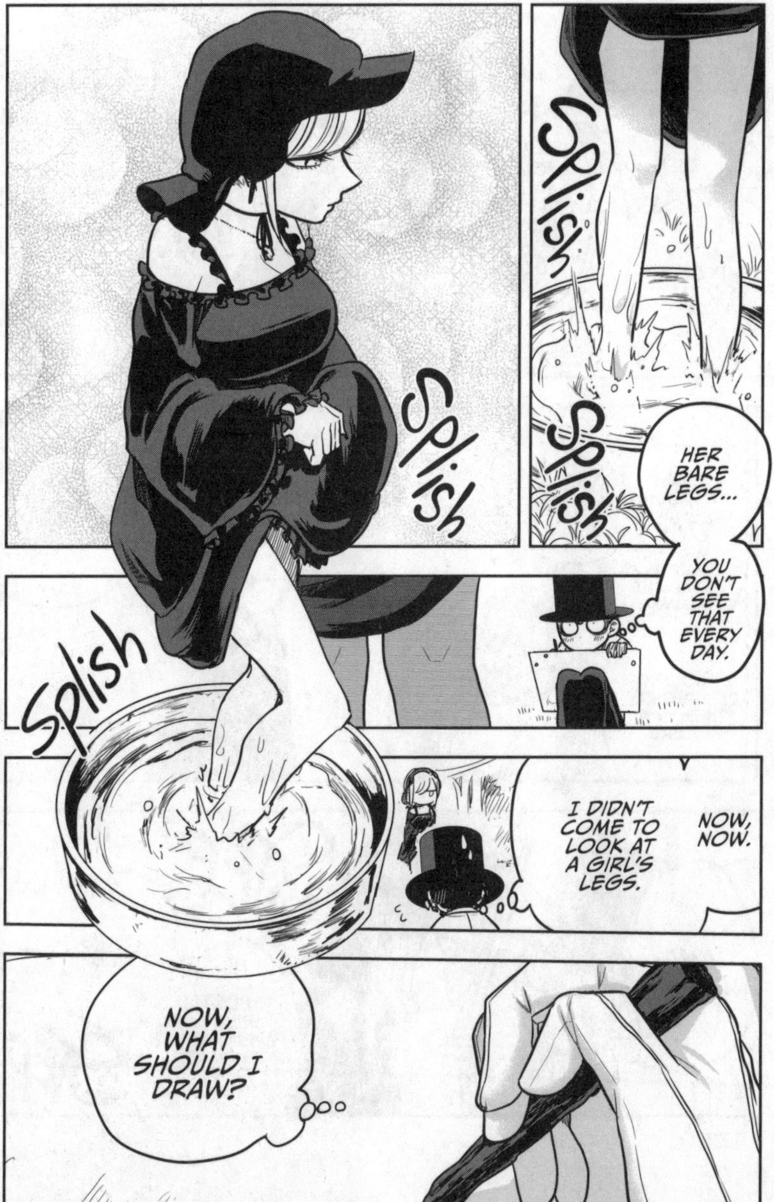
Splish
Splish
HER BARE LEGS...
Splish
YOU DON'T SEE THAT EVERY DAY.
Splish
NOW, NOW.
I DIDN'T COME TO LOOK AT A GIRL'S LEGS.
NOW, WHAT SHOULD I DRAW?

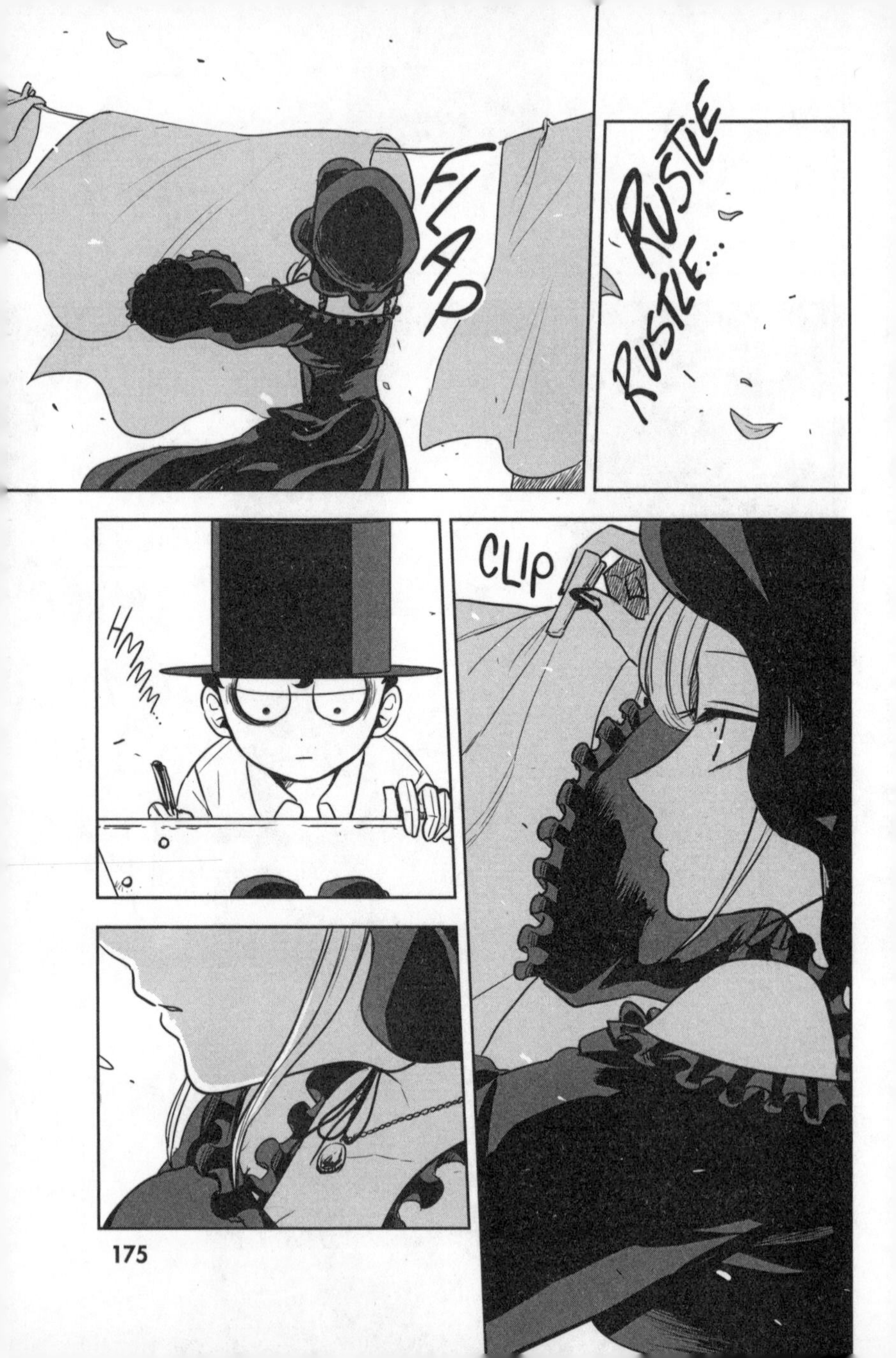
RUSTLE RUSTLE...
FLAP
CLIP
HMMM...

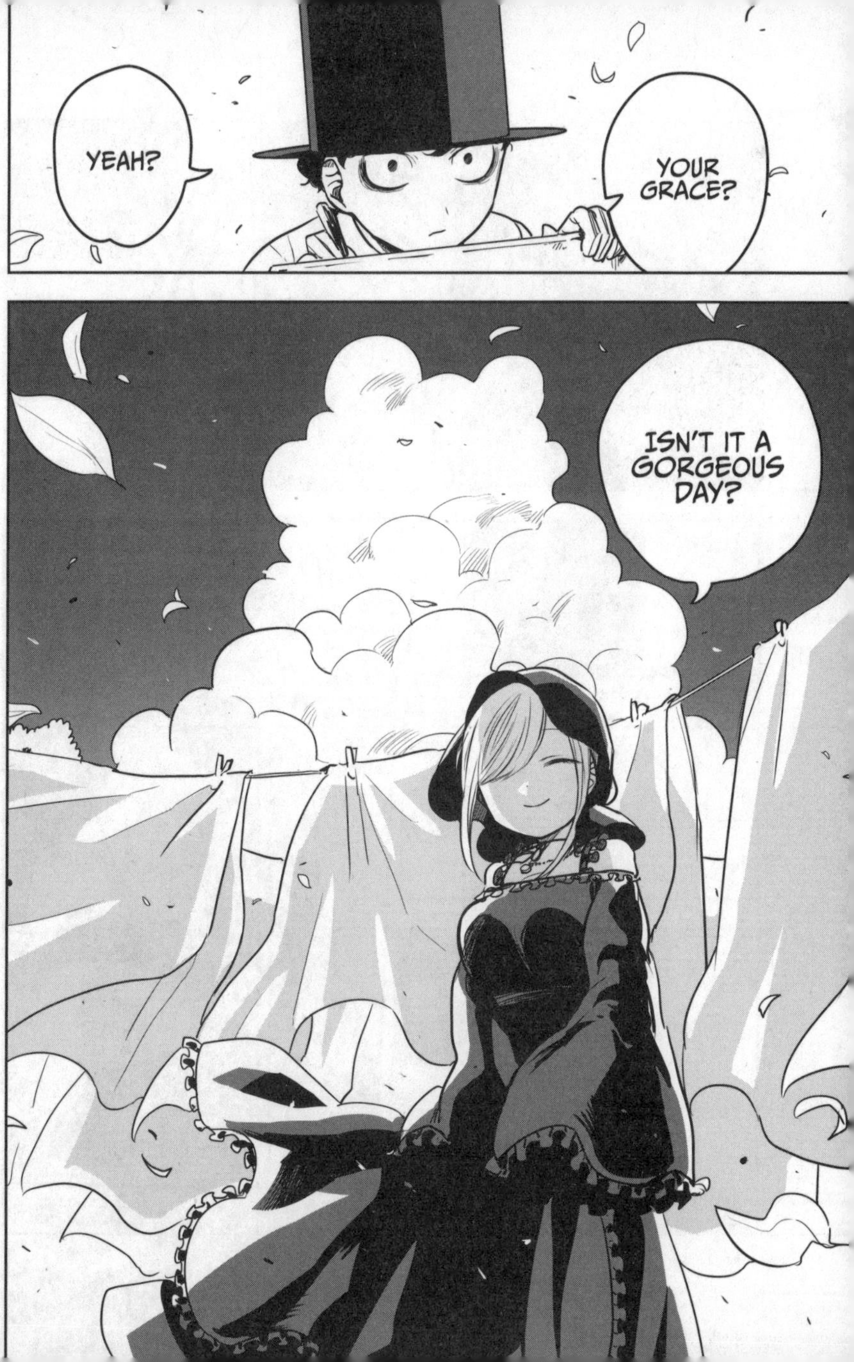
YOUR GRACE?
YEAH?
ISN'T IT A GORGEOUS DAY?

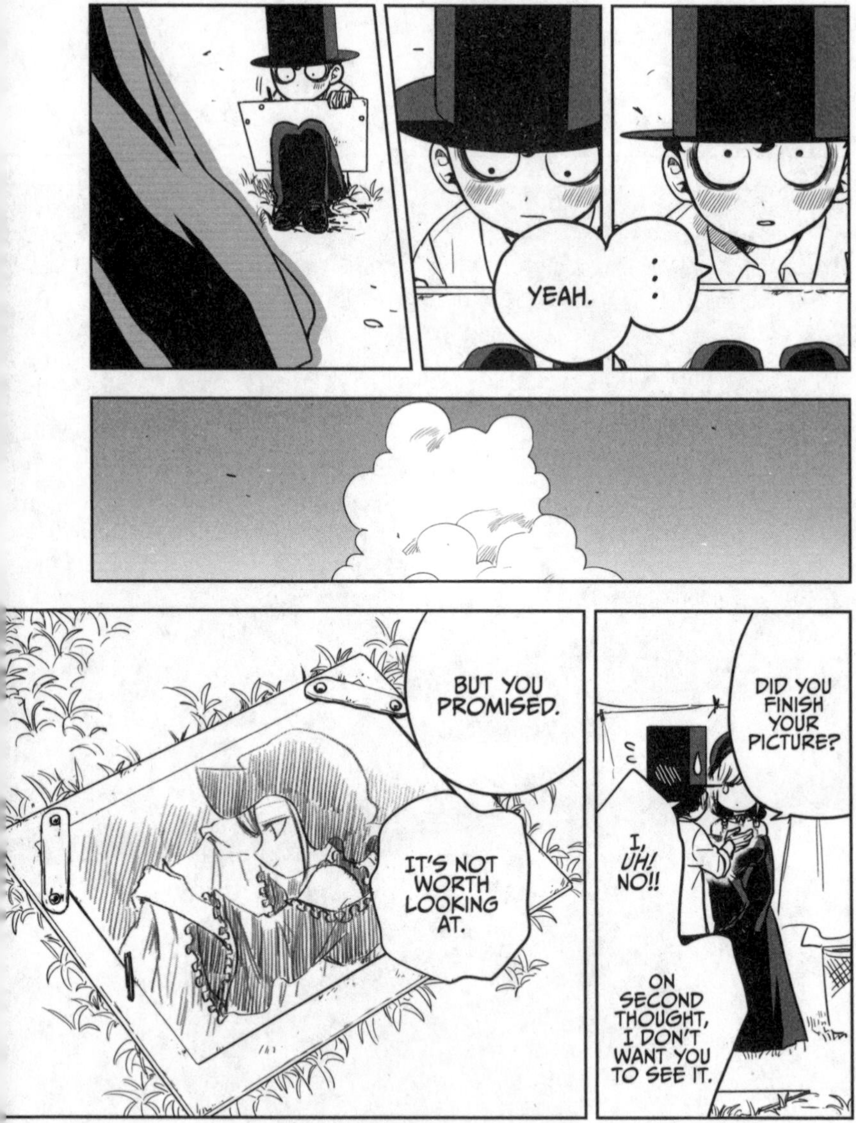
...
YEAH.
DID YOU FINISH YOUR PICTURE?
I, UH! NO!!
ON SECOND THOUGHT, I DON'T WANT YOU TO SEE IT.
BUT YOU PROMISED.
IT'S NOT WORTH LOOKING AT.

End of Bonus Chapter

THE DUKE OF DEATH AND HIS MAID

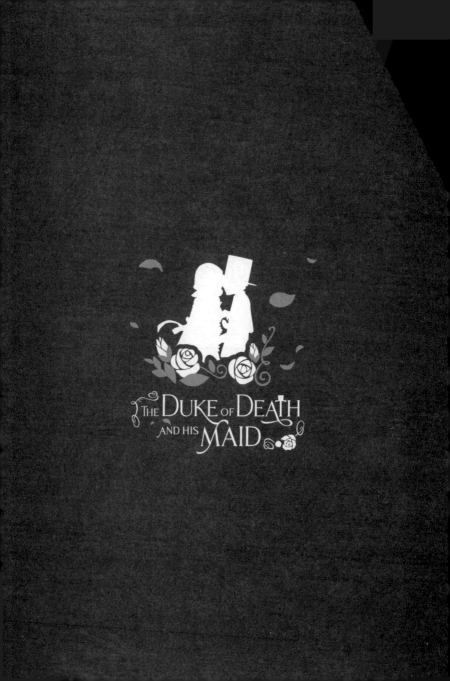

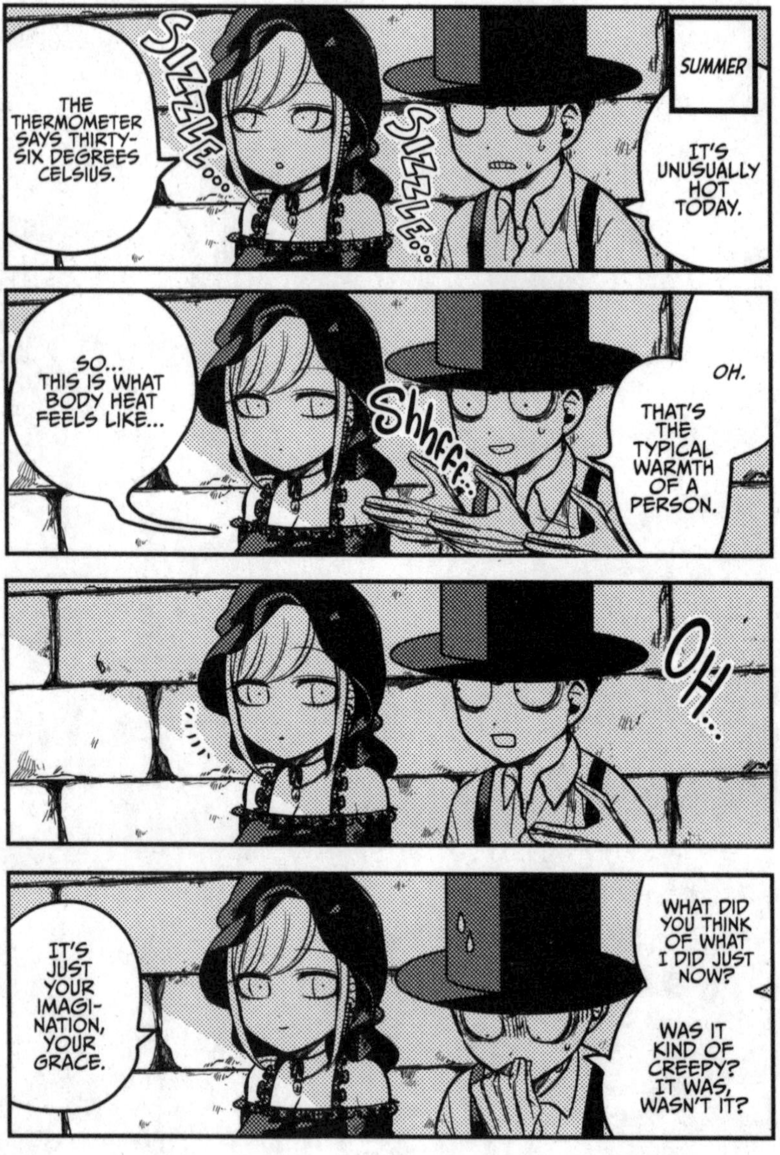
SUMMER
IT'S UNUSUALLY HOT TODAY.
SIZZLE...
SIZZLE...
THE THERMOMETER SAYS THIRTY-SIX DEGREES CELSIUS.
OH.
THAT'S THE TYPICAL WARMTH OF A PERSON.
Shhfff...
SO... THIS IS WHAT BODY HEAT FEELS LIKE...
OH...
WHAT DID YOU THINK OF WHAT I DID JUST NOW?
WAS IT KIND OF CREEPY? IT WAS, WASN'T IT?
IT'S JUST YOUR IMAGINATION, YOUR GRACE.

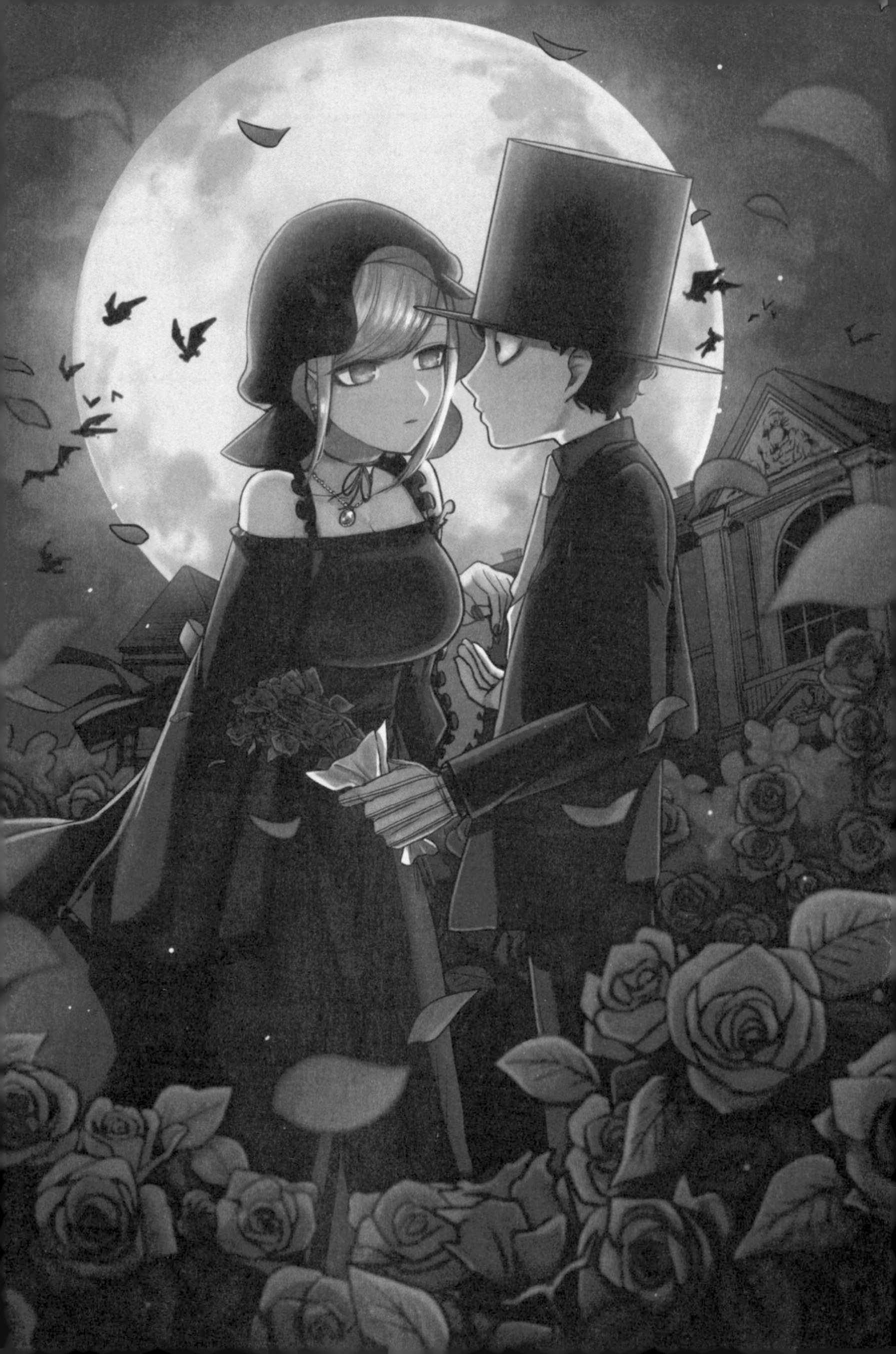

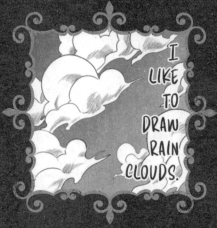

I LIKE TO DRAW RAIN CLOUDS.

INOUE

Nice to meet you.
This story is a little bit funny,
a little bit pervy, and a little
bit true love. I'm gonna do
my best with it.
Thanks!

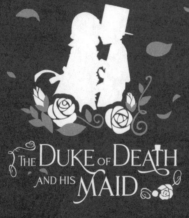

THE DUKE of DEATH AND HIS MAID

CONTENTS

INOUE PRESENTS

THE DUKE OF DEATH AND HIS MAID

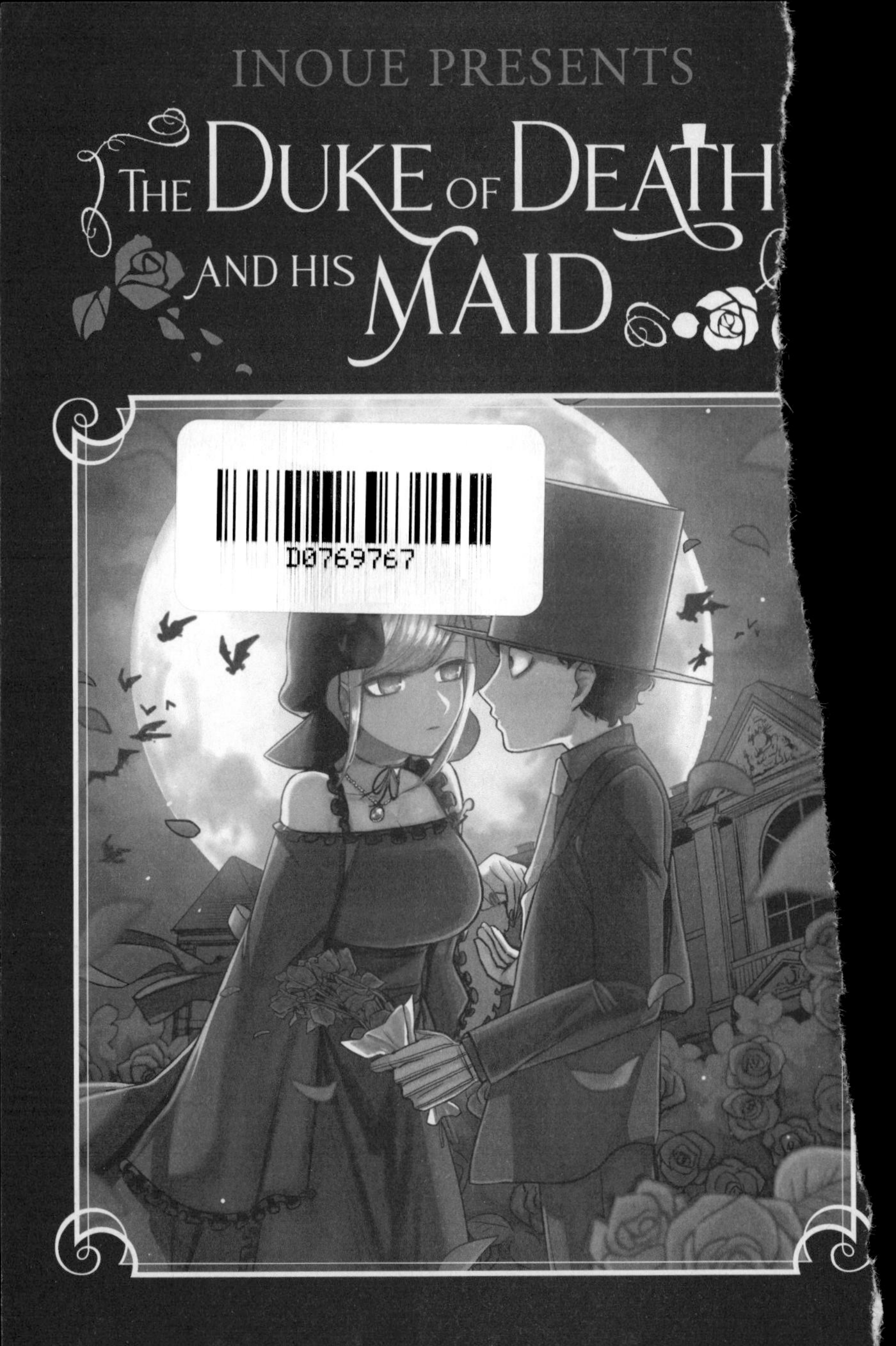